AF478156

OPERATION FREAK

Operation Freak

Narrative, Identity, and the Spectrum of Bodily Abilities

CHRISTIAN FLAUGH

McGill-Queen's University Press
Montreal & Kingston • London • Ithaca

© McGill-Queen's University Press 2012
ISBN 978-0-7735-4027-9

Legal deposit third quarter 2012
Bibliothèque nationale du Québec

Printed in Canada on acid-free paper that is 100%
ancient forest free (100% post-consumer recycled),
processed chlorine free.

This book has been published with the help of grants
from the Julian Park Publication Fund and the Canadian-
American Studies Committee at the University at Buffalo
– The State University of New York.

McGill-Queen's University Press acknowledges the
support of the Canada Council for the Arts for our
publishing program. We also acknowledge the financial
support of the Government of Canada through the
Canada Book Fund for our publishing activities.

Library and Archives Canada Cataloguing in Publication

Flaugh, Christian, 1968–
    Operation freak : narrative, identity, and the spectrum
of bodily abilities / Christian Flaugh.

Includes bibliographical references and index.
ISBN 978-0-7735-4027-9

    1. Godbout, Jacques, 1933– Têtes à Papineau. 2. Ben Jel-
loun, Tahar, 1944– Enfant de sable. 3. Ben Jelloun, Tahar,
1944– Nuit sacrée. 4. Condé, Maryse Moi, Tituba, sorcière—.
5. Abnormalities, Human, in literature. 6. Identity (Philosophical concept) in literature. I. Title.

PQ637.B63F53 2012   843'.914093561   C2012-904354-0

This book was typeset by True to Type in 10.5/13 Sabon

*For my parents, my grandmother, Ann, Carrell, Ernest,
Elaine (my Man Yaya), J.J., and especially for Mark.*

Contents

Acknowledgments

It goes without saying that there are many, many people I need and want to thank for their support. The initial ideas for this project came to light while I was a graduate student, and so I must recognize all of the students, peers, and friends of Middlebury College (in Vermont and in Paris) as well as in Madison and of UW-Madison (particularly of FRIT and of 666) who discussed the concepts with me – or listened to me work through them – and who continued to encourage its completion. I especially want to thank Mary (Conway) Bashir, Cora Fox, Sage Goellner, Christine Lemley, Gerry Milligan and Toja Okoh, who offered generous, consistent, and ongoing attention to me and to my pages. I also wish to thank all of my previous professors and especially my two advisors, Aliko Songolo and Soraya Tlatli, without whose expert direction and continued encouragement – and patience and good humour – this curious and adventurous project would never have begun. I am eternally grateful to Elaine Marks, whose spirit continues to guide and inspire me in all of my scholarly endeavours.

I also wish to thank the librarians who helped me find the right sources at the right time, from Madison to Buffalo and all the stacks in-between. This includes the staff of Madison's Memorial Library (especially Emilie Ngo-Nguidjol), the Bibliothèque Schoelcher (including the Pavillon Bougenot and Hélène Parfait-Verheyt) in Fort-de-France, the Bibliothèque et Archives nationales du Québec (particularly the Grande Bibliothèque) in Montreal, the Andrew L. Bouwhuis Library of Canisius College, the Buffalo and Erie County Public Library, and the University at Buffalo (UB) library system (and, most certainly, Ellen Urbanek, Bill Offhaus, Anne Bouvier, and Jean Dickson, for their patience, thoroughness, and good humour with my book and other requests). I add to this list Patrice Placoly, a most amazing resource, host, and friend in Schoelcher. I am forever grateful for the boundless knowledge, patience, and enthusiasm that you all possess and are more than willing to share.

Operation Freak took its most significant turn after I arrived in Buffalo, unfolding into a mediation I had not envisioned, and this transformation is due to the support of many. In fact, the list of names from the University at Buffalo alone is extensive, so I want to extend first a most sincere word of thanks to the entire UB community, past and present, for fostering an environment in which creativity and intellectual engagement come together across multiple disciplines. The College of Arts and Sciences has always been exceptionally generous, particularly through the Julian Park Fund, and without CAS support through semestrial leaves as well as financial backing, this book would not be a book. The same is true of the Canadian-American Studies Committee (and, notably, Lorraine Oak), whose support helped fund my work in Montreal as well as this book's publication. I certainly want to thank the Department of Romance Languages and Literatures for its varied forms of encouragement and endorsement, including but not limited to a semester's course release.

I also wish to thank my numerous classes of graduate and undergraduate students who were willing to do test runs of many of the ideas with me, even when the thoughts and my articulations were rather raw. I especially want to give a nod to Mike Duffy and Chantal Englert for the research that we did together, and another nod to Betty Brown and Amy Hardy who more than generously offered their services with books, citations, humour, and the like. These courses and the students in them helped me refine my interests, which led me to join the Transnational and Transcolonial Caribbean Studies Research Group (TTCSRG) in New York, and I thank every member (including co-founder Kaiama Glover) for their help with my thoughts and my texts. Julie Nack Ngue and Claire Barker, kindred spirits in new readings of disability, never hesitated to lend a hand. My colleagues and friends from UB – especially Sarah Bay-Cheng, David Castillo, Tim Dean, Maureen Jameson, Marieme Lo, Jeannette Ludwig, Amy Graves Monroe, Elizabeth Scarlett, Jean-Jacques Thomas, Claude Welch, and Cindy Wu – were also always eager to help and deserve more gratitude than I can offer for the time they spent carefully reading my drafts, interrogating my ideas, or suggesting necessary readings. I offer an additional note of thanks to Carine Mardorossian and Margarita Vargas, who read so many of my words.

The reading did not, of course, stop at UB. The editorial staff of McGill-Queen's University Press is stupendous. Kyla Madden spent remarkable amounts of time thoughtfully reading and commenting on the preliminary versions of the manuscript as well as on the related documents and then carefully guiding the project through the proper channels, and for that I am profoundly grateful. The anonymous readers who worked with Kyla are due a special note of thanks for their time as their suggestions for how to restructure certain aspects of the work were exactly what it needed. Joan McGilvray and Ryan Van Huijstee provided me with expert and swift explanations of the editorial process. And Joanne Richardson provided the most expert attention and advice on every single word, a feat that was a most welcome operation in all senses of the term.

Some portions of the project first appeared in articles, and revised versions of the selected portions appear here by permission, for which I am grateful: (by permission of Oxford University Press) "Operating Narrative: Words on Disability and Gender in Two Novels of Tahar Ben Jelloun." *Forum for Modern Language Studies* ("Perspectives on Africa") 45, 5 (2009): 411–26; (by permission of Taylor and Francis) "On Normalities: Narratives of Bodies, Ability, and Freaks of Culture in Twentieth-Century Francophone Literature." Invited contribution. *Contemporary French and Francophone Studies/Sites* 10, 2 (2006): 217–25. http://www.tandfonline.com/toc/gsit20/current; (by permission of *Equinoxes*) "Identity Betrayed: Negotiations of the Freak in Tahar Ben Jelloun's *L'enfant de sable*." *Equinoxes* (Fall/Winter 2003).

Last, I want to again thank all of my friends as well as my family for their contributions and encouragement. David Calaiacovo, Janet Murphy, Michelle Murphy, and Gina Calaiacovo helped at crucial moments with close readings and references. Specifically and sincerely, I wish to thank a fellow Madison alum, TTCSRG co-founder and my friend Alessandra Benedicty, whose words of wisdom and endless encouragement guided me through every page of *Operation Freak*. I also wish to recognize the tireless and loving support of my immediate and extended families – in the Buffalo area as well as in Florida, Illinois, Michigan, California, Washington, Ohio, and beyond – who understood when I had to step away (and who were probably better for it).

And most certainly, I thank Mark, who walked, ran, and jumped with me every day, and who continues to do so. You are the best man. Thank you for J.J., the Thomas Edison, and the help in seeing how I'm capable of astounding myself.

OPERATION FREAK

Il n'y a pas de récit sans événement, sans une quelconque rupture de la
norme.
[There is no narrative without an event, without some breach of the norm.]
Marc Gontard, Le moi étrange

Freaks are above all products of perception: they are the consequence of a
comparative relationship in which those who control the social discourse
and the means of representation recruit the seeming truth of the body to
claim the center for themselves and banish others to margins.
Rosemarie Garland Thomson, Extraordinary Bodies

Introduction:
Freaks, Spectrums, and
Francophone Narratives of Ability

This figure of reproductive variety is never specific, but more like a trick
of nature or, as Buffon puts it, a "monster by default."

Joan (Colin) Dayan, Haiti, History, and the Gods

You have to start with a kind of shock.

Maryse Condé, "Afterword"

Louis-Auguste Cyparis. Sanson. Joseph Sibarace. Ludger Sylbaris. Samson. Sylbaris. Ciparis. Cyparis. These are the varied names of the (alleged) sole survivor of montagne Pelée's 8 May 1902 *nuée ardente* – an avalanche-like eruption in surging clouds of superheated gas containing rock and ash, that wiped out the neighbouring city of Saint-Pierre, an approximate 29,000 people in and around it, everything in the eight-kilometre (five-mile) path between the volcano and the city, and a total area of 58 square kilometres (22 square miles) in the northwest region of Martinique.[1] The list of names also includes some of the labels that refer to the individual whom the Barnum and Bailey Circus brought to the United States the following year to tour with an assemblage of performers billed as freaks due to their extraordinary bodily abnormalities. Cyparis's inclusion was due in part to his survival of the pyroclastic storm and in part to the related scorching of his body, both of which made of him a living testament to the events of a most transformative 8 May and strangely ironic Day of Ascension.

Although Cyparis's experiences brought him an instant claim to some fame, his story today has a smaller audience. Conversations with individuals either from or familiar with Martinique associate him most often with 1902, less frequently with Barnum and Bailey.[2] The documented written sources are varying. Some of them are websites that touch on details in sensationalist ways, while others are more extensive book-length historical studies of the montagne Pelée disaster of which Cyparis is just one part.[3] Still, the portions of Cyparis's tale that continue to circulate – both the sensationalist and the historical, the written and the oral – speak of narrative, identity, and bodily abilities.

The various online web pages that are the most immediate means of gaining access to Cyparis's narrative today map out concrete yet eye-catching details. Because of two misdemeanors, Cyparis had been locked in a *cachot*, a solitary cell made of thick stone with only a small barred grate and a wooden door as openings.[4] Printed sources reveal similar and further details: that same incarceration in the enclosed cell of the prison – along with its location, wedged at the foot of the morne Abel, behind several higher buildings, and with all openings facing the opposite direction of montagne Pelée – helped to save Cyparis's life (Chrétien and Brousse 192–3; Lacroix 299–301). The 30 June 1902 letter of Père Mary, a parish priest of the nearby Morne-Rouge, to Martinique's acting governor, Georges Lhuerre, reveals more.[5] Three individuals walking amidst the Pompei-like ruins discovered Cyparis nearly four days after the eruption. They freed the severely burned prisoner from the still-standing *cachot* and then transported him to Morne-Rouge, where Mary orchestrated care for his extensive wounds.

In the absence of any other written account, Mary's letter is the source from which most details of Cyparis's experience are now pulled, a narrative based on Cyparis's recounting of what he heard and experienced: large and loud booms in the sky with formidable darkness, people's cries, scalding ash and bits of fire attempting to work their way into his cell, and eventually utter silence.[6] In words that testify to his intellectual abilities, Cyparis also told of his efforts to prevent his injury and even his death. He covered his face with clothing, wetting it however he could so as not to allow the heat to burn his lungs, and he drank rain water whenever available so as to stave off almost ninety-six hours of hunger and thirst (Bennett "On-Site Martinique," Nield "Le cachot de Cyparis," "Louis Auguste Sylbaris," "The Prison Cell").[7] Sceptics of the day scoffed at the possibility of survival, claiming, for example, that Cyparis was a looter in the days immediately following 8 May. However, Mary's transcription of

Cyparis's words – a text intended to validate the details of his rescue and survival for Gouverneur Lhuerre – offered proof to the contrary.[8]

In a way, this epistolary justification became Mary's unwitting sharing in the telling of Cyparis's remarkable tale. It also reveals the pliability of narrative. For example, he briefly acknowledges the nickname of Sanson, one that other sources suggest is a name that residents of the region gave to Cyparis, perhaps to acknowledge the strength it took for him to survive and thus associating him with a biblical tradition of virile masculinity. Mary connects to a collective narrative while at the same deciding how to effectively spotlight narrative voice: Cyparis's words dominate for at least half of the narrative, as he emphasizes his ability to survive ("Martinique 1902–2002: Documents"; Scarth 185).[9]

The opening of Mary's letter also nods to narrative transformability. He insisted that he believed he had transcribed Cyparis's story as precisely as possible: "je recueillis son histoire que je crois reproduire aussi exacte que possible." However, Mary's statement that he himself composed this letter for a new audience (Martinique's governor) after listening to Cyparis recount his own version, while at the same time offering up a slight doubt regarding his narrative's fidelity to Cyparis's, highlights the potential for another version of the narrative and, thus, signals the impermanence of any narrative. Specifically, it renders apparent how the act of manipulation – *opération*, or operation – of narrative is in ways every bit as prevalent and unavoidable as is the discourse of bodily abilities in the story of Cyparis.

At the same time that Cyparis's tale told of his survival, it also showcased montagne Pelée's imprint on his body. Cyparis did not survive the *nuée ardente* without harm: the heat ranging from 200 to 450 degrees Celsius (390 to 840 degrees Fahrenheit) is said to have produced the burns on a significant portion of his body while leaving his clothing unscathed, a common phenomenon of the eruption and listed as further evidence to his presence in Saint-Pierre. The explosion and the subsequent four-day isolation transformed Cyparis's own abilities to ambulate, as attested by the very act of the individuals who had to transport him to Père Mary for treatment. Given the extent of his burns and the alteration of physical capacities, he would need a series of palliative medical operations as well as bedrest to help restore any portion of his pre-May 8 bodily abilities.

At that moment in history, Cyparis's audience grew as people yearned to both see and hear how he was able to survive. Records of the aforementioned regional visitors do not appear to be available (and if any existed in Morne-Rouge, they may well have perished in montagne Pelée's subsequent eruptions that same year). Primarily for these reasons, Cyparis's post-eruption experience lives on most prominently in images and, especially, in printed texts of visitors from outside of the area. Cyparis even won an international audience, including the above-cited Alfred Lacroix, a metropolitain French geologist sent to Martinique to study the blast. In his over six-hundred-page report published in 1904, Lacroix dedicates a page to Cyparis whom he provides very basic biographical information about the survivors of the eruption.[10]

Another individual to meet with Cyparis was George Kennan, the journalist from the United States who, in *The Tragedy of Pelee* (1902), transmitted his interaction with the famed survivor in Morne-Rouge.[11] Specifically, Kennan notes that, on the first visit, which occurred three weeks after the eruption, Cyparis was in a house turned lazaret. To Kennan, Cyparis was a remarkable sight: "He had been more frightfully burned, I think, than any man I had ever seen" (75). In addition to listening to Cyparis's tale, Kennan observed his body. It oozed blood and other fluids and it reeked of an overwhelming odour. Cyparis's "feet and hands were covered with yellow, offensive matter which had no resemblance whatever to human skin or flesh" (75–6). However, Cyparis's profoundly charred body held, in Kennan's eye, one curiously normal distinction: "His face, strangely enough, had escaped injury, and his hair had not even been scorched" (75). Kennan's second visit tells briefly of a Cyparis significantly transformed and on the path to recovery due in part to medical supplies sent from the military hospital in Fort-de-France, an assessment with which Mary's letter concurs and that shows the impermanence of Cyparis's bodily abilities (80).[12] Clearly, readings of Cyparis's body informed scientific as well as journalistic discourse. However, they also continued to supplement his own narrative: onlookers affirmed the natural disaster's power and Cyparis's survival at the same time that they further accounted for his extraordinary abilities to survive despite Kennan's indication of his "average intelligence" (80).

In addition to detailing Cyparis's survival, nearly all written sources of his narrative document the subsequent change in his life when he worked for the Barnum and Bailey circus beginning in March 1903. Even before Cyparis was physically involved in this entertainment enterprise, the US media highlighted his extraordinariness. For example, on 25 February 1903, the *New York Times* released a short account entitled "Survived Mt. Pelee's Fire," which announced Cyparis's arrival in the United States. This narrative referred to him by the name of "Joseph Sibarace" and explained as well as expanded upon what made this human marvel marvellous: his status as a survivor and his abilities to survive. However, the piece also depicted in Cyparis a raw, outdated, and impoverished state of being. He was wearing "a rather ancient straw hat," "a suit of clothes of the thinnest of texture, and a threadbare and ragged overcoat."[13] Such an appearance is, in part, attributed to the speculation that Cyparis had not yet had contact with the Barnum and Bailey staff, who might have provided him with attire not so seemingly ragged and inappropriate. The almost other-worldly description is furthered into the strange and the exotic by what would be part of his claim to fame: his skin was recorded as especially distinguishable, with his bare and burned feet that "were scarred with frightful marks" and the "white scars on the black skin" that gave him "an uncanny appearance."[14]

References to Cyparis's abilities also permeate the narrative, with emphasis on his then present intellectual and (especially) linguistic abilities involved in his captivating recounting of "awful sufferings." The report accentuated his capacities as even more curious due to his "peculiar West Indian French" (resolved by a translator) as well as deficient as he "tried to tell his story" (a tale whose recounting is offered in extensive detail for such a short publication). The article concludes by stating that Cyparis was taken to Ellis Island before being allowed to come ashore and "take his place among the freaks of Barnum and Bailey's Circus" ("Survived"). From that point forward, he would be known in anglophone contexts as "Ludger Sylbaris," particularly in the numerous historical studies of montagne Pelée. Advertisements for his role in the circus listed "Samson," the US version of his Martinican nickname that connects him again to the legendary virility of his biblical counterpart.

Once Cyparis is in the circus, reports on his life eventually diminish in lustre. A few imply that this Samson's unburned hair was never cut and that he died in 1929 due to natural causes (Nield "Le cachot"). Others tales would have it that his previously unsinged locks had been, metaphorically if not prophetically, cut clean off: some insist that he died weakened and impoverished (and perhaps in Panama) in 1955; others that he stabbed a Barnum and Bailey employee in 1903, which brought a premature end to his tour that year and likely to his career as a performer (Bennett "On-Site Martinique"; Scarth 189; Zebrowski 267; Morgan 221–2).[15]

Despite his shift in direction and his disappearance, Cyparis's scorched skin and negotiated narrative attest forever to the real and the recounted, the optimal and the operated bodily abilities employed in the production of his identity. Offender turned miracle, he was the phenomenon who became a freak. But he was a freak of culture – defined by his survival abilities, his varied performances, and especially the varied sociocultural codes with which he came into contact – who arose from the rubble of a freak pyroclastic eruption and fell into the hands and the pages of multiple individuals. Such concepts only begin to capture the complexity of Cyparis and his extraordinary identity as situated within spectrums of abilities and sociocultural narratives.

Cyparis's narrative, as much as it has been or can be concretized and as much as critics can examine it, is significant to the contemplation of normative, somatically charged identification processes. Its abridged engagement here certainly merits further exploration. However, such a perspective also highlights how a body, after being operated on by the ardent forces of nature and subjected to the unintended shelter of society's stone-and-iron construction, moves away from varied sociocultural norms of appearance and informs narrative. It attests to the ways in which Cyparis as an individual uses several different abilities – intellectual, physical, and psychological – to survive montagne Pelée's pervasive presence in his cell. It also reveals how that same individual is moved – by himself and by others – throughout a spectrum of ability types in order to create the eventual circus narrative that would identify him.[16] Rereading Cyparis's tale also demonstrates how various identity categories intersect with various types of abilities. His intellectual ability to survive the eruption is, in the opinion of some, associated with the race of the *nègre* and, in the opinion of others, with a Samson-like masculinity. Similarly, his supposedly mediocre linguistic abilities are connected to his journalistically labelled "West Indian" citizenship. In tandem, Cyparis's narrative underscores, through its multiple versions (including his varied names) and numerous audiences, how individuals regularly operate narrative in order to enhance various forms of profit. Further, it reveals how Cyparis has been incorporated into multiple narratives – the Martinican, the French, the American – all either literary or historical. Ultimately, the multiple facets of Cyparis's tale reveal how bodies and their abilities are a recurrent component of such narratives and the identities they produce.

In sum, Cyparis's narrative, which hinged on and sold his extraordinariness, becomes one way to begin a discussion of identification and narrative. It exemplifies how humans are identified as freaks: as *monstres* and *bizarreries*, gawked at on or off-stage for a disordering of norms; as *chaos*, which the individual represents within particular social contexts; as *parias*, read as untouchable, liminal, or deviant; as *phénomènes* that defy natural or cultural codes. It also opens up a reflection on how freak identification, whether self-authored or externally writ, becomes a salient means for exploring the role of narrative and bodily ability in, but not unique to, Francophone studies.

The works that I have chosen to study provide representations similar to those of Cyparis's tale. I engage in this reflection through close readings of four characters from different novels who encounter exceptionally normative identification processes: citizenship production through the use of linguistic abilities required of the citizen and for the nation-state in Jacques Godbout's *Les têtes à Papineau* (1981) [*The Papineau Heads*];[17] gender and biological reproduction for the preservation of faith and fortune in two novels by Tahar Ben Jelloun, *L'enfant de sable* (1985) [*The Sand Child* (1987)] and *La nuit sacrée* (1987) [*The Sacred Night* (1989)]; and race, spirituality, and the fabrication of control over supernatural abilities in Maryse Condé's *Moi, Tituba sorcière … Noire de Salem* (1986) [*I, Tituba, Black Witch of Salem* (1994)]. The protagonists' formations of identity are nothing if not visceral. Perceived as the monster, the pariah, or as chaos, the characters endure recurrent operations that alter abilities, and, as a result, the gamut of represented bodily abilities becomes, as their tales tell, understandable as undeniably pliable. The abilities constantly shift or are shifted, and, as such, they exist within what I propose to call a spectrum of bodily abilities. This spectrum includes but is not limited to varied categorizations of disabilities (as I discuss below) as well as inabilities and extraordinary abilities, all of which factor into the production of identity and which may have other labels (such as "capacities" or "faculties"). The protagonists of these novels move or are moved throughout the spectrum in the production of their identities. Although not all are exclusively Francophone in their contexts, the studied tales are represented in Francophone novels, occur in various regions of the world, and come to light because of operations on bodies and master sociocultural narratives that speak about related identity categories such as citizenship, gender, and race. Given this convergence, Francophone studies becomes a rich space in which to explore the questions at hand as it is a field in which reflections on ability have yet to be fully explored but in which these abilities continuously appear.

To undertake a study of freaks, abilities, and operations in Francophone literature might, of course, suggest at one level that there is something "abnormal," "deviant," or even "freakish" about this literary grouping.[18] Many voices have made similar claims about the rubric itself. One example is undoubtedly the 16 March 2007 publication of "Pour une 'littérature-monde' en français" ["For a 'World Literature' in French"], also known as the Manifeste des 44, a text composed by a collection of forty-four authors whom critics frequently affiliate with *la francophonie* (Le Bris and Rouaüd).[19] Readers familiar with the "manifesto" recognize it as the signatories' now famous gesture to separate themselves and their written work from *la francophonie*. The authors' motivations are varied, and they include an interest in, for example, seeing themselves as voices of the "inconnu" [unknown] that exist around the world and not as the "variante exotique tout juste tolérée" [exotic variant simply tolerated] that they feel *la francophonie* transmits.[20] Another important and earlier meditation on *la francophonie* appears in Aliko Songolo's "Présentation" to the 2003 *Présence Francophone* collection entitled "Littératures francophones: Un corp(u)s étranger?" ["Francophone literatures: A foreign corp(u)s?"].[21] Writing of what he gauges as the field's still tenuous position at the beginning of the twenty-first century and the need of certain entities to harness it, Songolo describes Francophone literature as follows: "bref, il s'agit d'un corp(u)s étranger qu'il faut gérer, contrôler, limiter. Par conséquent, elle [la francophonie] a dû faire face à des mécanismes d'exclusion de tous genres" [In sum, this is a foreign corp(u)s that must be managed, controlled, and limited. As a result, *la francophonie* has had to face exclusionary forces of all kinds] (7).

The Francophone debate and its surrounding polemic, although in ways relevant to the present discussion, are not the focus of this study. My introduction and the following chapters and sections clearly study Francophone texts from varying regions of the world while, at the same time, recognizing that "Francophone" refers to a rubric as well as to a multilayered field of study (especially with respect to cultural and literary production) while "francophone" refers to a linguistic appellation. The "inconnu" of the 44 and Songolo's "étranger" have important connections to this work. They both recall the abnormal, the deviant, the curious, the other-worldly, and the freakish, all elements of literature that writers (e.g., those of the 44) often claim to share with their readers through their texts. Similar to what individuals such as Lennard Davis and Ato Quayson argue in their respective works about "strange" disabled bodies in literature, such representation draws readers to texts.[22]

As it stands, I do not make an effort to read "Francophone literature," or *la francophonie,* as a cohesive collective; rather, from its earliest conception, my purpose in *Operation Freak* has always been to examine the ways in which Francophone texts are representations of varying parts of the world, regardless of whether the latter are (exclusively) francophone. I also examine the ways in which narrated, fictional experiences of identification, operated by varying agents and through the support of master narratives that speak of or rely on bodily abilities, reveal similar but not universal processes of sociocultural identification in the same world regions. Such operations depend in multiple ways on the human body and on narrative; similarly, as the collection of works studied here indicates, these operative gestures can and do exist in more than one, and thus arguably in any, region of the world.

Moreover, by focusing on the spectrum of bodily abilities involved in identification, I open up the Francophone novels explored here and, thereby, Francophone studies to the detection of patterns that account for the crossing of multiple identities in ways that neither separate nor compartmentalize. As such, *Operation Freak* continues in the spirit of Carine Mardorossian by demonstrating how "diverse configurations of difference cannot be read in isolation since they acquire meaning through one another," and it thereby "challenges our deep-seated investments in normative figurations of identity" (16). I ask what kind of world is suggested or even imaginable through juxtaposing various literary freaks and by exploring related processes of identification. I assemble literary texts and sociocultural narratives from varied world regions, all of which point in at least one very clear way to the perpetual operation of identity, narrative, the body, and bodily abilities.

It is here, at the crossroads of culture and bodily abilities, of production and operation, that the Francophone literary works under study can be said to represent identity production. Through a close reading of various bodies and regions of the world imagined in Godbout's, Ben Jelloun's, and Condé's novels, I show how operated bodily ability, in the spirit of Catherine Kudlick (2003), becomes one of the identity-centred means by which all individuals and collectivities attempt to make sense of themselves and the world. Such attention to text also provides a further means for understanding Songolo's *corp(u)s francophone* and the 44's *monde francophone* and how they connect to Kudlick's world. Specifically, such insight arises from the ways that the texts represent freak protagonists and their bodily abilities, a concept that Rosemarie Garland Thomson helps us to understand and that I explore later.[23]

In this repsect, the concept of abilities that I touched on earlier emerges from the field of disability studies. I expand upon how, in *Critical Conditions* (2012), Julie Nack Ngue astutely summarizes existing theoretical reflections on the category of disability itself: "Disability should be understood as varying health and body states on a continuum of normative health, rather than as a fixed state of being with clear borders and contours" (12). Nack Ngue, in addition to Kudlick and Garland Thomson and many others, has extensively and rigorously explored the multiple states of disability. The concept of disability that I use echoes theirs: it designates both a physiological state (with and without the normative implications of physiology, as determined by the context) and the experiences lived in relation to it. It also includes such states, both assigned and appropriated, in their theoretical, fictional, and lived contexts, which are recurrently read or represented as non-normative. I use the same definition when speaking of all of the types of ability, noting especially when they are read negatively or pejoratively.

Through its readings of the aforementioned novels' characters, *Operation Freak* expands disability-grounded discussions in order to speak of the spectrum of abilities. I use the concept of disability as a framework within which I define abilities. I also suggest that abilities are neither forcibly nor always situated within a context of normative health (as do Nack Ngue and others) and, thus, not solely within a context of disability. Normative sociocultural codes of healthy bodily abilities do at times factor into the readings, as do related states of disability. However, I look closely at a broad range of abilities into and out of which individuals move, are moved, and can be convinced to move, whether it be from disabled to able-bodied, from extraordinarily abled to disabled, or otherwise. Within this spectrum, there are no inherent valorizing or valorized mid- or end points: worth is designated or interpreted only in the context of master sociocultural narratives that are equally operated and that reveal both covert and overt production-rooted motivations. This mutability is particularly evident and revelatory in the novels under study when attention is paid to the rhetorical and surgical nature of the operations that shift or alter abilities. Quayson's words (2007) with respect to a state of ability as impermanent and transitory are particularly useful as they essentially help to emphasize how every individual *does, can,* and *will* move across any given spectrum of ability.[24]

Such shiftability is not without parallels in other critical and theoretical contemplations of identity and its formation.[25] It can be seen in the work of, for example, Alfred Kinsey (1948), who argues that sexual behaviour is part of the living world and thus "a continuum in each and every one of its aspects"; or of Judith Butler (1990), who presents gender as "a complexity whose totality is permanently deferred" (Kinsey 639; Butler, *Gender,* 22).[26] Within the field of disability studies, such impermanence also finds an echo in reflections on the cognitive abilities identified with and as autism. Mark Osteen (2008) argues that spectral positioning can happen in two ways: either various people fall in differing places or "any given autistic person's abilities ... occupy different locations on [the spectrum] at different times" (7). Stuart Murray's work (2008) on narrative and, specifically, autistic biography concurs regarding the breadth of the autistic spectrum (i.e., its being as wide as that of the non-autistic spectrum) when he posits that "life writing by those with autism illustrates this kind of variation" (*Representing* 45).[27]

As such theories of identity speak to each other, the various forms of identity have contact with one another in the spectrally conceived formation of identity. The readings that I conduct demonstrate how the abilities that exist within a spectrum regularly intersect with other identity categories. They all take root in master sociocultural narratives of various identities that are fundamental to the formation of both individual and collective identities. Such identity formation occurs, as depicted in the novels under study, with respect to citizenship (within the nation or the nation-state), gender (within the religious community), and race (within the trans-regional politico-economic structure). The same novels testify to such forms of identification through their depiction of the various physically mutilating (typically surgical) as well as discursively manipulating operations that the protagonists endure and recount. Furthermore, because the master sociocultural narratives that speak to bodily abilities and that inform the operating agents' motives differ, none of the resultant identificatory processes and products in the varying regions is the same. However, spectrums of bodily ability remain recurrent factors in identification processes around the world – a world for which the novels serve as allegories and within which they underscore lived experience.

Through such critical engagement with the novels of Godbout, Ben Jelloun, and Condé, I bring to light a hitherto unrealized discussion of bodily abilities in the world. Certainly bodily abilities, and especially disabilities, have been the topic of many book-length studies. Contemporary works that explore representations of disability in the literature of varying world regions do exist. However, for some time now the mainstay in studies of disability has tended to concentrate on what are deemed "highly industrialized" (and usually anglophone) regions of the world such as Australia, France, the United Kingdom, and the United States. Such projects reveal that discourses of disability (English) and *handicap* (French) were, since at least the First World War (with respect to government-distributed benefits), articulated in terms similar to those at use at the time of the publication of this book, with certain sociocultural contexts particular to each region. However, in cultural documents such as literature, film, and the fine art of that era, disability rarely entered the critical arena.[28] Since the 1970s and 1980s, when readings of bodies and of the narratives about them tended to move from Marxist discussions of class conflict towards the lived experience of the cultural body (as theorized by, among others, Hélène Cixous, Michel Foucault, Edouard Glissant, and Julia Kristéva), conditions identifiable in terms of bodily abilities, including disability, became increasingly recognized within various contexts (political, social, cultural) and regularly studied in literature.[29]

Yet disability – and the spectrum of bodily abilities that includes it as well as the narratives that speak of it and the spectrum – had not gained much attention in the multiple discussions of various sociocultural configurations and identifications of bodies. Over the past two decades, however, an increasing number of scholarly works on disability and *handicap* have brought more attention to the spectrum of bodily abilities, particularly to disability, as they are lived and written. Such studies reach into literary and other cultural representations of disability and also explore the intersections of disability with multiple categories of identity.[30] After such Western-focused works appeared, other studies eventually arose to examine literary representations of disability in regions of Africa and (later) Latin America, although not always in a postcolonial context.[31]

With the exception of Nack Ngue's work, there have been almost no projects on sociocultural representations of disability in Francophone studies, let alone on bodily abilities across a spectrum in texts and in history.[32] Such a lack is surprising, given the wide-reaching corpus of Francophone literature. Like many other texts, Francophone works often focus on the human body as a malleable element necessary to the narrative of the work and to the sociocultural narratives historically relevant to varying world regions represented in literary texts. In some cases, the emphasis on the body and its abilities arises from the numerous regions of the Francophone world born of France's three-century-long efforts at imperial expansion.[33] The relevance of such discourse appears in the range of historical projects that served, altered, and thereby operated the abilities of the colonized as well as of the colonizing bodies forced to advance such a mission. In other cases, the spectrum of bodily abilities becomes apparent within the narrative through an individual's efforts at self-identification and autonomy, which are informed, in part or in whole, by the variety of sociocultural narratives relevant to the regions within which he or she is represented.

The speaker of Aimé Césaire's *Cahier d'un retour au pays natal* (1939) [*Notebook of a Return to the Native Land* (2001)] emphasizes varying states of altered or damaged psycho-corporeal abilities (represented largely as melancholia) of the "nègre" as caused by colonialism.[34] The protagonist of Amadou Kourouma's *Les soleils des indépendances* (1968) [*The Suns of Independence* (1981)] and his wife are, in part, due to the protagonist's concerns over lineage, largely challenged by his wife's severely diminished abilities to procreate, which are directly related to genital cutting gone awry and, therefore, her failed operative introduction into womanhood. And the protagonist of Ying Chen's *Le mangeur* (2006) [*The Eater*] works to negotiate a patrilineal and cultural history of extraordinary consumption that bears certain similarities to the eating disorder classified as bulimia. Such stories involving the spectrum of operated bodily abilities (disabled and able-bodied, acquired and congenital) continue to fill the pages of *le corpus francophone*. In *Operation Freak*, I look at similar representations of bodily ability as well as at the related spectrum by offering a close study of the above-referenced novels of Jacques Godbout, Tahar Ben Jelloun, and Maryse Condé, which speak of specific world regions – Quebec, North Africa (particularly Morocco), and the Caribbean (notably the Lesser Antilles). My explorations are accompanied by an examination of related juridical, legislative, religious, and scientific texts (specifically, what their narratives spell out) as well as of the social customs that are apparent in the novels and that are the master sociocultural narratives referenced and operated during ability-altering manipulations.

The prominence of operated bodily abilities in identity processes does not by any means exist solely within fictional worlds. It also appears in the lived experiences of individuals from regions the same as, near, or related to those represented in the works under study. Contemporary examples – Francophone and otherwise – occupy the three interludes and the conclusion of *Operation Freak*. My intent is to further bridge the relationship between the imagined and the lived as well as the local and the global in the thinking of the intersection of bodily abilities, related operations, narrative, and identity, as with Cyparis's tale. The lived stories of individuals from earlier periods and varying world regions also further demonstrate how, as various forms of operations reveal, identificatory processes have always been informed in some way by bodily ability. Saartje Baartman, the "Hottentot Venus," became – at least during her short early nineteenth-century life, which was spent in the West (particularly in London and Paris) – a quintessential staged and somatic sign of heightened sexual abilities associated with race.[35] The postmortem dissection of her body and the casts made of some of her bodily parts, all by French anatomist Georges Cuvier, offered her genitalia as proof not only of her sexuality but also of her exaggerated sexual abilities, which are forever linked to questions of race. As early as 1685, in the first version of France's *code noir* [*Black Code*], Africans bought and branded as slaves for the French-owned farms and plantations of the Caribbean were defined as "meubles, & comme tels entrer en la Communauté" [charges, and as such enter(ed) into community property]; they were non-thinking subhuman objects of property valued for their ability to labour, and they suffered bodily mutilations as punishment for violations of the code.[36] The leagues of labourers and the caravan of "King's Daughters" (*filles du roi*) in seventeenth-century New France were appreciated for their abilities to produce as well as to reproduce, particularly as the colony fought to keep itself alive amidst decades of obstacles.[37] And there were the thousands upon thousands of castrated boys and men from varying regions of Europe and Africa during the years of the Ottoman Empire who were valued for their presumed sexual and procreative inabilities when serving as guards and advisors within family structures.

How, then, might all of the examples thus far presented and the protagonists in the novels under study come together through a discussion of bodily abilities, identity, narrative, and operation in the discursive arena of the freak? And why is this of importance? Certainly, it may appear that there exists a tendency towards conflating individuals from disparate regions of the world as well as the sociocultural lenses through which their bodies are read. It may even seem that such observations unintentionally identify all of the individuals listed above as abnormal and, given the title of this work, thereby collapse them all under the category of "freak," which, as is often discussed (and is addressed below), has typically been associated with Western capitalist endeavours.

Such readings are not, however, indicative of my intent; rather, I aim to demonstrate how individuals are identified – or operated – in terms of both their bodily abilities and the normative sociocultural spectrums of bodily ability. As many other studies of identification determine, *Operation Freak* argues that certain individuals are identified and singled out from the norm. Here they are the *lusus naturae* (freak of nature), or, as Michael Chemers's useful etymological study of the term "freak" reveals (see chapter 1), they are a sudden cavort within the average (6). Joan (Colin) Dayan approaches a related question when investigating eighteenth-century operations to scientific and legislative narratives in colonial Saint-Domingue with respect to race and blood, which also reproduce convenient forms of degeneration and oddities (*Haiti* 234). In such a context, identity becomes increasingly (but not solely) understandable for the ways that the body's abilities are determined to exist farther from such a norm than do those of most other identities. Through such remarkable embodiments, the prevalence of the spectrum of abilities in identification processes is much more clearly represented.

My engagement with the chosen novels also reveals a consistent relationship between the body, identity, and various forms of production: the tendency of the protagonist's bodies to be discursively or physically (and often surgically) operated in the context of bodily ability has a direct correlation to varying goals of production that realize profit and that are later discussed as "reproduction." The novels disclose how the correlation exists globally, despite the recurrent tendency to associate such performative aspirations with the strictly capitalist endeavours of Europe and the United States. Such an identity phenomenon stems from what Rosemarie Garland Thomson suggests in her introduction to *Freakery* (1996) as the penultimate manifestation of an ability-charged identification process rooted in performative and sociocultural constructs of abnormality and production. It results in what she terms the "freak of culture," which I understand as *monstre de la culture*.[38]

Although the use of the term *monstre* is almost entirely absent from the novels under study, the multifaceted identificatory processes of the freak that harmonize with what Garland Thomson proposes, and with what I explore in chapter 1, are clearly apparent.[39] Indeed, their presence allows for an engagement of French-language cultures with freak discourse studies, a connection that thus far has only been established in non-literary projects.[40]

Specifically, the novels of Godbout, Ben Jelloun, and Condé correspond acutely and extensively to the aforementioned conceptualization. First, they are based on eye-grabbing phenomena reported and at times sensationalized via the media or word of mouth: the existence of multiple births and the surgical operation on conjoined twins living in Canada and the United States; the *fait divers* of a Moroccan girl raised as a boy; and a black female slave who, unlike her white counterparts, escaped execution during the Salem witch trials. Second, the novels were composed in the 1980s and therefore during the aforementioned critical and ideological shift from social class to the body.[41] Third, they contain protagonists who, because of their staged abnormal bodies (which are intended to produce profit) and because of the numerous norm-based operations across the spectrum of bodily abilities that they experience, are considered to be *monstres de la culture*. The character construction of performative protagonists – Godbout's media-hopping and gifted conjoined twins, Ben Jelloun's circus-working gender-switching *homme/femme fatale*, and Condé's staged and gazed-upon exotic witch – confirms the connection.[42]

Yet these protagonists are not conceived of as freaks simply because they embody the absolute Other of mass culture, that objectified performative individual through whose on-stage body anyone and every-one was encouraged to affirm their normality.[43] Through the recount-ing of the events they lived both on and (especially) off their stages, the novels demonstrate how the operations to the characters' extraor-dinary bodies, justified in the name of master sociocultural narratives, showcase the role of bodily abilities in their identificatory processes. Relying on the testimonial potential of diaries and storytelling, and opening up enclosed or private spaces (operating rooms, prison cells, bedrooms) where the operations occur, these novels zoom in on the ability-targeted operations that the protagonists endure at the hands of agents from medical, economic, religious, and even familial socio-cultural structures. The protagonists become the hyperbolic embodi-ment of ability-charged identity formation as their bodies are shuttled throughout the spectrum of bodily abilities. Although the novels reveal how these characters work to reclaim their identities by com-bating the effects of the operations (and in certain ways by appropri-ating their "freak" identities, a topic equally worthy of critical explo-ration), I focus on the external sources of identification in order to demonstrate how and why a freak-of-culture identity can still carry negatively charged connotations.

To demonstrate the occurrence and importance of such opera-tions, I trace the ways in which both physical (surgical) and discur-sive procedures reveal and reinforce the operative process of identifi-cation rooted in bodily ability. The style of each of the novels contains rhetorical constructions that echo and, in various ways, rein-force the tone of operation. The novels depend on the genre-based associations of intimacy between reader and text so that they can confidentially relate the characters's presumably private lives. Within the narrative that is each novel, the operative procedures are repre-sented as penetrating and often as akin to surgery in order to under-score the invasive, normative manipulation of the human body that, here, is read in the context of bodily ability. The manipulation may not always necessitate a surgical blade; however, it regularly involves mutilation of the body through penetrating and, at times, disfiguring measures. The operations also arise from various agents' adaptations, and thus operations, to master sociocultural narratives as well as from the ways in which the protagonists' bodily abilities are rhetori-cally presented as ripe for operation. Ultimately, such operations reveal the arbitrary means by which categories such as "citizen," "woman," "healer," and "freak" are perpetually constructed. Simultaneously, it highlights how the operations are intended to perpetuate – or "reproduce" – the agents' profit-based agenda through an assertion of power that alters bodily abilities and related sociocultural narratives.

"Reproduction" – the continued efforts on the part of the agents to benefit from the repeated operations on freak characters in varied contexts of production – summarizes the operators' profit-centred goal in the complex and capricious processes of identification. Because reproduction depends on operations that emphasize and often target bodily ability, I discuss how the spectrum of bodily abilities at play in such identification processes are always perceived in terms of what the bodies – because of their abilities – can or cannot produce. The strategic echo of the iconoclastic capitalistic production in the sideshow freak's display and performance is, again, undeniable, and similar forms of production are invariably replicated in the lives and goals of the protagonists. By exploring how operating agents pretend to safeguard sociocultural structures, I reveal how their operations are only ever concerned with achieving *their* profit-focused goals – the production of offspring, language, labour, or financial gain – never those of the protagonists.

In chapter 1, "Locations and Locutions of Ability Operations," I begin to develop such ability-centred thought. I point to theoretical and philosophical trends in which the body and its functions, as objects of discourse and subjects of experience, have played and continue to play a crucial role in the formation of identity and the understanding of human experience. I pay particular attention to the ways in which identification hinges on and speaks of bodily ability, how and what operations highlight the importance of such abilities, and how forms of reproduction remain the primary goal in such operations. Specifically, I demonstrate how the freak, as a form of identity, is, again in the words of Garland Thomson (1996), grounded in sociocultural constructions of normality and bodily ability that work towards various profit-oriented forms of reproduction.

In chapter 2, "Excising Conjoined Citizenship; or, the Beheading of Linguistic Abilities in Jacques Godbout's *Les têtes à Papineau*," I explore how linguistic abilities – those simultaneously intellectual and physical, of the mind and of the body – play a crucial role in the identification of the citizen. Such identity formation is emphasized in a series of ability-altering operations endured by the protagonists, most notably the reduction of their two heads into one by the anglophone Dr Gregory B. Northridge.

The question of biological reproductive bodily ability takes centre stage in chapter 3, "Regenerating Family Fortune: Incising Religious Orders of Gender and Procreation in Tahar Ben Jelloun's *L'enfant de sable* and *La nuit sacrée*." I examine how the ability to biologically reproduce plays a fundamental role not only in the gendered processes of identification of the novels' protagonist but also in the operating agents' motivations for manipulating the human body in terms of these procreative abilities.

In chapter 4, "Witchy Ways: Transregional Mutilations of Race and Supernatural Abilities in Maryse Condé's *Moi, Tituba sorcière ... Noire de Salem*," I address how the individual is identified in relationship to categories of race and the ability to care for the human body. I take a step away from the scientific and sociological conceptions of linguistic abilities associated with the citizen and the procreative abilities associated with men and women (all addressed in previous chapters) to explore how an individual's abilities to heal are read on and in the body. More specifically, I examine how the novel's eponymous protagonist is operated in terms of her supernatural abilities (which are shown to be of the mind, soul, and body) at the same time that she is manipulated with regard to sociocultural constructions of race.

At the end of his introduction to *Staging Stigma*, Chemers explains his motivations for examining in depth the history of the US freak show, the freak performer, and, thereby, the "ugly" word "freak." He underscores that his discussions of the marginalized group of performers recognize the undeniable connection to bodily abilities just as they realize the liberation of a performative type of identity:

> Freakeries are, without doubt, a representation (even a heuristics) of disability in its most stigmatized form and, although we may find it odious and possibly even dangerous to handle, it is within that precise context that we find its most productive analysis. Disability may never be liberated from the history of the freak show, but the freak show can and must be liberated from its historical neglect, so that the freak, hitherto visible only as a victim of conscienceless managers and degenerate audiences, can be recognized as an active agent ... To conceive of freaks in such a way

has a magnificent potential, not only for illuminating the history
of the freak show but also for raising important questions about
the formation of the American concepts of "normal" and
"abnormal." (9)

Commenting on freakery as the category under which such
diverging bodies are listed, Chemers's statements lean directly
towards a rethinking of the identificatory value of freak performance
and the agency of the performers. However, as his words on
American notions of "normal" and "abnormal" indicate, he also seeks
to reveal the means by which such categories are thought, especially
as they relate to stigmatizing conceptualizations of disability.
Furthermore, where Chemers sees his discussion of freak history as
liberatory for performances and performers, he also admits that it
may, in certain ways, "[strike] a blow at mainstreaming persons with
disabilities" (9). The need to examine the past (especially that of the
performer), Chemers claims, is what merits study.

Operation Freak works in ways parallel to yet distinct from *Staging
Stigma*. The questions of agency that Chemers raises do factor into my
close readings of the novels, much as they have in the different critical
optics of earlier studies of these authors and their works.[44] However,
by exploring the stories of marginalized characters as well as the
master sociocultural narratives that contribute to their tales through
agent-conducted operations, I demonstrate how private operations of
publicly staged bodily abilities regularly factor into constructions
of identity. And I do so outside of the purview of the colonial
metropoles that are analyzed in the numerous essays in Bancel et al.'s
Zoos humains (2004), which discuss the spread of freakery across
Europe and the United States. *Operation Freak* does not prioritize the
freak as a model of identification, nor does it propose an effacement
of such an identity formation model. Instead, through discussion
of the novels' characters, it reveals how such Francophone representations – with or without all of their intended political, moral, or
ethical commentary – are in fact a heuristics in their own right. They
provide a means for understanding the ways in which the spectrum of
bodily abilities and the sociocultural norms attached to them are
consistent components of identification processes throughout the
Francophone world and, by extension, around the world.

I

Locations and Locutions
of Ability Operations

Toute œuvre est plus ou moins amputée dès sa véritable naissance, c'est-à-dire dès sa première lecture.
[Every work is more or less amputated right from its true birth: that is to say, from its first reading.]

Gérard Genette, Palimpsestes

Human bodies and the societies they live in are by nature unstable.

Catherine Kudlick, "Disability History"

In *Le corps en Islam* (1999) [*The Body in Islam*], Malek Chebel offers the following comment on the human body: "Le corps est un élément actif du conditionnement social et culturel. Sa plasticité en fait un support de mémoire, une sorte d'archive vivante qui permet à l'observateur, des siècles après, de mesurer le degré d'acculturation de la société où il est immergé" [The body is an integral element of social and cultural conditioning. Its plasticity makes of it a memory aid, a sort of living archive that allows the observer, centuries later, to measure the degree of acculturation in the society in which he is immerged] (35). As the title of Chebel's work shows, he reads the body in an Islamic sociocultural context. The content of his work (as well as the work's original title for the 1984 edition, *Le corps dans la tradition du Maghreb* [*The Body in the Maghrebian Tradition*]) provides a more specific but still somewhat general framework – North African – within which the body is, according to Chebel, to be understood. The citation speaks undeniably of the body of the Arab-Muslim Maghrebian who has lived in, and is therefore marked by the sociocultural experiences of living in, an Arab-Muslim region.[1]

And yet the citation offers something other than a snapshot of a specific cultural context in which individuals live and according to which their bodies, and thus their identities, may be formed. It provides a means for understanding how the living body is one element in a process of sociocultural conditioning at the same time as it implies that other elements contribute to the body's formation. The citation also provides a means for thinking of the body as a living visual referent – an archive – through which anyone may be able to read such a process. The body, as an active and living repository, testifies to a sociocultural process of identification that is not only theorized but lived.

What the Chebel citation does not discuss directly, but which his project does, is how concepts of bodily ability (which include disability) factor into such somatically grounded meditations. Because of its attention to abilities as well as its concurrent emphasis on related exclusionary sociocultural powers, Chebel's work is in dialogue with that of specialists of both disability studies and freak discourse studies.[2] In her introduction to the collection *Freakery* (1996), Rosemarie Garland Thomson writes in a similar fashion of the staged bodies in various human exhibits, many of whom would be considered disabled and all of whom she considers "extraordinary." When reflecting on ability-charged bodies displayed as sociocultural abnormalities, or "freaks of culture," she explains that "the extraordinary body is fundamental to the narratives by which we make sense of ourselves and of our world" (1). Like Chebel, Garland Thomson speaks of the readability of the body and of its importance to processes of identification that are normatively operated. Unlike Chebel, she speaks of the body and its importance to the variety of narratives used in various forms of identification typified by the spectacle of freaks. Such identificatory processes are, for Garland Thomson, connected not only to bodily abilities but also to the narratives that agents use to define bodies in terms of their abilities. Chebel and Garland Thomson together point to the ways in which bodies are understood in terms of both narratives and abilities, with one of the latter being a capacity to produce – be it capital, identity, a fundamental sign in the interpretation of materiality, or the perpetuation of narratives that undergird sociocultural structures.

In this chapter I continue to tease out such a theoretical discussion of bodily abilities – conceptualized in my introduction as many abilities within a spectrum that are also thought of as capacities or functions – and sociocultural narratives in order to explore their role in identification processes and, thus, in human existence. The ways in which specific identity categories – such as citizenship, gender, and race – along with bodily abilities factor into identification in specific sociocultural contexts appears in following chapters. Here, I discuss how operations of and on the body reveal the workings of an externally manifested identity formation often associated with freaks of culture, the penultimate Western sociocultural signifier of bodily ability and production, and how this identification process is always located within the spectrum of abilities. Reflection upon the concept of an operation as a surgical act, as an activity that probes in order to acquire knowledge but that seeks to modify in order to heal (at least in the context of normative sociocultural constructs of health), helps to understand how the act of operating is crucial to the present discussion.

The operations themselves are thus acts that cut, penetrate, and deform the body and that are conducted by agents external to it. However, the operations are also simultaneously discursive in that the same agents manipulate master sociocultural narratives in order to accomplish and to justify the corporeal manipulations. The goals that such forms of identification realize are those of reproduction, or what is to be understood as the perpetuation of various profit-aimed normative structures that can be repeatedly achieved through alteration of the body. These reproductive goals also reveal a potential for operation not only of the human body but also of narrative, and the manipulated legacy of bodies and the related narratives bear witness to the identification process. Focusing on bodily and narrative operations conducted by external agents is not intended to overshadow the agency of the operated individuals who are the novels' protagonists, which I explore in the following chapters. On the contrary, such an approach provides a method for thinking through the complex identification processes detailed across each of the novels and that includes, at times, the protagonists' participation for their own benefit.

Moreover, I want to allow for a deeper, more contemplative probing into the ways that operations of bodily abilities and of narratives live on in varying regions of the Francophone world. To do so, I explore various representations of bodily abilities, their relationship to various forms of narrative (including that of the freak), and the multiple means by which operations are understood. I do not intend to present an exhaustive, finite reflection upon the questions at hand but, rather, to bring narratives from various time periods and of varying geographical regions into a dialogue that asks readers, as Edouard Glissant comments in his own contemplation on the writing of national literatures, to do this: "méditer ce nouveau rapport au monde" [to reflect on their new relationship with the world] (*Le discours antillais* 332; *Caribbean Discourse* 101).

PHYSIOLOGY, DISABILITY, AND THE SPECTRUM OF ABILITIES: INITIAL REFLECTIONS

Physiology is a frequent component of discussions of human existence. The ways in which a body moves or does what it does have often been explained as part and parcel of who an individual is and why she exists in the ways that she does. Such physiological capacities speak of what a body *does* (e.g., ambulate, gesticulate, masticate, procreate), thus denoting bodily abilities at the same time as they inform human existence. In their exploration of human nature, writers from regions considered highly industrialized and here referred to as the "West" (as Glissant's "project") reveal such a philosophical heritage – a heritage that, in ways, has informed contemporary projects on discourse and disability.

Think, for example, of the *Essais* (1588) [*The Complete Essays* (1958)] of Michel de Montaigne. Each chapter of each book encourages the efforts to know oneself, a knowing that often comes through the body's functions.[3] In many of the essays, Montaigne proclaims to be speaking from, and therefore of, his own physiological capacities, including those challenged by various health conditions. Because Montaigne's reflections begin from his subjective point of view informed by the status of his body and its altering abilities, his philosophical contemplations give substance to my articulation of the spectrum of bodily abilities and their inherent transformation. Furthermore, Montaigne's work also interrogates the multiple ways in which the individual's body is understood and therefore read. More specifically, Montaigne's reflections work to demonstrate how agents selectively assign a particular value as well as a type of production both to certain somatic forms and to the bodily capacities they perceive in them. Not unlike Garland Thomson's theory of the freak of culture, form becomes the means for determining, if not justifying, the production that is understood to arise from a body's functions or abilities.[4] This same conclusion is even true of the written word. As Richard Regosin writes in *The Matter of My Book* (1977), "Montaigne will insist on the word as substantive and on the fact that he literally resides in it … Like the ideal portrait, [the language of the *Essais*] seeks actually to participate in the nature, life, and properties of the man whose image it is" (199).

The chapter entitled "Des boyteux" ["Of Cripples"] in Book Three of the *Essais* is relevant to the present discussion because it speaks of types of bodies that, in many contemporary Western cultures, would be deemed either different, exploited, or disabled. Towards the end, Montaigne does write of the bodily abilities associated with individuals identified as cripples. But he does so by unveiling how such bodies have come to fulfill particular roles in society because of an accepted and acceptable non-normative physiology. For example, in the pursuit of their own interests agents have determined that the *boiteux* (cripples in general but, especially, male cripples) and, even more so, the *boiteuses* (female cripples) are better and even more productive sexual partners because of the ways in which their sexual and reproductive organs, due to presumed developments due to equally presumed limited abilities to stand and to walk, have been underused.[5] The result is that the *boiteux* come to be identified more in terms of their enhanced sexual abilities and less in terms of their apparent ambulatory disability, even though the latter remains a primary corporeal and therefore visual determinant in such a process of identification.

However, Montaigne's reflections become even more useful when he contemplates how easily the human mind can accept the sociocultural narrative associated with a somatic form that is charged with extraordinary abilities: "Nos raisons anticipent souvent l'effect, et ont l'estendue de leur jurisdiction si infinie, qu'elles jugent et s'exercent en l'inanité mesme et au non estre[.] Outre la flexibilité de nostre invention à forger des raisons à toute sorte de songes, nostre imagination se trouve pareillement facile à recevoir des impressions de la fauceté par bien frivoles apparences" [Our reasons often anticipate the fact, and extend their jurisdiction so infinitely that they exercise their judgment even in inanity and non-being{.} Not only is our invention flexible in forging reasons for all sorts of dreams, but our imagination is equally prone to receive impressions from the very unreliable appearances given by falsehood] (1034; 791).

Clearly Montaigne's argument aims to highlight the human mind's frequently facile acceptance of appearance – be it of the body of the cripple or of the proverb of a culture – with all of its sociocultural connotations. In this respect, his words on cripples engage in dialogue with the work of Chebel and Garland Thomson: not only may Montaigne's observers of the *boiteux* be prone to quick conclusions but they may also be swayed by somatic sociocultural significations that function within the context of bodily abilities.[6]

Friedrich Nietzsche's work provides another example of a way of thinking of human existence in direct relationship to physiology and bodily abilities. It has been said that Nietzsche encouraged philosophers who were interested in discussing human nature to be knowledgable about physiology because this would afford them greater awareness of the functions of the body that, in fact, inform human existence (and that affected Nietzsche's own health). Penelope Deutscher underscores the fundamental connection that Nietzsche drew between a philosopher's physiology and a philosopher's text, where a reader of said text can attest to the impact of the philosopher's body on the writing: "reading might well be a matter of listening for the posture of the writer's body, and … assessing the quality of the book might also be a matter of assessing the quality of the posture" (29).[7] Expressed in a context that employs the rhetorical overlap of the reader's abilities ("reading might well be a matter of listening"), Nietzsche's work suggests a link between physiology and text, where the former influences not just the quality of the work but also the ability to produce that quality.

The doctrine of eternal recurrence that Nietzsche develops in *The Gay Science* (1882) also alludes to movement between states of abilities. It posits that an individual's self-perception is definable and even alterable in terms of his awareness of his existence. Such awareness informs the individual's reaction to the theoretical possibility of reliving that existence throughout eternity, as is demonstrated in aphorism 341: "Would you not throw yourself down and gnash your teeth and curse the demon who spoke thus? Or have you once experienced a tremendous moment when you would have answered him: 'You are a god and never have I heard anything more divine?'" (194).

This reflection on human existence is filtered through what informs the individual's existence, and, in Nietzsche's work, such events include moments of health and illness (as related to pleasure and pain) in the human body. The conclusion is that the answer to the above hypothetical question will be guided by the impact that states of health and illness have on the body – not in its anatomical stasis but in its physiological fluidity. Furthermore, the answer will depend on how the individual thinks in terms of the ability to use her body as well as the body's abilities to function based on her already lived experience. From such statements, the individual's choice with respect to eternal recurrence may well demonstrate a willingness to possess a more normatively conceived healthy body – one immune from acquired conditions that might not only produce pain but also, as a result of diminishing abilities and potential pain, limit living. Such a state of bodily ability, then, could be seen as an impediment to activity and thus as a burden to the repetition of existence theorized in eternal recurrence.

A turn to reflections on disability in the late twentieth and early twenty-first centuries expands the present discussion, particularly since many works encourage a way of reconsidering various states of abilities as fundamental to human existence and as a consistent component of processes of identification. In *Narrative Prosthesis* (2000), David Mitchell and Sharon Snyder revisit what Montaigne and Nietzsche articulate regarding the body, including elements of the discussions above. They do this in order to demonstrate how bodily abilities have remained at the forefront of centuries of certain philosophical traditions. In a more general sense, Mitchell and Snyder shift the discourse from function (or physiology), which both Montaigne and Nietzsche emphasize in their discussions, to the recent referents of bodily abilities – specifically disability – and the normative contexts in which they have been conceived.

Mitchell and Snyder also concentrate on specific representations of disability, most notably the figure of the cripple in the works of Montaigne and Nietzsche. In so doing, they discuss how these philosophers troubled the conventional way of thinking about bodies that are today identified as disabled: "Both move philosophy toward a disruption of the tradition's formulas of ethical discourse through direct challenge to the normative expectations that surround disabled figures" (66). As demonstrated in my discussion of Montaigne, however, his work also engages in dialogue with my concept of the spectrum of abilities. Specifically, when he proposes the notion of a *boiteux* or a *boiteuse* as naturally inclined towards an enhanced sexual ability, the sexual ability itself comes across not as a disability or as an ability diminished (be it in terms of sociocultural or even moral value) but, rather, as various possibilities within the spectrum of one ability.

At the same time that Mitchell and Snyder underscore Montaigne and Nietzsche's respective breaks with such traditions, they also reveal the ways in which such apparent ruptures reinforce normative ways of identifying the self through perceived corporeal and physiological abnormality. Their discussion of Montaigne is of greatest relevance here for what it says of the identification process. Despite his argument's apparent efforts at challenging norm-based expectations, Mitchell and Snyder claim that it still highlights a negatively charged identity process: the viewer defines himself in contrast with a cripple who, observed, is understandable as decidedly specialized and therefore limited to certain bodily abilities. Although Montaigne's reflections do not intend to transmit a reductive reading of the cripple, it is the facile process of self-identification couched in differentiation and limitation of abilities (and, one might argue, Montaigne's own indication that he has felt the same) that Mitchell and Snyder find of concern. They claim that Montaigne's work continues to show how "the human will to knowledge is more readily exercised upon that which seems most unfamiliar" and thus reifies such distinctions (70). Although it may appear possible to interpret Montaigne's words as an indication that the *boiteux* and, specifically, the *boiteuses* are disabled in a negatively charged context (because they are, without doubt, limited to certain abilities), what becomes of more interest is the way that Montaigne's words on the power of the human will engage in dialogue with Mitchell and Snyder's. In other words, where they might disagree on the status of the abilities of the cripple, they would likely agree on the ways in which the human mind manipulates – or, in the context of the present work, operates – identity in the context of bodily abilities as such contexts are understood through engagement with sociocultural narratives.

As such reflections reveal, thinking of the impact of physiology on human existence implies thinking in terms of bodily abilities. The very notion of the body's functions is premised on the body's overall ability to function within a spectrum of abilities required, for example, to read, to write, to have sex and, thus, to think, to produce, or to feel. Such a perception exists in many contexts outside of those discussed thus far: the developing heart condition or the broken leg that, with or without prosthesis, may alter the ability to engage in physical activities; the presence of cerebral palsy that may require the use of speech-assisted devices to standardize linguistic abilities; the hyper-trained body of an athlete that typically possesses extreme physical (and at times psychological) abilities to compete and, thus, the chance to suffer injury or, over time, to exhaust one's abilities and return to a preconceived norm; a history of major depression that, with or without medication, informs an individual's psychological as well as physical abilities to engage in life's activities.

This short list of physiologically informed configurations shows how abilities are conceived as crucial to human existence and are movable within the spectrum of each ability through a variety of means. In this respect, an individual may determine acquired reduction in her own bodily ability to be positively or negatively charged, as either increasing or limiting her existence, and thus may encourage or avoid it. Such changes are typically thought of primarily in terms of disability (physical, intellectual, developmental) and, depending on sociocultural constructions of ability, as limiting or not limiting. The individual may also view another individual's bodily abilities – acquired or congenital disabilities or varying degrees of the same ability – as a means of self-identification. In either equation, the short list and other possible formulations of spectrums of bodily ability are most certainly understood as central to human existence and, thus, as fundamental to sociocultural processes of identification that are grounded in human interaction.

BODILY ABILITIES AND THE *MONDE FRANCOPHONE*

Although Mitchell and Snyder's collaborative work certainly remains pioneering, it is in fact one of many studies of disability that now ask for a reconsideration of various forms of bodily ability thought of in terms of disability. Most of the work that exists, as mentioned in my introduction, concentrates primarily on the sociocultural contexts of the United States, the United Kingdom, France, and other regions identified as part of the West. Projects by Lennard Davis (1995, 2002), Garland Thomson, and Henri-Jacques Stiker (1982, 2006), as well as those by Petra Kuppers (2003, 2007), Simi Linton (1998), and Tobin Siebers (2008, 2010), have resulted in groundbreaking studies that are anchored in similar sociocultural contexts. They reach into the forms of cultural production (e.g., literature, film, performance) coming out of these regions and inform many of the disability-focused projects in cultural contexts that appear today.

Such observations on the geographical limits of discussion do not imply that the questions of bodily ability in general and disability in particular have not been addressed in texts from varying regions of the world. In 1995, in a cultural context that does not focus on the literary text, Benedicte Ingstad and Susan Whyte's "Disability and Culture: An Overview" posits that cultural understandings about "the body and personhood must be seen in the context of … social [and cultural] interaction" (4).[8] As I discuss in the introduction, many explorations in the related fields of literary cultural studies exist. They include works such as Ato Quayson's (2007) as well as Clare Barker's (2006, 2012) and, for the *monde francophone*, studies by Julie Nack Ngue (2007, 2009, 2012). The *Journal of Literary and Cultural Disability Studies* is a key publication that regularly houses such projects from and about varying world regions. Such works are filling the shelves of critical studies libraries and are helping to demonstrate the varied ways in which disabilities are lived, represented, and conceptualized. On parallel levels (especially for the studies that also work to advance the representation of rights for the disabled), a discourse about (and, more recently, legislation concerning) disabilities continues to grow throughout the world, providing further proof that attention is being paid to such discourse and to such lived experiences.[9]

At the same time as the above works pay necessary attention to sociocultural contexts, they all tend to primarily explore states of disability. Their focus has drawn many a critical eye to the varied yet fundamental and consistent ways in which disability factors into processes of identification. Most notably, they have made readers understand, or at the very least contemplate, the ways in which identity and existence are profoundly informed by bodily abilities. The recurrent result, however, has been that other states of bodily ability within a particular spectrum, and their recurrent role in identification processes, tend to be discussed either incidentally or as they appear in conjunction with states of disability (be it, for example, the normative binary opposite they may represent in the determination of disability or the state out of which a body moves into acquired disability). There are, however, multiple instances in which varied forms of abilities – extraordinary abilities (acquired or congenital) or even inabilities (acquired, congenital, or neither) – factor into identification processes as much or more than states of disability. To understand more fully how bodily abilities play such roles, it is necessary to widen the current scope of critical engagement and to explore their varied states as well as the sociocultural narratives that inform them.

One narrative that helps us to think about the centrality as well as the malleability of bodily ability is the saga of the African slave trade that occurred primarily in the eighteenth century and that, for centuries, has spoken about bodily abilities. Throughout the history of the former French colonial empire alone, the estimated 1 million enslaved bodies that were valued for the productivity they realized, as Christopher Miller points out in *The French Atlantic Triangle* (2008), were also valued for their varied bodily abilities to produce (59). The same holds true of the enslaved bodies that laboured for France's colonial rivals.

Joan (Colin) Dayan's *Haiti, History, and the Gods* (1995) perhaps comes the closest to a discussion of abilities and, specifically, disabilities.[10] For example, the sections "Taxonomies of Enlightenment" and "Tools of Terror" provide a detailed reading of eighteenth-century texts by Moreau de Saint-Méry and the Comte de Buffon that rework categories of race and ability. She highlights the emphasis, particularly in Saint-Méry's elaborately imagined taxonomy, on the degeneration and monstrosity born of interracial mixing. The results included the "*gens de couleur* who are lighter" as well as (and as distinct from) albinos – all bodies that, in varied ways, presented a supposed menace to colonial white superiority, right down to its very blood (238, 240). In a vocabulary that speaks directly to bodily abilities, Dayan points out how, according to Saint-Méry, "false whites" could be detected by traits such as "effeteness, weakness, or debilitation," an eighteenth-century vocabulary that, through valuation, speaks to what could be considered lesser abilities if not disabilities (234). Her own summation of Saint-Méry's colour scales – a "colour continuum" – emphasizes the varied positions made available to his category of *gens de couleur* (232). This positionality, Dayan suggests, is both arbitrary (a constructed narrative) and mutable (due to further "mixing"), and, in these respects, it corresponds to the thinking of spectrums of abilities.

Many literary works, such as Aimé Césaire's *Cahier d'un retour au pays natal* (1939), attest to the identification of bodies of African origin alone, a process Césaire later connects to all populations living a colonized condition, as discussed in *Discours sur le colonialisme* (1955) [*Discourse on Colonialism* (1972)]. The related histories of mutilated colonized bodies (which in contemporary terminology would be considered disabled or *handicapé*) and the colonizer's anxiety over consequent loss of labour attest to a long-standing and extensive familiarity with the body, its abilities, and its worth in terms of capital.[11] The able-bodied slave was of significant value; the disabled slave or the slave perceived to be less capable of production (due to age, physiology, or other selected criteria) was considered to be of less value. However, in the production-oriented system that was the colonial empire (particularly the plantation, as Glissant argues in *Le discours antillais*, 1981 [*Caribbean Discourse* (1989)]), the enslaved were all and always identified in terms of their abilities.[12]

The historical valuation and transformation of such physical bodily abilities, which became a colonial hegemony, would eventually manifest itself psychologically in many of the descendants of the slaves. And it often manifested itself in a discourse akin to disability. Well known for his discussion of the "expérience vécue" (lived experience), Frantz Fanon was one of the first to speak in concrete clinical terms of colonialism's centuries-long devastation of colonized peoples (specifically, those of Afro-Caribbean and North African origin) due to slavery, forced labour, or torture, and their resulting psychological and physical disabilities. His discussion of the "complexus psycho-existentiel" (psychoexistential complex) in *Peau noire, masques blancs* (1952) [*Black Skin, White Masks* (1967)] is just one such example. In *L'odeur du père* (1982) [*The Scent of the Father*], V.Y. Mudimbe also speaks of the presence of psychological disabilities in the formerly colonized SubSaharan African body and the need for an ethnologically based psychotherapy, or an ethnopsychiatry, that pays particular attention to the sociocultural formation of the individual under treatment. What distinguishes such works from those written by Siebers, Quayson, or others is the recurrent claim that states of disability are caused by colonialism as well as the call to recover from such disabilities. Certainly such rhetoric and representation factored into a larger political agenda to end and, where possible, to renavigate (in Christopher Miller's terms) the machinations of the colonial enterprise in postcolonial contexts.[13] Such discourse continues today, as witnessed in the rhetoric of several union workers in the 2009 strikes in Martinique and Guadeloupe, who argued that the lower wages of the overseas departments were debilitating and that this fanned the familiar flames of anticolonial sentiment.[14]

The history of the French Atlantic slave trade and the productivity of ability-charged enslaved bodies provide, without doubt, one sociocultural (as well as one socioeconomic) context within which to think the spectrum of bodily abilities in processes of identification. As suggested above, slaves were valued not for their intellectual abilities but, rather, for their physical abilities to produce; as my introduction emphasizes, they were devalued when they could not (or, through rebelling or running away, would not) produce. However, such a context is, by virtue of originating within a slave trade marked by intersections of peoples, composed in fact of *multiple* master sociocultural narratives. These include those of the slavetraders and slaveowners, those of the various individuals of West African origin transplanted to the Caribbean islands, and those of the peoples who lived in the Caribbean Basin prior to Columbus's arrival and, especially, the ensuing colonial projects.

The influences on sociocultural narratives were varied: to the French narrative, for example, the need to save the lost souls of savages as well as the call to make a profit through finding new ways of subjugating human beings was added; from the West African narratives the solidity of regional sociocultural practices and a sense of humanity was subtracted at the same time as, in order to survive the whips and chains of Caribbean colonial practices, the mixing of ethnic groups and cultural practices (and a process often refered to as "creolization") was added. Notions of spectrums of bodily ability were modified to adhere to new formulations of sociocultural narratives and new forms of identification grounded in race, social stature, and economics; however, bodily ability remained a central component of these new narratives and new forms of identification.

The French colonial project, vast as it was, is one among many within which bodies were valued and identities constructed in terms of bodily abilities. Across the pan-imperial project of colonialism and the Atlantic slave trade, similar yet varied narratives would arise (e.g., within the United Kingdom, the Netherlands, and the United States). What appears to have resonated throughout, however, was the importance of the slave body as one that was able to produce.

ABILITIES AND IDENTITIES:
NORMS AND NARRATIVES

Colonialism would not be the only context within which the spectrum of bodily abilities would hold a key position in the various master sociocultural narratives that informed processes of identity formation in regions of the Francophone world. Other historical events, such as war, natural disaster, economic depression, and epidemics and pandemics, continuously contribute to the ways in which identity is formed and understood. Every day life outside of such calamities – life lived by human beings, by the intersexed, by women of ethnic minorities, by men of various socioeconomic standings, by children of athletic prowess, by individuals of religious faiths and spiritual practices, and by the disabled – makes its own mark on identity. As many studies argue, identification always involves the interaction of more than one identity category. Bodily ability remains one factor that is regularly present in such processes.

As many feminist scholars have long argued with regard to gender, women (as well as men, transsexuals, the intergendered, and individuals of other identities) have been and continue to be represented in normative master sociocultural narratives in terms of what their culturally gendered and biologically sexed bodies are supposed to be able to do. We know that Simone de Beauvoir (2010 [1949]) states that one is not born a woman but becomes one; and that Judith Butler (1990) argues that gender is scripted. In one of many recent and complementary studies, Todd Reeser (2010) discusses how masculinity is a complex, chameleonesque category of identity "often predicated on incoherencies" (11).[15] Amidst all of these discussions, biological reproduction is recurrently emphasized but not extensively examined within the context of bodily ability.

Of course such valuations of procreative abilities are to be thought within the relevant sociocultural contexts, which include the master narratives to which individuals refer in order to make such categorizations. Such observations do not intend to deny the very valid frustrations for which individuals, who choose to use their own bodies to procreate but are presented with biological impediments, seek some form of assistance with the reproductive process. Moreover, this series of hypothetical statements serves only to demonstrate some precursory ways in which another identification process – one typically associated with gender – is equally, and at times primarily, conducted in terms of a spectrum of bodily abilities that is not only lived by individuals but also living in the master sociocultural narratives that inform identity.

Narratives, then, remain a key component in such processes of identification. The first reason for their centrality is the similarity between their potential to be manipulated and the regular transformability of bodily abilities. Here the work of Gérard Genette helps us to think further about such alterability with respect to narrative, or text. In *Palimpsestes* (1982) [*Palimpsests* (1997)], Genette offers multiple and detailed means for categorizing reworkings of text and their relations – in short, of intertextuality. In his defining of "hypertextualité" (hypertextuality), the fourth of five types of "transtextualité" (transtextuality), he explains how a text B "se greffe" (is grafted) onto an anterior text A at the same that he distinguishes how text B has its own identity and content that does not (need to) reference text A (11–2; 5). Here, the original text is like a first layer not only of content but also of skin, as the verb *se greffer* suggests. It informs, even nourishes implicitly and/or explicitly, all subsequent layers that are, due to the process or "opération" that Genette calls *"transformation,"* placed over it and through which text A can be heard if not seen (12; 5).[16] In her own study of intertextuality and the "palimpsestic" process of writing with empire, Sage Goellner summarizes Genette well: "Genette explains intertextuality as a double voicing that can be understood through the figure of the palimpsest in which one can see a text transposed onto another one, not completely hidden but seen through the light" (34, 41). Text, at least hypertextually, exists neither in static forms nor in isolation; it is, like the human body and its abilities, impermanent, where the new text (the hypertext) as well as the one that comes before (the hypotext) are simultaneously palpable. Although the notion of layers does not explicity replicate the notion of a spectrum of abilities that I propose, the levels that are added on to the hypotext demonstrate a line-up of texts that, when looked at comprehensively, suggest a textual continuum.

One of the *opérations* Genette details, "excision" (excision), adds a particular twist to meditations on the relationship between narrative and the body. In proposing this term as one means of thinking rewriting and thereby rereading text (whether by the original author or by another writer or even editor), Genette expects that the word will evoke preconceived surgical notions of acts (primarily but not necessarily clinical) that reference a cutting out and thus removal or reduction. Specifically, he asks his reader to understand metaphorically but also viscerally his theory through a corporeally charged discourse evident not only in his use of "excision" but also in his use of related terminology like "intervention" and "amputation" (264; 229). Genette claims that such acts do not realize an absolutely negative alteration: "L'attentat n'entraîne pas inévitablement une diminution de valeur: on peut éventuellement 'améliorer' une œuvre en en supprimant chirurgicalement telle partie inutile et donc nuisible" [The assault does not inevitably include a diminution of value; it is possible to "improve" a work by surgically removing from it some useless and therefore noxious part] (264; 229). Instead, they are part of a common literary practice that involves selecting and thus leaving (out) what one finds useful for the hypertext, all the while harkening back to the hypotext (265; 230). The use of an altered body as metaphor – a body whose abilities will be altered by the excision – for the transformed text intends to underscore the specific abilities of the hypertext. Genette's own assessment is normative: it acknowledges that the excision might diminish an appreciable value found in the hypotext; and it recognizes that the post-excision hypertext may transmit its altered narrative in ways that are neither "inutile" nor "nuisible," as they might have been in the hypotext.

The second reason for the importance of narratives is their presence in sociocultural contexts. In particular, the notion of the "grands récits" (metanarratives) that Jean-François Lyotard discusses in *La condition postmoderne* (1979) [*The Postmodern Condition* (1984)] directly informs the concept of master sociocultural narratives throughout all readings in *Operation Freak*. Certainly Lyotard's reflections on fragmenting master narratives as a result of technological transformations in the transmission of knowledge are particularly relevant to the first reason for the importance of narratives, especially regarding how they demonstrate the undoing of a master narrative. As for the second reason, Lyotard's theory of the master narrative, as an authoritative means of providing answers to all questions and thereby of forming collective values to which individuals within communities adhere, provides the key and base definition of master sociocultural narrative for my project.

In these reflections on narrative, one of the first things I acknowledge is that the master narrative is a primary means through which individuals and communities are identified. This particular identification process occurs through totalizing efforts to measure individuals based upon such narratives. In this light, it becomes possible to think of how narratives that guide and maintain norm-based developments of sociocultural communities also regulate the identities that inform such communities. As Shelley Tremain shows in "Foucault, Governmentality, and Critical Disability Theory" (2005), Michel Foucault's work on bio-power and the power over life inform critical approaches to thinking identity that arise from norm-based constructs of bodily ability. Here is the citation from volume 1 of *Histoire de la sexualité* (1976) [*The History of Sexuality* (1978)] upon which Tremain bases her argument – an excerpt that speaks directly to the present discussion: "Un tel pouvoir a à qualifier, à mesurer, à apprécier, à hiérarchiser, plutôt qu'à se manifester dans son éclat meurtrier; il n'a pas à tracer la ligne qui sépare, des sujets obéissants, les ennemis du souverain; il opère des distributions autour de la norme … Une société normalisatrice est l'effet historique d'une technologie de pouvoir centrée sur la vie" [Such a power has to qualify, measure, appraise, and hierarchize, rather than display itself in its murderous splendor; it does not have to draw the line that separates the enemies of the sovereign from his obedient subjects; it effects distributions around the norm … A normalizing society is the historical outcome of a technology of power centered on life] (189–90; 144).[17] Foucault speaks of the enactment of power as huddled around a norm, realized through the process of active effect, or what is best articulated in French as "opère" (operates).

Such a conceptualization of master sociocultural narratives helps us to think further the emphasis on operations of narrative that are embroiled in identification processes in which bodily abilities are moved throughout a spectrum. It also aids in determining which master narratives, as understood within the normative sociocultural specificities of geographical regions, are part of such processes. In certain respects, master sociocultural narratives correspond to sacred texts, legislative acts, and even medical and surgical procedures as widely accepted normative discourses. However, I speak more generally of such narratives through their myriad interpretations within sociocultural communities. Such interpretations, which are themselves operations, do not always involve an inscribed form of the narrative; nor do they necessarily involve its literal reproduction. Through such engagement, a master narrative like Genette's palimpsest finds itself replicated in a somewhat altered state by the hands that manipulate in its name. At times, individual operations do eventually find themselves replicated by multiple parties, only to result in the subsuming of the pre-operation narrative by the post-operative versions.

In what master sociocultural narratives, then, has discourse on the spectrum of bodily abilities been located and how has it been discussed? In lexical terms, reflection upon abilities could involve exploration of other realms in which abilities appear, such as the emotional or sensorial faculties. However, the notions of bodily ability that I discuss fall into the categories of physical and cognitive (which includes all references to intellect and intellectual) as they are both thought in narratives and lived in life. As referenced in the earlier discussion of Garland Thomson (1997), Mitchell and Snyder (2000), and

Quayson (2007), the field that locates and examines such intersections is primarily that of disability studies. Many works from this field explore the ways in which disability and, thus, ability factor into or expose the master sociocultural narratives upon which processes of identification rest.

Stiker's *Corps infirmes et sociétés* (1982) is one of the earliest book-length works on representations of disability. It studies concepts of the master narrative as a written text and the ways in which it affects perceptions of bodily ability. He starts with the myth of Oedipus and with the Judeo-Christian tradition and works his way through historical periods up to the time in which he published his work. In this respect, Stiker situates his exploration within the confines of the Western sociocultural tradition (with emphasis on the French).[18] His study also relies upon two key terms for thinking through the presence of bodily ability: (1) *handicap* (disability), as recently defined within a concrete social context and presumably free of negative connotations yet imprecisely used in the sociocultural system; and (2) *infirmité* (impairment) as linked to a long-standing exclusionary identification process rooted in difference that has an impact on and is thus linked to individuals (1, 3, 7; 1, 3, 8).[19]

Stiker's tracing of disability and impairment-informed ideology in, for example, Judeo-Christian history is particularly useful for the ways in which he reads narrative. Specifically, he studies the master narrative of the Judeo-Christian sociocultural tradition: the Bible. His readings of disability or of disability-type states of the body, whether read for literal or figurative meanings, are not of primary importance to my discussion. What is of relevance are the ways in which Stiker talks of the Bible as a master sociocultural narrative. For example, when he writes of Judaic thought, he refers to various portions of the Old Testament that historically helped to determine the complex and conflicting ways in which impairment (specifically) was thought within a specific sociocultural context. Most notably, Stiker underscores how certain passages were used to enact religious prohibitions as well as ethical obligations with respect to the impaired. By highlighting such interpretation, he reveals not only the centrality of this narrative in processes of identification but also the ways in which it could be selectively operated (both to include and to exclude). In certain respects, Stiker argues, the lack of integration realizes a very particular form of exclusion: "On peut dire sans presque de paradoxe que la non-intégration culturelle est la condition de leur non-exclusion culturelle" [We could say, almost without paradox, that the non-integration of the disabled in religious practice is the precondition of their non-exclusion from the culture] (29; 31).

Stiker's engagement with this one example of a master sociocultural narrative helps to explain the legacy of such identification, particularly as it is related to narrative and bodily abilities. Starting from sacred text, moving into religious practice, and expanding into general sociocultural application, the identity formation process has at its core a master narrative. When interpreted, it morphs into a narrative of cultural customs and written words that continues to guide conceptualizations of individuals and, in this context, their bodily abilities.

Another of the noteworthy discussions of bodily ability appears in Garland Thomson's *Extraordinary Bodies: Figuring Physical Disability in American Culture and Literature* (1997). In her first single-authored book, Garland Thomson examines the sociocultural concept of normality and its relationship to physical disability in untranscribed yet sedimented (to borrow from Judith Butler) master narratives of the United States. To put it in Garland Thomson's terms, she aims not at dismantling stereotypes but, rather, at "interrogat[ing] the conventions of representation and unravel[ling] the complexities of identity production within social narratives of bodily differences" (5).[20] Narrative, then, becomes a pivotal means for constructing the normality, or even normalities, that are associated with bodies; the study of it helps, if not to undo such processes, at least to deconstruct the hegemonies that inform them.

Garland Thomson contextualizes her project by first highlighting the sociocultural exclusion that is made to pivot on ideologies of bodily ability. This process is based to a large degree on the insider/outsider, or superior/inferior, narratives used in related discussions of individual identity categories such as race, gender, and sexuality. She writes: "The 'physically disabled' are produced by way of legal, medical, political, cultural, and literary narratives that comprise an exclusionary discourse. Constructed as the embodiment of corporeal insufficiency and deviance, the physically disabled body becomes a repository for social anxieties about such troubling concerns as vulnerability, control, and identity … Disability, then, is the attribution of corporeal deviance – not so much a property of bodies as a product of cultural rules about what bodies should be or do" (6). Here Garland Thomson maintains that bodies are not inherently deviant or disabled but, rather, are classified as such through the use of particular sociocultural narratives. The result is that these bodies are deemed insufficient by "cultural rules about what bodies should be or do," where the "do" points directly to the body's expected, if not commanded, abilities.

Culture and narrative, then, play significant roles in constructing the normative identity of those who are included as well as, because of the body's contrived deviance, the non-normative identities of those who are excluded and, thus, deemed abnormal. As Garland Thomson puts it: "one group is legitimated by possessing valued physical characteristics and maintains its ascendancy and its self-identity by systematically imposing the role of cultural or corporeal inferiority on others" (7). She works to demonstrate the machinations of such a normative process by discussing the representations not only of the disabled (like the crippled and the invalid) but also of the freak (to be discussed shortly), the queer, and other figures. Garland Thomson positions all such labelled individuals under the rubric of the "extraordinary body" and then demonstrates how such an identity is defined through the body's violation of the master sociocultural narratives (5).

Before Garland Thomson would finish her theory of the extraordinary body, Lennard Davis would already have taken up the pen to address similar questions of disability. Published in 1995, his *Enforcing Normalcy: Disability, Deafness, and the Body* examines the construction of normality, or, as he chooses to consider it, normalcy. Like Garland Thomson, Davis believes that normalcy is a cultural construct. He also posits that the late twentieth-century concept of normalcy, as he reads it in cultural representations pertaining to the United States, first arises most notably in earlier periods. In words similar to Garland Thomson, Davis writes: "the social process of disabling arrived with industrialization and with the set of practices and discourses that are linked to late eighteenth- and nineteenth-century notions of nationality, race, gender, criminality, sexual orientation, and so on" (24).

However, Davis's argument distinguishes itself from Garland Thomson's in that he links the identification process to the industrialization of Western societies as well as to the advances in eugenics. What he finds of particular interest are the ways that these two phenomena have been used to inform the building of the nation.[21] According to Davis: "The emphasis on nation and national fitness ... plays into the metaphor of the body. If individual citizens are not fit, if they do not fit into the nation, then the national body will not be fit … [T]he eugenic notion that individual variations would accumulate into a composite national identity was a powerful one. This belief combined with an industrial mentality that saw workers as interchangeable and therefore sought to create a universal worker whose physical characteristics would be uniform, as would the result of their labors – a uniform product" (36). Bodies, then, are also about productivity and, to a greater degree, about usefulness. Their ability to produce is what determines their worth as well as their normality. If they can produce according to an industry standard, they are useful and normal; if they cannot live up to that standard, they "fall short" of the norm and are both useless and abnormal.

The historical development of statistics also plays an important role in Davis's theory of the narrative of normalcy, particularly for its reliance on the bell-shaped curve used in determining averages. This instrument of measurement supports the norm, he argues, by working as an umbrella, which enables those who do not fit within the middle of any chosen construct of normality to still place themselves within its boundaries: "The concept of a norm, unlike that of an ideal, implies that the majority of the population must or should somehow be part of the norm. The norm pins down that majority of the population that falls under the arch of the standard bell-shaped curve" (29). What is interesting to note, particularly because it remains crucial to the definition of normality that I propose, is that even those who deviate from the norm are not excluded from the bell-shaped curve; rather, they fall at its extremities and are thus still part of normality. If a society or a culture follows such a model, as I maintain that they do, those whose bodily abilities do not comply with the norms (and are subsequently manipulated) are not wholeheartedly excluded because they are seen as necessary components of normality's definition. Because the bell-shaped curve permits a specific and rigid demarcation of place for any entity approaching or departing from a norm, its use with regard to the human body's relationship to normality makes it oppressive, or what Davis refers to as "a symbol of the tyranny of the norm" (29).

What arises from Garland Thomson's and Davis's arguments, then, is a theory of the normal individual who becomes a sociocultural means of measurement for determining normal and abnormal individuals based on bodily ability. The discourses that support this normal individual seek to maintain that such bodies run rampant in societies, that they can be found in great numbers and therefore outweigh the abnormal by leaps and bounds. However, both Garland Thomson and Davis object to the idea of such a teeming existence. For Garland Thomson, this "normate" is the arbitrary standard individuals use to position themselves within normality but to which very few belong: "If one attempts to define the normate position by peeling away all the marked traits within the social order at this historical moment, what emerges is a very narrowly defined profile that describes only a minority of actual people" (8).

And for Davis, as he writes in his later work, *Bending over Backwards* (2002), this standard is the "average citizen" who is rooted in a fiction: "the average citizen, like the average family with 2.5 children, is a kind of fiction, a created character that fits the national mold" (109).[22] Indeed, normality depends not on a clearly defined *normal* body but, as Garland Thomson indicates in her further discussion of the normate, on the "array of deviant others [with] marked bodies." Fiction or narrative, normalcy or normality – these projects demonstrate how the agents who secure boundaries of identity engage (with), and thus operate, master sociocultural narratives in order to reinforce categories of distinction necessary to the maintenance and perpetuation of sociocultural order. All such narrative- and operation-grounded systems are built upon constructs of bodily abilities and the corresponding sociocultural contexts within which they fall.

ABILITY AND THE FREAK OF CULTURE

One arena in which the interplay of sociocultural normality and bodily ability has become most apparent in Western traditions of the body is the now extremely varied but once historically specific figure of the freak. First, it is important to mention that the connection made here between the freak and the disabled does not suggest that they are synonymous, nor does it conflate the study of disability and the study of freak discourse. The connection is made because the two fields address very similar notions of normality as they relate not so much to bodily appearance as to bodily ability. Robert Bogdan traces one historical and ideological line between the two fields in *Freak Show: Presenting Human Oddities for Amusement and Profit* (1988) when he states: "freak shows contributed to the imagery of disability" (viii). To expand on this notion, the two fields explore the ways in which bodies must possess specific abilities – the ways that bodies must be able-bodied – in order to be deemed normal, and they also demonstrate what happens to the bodies that are not normally abled.

Freaks, as objects of display with bodies billed as bizarrely abled, were used to build a highly profitable industry. The popularity and financial gain associated with such a "meat market," which occurred almost exclusively in the Western hemisphere, assured its own existence as well as the success and empowerment of the many individuals involved. These individuals include, in some cases, the freak performers themselves, as convincingly argued in studies as recent as Michael Chemers's previously cited *Staging Stigma* (2008). Furthermore, the freak body became a regular means not only by which an observer could define her normality as it functions within the context of master sociocultural narratives but also by which she could read the bodily abilities that should not be possessed. Because of the strategic use of freak bodies, the notion that their advertised abnormality was born of nature reveals itself to be a fallacy. This is because these individuals were, as Garland Thomson shows (see below), freaks of culture.

It is also necessary to mention that studies identified as part of or contributing to freak discourse and freak culture, like disability studies, sit largely but not solely within a Western context – specifically, within the United States and certain regions of Western Europe. These are the regions where modern freak shows, sideshows, world fairs, and the like became the choice locales for displaying the bodies of otherwise abnormal appearance and abilities. Early interpretations of the same bodies correspond more to historically and socioculturally specific conceptualizations of the monster or *monstre*, words that etymologically mean, inter alia, "to show" or "to demonstrate" (from the Latin root *monstra* and also the Latin verb *monstrum*) or, in other cases, "to warn" (as with *monere*).[23] Terminology regarding the notion of the freak would crystallize in the eighteenth and nineteenth centuries, when the aforementioned venues of display engaged the public eye with freak bodies.

As the earlier discussion of Chemers alludes to, the word "freak," with its origins in the Old English *frician* (a dance of sudden jumps or gestures), would come to mean something uncanny or unique only to then become a term that, even today, refers to the corporeally extraordinary – those who recall the performers on freak show stages (6). What was once the monster would now be the freak of nature, expressed in Latin as *lusus naturae*, a variation of what nature normally produces and that which is deviant. In French, a shared heritage appears in expressions such as *merveille de la nature, phénomène de foire*, or, quite simply, *monstre*. The etymology and signification of this lexicon seems to foretell the exhibition of unnatural bodies: *monstre*, meaning "démontrer" (see *Dictionnaire de la langue française*); *phénomène*, from the Greek noun *phainomena*, which, in French, is *ce qui apparaît*, or that which appears; and *merveille*, stemming from the Latin *mīrābilis*, meaning "admirable, merveilleux" (see *Le Trésor de la langue française*).[24]

One of the first comprehensive contemporary studies of the freak as an individual is Leslie Fiedler's *Freaks: Myths and Images of the Secret Self* (1978). Fiedler examines the spectator's viewing of the spectacle, which becomes the recognition of the secret fears and even terrors within the self. To give evidence to his experiential theory, Fiedler places himself in the equation when he writes of "the wonder of seeing for the first time my own private nightmares on public display *out there*" (22). Fiedler's argument is relevant to my work because it discusses the viewer's perception of the abnormal in the human body. However, given its emphasis on visual phenomena, his reading is blatantly reminiscent of a viewer's perception of external representations of internal fears, not too dissimilar from what Freud discusses (1919). As such, Fiedler's study perpetuates a theory of identification in which the individual deemed abnormal is excluded from participation in the identificatory process, except for the metaphoricity of the body (but not of bodily abilities).

Bogdan's *Freak Show* provides one of the first important analyses of how the individual is constructed, or manipulated, into the role of the freak and the implications of such identification. In his detailed historical analysis of American freak culture, Bogdan not only outlines the historical rise of the freak show in the United States but also explains the forms of manipulation necessary to the success of the displays of the abnormal body. Among the many elements of categorization, he distinguishes an important form of bodily presentation that he classifies in retrospect (i.e., not as part of freak industry terminology) as "modes of presentation": "the *exotic*, which cast the exhibit as a strange creature from a little-known part of the world; and the *aggrandized*, which endowed the freak with status-enhancing characteristics" (97). These modes, Bogdan maintains, were either fabrications or exaggerations of identities associated with bodies that today are considered either disabled, as referenced above, or of presumably non-Western ethnicities. Furthermore, these identities were the products of the showmen of the exhibitions, most of whom were concerned only with the financial success – the production of profit, as Bogdan's book title underscores – of the spectacle that they obtained through the manipulation of the freak body as well as of the spectator.

Bogdan's study focuses only on freak individuals in the context of exhibitions. However, his demonstration of how showmen played upon contemporary sociocultural constructs of exclusion and distinction in order to attract an audience is of great use for further contemplation of the sociocultural formation of identity that is realized through the operation of narratives to realize profit. Bogdan's project also contributes to my discussion by focusing on bodily abilities in its discussion of historical freak performers. As referenced above, he states that many of them would have been clinically identified as having a cognitive or a physical disability. This includes the freak performers of the exotic mode of presentation, most of whom – despite how they were presented – came from various areas of the mainland United States. Before the public eye, such individuals became the human oddities billed as wild individuals from foreign lands that were coveted prizes in the battles between warring colonial empires (121–2). The physical manifestation of cognitive disabilities was at the basis of many of the performances and displays of the exoticized figures: only the individuals involved knew of and used such states of being in order to create the lucrative spectacles of abnormality (120).[25] As the gawking viewers continued to pour in, the abilities of these individuals, unbeknownst to the millions of viewers, remained at the core of such spectacles' success.

On the shelves holding French cultural studies resides a retrospective of freak discourse similar, in ways, to the work of Bogdan. Sponsored in part by the Centre national de la recherche scientifique (National Centre for Scientific Research), Nicolas Bancel et al. would organize a collection originally entitled *Zoos humains: De la Vénus hottentote aux* reality shows (2002), retitled in its second edition as *Zoos humains: Au temps des exhibitions humaines* (2004) [*Human Zoos: Science and Spectacle in the Age of Colonial Empires* (2009)]. The work was organized as a series of essays (in which excerpts of Garland Thomson's and Bogdan's works appear in translation) that examines the nineteenth- and early twentieth-century displays of the exotic colonial body in the Western world, with specific emphasis on France. *Zoos humains* has as its goal the analysis of visual culture in the form of human spectacles – the *zoos humains* that, at world fair exhibitions or in the form of ethnographic displays and *villages nègres* (Negro villages), were concretized in the nineteenth century and that continue, albeit transformed, into the twenty-first century. It also outlines the importance of such visual culture to the construction of identity in nineteenth-century France.

One early example in the collection of the role of visual culture is an excerpt from William Schneider's *An Empire for the Masses: The French Popular Image of Africa, 1870–1900* (1982). Schneider's study foregrounds and outlines the accidentally profitable nineteenth-century displays of human beings from primarily SubSaharan African colonies at the Jardin zoologique d'acclimatation and the world fairs in Paris. Looking largely at the interplay of financial profit and visual forums (such as static images and live spectacles) in the late-nineteenth century, Schneider points to both an increased presence of and preference for these newer forms of visual culture and to France's efforts to make its outer regions better known and more profitable to the empire.

Zoos humains continues to emphasize the recurrent importance of visual culture (and, thus, of the body) to society by concluding with an article on variations in the exhibitions (e.g., reality shows) in twenty-first century France and the Western world. However, the other main thrust of the collection is the sociocultural reinforcement of European colonial logic concerning the binary-driven hierarchy of the races, which many of the essays argue continues today due, in part, to such exhibitions. The following citation best expresses this hegemonic transformation: "La vision de l'Autre dans des mises en scène visant à confirmer le sentiment d'étrangeté a produit un grand nombre de stéréotypes à caractère raciste qui imprègnent largement les opinions publiques" [The vision of the Other in staged displays aiming to affirm a feeling of strangeness produced a large number of racist-based stereotypes that permeated public opinion] (17).[26] Indeed, these stereotypes would continue to feed public opinion, conflating both the exhibited "savage" bodies and those of the colonies from which (truthfully or not) the individuals on display originated. The result is, as much of *Zoos humains* argues, the extension of the colonial gaze to the individual viewer in metropolitan France and thus a sedimentation of such identification practices, which continue to appear in visual culture.

The connection to bodily abilities through the constructs of disability, as discussed in Bogdan, is not immediately apparent in the displays studied in *Zoos humains*. However, my earlier discussion of the enslaved and colonized body as always already a body signified by and for the sociocultural constructs of its desired physical abilities (and, by extension, its undesirable psychological and physical disabilities) provides a means for thinking how the observers of the exhibits would identify both themselves and the bodies in terms of the varying spectrums of bodily abilities represented by the various bodies in the exhibits. Aware to varying degrees of the history of slavery and forced labour in many colonies, the gawking Westerners would be able to compare and contrast their bodies with the objectified individuals before them in terms not only of how they lived (communication, ingestion of foodstuffs, ambulation, etc.) in their recreated "natural habitats" but also in terms of what they laboured to produce. Furthermore, because the civilizing mission became one of the primary means by which the French colonial empire convinced its metropolitan population of the "savagery" of the colonized, this savage state took on significant semiotic value in the human zoos.[27] It would be seen not only as a form of the abnormal against which the colonizers purported to work. Couched in a spectrum of human development, the supposed savagery of the bodies would also be read as a profound developmental disability, which, according to colonial discourse, the colonized could never truly overcome.[28]

Bogdan's as well as Bancel et al.'s works take important steps towards designating the role and the manipulation of the body for the success of bodily displays. Their studies, as preliminary reflections on such bodies, contribute significantly to the understanding of identity as performed and performable and certainly as malleable. However, they do not typically address either the impact of manipulations upon bodily abilities outside of (or even unrelated to) the exhibit or the way in which said bodily abilities exist within spectrums. In other words, they do not explore how the bodies of off-stage *monstres* – the *bizarreries*, the *parias*, and the *phénomènes* as the extremely marginal – are in personal, intimate contexts also normatively identified in terms of specific sociocultural contexts that hinge on bodily abilities. No significant attention has yet been given to the ways in which such individuals are operated, as I define it, in relation to sociocultural spectrums of bodily abilities in order to realize the notion of reproduction.

Nevertheless, the existing work on freak discourse that emphasizes such normative processes is of great importance with regard to helping us think through *Operation Freak*'s ability-charged discussion of identification. Such work has already been conducted in various ways not only by Chemers and Garland Thomson but also, I would add, by Dayan. At the same time as they examine the emerging discourse of bodily normality and bodily abilities in displays, they also, in an attempt to rethink the term and the body of the freak, address the hegemonic incorporation of such discourse into society. Chemer's *Staging Stigma* (2008) does this in its discussion of the freak performance industry in the United States. At the same time, it also moves towards a new goal: a demonstration of what Chemers calls a "transgressive and liberating potential" (particularly for conceptualizations and hermeneutics of the disabled) through the rehabilitation of the freak tradition of performance (25).[29]

Although not formally associated with studies of freak discourse, I add Dayan to this discussion because of her early reflections on these questions. She does not emphasize the notion of freak shows, as do Chemers and Garland Thomson; however, she does discuss how the bodies upon which she reflects were, in the eighteenth century, decipherable in concepts of abnormality and are readable in terms of abilities. Dayan's *Haiti* (1995), in its analysis of the identification realized through racialized corporeality, demonstrates that particular strains of the freak and freak discourse were already prevalent in eighteenth-century French discourse. An emphasis on the abnormal as connected to freak discourse surfaces in terminology associated with, for example, the bodies that Moreau de Saint-Méry categorized as "oddities" and that Buffon labelled as "corporeal surprises" or assessed as degenerates. Dayan posits that the arguments that Saint-Méry and Buffon offered were intended to reestablish if not manufacture the social, moral, and economic superiority of whites by inventing racalized distinctions between bodies of colour that were not, in Saint-Méry's and Buffon's terms, of culture but of nature (234, 238). Specifically, her unpacking of their work on natural monstrosities reveals how profoundly their words repositioned sociocultural processes of identification that highlighted, as they hinged on, a fictional weakening of certain physical abilities realized by the enactment of inter-racial procreative abilities.

Garland Thomson remains one of the frontrunners in this endeavour with her work as editor of the collection *Freakery: Cultural Spectacles of the Extraordinary Body* (1996).[30] Garland Thomson first outlines her theory by combining the analyses of, among others, Bogdan and Fiedler, synthesizing in her introduction the elements of their work crucial to her own and to the larger project of *Freakery*: "The exaggerated, sensationalized discourse that is the freak show's essence ranged over the seemingly singular bodies that we would now call either 'physically disabled' or 'exotic ethnics', framing them and heightening their differences from viewers, who were rendered comfortably common and safely standard by the exchange" (5). Here she recalls Bogdan's general categorization of bodies as well as Fiedler's argument that the viewing of the freak on stage comforts the viewer by showing her a strangeness that is safely distant. Garland Thomson argues similarly that the separation of viewer and viewed is an indication that the observed individuals were "cordoned off from the rest of humanity," a clear indication that these bodies – and their bodily abilities – were to demarcate the abnormal (17).

Garland Thomson extends her project by revealing that the processes of bodily distinction initiated by the exhibitions are incorporated into and perpetuated by the collective consciousness of today's society. She does this to justify the study of the freak as a way of exploring constructions of bodily difference and deviance in the past and in the present: "Taken together, they [the essays in the volume] demonstrate how the social ceremony of the freak show sits at the crossroads of all systematic discourses – race and gender, for example – that underpin sociopolitical subordination by representing difference as deviance. The volume thus comprises a wide-ranging, interdisciplinary conversation that charts the interconnections among a profusion of both muted and blatant discourses of the freakish body" (13). What resonates here is the designation of the exhibitions as key to conceptions of human deviance connected to the visual body. However, she also points to the impact of this process on the "freakish body," positing it not as the object but as the subject of varied discourses that are far-reaching and interdisciplinary.

At the same time as these discourses are sociopolitical, they are also (and even more) sociocultural. Garland Thomson maintains that these operations – grounded in the various sociocultural processes of identification – reveal how "a freak of nature was instead a freak of culture" (10). She also states that the individuals identifiable as freaks lived, along with their "normal" viewers, in an era of modernization that significantly transformed the perception of the human body. As a result of the multiple developments she associates with the modern era, Garland Thomson posits that "the way the body looked and functioned became one's primary social resource" (12). The functioning to which Garland Thomson refers recalls, again, the use of the body's abilities to function as required within the sociocultural context. Where Garland Thomson calls the freak of culture the "hypervisible text" against which the spectator's normality is reinforced and autonomy is strengthened, it becomes clear how to read the freak – as the antithetical text of the accepted bodily abilities required of the normal individual (10).[31] Nevertheless, the freak's abilities, although understood as abnormal within the larger sociocultural structure, become a normal and necessary component of such an identification process.

OPERATIONS, BODIES, ABILITIES

Thus far I have discussed how the body's functions may be and have been considered in terms of bodily ability and how the latter refers to various spectrums of abilities, which include but are not limited to types of disability. I have reviewed various ways in which the two intertwine in processes of identification, and I have explored how the identity of the freak is regularly conceived in terms of bodily abilities that are specific to the sociocultural contexts in which the freaks exist and that are informed by norm-based master sociocultural narratives.

The notion of operation that I have evoked intermittently has a very specific meaning here. Generally speaking, it transmits the act of producing an effect and of doing so by operating on the body. Although this may immediately conjure up the image of a surgical operation as performed in the practice of what is called modern medicine, operation of the body, as I discuss it, does not limit itself to processes of preparing, anaesthetizing, opening up the body through the use of a surgical tool, and then suturing up the surgical site. Such aspects do factor into the ways in which operation is thought here; however, what is of overarching concern are the various reasons agents have for operating a body, the multifaceted means (tools, powers) by which bodies are operated, and, more important, the repeated emphasis on bodily ability that arises from such operations. A discussion of such phenomena also demonstrates the varied historical, theoretical, and cultural connections between operative acts and the spectrum of bodily abilities.

The force and the power associated with operations appear in various contexts and have an array of meanings. The general terms of the concept of operation are spelled out in, among other resources, *Le Trésor*: "Action d'une puissance, d'un pouvoir qui produit un effet physique ou moral" [An action of strength or of a power that produces a physical or moral effect]. Derived from the Latin *operari*, meaning "activity" or "working," and passing from French into English, the word "operation," as defined in the *Oxford English Dictionary*, has a similar meaning: "Power to operate or produce effects; efficacy, force." Synonyms in English include an act, a campaign, or a transaction.

Other definitions of operation point to the various means by which an operation is conducted. See, for example, the definition found in the *Dictionnaire de l'Académie française* (9th ed., 1992/2000): "Suite d'actions par lesquelles on combine, selon un ordre précis, divers moyens en vue de parvenir à un résultat déterminé" [Series of actions by which one brings together, following a specific order, various means for achieving a specific result]. With one of its English synonyms being "process," this definition of operation recognizes the variety of means by which operations (including but not limited to traditionally conceived surgical operations) are realized. It corresponds to the variety of operations represented in the novels I explore in subsequent chapters: the actual surgical operation as well as the simulated operation, both involving the presence of a surgical blade; the planned and the prepared process conducted in traditionally acceptable spaces of operation; the surprisingly enforced acts of mutilation in unconventional quarters realized through cutting or penetration; and their effects.

What is also pertinent to my discussion are the ways in which such operations become fundamental to processes of identification and production. When I discuss the novels, what I am interested in is how they reveal the profundity of an ability-informed identification through severe and violent operations, and how the representation of such operations asks the reader to contemplate various forms of the human condition that are always connected to varied norm-based constructs of bodily ability. Such reflection demands that the reader pay attention to both the operator and the motivations for the operation: that is, what is it about the operator that leads to the act of operating? It also requires that the reader take note of the protagonist as an operated body and the reasons he/she is chosen: that is, what is it about this protagonist's body that makes it an ideal candidate for an operation and how specifically is this identification motivated by bodily ability?

A discussion of various historical motivations for similar operations helps to tease out a broader conceptualization of operation itself, and this, in turn, allows for a way of conceiving of its varied yet consistent relationship to sociocultural structures. Along with various theoretical, historical, and anthropological documents, other sources that inform the discussion of operation appear in the collections of various schools of medicine in metropolitan France, Morocco, and Quebec. Such investigation and reflection reveal how the operations themselves are conceived in two distinct yet mutually dependent manners: (1) surgically (i.e., of the human body, which, as a physical site, demonstrates to the reader the ability-targeted operation and the resultant often painful alteration); and (2) discursively (i.e., of narrative, which, as a modified written work or sociocultural custom, becomes the means by which the operation on bodily ability is justified and codified).

To understand such acts, it is useful to focus first on a sampling of ways in which surgical operations to the body intend to transform that body. One place to start, at least with regard to colonial and linguistic expansion, is metropolitan France. Defined as early as the first decades of the fourteenth century, operations have as their goal a transformation that typically moves towards a presumably healthier and thus normative functioning of the body. For example, with the developments in what is referred to as "modern medicine" – considered largely to be the by-product of nineteenth-century Western scientific innovation – the focus of surgical operations was aligned with what was considered to be the maintenance and the reestablishment of the body's normative functions and abilities. René Leriche points to this in citing François de la Peyronie's preface to *Mémoires de l'académie royale de chirurgie* (1731) [*Memoirs of the Royal Academy of Surgery*], which reveals how the eighteenth-century surgeon spoke of the rules by which "on doit se conduire dans la cure des maladies" [one must conduct oneself in the curing of illnesses] (qtd. in Leriche 18).

In *L'acte chirurgical* (1990) [*The Surgical Act*], Jean-Paul Binet outlines a similar curative discourse. In defining the concept of a medical operation, he writes: "'opération' implique la thérapeutique qui nécessite l'ouverture et la manipulation [du corps] pour traiter, réparer ou guérir ce qui ne peut l'être par la médecine" ["operation" implies the therapeutics that require the opening and the manipulation {of the body} in order to treat, repair or heal what cannot be handled by {non-surgical} medicine] (8). Presented as an option akin to non-surgical medical treatment, the operation shares the same goals as the former: treating, repairing, and healing. Repairing and healing emphasize the notion of a lost normal bodily state – one that the operation works to recover or, at the very least, to partially regain. All three goals ultimately target the functioning of the human body. More specifically, they zoom in on affected bodily abilities: the heart's reduced ability to send out and receive blood due to arteriosclerosis; the hip's inability to allow for easy or painless ambulatory movement due to having been fractured; or the brain's diminished ability to command all of the body's abilities due to a stage-three brain tumour. The same or similar goals exist, with various modifications depending on sociocultural context, in regions of the world where similar surgical operations are performed.

Given a recurrent emphasis on treatment aimed at healing or alleviating medical conditions in such discourse, the surgical operation may also be understood as associated with care for the body realized through openings and manipulations – a form of care that becomes the surgeon's call.[32] The agent typically and primarily responsible for the operation in this context is that same surgeon who, as James E. Goodnight writes, bears the responsibility and possesses the privilege to take part in the surgical operation: "It is the treasured province and privilege of surgeons to visit in the flesh that express and admirable form. With reverence, humility, and intent to do good, the visitation is an act of grace" (vi). As such, the surgeon must not only ethically but also reverentially conduct the surgical operation that involves the "ouverture," or "manipulation," of which Binet speaks.

In thinking of the actual means through which operations occur, it is useful to return to Binet, whose conceptualization of surgery is very specific. He talks not of the operation that, in medical contexts, includes all services (e.g., anaesthesia) but, rather, of the act of "intervention" that the surgeon executes with her/his hand: "munie ou non d'un instrument" [with or without an instrument] (8). My use of the term "operation" and of its variants does not always respect the distinction that Binet makes because not all of the literary protagonists' experiences that I examine fall within traditionally Western conceptualizations of surgery or surgical operations. However, Binet's reference to the use of the hand, with or without an instrument, speaks to the varied means by which all operating agents in the novels perform: not always with an instrument used within the modern surgical context but always with the hand and always with an instrument (e.g., sticks, rope, and even computer screens). Ultimately, the operation is always intended to manipulate the body, and it does so by gaining access to existing openings and/or by creating new ones.

KNOWLEDGE BY OPERATION

Operations on bodies have also been a means for expanding knowledge of human existence. While some thinkers have concentrated on the integral organism of the body as their means of reflecting on human existence, others have preferred to explore the body more deeply and more selectively. Literally. In *The Scar of Visibility* (2007), Petra Kuppers traces how contemporary Western interests (particularly those of the United States) have come to focus on the hidden regions inside the body – regions that modern technology now makes available. She concludes: "The proliferation of medical vision machines, not only in the history of modern Western medicine but also in many of popular culture's accompanying translations and reimaginings, testifies to the problems and desires of vision itself. The inside of human bodies is one of the latest frontiers of knowledge" (32). Such a development, Kuppers maintains, realizes a change in the human's perception of the self – a change that makes the senses "unreliable in relation to our bodies." This transformation also plays itself out in the composing of narrative: "Western biomedical science, with its visualizing power, sometimes tells different stories about our insides than the narratives that common sense can make knowable" (33).

Where Kuppers focuses on the devices that peer in or that enter, other thinkers focus on the most marked form of exploration: dissection. They engaged in such meditation, of course, prior to the time frame that Kuppers signals as the moment when vision machine exploration simultaneously begins and transforms. Religiously oriented and secularly driven individuals alike turned to the kind of exploration that the dissection of cadavers allowed. Their interest in dissection helped them to theorize how the body's internal functioning – or at least what appeared to be its internal functioning – informed, separately and together, the body's and the mind's functions and reflexes. The act of cutting open and cutting apart the body would be put forward as a means by which human existence and, thus, the individual's identity and existence, could be understood. To dissect was to understand. Specifically, it was to understand nature through the study of the ways in which bodily abilities, as understood in their respective sociocultural contexts, occurred.

Religious perspectives underscore how the dissection of the body functions as a means to understanding a supreme being's power. In "Attitudes toward Dissection in Medieval Islam" (1995), Emilie Savage-Smith argues that, in two works from the late eleventh and early twelfth centuries – *The Revival of the Religious Sciences* and, in particular, *The Deliverer from Error* – Abu Hamid Al-Ghazali praises the study of medicine.[33] Savage-Smith also affirms that Al-Ghazali appears to valorize the study of the fruits of dissection (or, at the very least, of the anatomical exposition of bodily parts) as a means of engaging in self-reflection and drawing nearer to God. As Savage-Smith argues, the study of dissected anatomical components, the investigation of their complexity and their inter-workings, reveals what Al-Ghazali claims to be "the wonders of God's design and the marvels of His wisdom" as well as "a wise Creator Who is aware of the ends and purposes of things" (qtd. in Savage-Smith 96).

Savage-Smith carefully notes that Al-Ghazali's words provide no clear endorsement of dissection. She deduces this through an ambiguity surrounding the use of the Arabic word *tashrih*, which, in that historical period, meant both anatomy and dissection; and also through the controversy surrounding the conflict between the wholeness of the human body (as advanced in Islamic jurisprudence [*fiqh*]) and the dismemberment of that same body. Al-Ghazali's praise of the study of anatomy may also have been in reference solely to the study of the bodies of animals, which, under Islamic jurisprudence, were not regulated in the same manner as were human bodies. Nevertheless, the process of dissection, or at least the thinking of the body in parts and in terms of faculties, remains fully valorized as a means for understanding human nature.

Secular musings on human existence have also hinged on observations of the surgically explored human body. Some six centuries after Al-Ghazali, for example, Francis Bacon speaks of dissection as a way of reflecting not on God's powers but, rather, on nature's secrets. Such observations of the dissected body would, as Carolyn Merchant shows in her study of *Novum Organum* (1620), lead Bacon to build "in the human understanding a true model of the world, such as it is in fact" (qtd. in Merchant 158). Merchant also cites the moment in Bacon's *Advancement of Learning* (1605) in which he praises the power of dissection by lamenting the inability to conduct it on living bodies: "Wherefore that utility may be considered as well as humanity, the anatomy of the living subject is not to be relinquished altogether, nor referred (as it was by Celsus) to the casual practices of surgery; since it may be well discharged by the dissection of beasts alive, which, notwithstanding the dissimilitude of their parts to human, may, with the help of a little judgment, sufficiently satisfy this inquiry" (qtd. in Merchant 158). In other words, the living anatomy (albeit of "beasts") could allow for an approximate means of understanding hidden truths.

Over three centuries later, Michel Foucault would investigate the politics of autopsy and dissection in nineteenth-century Western Europe. In *Naissance de la clinique* (1963) [*The Birth of the Clinic* (1973)], he speaks of clinicians' efforts to justify their work by painting a false portrait of a pre-1789 period that forbade dissection and to thus make the scientist the pioneer in a quest for finding hidden knowledge: "Le savoir file où se formait la larve" [Knowledge spins where once larva was formed] (126; 125). The end result of this was the glorification of nineteenth-century clinicians/scientists: "si les vieilles croyances ont eu, si longtemps, un tel pouvoir d'interdiction, c'est que les médecins devaient éprouver, du fond de leur appétit scientifique, le besoin refoulé d'ouvrir des cadavres" [if the old beliefs had for so long such prohibitive power, it was because doctors had to feel, in the depths of their scientific appetite, the repressed need to open up corpses] (126–7; 125–6).

Aimed at demonstrating the manipulation of medical history, Foucault argues:

Du jour où il fut admis que les lésions expliquaient les symptômes, et que l'anatomie pathologique fondait la clinique, il fallut bien convoquer une histoire transfigurée, où l'ouverture des cadavres, à moins à titre d'exigence scientifique, précédait l'observation, enfin positive, des malades ; le besoin de connaître le mort devait exister déjà quand apparaissait le souci de comprendre le vif. De toutes pièces, on a donc imaginé une conjuration noire de la dissection, une église de l'anatomie militante et souffrante, dont l'esprit caché aurait permis la clinique avant de faire surface lui-même dans la pratique régulière, autorisée et diurne de l'autopsie. (127)

[The day it was admitted that lesions explained symptoms, and that the clinic was founded on pathological anatomy, it became necessary to invoke a transfigured history, in which the opening up of corpses, at least in the name of scientific requirements, preceded a finally positive observation of patients; the need to know the dead must already have existed when the concern to understand the living appeared. So a dismal conjuration of dissection, an anatomical church militant and suffering, whose hidden spirit made the clinic possible before itself surfacing into the regular, authorized, diurnal practice of autopsy, was imagined out of nothing. (125–6)]

What is relevant here is Foucault's highlighting of the emphasis that nineteenth-century practitioners placed on dissection and on autopsy. Clearly, the operative act was fundamental to the practices of the clinic and, thus, to the knowledge that clinicians needed to work on the human body in an effort to understand (if not cure) pathological anatomy. However, the same clinicians operated the narrative about dissection in order to portray it as dark or dismal and thus to justify "autopsy" as its cleaned up, clinical, and therefore acceptable version. Furthermore, Foucault's argument paints these scientists in a discursive light similar to that advanced by Bacon: their aim was to obtain knowledge that would lead to the managing of the body and its functions. Ultimately, the operative act is highlighted as the most probing means by which to realize both the cure and the contemplation of the body as it functions within spectrums of abilities.

TEXTUAL OPERATION MARKS

The written work also relies on operations to bodies that inquire into the nature as well as the state of human existence. Operations would not necessarily be limited to the dissected, dismembered, manipulated, and mutilated bodies of characters in literary works (although they were not necessarily excluded). They would also be transmitted in the vivisection of elements of the body of a narrative as well as in the strategically structured components of theoretical works. The varied presence of such operations demonstrates not only how bodies are key components of text but also how abilities – through their altered and emphasized states – offer a palpable if not visceral means for a text to make its mark.

Authors working within nineteenth- and twentieth-century French-language literary traditions, such as Honoré de Balzac, Gustave

Flaubert, and Eugène Ionesco as well as André Breton, Aimé Césaire, and Léon Gontran Damas, would use or represent varying forms of such identifying operations in plot (including character construction and deconstruction) or style in order to transmit a certain effect to the reader. For example, the form of the text, and in particular its distribution on the page, would work to represent operated and even mutilated bodies not only through imagery but also through the use of free verse. Such choices would transmit various forms of the altered body (animal or human) in, for example: Breton's "Dans la vallée du monde" (1923) ["In the Valley of the World" (1993)] with the "animaux disjoints" (disjointed animals); (77; 69); Césaire's *Cahier d'un retour au pays natal* and the overlaboured colonized bodies demonstrating corporeal alteration; and in Damas's "Hoquet" (1937) ["Hiccup"] with the disaster-afflicted, hiccupping body of the speaker.

As some texts altered their format to transmit the sense of operation, others acknowledged or even depicted operations on the human body. Many of these operations result in an underscoring of the fundamental importance of bodily ability in the identificatory operation. Balzac's works most certainly offer examples, with one of the most notable being la Zambinella, the castrato from *Sarrasine* (1830; n.d.) whose ability-altering operation was funded by Cardinal Cicognara in order to generate fortune and pleasure through the performance and fame of the genitally excised singer. In Flaubert's work, the failed surgical treatment of Hippolyte in *Madame Bovary* (1856; 2010) relates not only to the character's clubfoot but more generally to the novel's subtitle, *Mœurs de province* [*Provincial Ways*]: the operation testifies to the hunger for success living in the protagonist and her neighbourhood apothecary, M Homais, who encourage the gullible and professionally unqualified Charles, "officier de santé" [public health officer], to execute an experimental and doomed surgical cure (69; 10). It also shows how profit is perceived in terms of productivity and conceived through exploration of the bodily abilities of an individual identified, in today's terms, as disabled.[34] In *La leçon* (1951) [*The Lesson* (1958)], Ionesco speaks of the loss of sense in language and communication. More specifically, he emphasizes a diminishing ability to communicate reminiscent of aphasia and a resulting potential for violence. The Professeur's repeated rape-like stabbing of his young Elève's body becomes, most certainly, his slicing up of her, and thus all, linguistic production.

The interests and effects of representing such operations do not relate solely to the efforts to understand the nature of the operated body and thus of existence: they also relate to an interest in revealing the status of the operated body and of the states that motivate such operations. Works that speak through the operation of the human condition and even of a human plight might be said to have connections to the tradition of the picaresque. As Ellen Turner Gutierrez explains: "the picaresque novel was interpreted as a work of social criticism and greatly admired for its realism, wit and satire" (2). Examples of works inspired by this tradition include, again, Balzac's *Sarrasine*, but also Victor Hugo's *L'homme qui rit* (1869) [*The Man Who Laughs*, n.d.] and its surgically disfigured protagonist. These texts by Balzac and Hugo are particularly noteworthy for their romantic sensitivity – subtle in the former, pronounced in the latter – towards human suffering, which, it is suggested, is caused by a presumably unresolvable disparity between members of different sociocultural structures. Gone from these operations are the goals of therapy and care. Here we have ambition and greed for success and profit, which agents justify through their references to master sociocultural narratives that, in many ways, inform and are informed by norm-based constructs of bodily ability.

The same works, along with Ionesco's *La leçon* and many of Jean-Paul Sartre's and Albert Camus's texts, may also be seen as products of an *écrivain engagé* (engaged writer) responding directly to historical events such as the Holocaust.[35] Although their works may or may not represent operations as addressed here, they do speak to historical developments that manipulated and mutilated bodies. Another example from Hugo's corpus is *Les misérables* (1862; n.d.), with its collection of malnourished and overlaboured workers as the product of industrial development. Turn to Emile Zola and Guy de Maupassant just a short time later, and similar thematic representations appear in their uniquely crafted style.[36] What such works provide is a way of thinking the literal yet varied representation of operation in terms of its figurative potential with respect to sociocultural as well as temporal contexts. They also offer a means for contemplating the various ways in which operations' contexts are understood. For, although I maintain that the operation need not always be read in terms of the surgical operation, it is certainly understood in the context of the afflicted, penetrated, and thus manipulated body that has been operated by external forces.

Discussion of the notion of operation in terms of manipulation by external forces and as manifested through the body also appears in theoretical works. Some of the most readily apparent and extensive discussions are, in addition to *Naissance de la clinique*, found in Foucault's corpus: *Les anormaux: Cours au Collège de France, 1974–1975* (1999) [*Abnormal: Lectures at the Collège de France, 1974–1975* (2003)]; *Naissance de la biopolitique: Cours au Collège de France, 1978–1979* (2004) [*The Birth of Biopolitics: Lectures at the Collège de France, 1978–79* (2008)]; and, in certain ways, *Histoire de la folie à l'âge classique* (1961) [*The History of Madness* (2006)].

Surveiller et punir (1975) [*Discipline and Punish* (1977)] is, however, the work most relevant to my discussion of operation and text. As readers of Foucault know, *Surveiller* speaks of where power manifests itself: in various institutions and, thereby, in the agents of such institutions, agents who can be considered not only surgeons but also law enforcement officers (broadly speaking), slaveowners, and even family members; and in the ideologies of the master narratives upon which the institutions depend – narratives that can be in the form either of, among others, written legislation, sacred texts or oral traditions. Due to the intersections of such manifestations, power becomes what Foucault describes in the first volume of *Histoire de la sexualité* (1976) [*The History of Sexuality* (1978)]: "c'est le nom qu'on prête à une situation stratégique complexe dans une société donnée" [it is the name that one attributes to a complex strategical situation in a particular society] (123; 93). In addition to being strategic, the "situation" is also particular to the society within which it is operated. In other words, such a conceptualization of power refers not only to social but also, I would argue, due to the reciprocal and interdependent production of society and culture, to cultural specificities of each instance of operative identification.

In examining discourse and power in *Surveiller et punir*, Foucault discusses, at least symbolically, how agents operate bodies and the impact of such acts on processes of identification. The presence of an operating power in what Foucault specifies as a political space is especially apparent in a well-known passage found in the first chapter, "Le corps des condamnés" ["The Body of the Condemned"], in which he speaks of powers that mark the body: "le corps est ... directement plongé dans un champ politique; les rapports de pouvoir opèrent sur lui une prise immédiate; ils l'investissent, le marquent, le dressent, le supplicient, l'astreignent à des travaux, l'obligent à des cérémonies, exigent de lui des signes" [the body is ... directly involved in a political field; power relations have an immediate hold upon it; they invest it, mark it, train it, torture it, force it to carry out tasks, to perform ceremonies, to emit signs] (30; 25). Clearly, the acts of operating – written as "opèrent" but translated as "have a hold" and thus indicative of the operation as a controlling, redirecting process that has a physical and moral effect – are social in that they occur when human beings come into contact with one another. John Caputo and Mark Yount explain this well: "power relations are embedded in the very heart of human relationships, springing into being as soon as there *are* human beings" (5 [emphasis in original]).

Equally important to the argument of *Surveiller* and to my work is the way in which Foucault develops a notion of the subjugated and productive body. To underscore this state of the body, he designates the various instruments used in operations:

Cet assujettissement n'est pas obtenu par les seuls instruments soit de la violence soit de l'idéologie; il peut très bien être direct, physique, jouer de la force contre la force, porter sur des éléments matériels, et pourtant ne pas être violent; il peut être calculé, organisé, techniquement réfléchi, il peut être subtil, ne faire usage ni des armes ni de la terreur, et pourtant rester de l'ordre physique. C'est-à-dire qu'il peut y avoir un "savoir" du corps qui n'est pas exactement la science de son fonctionnement, et une maîtrise de ses forces qui est plus que la capacité de les vaincre: ce savoir et cette maîtrise constituent ce qu'on pourrait appeler la technologie politique du corps. (31)

[This subjection is not only obtained by the instruments of violence or ideology; it can also be direct, physical, pitting force against force, bearing on material elements, and yet without involving violence; it may be calculated, organized, technically thought out; it may be subtle, make use neither of weapons nor of terror and yet remain of a physical order. That is to say, there may be a "knowledge" of the body that is not exactly the science of its functioning, and a mastery of its forces that is more than the ability to conquer them: this knowledge and this mastery constitute what might be called the political technology of the body. (26)]

In true Foucauldian fashion, the political technology of the body is wide-reaching and is void of any concretely identifiable source. Various terms describe its variegated nature: "diffuse, rarement formulée en discours continus et systématiques"; "de pièces et de morceaux"; "une instrumentation multiforme" [diffuse, rarely formulated in continuous, systematic discourse; made up of bits and pieces; a multiform instrumentation] (31; 26). It is also a technology that is intended to dominate and that is put into motion not by but through the rather obscurely defined institution known as an "appareil étatique" [state apparatus] (31; 26). The validity of the technology lies somewhere between two entities: "ces grands fonctionnements [les appareils et les institutions] et les corps eux-mêmes avec leur matérialité et leurs forces" [these great functionings {the apparatuses and the institutions} and the bodies themselves with their materiality and their forces] (31; 26).

Reading Foucault in relation to the "real" body is of course not free from problems, particularly when, in *Surveiller et punir*, he speaks primarily of the subjugating powers. Post-Foucauldian critics claim that he speaks much more of a discourse of the political body than of the lived body, a concept more frequently associated with, for example, Fanon and the "expérience vécue" (lived experience) of the body.[37] Work accomplished in the context of disability studies offers further insight. In "What Can a Foucauldian Analysis Contribute to Disability Theory?" (2005), Bill Hughes concurs with the critics who maintain that Foucault speaks neither of the lived experience nor of the lived body. He argues that Foucault's work may not allow for speculation either about the individual (and thus the lived [including the operated] "fleshy" body) or about the individual's efforts to claim bodily agency. Yet he does think that Foucault's conceptualization "can shed some light on the historically contingent set of practices that restrict the actions of humans in general and disabled people in particular" (80). This interpretation becomes apparent when we revisit Foucault's words on the body operated in the "champ politique" and when we think of how this encounter appears in marks on bodies that inform the individual's identity.

Such operations, like those represented in literary works, have a very real effect on bodies and thereby on bodily abilities. In other words, discursive disciplining ultimately forces the body to engage (through labour or other means) in many contexts and in varying ways, and such engagement is what results in actual marks upon the body. These marks may be due to excessive demands on the body or an injury, both of which can result in a modification of bodily abilities and both of which are incorporated into the theoretical and the literary text alike. As I discuss, such transformations also arise from surgical and discursive operations that force individuals – real and fictive – to come into contact with manifestations of power that, in turn, have an impact on bodies and their abilities.

OPERATING MASTER NARRATIVES OF BODIES

Reading Foucault's work demonstrates, then, that institutions (loosely defined) contribute to the operations of power associated with the body. Equally important to the process are the individuals who interact with these institutions, the same individuals through whom power passes in each complex and strategic situation. The bodily manipulations realized through such power relations and, specifically, by the agents of such power become, under certain conditions, documented and thus constitute histories of the operations: "aucun de ses épisodes localisés ne peut s'inscrire dans l'histoire sinon par les effets qu'il induit sur tout le réseau où il est pris" [none of its localized episodes may be inscribed in history except by the effects that it induces on the entire network in which it is caught up] (*Surveiller* 32; *Discipline* 27). Clearly, Foucault offers a selective means of documenting or of representing these acts, stating that they must affect the entire network of power relations in order to be recorded. The accuracy of this rather general assertion may be debatable, particularly when it comes to considering who or what constitutes the "réseau" and, thus, who documents what.

However, what Foucault's statement also points to is the notion that such operations can and do become documentable in history. From such an observation can be extracted the creation of narratives that not only recount the manipulations but also the sociocultural contexts ("tout le réseau *où il est pris*") [the entire network *in which it is caught up*] within which they occur.[38] In sum, the operations that said agents perform on bodies in the name of power inform and become narratives of power and bodily operations.[39] Furthermore, the repeated enactment of manipulations within sociocultural contexts creates narratives that become forms of Lyotard's previously discussed "grands récits." In other words, the narratives begin to serve as testaments of sociocultural directives, particularly when operating agents look to them for guidance and inspiration with regard to their interaction with other human beings.

The master sociocultural narratives are, as the discussion of Foucault demonstrates, social and political; but they are also, among many options, juridical, legislative, religious, sexual, and economic. Within such contexts these narratives are also malleable. Agents themselves often manipulate them to meet their own needs, bending and cutting the text and the context to satisfy the agenda they envision. Such operations often repeat, and, as a result, the master sociocultural narratives become as pliable as the bodies themselves, reciprocally demonstrating the impermanence of any singular state of body or of narrative that is most readily and regularly transmitted through the alteration of abilities. Such a conclusion speaks largely to the operations as they are thought within a systemic framework, ultimately reinforcing the experience of the collective in terms of activity. It tends to elide the individual operations, or activities, that may either be at the foundation of such narratives or that may contribute to their transformation. However, the operations discussed here depend on individual agents who operate not just the bodies but also the narratives. The notion of the agent as the operator – here the operator of the master narrative – in many respects involves the agent's act of reading the narrative.

Roland Barthes's theory of reading text provides a useful means of considering such an individuated process of narrative production. In reflecting on the relationship between narrative, identity, and the body, I have already demonstrated how Genette refers to a type of textual pliability that is realized through *opérations* and how, at least metaphorically, he brings the body into the discussion. Some fifteen years earlier, in *S/Z* (1970; 1974), Barthes designates two overarching and consequential operations for reading text: "évaluation" [evaluation], by which texts as narratives are understandable as "scriptible" [writerly] and therefore ripe for production; and "interprétation" [interpretation], which demonstrates the limitless potential of a text (9–11; 3–5). Evaluation helps to see beyond the "lisible" [readerly] texts, which are only of reactive value (10; 4). It also aids in experiencing how texts produce and are reproducible by a reader as well as how that same reader chooses which texts to read or, rather, "ré-écrire" [to re-write] (10; 4). Interpretation is largely an engaged reading that opens up the text, as well as the language and the signifiers that constitute it, to an inherent plurality: "Interpréter un texte, c'est … apprécier de quel pluriel il est fait" [To interpret a text is … to appreciate what *plural* constitutes it"]

(11; 5). As text is always without limit and is always engaged by a reader, it is always in operation.

The role of the reader in Barthes's theory is as important as is the narrative, and the reader also provides ways for a particular form of production. To realize such an operation, the writerly texts require a reader who is not a passive "consommateur" [consumer] but, rather, an active "producteur" [producer] (10; 4). The reader's own productivity is due in large part to what Barthes calls "d'autres textes" (other texts), and what I consider the myriad cultural narratives that inform her existence and therefore her approach to text: "Ce 'moi' qui s'approche du texte est déjà lui-même une pluralité d'autres textes, de codes infinis" [This "I" which approaches the text is already itself a plurality of other texts] (15; 10). Inevitably, the reader will only ever mix the text and the other (cultural) texts or narratives, recycling them in varied ways and thereby demonstrating that they are both perpetually *scriptible* and productive. In this sharing of critical readership, the unlimited engagements of which Barthes so hopefully writes avoid the impossible single, comprehensive, and therefore dominant reading ("il n'y jamais un *tout* du texte" [there is never a *whole* of the text]) and, because of the productive writing involved, provide new versions of any narrative (11; 6).

Like Barthes's reader who rewrites the writerly text with each reading and reveals that a text's potential can never be exhausted, operating agents rewrite the master sociocultural narratives with each operation and reveal that such narratives can never be depleted of meaning but can always be refashioned. Here Barthes's work helps in understanding operator engagement with narrative and with its pliability. Furthermore, "operation," in my usage, speaks in ways to Barthes's thoughts on ideology as narrative and its connections to culture and nature. Terry Eagleton summarizes Barthes's position well when he writes that he believed ideology served "to 'naturalize' social reality, to make it seem as innocent and unchangeable as Nature itself. Ideology seeks to convert culture into Nature, and the 'natural' sign is one of its weapons" (117).

However, where the distinction between the two processes of narrative manipulation arises is in the intent and the product of such operations. The operations that agents conduct in the works I discuss do not, like those of Barthes's readers, lead to a liberation of language and narratives (and, by extension, peoples and cultures) from monopolistic, singularly visioned readings of text. In fact, liberation and freedom are rarely the goals at all. Intent takes on a particular meaning here: the operating agents rarely wish their operations to be considered as acts born of culture but, rather, as a requirement for restoring what they believe to be the order of nature. Moreover, the objective of the incising acts is to operate narratives as well as bodies such that they reproduce, or aid in reproducing, in the manner that the agents wish them to reproduce. Typically, if agents operate narratives in this context, they also operate bodies and their abilities to reproduce.

Operations to narrative are not restricted to individuals external to the operated body, nor are they restricted to the master sociocultural narratives that inform the operations. As agents in the novels I study produce their narratives, so protagonists manufacture their own, all of which are connected by a similar theme. The end result is, as thought within the context of Gerald Prince's *Narrative as Theme* (1992), the creation of a main narrative (41). However, the protagonists' operations materialize in different manners and for different reasons: they recount or write their own narratives (for some are oral and some are written) that have, in part, been informed by the operations to master narratives and to their bodies. They also recount or write them in order to testify to the extraordinarily ability-altering experience of the operations – gestures that also continue to underscore the role of bodily abilities in identification processes. Their bringing together of implausible yet realized narratives in the main narrative is also, to return once more to Prince, what makes of them the singular narrative: "It affirms the essential kinship between an exceptional truth and a narrative that dares to be exceptional" (50). The representation of the outrageously "real" within the narrative is what renders the novels novel.

The transmission of the tale formed by the encounter with other individuals and with the master narratives is only one form of the protagonists' operations to narrative. They and their narratives also demonstrate a constant reworking, manipulating, and, thereby, operating of the narrative. At times the protagonists, as well as other characters and storytellers who speak with or about the protagonists, demonstrate a concrete awareness of the means by which operating narratives (style, voice, organization, rhetoric, inclusion or inference of details) realize a productive narrative. Such a narrative is one that, in the context of Barthes's writerly text, which is itself "productif" [productive], informs the reader of the operability of the body, the narrative, their abilities, and how they come to reproduce (10; 4).

OPERATION, REPRODUCTION

The opportunity to meld narrative with a specific set of objectives has production as its primary goal. The operations lead to the various forms of production previously discussed, or to what I call "reproduction." The emphasis on the repeated efforts to produce is the primary reason I speak of *re*production, and I do so taking into consideration the intertwined relationship of tangible results and the processes of production. Because of the teleological history and the visceral visibility of freaks of culture, narratives that inform their existence become the most poignant means not only for representing but also for thinking them. In the novels under study, the involvement in such a system of reproduction contributes to the identification of the protagonist in norm-based terms of bodily ability at the same time as it realizes various forms of production, all of which revolve around some notion of profit. Such operations involve the meeting of bodily ability and another category of identity. When an individual is situated at some point on a spectrum of abilities that is outside the normative position of both categories, and when that position is remarkably and dangerously distant from the sociocultural norm, individuals within range of the norm decide to operate the non-normative body in terms and in hopes of maintaining reproduction.

Rudimentary definitions of "reproduction," the base term of reference for reproduction, help to begin thinking such a concept. *Le Trésor* indicates that "reproduction" is in one context connected to a political economy (including financial) as well as to a house or a family. The latter concept and its often quick connection to biological reproduction, which I do discuss elsewhere in *Operation Freak*, is one of the pragmatic reasons for my use of the term "reproduction." The *Oxford English Dictionary*'s definitions are also useful: "action or capacity of enabling productive economic activity" and "the cyclical recurrence or perpetuation of conditions which allow this."

Attention must also be drawn to the conditions that encourage the action and the capacity to reproduce as well as to the cyclic nature of both macro- and micro-structures of order that perpetuate such efforts. The initial tendency might be to move directly to a discussion of, for example, Walter Benjamin (1936), Rosemary Hennessy (1992), Frederic Jameson (1991), or Herbert Marcuse (1964) in order to flush out the ways in which narratives of production intersect with narratives of collective bodies (often associated with Marxist thought).[40]

However, because I focus on the numerous ways in which varying bodies (individual, although in ways metonymic of a collective) and their abilities are operated in the discursive space of identity politics and narrative, studies generated in the context of the body and body criticism and speaking to numerous forms of identification take the spotlight.[41]

Again, one way to approach these issues is through the work of Foucault. As mentioned in the earlier reading of *Surveiller et punir*, his discussion of the operation to the body is intended to lead to forms of production.[42] He writes: "Cet investissement politique du corps est lié, selon des relations complexes et réciproques, à son utilisation économique; c'est, pour une bonne part, comme force de production que le corps est investi de rapports de pouvoir et de domination" [This political investment of the body is bound up, in accordance with complex reciprocal relations, with its economic use; it is largely as a force of production that the body is invested with relations of power and domination] (30; 25–6). Following Foucault's argument, the operations underscore the body's usefulness to a production that is largely economic: they are connected to the proper governance of bodies within the system of production and, thereby, the continued and perpetual governance of such bodies. As with Barthes's discussion of writerly texts, the notion of production as a process and as an ongoing activity takes priority over the notion of a product as a concrete end goal: the body is continuously invested with meaning through power relations. Tangible results remain, however, a key component of the process, for there is always a product of such production that, as the Chebel citation at the beginning of this chapter attests, serves as an archive of the process. Furthermore, at the same time that the operated body produces, it aids – unwittingly or unwillingly – in a reproduction of narrative and bodily operations.

Freak discourse exemplifies such a reproductive phenomenon, and that parallel is of interest both pragmatically and strategically. The novels under study all contain displays of and performances by the protagonists that correspond directly to a freak of culture and that play a key role in the related identity formation processes within specific sociocultural regions. Two developments arise from this: (1) the delineation of acceptable spaces of normality and abnormality and, thus, (2) the perpetual institutionalization of constructs that are thought in terms of bodily ability and that are used in processes of identification.

The developments become relevant to reproduction because the displays and the performances generate revenue that is financial and, more largely, economic. Sideshow barkers, circus tycoons, fair organizers, and the performers engage in contractual relationships whose primary goal is to create capital. The century of spectacles and their related forms not only grew in number but also repeated their performances, which were anchored significantly in constructs of bodily abilities, thus providing a way for an increasing number of audiences to observe – and observe and observe – as much as their own cash flow allowed. In different venues but in almost simultaneous time frames, scientists emphasized, through other forms of display, an alleged progress in the development of human capacities, thereby demonstrating not only how but also what and in what quantities science could produce (and thus needed to produce).

In the novels discussed in the following chapters, the operating agents function in a similar manner. At times they coerce the protagonists to take part in such productive performances, operating sociocultural narratives of identity and of profit to realize the characters' participation; at other times the agents simply show the characters the path. Through their involvement in the performances, some characters intend to realize a process of self-identification, while others intend to reap financial gains from the institutions with which they engage. However, the repeated operations through which such production is realized are most frequently the domain of the operating agents. The ensuing engagement of the freak characters rarely involves a single performance; instead, it involves returns to the various stages on which their bodily abilities are displayed and through which spectrums of abilities are highlighted.

In addition to the economic goal-oriented forms, other types of reproduction within varied sociocultural contexts are also represented in the novels. The efforts to perpetuate these signal economic production and the importance of such production; however, they also emphasize the utility (and, in some cases, the lack of utility) that the agents literally operate onto or into the protagonists and their bodily abilities. Furthermore, their acts are based not solely on bodily ability but also on norm-based sociocultural narratives that inform other categories of identity. The crossroads can occur with any category of identity; however, I focus on the intersections between citizenship, gender, and race. Each of these categories factors into the reproduction of identity in diverse ways as elements of one identity category are made to speak to or against the varying positions each individual occupies within a spectrum of bodily ability. This process is most acutely transmitted through the lived experiences of the highly ability-charged protagonists.

One example of such intertwining can be found in the representation of gender, the abilities associated with it, and the forms of production that are claimed to arise therefrom. As mentioned earlier, Simone de Beauvoir and Judith Butler have written about the ways that gender is formed. Alongside them, Hélène Cixous (1975), Elizabeth Grosz (1994), and Julia Kristéva (1980, 1993) have, in their respective manners, spoken of the ways in which bodies – particularly the bodies of women – have historically been identified and subjugated because of patriarchal assumptions about their biological abilities to reproduce. Grosz argues as follows: "Relying on essentialism, naturalism and biologism, misogynist thought confines women to the biological requirements of reproduction on the assumption that because of particular biological, physiological, and endocrinological transformations, women are somehow *more* biological, *more* corporeal, and *more* natural than men" (*Volatile* 14). These types of assumptions have often been at the base of various master sociocultural narratives of gender. However, it becomes apparent that both the narratives of the body's ability to produce (and, as Grosz shows, to reproduce) and of the body's gender are necessary to the reproduction of institutions that govern human interaction and the related goals of production. Such claims become apparent when the procreative capacities do not function as they are expected to within specific sociocultural contexts. As a result, anxiety and frustration arise over the body's inability to satisfy the demands of the related master narrative. Treatment is frequently sought for a state of being that, in clinical terms, often becomes a negatively charged disability in need of resolution or repair. As a result, an individual finds herself multiply situated within the procreative spectrum of abilities as well as within the variations of gender.

Similar reproductions of identity have often ignored the woman's choice to procreate or not, a phenomenon that Butler (1993) and Cixous (1975) both highlight.[43] However, their readings and others have not always delved deeply into the question of the woman's ability to procreate; nor have they fully discussed the ways in which such a reproductively unable or disabled woman is identified. The potential for what is a scientifically abnormal reproductive ability, which can be used to infer diminished or absent productivity, is what often leads to the agents' operations on the protagonists' bodies. Scenarios such as this regarding the reproduction expected due to norms of gender and bodily ability are, like the freak performances of the protagonists, part and parcel of the processes of reproduction. Such an unfolding occurs particularly in contexts within which sociocultural structures are represented as fundamentally patriarchal and within which agents monitor the individual's production in terms of economic utility.

The same conclusion holds for the reproductively minded operations that are connected to citizenship and race. In my earlier discussion of French colonial history and slavery, I begin to think the ways in which the spectrum of bodily abilities and race always already come together with regard to labour production. This is further explored in a later chapter, where I address multiple forms of production in the context of race, spirituality, and bodily abilities and arrive at conclusions similar to those of Glissant: "Un peuple ne supporte pas très longtemps à la fois une aliénation brutale ou insidieuse de son arrière-pays culturel et une réduction systématique de son circuit de production" [No people tolerates for a very long time both cruel and insidious alienation from its cultural hinterland and a systematic reduction of its productive capacity] (*Le discours antillais* 326, 335; *Caribbean Discourse* 97, 103–4). Another chapter undertakes an extensive reflection upon the multiple meeting points between ability and citizenship with respect to linguistic production, signalling how operated narratives of science and nation aim to reproduce the normal citizen.

Ultimately, in the following chapters I explore the operations that realize and highlight reproduction, the narratives that inform those operations, the bodies and the narratives that are operated in the process, and the bodily abilities that are shuttled along various spectrums in order to accomplish these acts. In reading the tales of ability-charged protagonists from varying Francophone regions of the world, I discuss identification processes in ways similar to Garland Thomson: "I intend to introduce such figures as the cripple, the invalid, and the freak into the critical conversations we devote to constructing figures like the mulatto, the primitive, the queer, and the lady" (*Extraordinary Bodies* 5). Here the novels that contain the tales of individuals freakishly identified as a "Siamese" twin, a cross-dressing transgendered person, and an exotic witch reveal the many ways in which bodily abilities and the narratives that inform them operate identity in various regions of "le monde francophone."

Conjoined twin separation surgeries purport to offer a "normal" independence through the corporeal demarcation not just of bodies but also of their abilities. As practised in the West, surgical separation is claimed to be informed by a democratically conceived individualism, particularly that associated with the United States.[1] However, a shift has occurred in the international venues for the surgeries and the pursuit of normative and individualized able-bodied bodies. Surgical separation also occurs in the Kingdom of Saudi Arabia at the King Abdulaziz Medical City (KAMC) in Riyadh.[2] Parents from around the world – and at times of different religious faiths or from economically disadvantaged regions of industrializing countries – bring their children to the medical campus in the hope of providing them with what has been billed as a normal and individualized existence.

The post-surgical assessments of success typically depend on the children's capacity to exercise their bodily abilities independently. On 20 June 2009, KAMC conducted its twenty-third successful operation with the separation of Moroccan twins Azizah and Saeedah. Three days after the operation, the Kingdom reported that, for the first time, Saeedah's mother was able to carry her daughter independently of Azizah (23 June 2009).[3] On 5 August 2009, the twins were discharged from the medical facility, and Dr Abdullah Al-Rabeeah, the head of the surgical team, stated that they could now "continue their lives normally" and that all of their bodily abilities would be and could be exercised independently (16 August 2009).[4] Here the newly independent Moroccan girls were identified in terms of separate bodies and abilities – including those of independent ambulation – that they were reported to have gained with surgical separation. The Kingdom has published similar reports of successful independence for previous KAMC-orchestrated surgical separations of twins from other world regions, including Poland, the Philippines, and Cameroon.[5]

2

Excising Conjoined Citizenship;
or, the Beheading of Linguistic Abilities in
Jacques Godbout's *Les têtes à Papineau*

One of us, one of us!

Tod Browning, Freaks

Les comètes font jaser. Les monstres aussi.
[Comets cause chattering. Monsters, too.]

Jacques Godbout, Les têtes à Papineau

Jacques Godbout's 1981 novel, *Les têtes à Papineau* [*The Papineau Heads*], opens with the question of surgery for the conjoined twin protagonists, Charles and François Papineau, who describe their corporeal state as a form of imprisonment: "nous sommes condamnés, comme personne au monde, à un perpétuel tête-à-tête" [We are condemned, like no others in the world, to a perpetual tête-à-tête] (15). Out of this comment is born the nine-chapter narrative of their life, led largely in Montreal and operated radically in Vancouver, which includes all the events a late twentieth- or early twenty-first-century reader influenced by contemporary freak discourse might suppose typical of conjoined twins: instant celebrity at infancy, friendships with other freak characters, regular exposure to the media, periods of examination by various medical professionals, and, ultimately, a decision about having an operation to realize normative, corporeal independence. Each chapter's witty recounting of adventures culminates in the events' relationship to the protagonists' first-person plural contemplation of surgical modification. Talking over their array of extraordinary abilities, Dr Gregory B.

Northridge, anglophone surgeon, argues that the operation is the means to arrest their existence as "moitié d'hommes" [half-men] (21). His ambition: to provide them what he defines as "une vie normale" [a normal life] (19). Anchored in normality, the operation covertly intends to alter, and overtly does alter, an array of bodily abilities related to the production and the comprehension of language in which French is "enfin" [at last], as the final chapter is entitled, obliterated.

Since its publication, Godbout's novel continues to be read as an allegory for sovereignty, particularly for Quebec as a nation.[1] Published the year after Quebec's 1980 referendum on sovereignty association resulted in a "no" majority, and containing an anglophone surgeon who wants to amalgamate the heads of the conjoined bilingual (but largely francophone) protagonists (which "accidentally" erases French), how could the novel *not* be such an allegory? Its representation of Charles and François as conjoined protagonists, with the former yearning to leave behind his French heritage and the latter preferring to retain it, becomes a way of recognizing Quebec's voting population in 1980 and the thorny dilemma of cultural and linguistic heritage that ensnared the Québécois. In order to provide background to the characters' imprisonment, the novel also strategically revisits many of the significant moments in what appears as a battle between French and English. In a context that recalls yet differs from Foucault's discussion in *Surveiller et punir* (1975), it is possible to consider Charles and François the *corps des condamnés* (bodies of the condemned), with their shared body imprisoning English (or "brittanique") and French (or "gaulois") souls.[2]

Amidst all such discussions there emerges the recurrent and central figure of the somatic form that, through its repeated presence, emphasizes the body's importance in such normative discourse on belonging to a community. In *Les têtes à Papineau*, the discourse is plainly situated within the context of the nation and the citizen, and it includes philosophical reflection not just on individual but also and simultaneously on civic identity and the connection to the body. Certainly the normality of the body's appearance plays a significant part in the debate, if only metaphorically, as an indication of the potential for the erosion of a previous peaceful coexistence. However, as the novel's content suggests in nearly every chapter – especially in the final chapter, where the post-operative single-minded protagonist produces and comprehends only English – such notions of the nation (and particularly of the citizen) are conceived largely in terms of bodily abilities. More specifically, the spectrum of linguistic abilities (informed by the physiological, neurological, and other abilities required to produce and to comprehend language as well as the cognitive and intellectual abilities to create with language) becomes the means by which a citizen's identity can be transmitted and understood.[3] Charles and François are metonyms of that citizen. It can of course be argued that Godbout's choice to represent the protagonists as conjoined twins serves to replicate the peculiar condition of Quebec's own state and thereby gives life (albeit perhaps a diminished life) to conjoinment for political and rhetorical profit and not for representation of bodily abilities. However, it is the novel's particular emphasis on language, on the body's abilities to produce language, and on the normative concerns of the reproduction of such language that allows for a reading within the context of identification as related to bodily abilities.

To demonstrate how the spectrum of such abilities (and the operations to them) inform the identification of the citizen, I explore the ways and contexts within which Charles and François are connected to operations, to abilities, and to language. I begin by discussing the forms of operated text or narrative that exist in *Les têtes à Papineau*, including those that the protagonists, through the use of their extraordinary linguistic abilities, conduct in their *récit*. I then outline the various historical events that have resulted in the production of sociocultural master narratives, specifically the production of language, as implicit to but necessary for the preservation and, thus, reproduction of the nation and the citizen. This demonstrates the ways in which linguistic abilities are woven into such narratives and processes. I go on to explore how the novel connects the citizen and language production to two traditions: (1) the freak show and profit and (2) monstrous prodigy and foretelling. I reflect on how corporeality that is deemed socioculturally abnormal is seen as detrimental to the narrative of the productive citizen. I then delve into the ways in which the gamut of discursive and surgical operations (most notably, Northidge's) have repeatedly informed Charles's and François's identities, particularly as a citizen, in terms of abilities. Finally, I show the specific ways in which the spectrum of linguistic abilities informs the twins' pre- and post-operative identities, the latter of which, in the form of the reborn citizen, is refashioned into a new and monstrous state of abilities for the nation.

"TEXTE OPÉRATOIRE";
OR, OPERATIONS OF (THE) NARRATIVE

In a novel that begins with and follows the developments towards and through an amalgamating surgical procedure, the question of operating a narrative, in the sense of both Barthes's and Genette's readily transformable if not palpable text, becomes almost redundant. Recognizing that the text is itself built around a surgical operation would seem, at first glance, to justify the claim that *Les têtes à Papineau* is without a doubt an operating narrative. Such claims are certainly true. However, the representation of the surgical operation that realizes the proposed amalgamation of Charles and François Papineau speaks primarily to the content of the narrative, something I analyze in greater detail later in this chapter. Right now I intend to explore the presence of rhetorical, stylistic, and discursive procedures in the novel that regularly demonstrate the ways in which individuals – characters, narrators, and authors – manipulate, or "operate," a narrative in order to achieve profit.

In addition to discussing how Godbout's style echoes this notion of operation, I also examine how narrative production within the novel always requires more than one tone, voice, and hand to communicate a message. Such an operated process of writing, what the protagonists call a "*journal* de notre évolution, jusqu'au scalpel" [*diary* of our evolution, right up to the scalpel] and a "récit bi-graphique" [bi-graphic narrative], reminds the reader of the process and the power of operating and operated words in any text.[4] In the end, this discussion shows *Les têtes à Papineau* to be an example of the operating of narrative: writing can be thought as an operation requiring the use of linguistic abilities, whereby the writers operate and, at times, reveal their motives for doing so. Echoes of the operation to bodies appear at times, and I discuss these below.

One critically discussed aspect of the novel that factors into the operating of narrative is that of the author's stylistic choices. In his first book-length study on the author, *Jacques Godbout, romancier* (1984) [*Jacques Godbout, Novelist*], Yvon Bellemare, perhaps Godbout's most favourable critic, spells out the multitude of ways in which a critical reader can appreciate the discursive, rhetorical, and stylistic facets of Godbout's novels, both within and without their thematic content. One element that relates directly to the reflection on operating narrative is Bellemare's discussion of Godbout's abundant uses of ellipses and how they aid in communicating the content and the mood of the novel. Before even addressing the surgical procedure as an act of linguistic and cultural suppression vis-à-vis a state of cultural multiplicity, Bellemare writes of how the ellipsis (understood as the omission of words, details, or utterings) itself indicates the act of narrative suppression: "L'ellipse ... consiste à supprimer un élément important d'une phrase, comme le verbe, par exemple" [The ellipsis ... consists of removing an important element of a sentence, like the verb, for example] (182). Bellemare himself affirms such absence as having an effect on the reader: "[l'ellipse] ne laisse pas la possibilité au lecteur de compléter logiquement la phrase" [{the ellipsis} does not allow the reader the possibility to complete the sentence logically] (183). The verb is the grammatical element of a sentence upon which hinges the transmission of meaning, action, and thought. It may be considered the hub of the sense of a sentence and the transmitter of meaning to all of its dependent parts. With a verb removed, the sentence may be said to have had the head, which gives it meaning and which regulates its dependent limbs, severed from its body. As such, a sentence becomes like the protagonists at the end of the novel, evacuated of a crucial element that helps a structure to transmit its meaning.

Bellemare's analysis is not limited to interpretations of the ellipsis; rather, he demonstrates the ways in which it allows the text to expand upon various themes and moods. Through the repetition of words or expressions in the sentences that precede the ellipsis, certain functions of the latter arise: it is a "rappel globalisant" [all-encompassing reminder], a "jugement" [judgment], and, thereby, "une entité ... concluante et irrévocable" [a conclusive, irrevocable entity] (182–3). More specifically, it underscores the power of such use of the device: "[elle] dicte l'importance de l'essence même du mot répété" [{it} dictates the importance of the very essence of the repeated word] (183). Bellemare makes a poignant and strategic choice in his example from the novel's first paragraph, which, in speaking already of Dr Northridge's intent, prophetically emphasizes the amalgamating surgical procedure's outcome: "Il désirait procéder à quelques examens dont il avait seul le secret, et peut-être par la suite allait-il nous offrir une intervention chirurgicale définitive? Définitive" [He wished to move forward with some exams about which only he held the secret, and perhaps subsequently he would offer us a definitive surgical operation? Definitive] (Godbout 13). From the outset the sentence operated into an ellipsis speaks to the surgical operation that, as discussed later, reduces the protagonists into a *protagonist*, what Bellemare himself calls "la finalité monstrueuse qu'un processus sans appel transformera" [the monstrous finality that an irrevocable process would come to transform] (183). Further textual construction reinforces such finality not only through the last chapter's title ("enfin") but also through the numerous uses of the chapter title as ellipses throughout the novel (five times this occurs at the end of paragraphs). To this end, the references serve as an operated, refrain-like call to finality, and the novel's regularly truncated style announces and embodies operating narrative.

In addition to signalling the cutting (out) of words, *Les têtes à Papineau* also draws attention to voice through the two protagonists, Charles and François, whose presence and dialogue constantly remind the reader that the characters are both narrating and writing a text. Later I highlight the importance of such multiplicity within the Quebec sociocultural context of operating normality. What is of interest here, though, is what such vocality signals as an operation within the narrative. Certainly it underscores the multiplicity of voice in the text, which can be read retroactively in terms of a postmodern decentring, or destabilizing, of the subject.[5] However, the movement between the two voices and their mutual editing speaks most directly to my discussion of operating narrative. This is because the movement and the alterations show how narrative is operated: through movement between or among narratives and through the characters' editing (together) of the narrative(s). Such processes of editing voice also find links to the body and the history of the protagonists. As Alain Piette argues, the very acts of writing and editing and, therefore, textual production are familiar if not genetic to the twins as their father was a journalist (118).[6]

The novel contains multiple examples of such movement of voice, like the protagonists' first conversation with Northridge, in which Charles editorially "translates" for the surgeon one of François's poetic interludes: "Il n'y a rien à comprendre, ... quand François phrase il s'écoute, il frappe les mots comme des cymbales, peu importe si leur musique a un sens ou non, il fait du bruit, il publie ..." [There's nothing to understand, ... when François forms sentences, he listens to himself, he bangs words together like cymbals regardless of whether their music makes sense, he makes noise, he publishes ...] (22). Another appears in the scene in which the voice of an omniscient, collective narrator encourages the reader to watch, along with the gawking hospital nurse, the spectacle of interwoven arms as the protagonists compose answers to the questions that Northridge transmits through a computer system: "Elle les regarde faire, incrédule, la main droite sert à Charles, la gauche à François. Nous écrivons les bras croisés" [Incredulous, she watches them doing this, the right hand working for Charles, the left for François. We write with our arms crossed] (121). I explore the left/right corporeal composition of the protagonists (including its inconsistent representation of in the novel) later in this chapter. Here, what is of greatest importance is the fact that the novel's image of the overlapped arms suggests how one narrative (of fiction, of history, of the nation) is created simultaneously of and by voices and bodies and, thus, how the twins, with their extraordinary linguistic abilities, operate it into existence.

One of the most telling instances of voice involved in the operating of narrative, however, appears when the protagonists talk about the writing of the aforementioned *journal*, the "récit bi-graphique." The first impression is that the protagonists are, as Bellemare argues with regard to their dialogue throughout the novel, reflective beings who, in writing, live. This being the case, their writing speaks to the blending of individual life and milieu to produce the *cahier personnel*. Bellemare discusses this concept in his second author-focused study, *Jacques Godbout: Le devoir d'inquiéter* (2000) [*Jacques Godbout: The Duty to Disturb*]. It is a process that, in other Godbout novels, such as *Salut, Galarneau!* (1967) [*Hail, Galarneau!* (1970)], mixes life and writing and is identified as "vécrire," the combination of "vivre" and "écrire" ("to live" and "to write") (Bellemare 73). The scene also reveals how *vécrire* results in the coming together of dialogues and the compromises that such a union (whether temporary or permanent) involves.

Such writing appears in the following citation, in which Charles and François discuss the means by which to write life and effectuate the text's voice, given their own preferences of style and tone: "– Pendant que tu dormais j'ai relu notre texte, dit Charles, nous avons une fâcheuse tendance à nous épancher. – … [Ce] n'est pas grave si on déborde parfois ici et là. – Je déteste le mélo, soupira Charles. – Je n'aime que ça, dit François" [– While you were sleeping I reread our text, said Charles, we have a tiresome tendency to vent. – {I}t's not that bad if we go over the top from time to time, here and there. – I detest melodrama, sighed Charles. – I love nothing but, said François] (64). As a compromise to their conflict in which they work and even (with

Charles's sigh) breathe, Charles proposes a clearer separation of voice: "Est-ce qu'on ne pourrait pas … chacun écrire notre version de l'aventure?" [Could not each one of us write our version of this adventure?]. The passage is certainly heavily allegorical with respect to nation building as it speaks through François's existentially grounded statements regarding his concerns for collectivity and how it is written: "Tu chanterais les vertus de la solitude, je crierais pour deux" [You would sing the virtues of solitude, I would cry out for two] (64).

The outcome of their debate favours a collective *vécrire*, but only due to the guilt-triggered and self-motivated interests that Charles anticipates in the eventual realization of the surgical amalgamation: "- Tu n'es déjà plus avec moi, répondit tristement François. – Je te demande pardon, fit Charles, il fallait que nous en parlions. Nous le ferons à deux, si tu insistes. Sans coups bas. Nos quatre yeux ouverts. Mots à mots." [– You've already disconnected from me, responded François sadly. – I apologize, uttered Charles, we had to talk about it. We will do it together, if you insist. Without low blows. Our four eyes open. Words for words] (65). Through the discussion and, in particular, through Charles's acquiescence, the narrative demonstrates the editorial choices that are made in the writing of the officially documented history that *Les têtes à Papineau* allegorizes. Such choices in writing a lived history are, according to Michel de Certeau, in and of themselves operations, even in the separation of a present from a past: "Dans le passé dont il [le travail de cette séparation] se distingue, il opère un tri entre ce qui peut être 'compris' et ce qui doit être *oublié* pour obtenir la représentation d'une intelligibilité présente" [In the past from which it {the work of such separation} is distinguished it promotes a selection between what can be "understood" and what must be *forgotten* in order to obtain the representation of a present intelligibility] (10; 4 [emphasis in original]). For the *journal* and, thus, the narrative, the voice – and even the words, as underscored in the pluralizing of an otherwise singular "mot à mot" [word for word] – involves an operation undertaken by more than one and in the name of more than one. As such, Charles's and François's living/writing can only ever involve the operation of more than one narrative that, in the end, produces one text, the narrative in the singular.

The operating of narrative in the above excerpts realizes precisely what Piette describes in teasing out the multiple discourses that make up *Les têtes à Papineau*. In what appears to be an echo of the aforementioned crossed arms of the protagonists, he refers to "un entrecroisement de discours" [an intertwining of discourses] (113). With such examples, the two voices of the novel remind the reader that neither of the protagonists' versions is stable on its own but, rather, depends on that of the other. The input of the two voices concerning a composed narrative also suggests that the two versions are constantly edited and editable. Similarly, as Charles and François have different and at times differing motivations, their two voices reveal how the two versions are charged with multiple meanings (and even with the possibilities of *double entente*). Furthermore, the two voices intend to demonstrate, through references to style and tone and, thus, in the approach to writing and to word choice, the inferred "French" (François) and "English" (Charles) sociocultural distinctions. The demarcations associated with the protagonists run throughout the novel at the same time as both characters are presumed to be fluent in both languages.

The production of a narrative itself becomes a form of reproduction that, on one level, the twins' narrative operations intend to realize. It gives form to what they baptize the "récit bi-graphique," or a bi-graphical narrative, that they are under contract to publish. Their narrative operations, then, serve as the means to realize not only an object of creation but also the obligation of publication, which, in the best of scenarios, gives life to another form of reproduction – that is, financial production. During the process, the twins' hands, voices, and preferences of tone operate the narrative as they produce multiple textual components that make up the larger narrative that will be the published work.

Some of these components only appear as representative fragments that the protagonists produced, including keyboard-composed responses to Northridge's queries during their pre-operative hospital stay. The operating appears in scenes in which the twins discuss and edit, such as the one in which they realize how their responses are sorted by Northridge's computer program according to the use of singular and plural pronouns. Once discovered, they strategize how to compose answers that will prove their theory (94–5). Another example is the scene with the gawking nurse, in which the reader not only sees the protagonists compelled to compose but also learns that the twins value their operated narratives enough to guarantee their rights of ownership: "nous avons gardé les droits sur la publication de nos réponses!" [we retained the rights on the publication of our answers!] (94).

Other instances of the reproduction that arises from the operated narratives include the ways in which *Les têtes à Papineau* clearly steps into genres other than that of the *journal* that it is explained as being. For example, the novel shows François eventually conceding, in his own manner, to Charles's wish to compose portions separately. The chapter entitled "huitièment" ["eightly"] contains the most notable example of reproduction, and it is in the form of the at times dramatic scientific reporting of a violent, battle-like representation of the surgical amalgamation. Presented at first without any indication of its source (and thus intended to camouflage itself as the actual report), three pages later the reader learns that it is, in fact, François's independent imagining of the surgery. After reading the "récit sanguinaire" [bloody narrative], Charles calls it "un texte opératoire" [an operative text] because of the way it attempts to convince its reader of the violence of the impending surgical operation – an effect not realized on the scornful Charles (143, 145).

The most pronounced genre-based change appears in the final chapter, where the novel, like François with the imagined surgical operation, attempts to operate its reader. Without any documentation of the actual surgical amalgamation, the narrative advances from François's imagined version to its concluding section. What appears is a letter that serves, as Bellemare explains, as "un moteur à la progression de l'histoire" [a driving force in the progression of the story] [*Jacques Godbout* (1984) 195]. As a result, the narrative switches from the *récit biographique* to the epistolary response in the singular, from *journal intime* to what Piette calls a "lettre d'affaires" [business letter] addressed to a publisher concerning the protagonists' aspired publication of their *journal* (125). Despite all such operations in the name of production, a published *journal* becomes something that the socioculturally charged protagonists Charles and François Papineau are, *enfin*, linguistically unable to produce. In sum, the novel emphasizes that – with the exception of reproducing the life stories, as a *journal* or *récit de vie* is intended to do, and of reproducing the satirical awakening Godbout's fiction is known for – the operation to narratives can do nothing to preserve or to continue the narratives, the lives, and the abilities of Charles and François Papineau in the states in which they begin.

ONE WITH US, ONE OF US:
QUEBEC'S CULTURE OF LANGUAGE

Whereas *Les têtes à Papineau* underscores the operation of narrative and of language in the production of written text, as sociocultural repository it speaks directly to the status of the nation and thus of Quebec in the era of the 1980 referendum on sovereignty-association. As previously mentioned, many of the earlier critical readings of the novel have successfully addressed the ongoing heritage of colonial history and the frequently stated postcolonial status of Quebec. This spans the time from the 1759 battle between France and England to Quebec's current relationship with Canada as a federal state governed as a parliamentary democracy and a constitutional monarchy. The very history of Quebec as connected to Canada plays a central role in the operations involved in the ability-charged identification of the twins as citizens. However, because I focus on the ways in which bodily ability factors into the same process, and because the aspects related to Quebec's postcolonial status operate in tandem with others that function outside of the postcolonial context but within the context of Quebec itself (e.g., the protagonists' birth, their relationships with other characters and so on), the normative operating of abilities is a process to which the postcolonial condition contributes only in part.

There is no doubt that Godbout's novel recalls multiple aspects of the historical struggle for recognition of what some have called the "cultural essence" that constitutes and preserves Québécois identity and, thus, makes of Quebec a nation (R. Handler 37; Vallières, *Un Québec*, 86). Such history appears in the novel's title, the aforementioned reference that signals the historical figure of Louis-Joseph Papineau, "défenseur du pays" [defender of the country]. Papineau was a nineteenth-century endorser of the Canadiens Français and one of the architects of the 1837 *rébellion des Patriotes* (Patriots' Rebellion), which denounced the menacing expansion of English practices in what was still a predominantly francophone-populated region, particularly Bas-Canada (Lower Canada) (Denis 134; Lanctôt 188).[7] The character of Dr Northridge, the surgeon who proposes to amalgamate the protagonists (and, thereby, efface the French language), can also be said to recall the concrete efforts towards French effacement most frequently associated with the 1759 British victory on the Plains of Abraham. As one more example, inhabitants of Acadia endured London's efforts to expel the bodies of French speakers who refused to abort their culture to ensure the predominance of another. One of the most significant of these efforts was the "Grand Dé-rangement," an act of population redistribution that took place between 1755 and 1763 and that fractured the colony's French-speaking population by shipping francophones to, among other places, many of the British colonies, to France, and to Louisiana (Louder, Morissonneau, and Waddell 2).[8] An estimated thirteen thousand Acadians died as a result.

As most anthropologists, historians, and political scientists agree, one of the factors in historical struggles against assimilation is the French language and its multifaceted position as a fundamental, and in some cases natural, component of the culture. According to Piotr Sadkowski: "The community memory borne by the language of spontaneous communication (vernacular language), the works of the collective past (referential language) and the myths (mythic language) determine the cultural contemporaneity of the nation and assure its continuity" (153). The ultimate responsibility of such a social contract is entrusted to the citizen who, according to Alain-G. Gagnon and Raffaele Iacovino, is to reproduce that nation's interwoven and interdependent culture-language formula (*Federalism* 96). The duty is itself premised upon the ability to produce and to comprehend the language that is historically presented as a natural component of (being) a Québécois.

Published in 1981, Godbout's work about the English- and French-speaking conjoined twins was penned in the aftermath of the 1980 referendum. The call to vote asked whether or not the Quebec government should negotiate a relationship of legislative sovereignty-economic association with the federal Canadian government seated in Ottawa, not whether the referendum would provide for such a political state. As all reports show, just barely four years after the Parti Québécois took a majority in the Quebec government, the referendum results were a decisive 59.56 percent in opposition and 40.44 percent in favour. As the same studies show, the 1980 referendum would be only one in a series of efforts made by Ottawa and Quebec to map out whether the latter's land of francophones, which had been labelled *Nouvelle France* two centuries earlier, was to be a province of French Canadians or a nation of Québécois. The series would begin with the Révolution tranquille, would testify to various political bodies (such as the Front de libération du Québec (FLQ) and the Parti Québécois [PQ], which Godbout himself helped found), and it would carry through to discussions that the PQ continues to initiate.[9] Language remains at the heart of such arguments, which, even today, often turn to polemics. Frequently the rhetoric of the Québécois as colonized echoes Pierre Vallières and Denis Monière. For example, PQ leader, Pauline Marois, spoke fervently about the limited use of French during the opening ceremony of the 2010 Vancouver Winter

Olympics, accusing Premier Jean Charest – a francophone Québécois by birth – of sticking his head in the sand rather than defending the "autre langue officielle du pays" [other official language of the country] ("Vancouver").

With Marois's statement built both on pride of and political jockeying for one's language, language may be said to be both the heart *and* the head of Quebec's project for independence and, thus, its national identity (Vallières, *Un Québec*, 86). This may seem unsurprising given the volumes written on the central, if not corporeal, role that language plays in Quebec identity. Conceived for decades in biologically grounded theories of "Latin blood" and "Latin temperament," certain arguments tie language to the body just as they reinforce the francophone culture's contact with and evolution within the North American region. In the most ontological reading of the arguments, language appears to be not simply of but *in* the body. As Richard Handler's 1980s anthropological research posits, some Québécois feel that language passes from the speech rhythms of the mother to the unborn child, while others believe that it is transmitted through bloodlines from generation to generation of *Nouvelle France* settlers. In the same vein, language is said to be what constitutes Québécois identity; without it a Québécois would not be a Québécois (38). Most certainly, language is at the centre of the identification of both the nation and the citizen.

The citizen of the Quebec nation – be it the francophone immigrant that Quebec continues to work to attract or the Québécois "de souche" or rather, "pur laine" (indigenous to *Nouvelle France*) – is called upon to reproduce the French language. Such a call would eventually become concretely mandated by legislative operations. Previous bills from the National Assembly of Quebec, such as *loi* 22 (Bill 22) or *loi sur la langue officielle* (the Official Language Act), required that French be the sole official language of Quebec. Effectively replacing the earlier bill, *loi 101*, *Charte de la langue française* (Bill 101, the Charter of the French Language), adopted in 1977 and much scrutinized since, qualified the way in which French was the official language of Quebec. More specifically, the law served to effectuate the call to Quebec's citizens by assuring the presence and permanence of French in public life. Exempting the Inuit communities, the bill encouraged if not controlled citizens' interaction in French in state-sanctioned spaces such as government offices and most schools (as specified), with regard to public utility providers, and even through public signage within Quebec. Richard Bourhis and Rodrigue Landry write, as the first piece of legislation put forth by the PQ after taking power in 1976, the law intended to make a clear and direct statement about the presence of English: "la loi 101 se devait d'avoir un impact immédiat et positif sur le statut du français par rapport à l'anglais, surtout à Montréal" [Bill 101 had to have an immediate and positive impact on the status of French in relation to English, especially in Montreal] (107). According to Vallières, *loi 101* also worked to prevent the effacement of French within Quebec itself due to the presence of English-speaking Quebec residents whose language rights and production would be protected by Canadian federal laws (84).

The opening of the preamble to *loi 101* attests to the need to preserve the francophone heritage through the preservation of the French language: "Langue distinctive d'un peuple majoritairement francophone, la langue française permet au peuple québécois d'exprimer son identité. L'Assemblée nationale reconnaît la volonté des Québécois d'assurer la qualité et le rayonnement de la langue française" [WHEREAS the French language, the distinctive language of a people that is in the majority French-speaking, is the instrument by which that people has articulated its identity; WHEREAS the National Assembly of Québec recognizes that Quebecers wish to see the quality and influence of the French language assured] (*loi 101*; Bill 101). Composed in reference to the historical military battles and the then contemporary cultural battles for the land of Quebec, written with the intent of mandating French usage in multiple sociocultural arenas, and devised for the representation of multiple linguistically and culturally charged bodies, *loi 101* is itself an operating of narratives. It is an assemblage of and reference to multiple discourses that were authored and approved by the many voices of a legislative assembly. It also has at its core the operation of the assembly members' intent – one that is remarkably norm-centred – onto the very bodies it works to make reproductive of such legislation.

Responses of non-francophone communities at the time of the legislation were diverse. For the anglophone population, they included, in the following decade, the self-selected geographical relocation of 120,000 anglophone individuals to English-speaking provinces and the creation of political parties to pursue the right for the representation of English (Bourhis and Landry 110). Works such as Garth Stevenson's *Community Besieged: The Anglophone Minority and the Politics of Québec* (1999) provide a detailed view of such developments.

Individuals who were allophone (i.e., individuals with first languages other than French or English, excluding Inuit) reacted similarly, also offering up statements in the decade to follow. These included works that would engage in dialogue with earlier works written during the Silent Revolution, like Marco Micone's poem, "Speak What" (1989), which offered a response to Québécois activist and poet Michelle Lalonde's call-to-action poem "Speak White" (1968). It goes without saying that, with so much linguistic variation unrepresented, *loi 101* was far from a "perfect" bill for all of Quebec's citizens.[10]

A LINGUISTIC CITIZENRY OF ABILITIES AND REPRODUCTION

A piece of legislation that aims at solidifying one cultural group also opens the door to questions regarding how the citizen, conceived in terms of language, belongs to a nation due to her ability to produce language. As conceived by the majority of sovereignists, represented by the PQ, the citizen's production of language is clearly and complexly part of and one with the reproduction of the nation. In sum, the language of *loi 101*, which established the rights of the Quebec citizen to communicate with government agencies, employers, and similar bodies in French, also obliged the citizen, through the need to encourage the "rayonnement" of French, to reproduce Quebec's cultural heritage through the production of French.

The notion of a willed capacity is clearly at work here, for the more obvious means by which citizens can and should respond to the duty spelled out in the legislation is through learning or mastering the use of the language. Such a process involves a choice and, if not a desire, at least a felt obligation to take part in this endeavour. One result could have been a converse *dérangement*, whereby non-francophone citizens felt compelled to flee and, as some actually did, to seek refuge among related linguistic and cultural communities. However, displacement on the same scale was not realized as it had been centuries earlier, with the Acadians. Moreover, as the efforts to link the French language almost genealogically to the construct of the Quebec citizen increased, it became clear that the citizen's body was implicated in this duty: it was to have the full range of abilities needed to produce the language required by law. As a result, the citizen's body is to be fully committed to the reproduction and the comprehension of such language – it is to be what Gagnon and Iacovino refer to as "the primary vehicle for the preservation and flourishing of Québécois identity" (97). *Loi 101*, then, does more than mandate language use and production: it conceives of the citizen and, thus, the nation in terms of bodily ability.

The anglophone and allophone populations are just two examples of communities that do not forcibly possess the aforementioned linguistic abilities. Another, perhaps more pronounced, way that a citizen's range of linguistic abilities becomes apparent and complex is within the context of immigration as it is thought within the context of nation-building. In speaking of questions of integration and cultural pluralism, Gagnon and Iacovino maintain that "the idea of Quebec citizenship cannot be divorced from the larger issue of Quebec's national affirmation" and that citizenship involves the duty to learn and to speak French (*Federalism* 96). With the increased emphasis on integrating francophone immigrants into the Quebec nation in order to expand the number of bodies that speak French, the essentialist "Latin blood" arguments at the base of French-speaking abilities has shifted. Nevertheless, the overriding concept remains the need for francophone bodies as individuals who, in producing French, reproduce the nation.[11]

Still there exist other communities that have not factored prominently into the language and citizenship debate but that point to the ways in which the ability to produce language may or may not be woven into the narrative of the citizen. For example, members of the deaf and the "mute" community, a portion of whom connect to language not through French but through langue de signes québécoise (LSQ) – a language about which there continues to be much debate in Quebec – do produce language and are citizens.[12] Where the deaf presence reveals an arbitrary, normative connection to French is through LSQ itself. According to a fairly succinct report, LSQ demonstrates a divide between English and French along gender lines: female students tend to learn LSQ as it is influenced by American Sign Language (ASL), and male students tend to learn LSQ as it is influenced by langue de signes française (LSF) (20 April 2010).[13] Focused on a population of citizens conceived in norm-centred terms, *loi 101* risks being problematic for populations that do not necessarily communicate using all forms of language production supposed by the bill. By insisting on set, produced forms of one language and the lexicons that compose them, the bill shows its inclination towards a specific set of abilities that the citizen must possess.

In light of and despite such demographic distinctions, contribution to linguistic reproduction for the preservation of a culture and the affirmation of a nation requires the engagement of the bodily abilities needed to produce and to comprehend the official language. As the history of French-language rhetoric regarding "blood" and "temperament" reveals, the importance of the citizen's body to such language production and comprehension and, hence, to cultural reproduction, becomes increasingly evident. The body is, most certainly, the vessel whose abilities originate and realize such reproduction. As any law that intends to provide order for a human collectivity, *loi 101* can only offer ideas of order about the body and its comportment. Subsequent modifications to any legislation, whether by popular vote or by juridical enactment, could (and would) stand to rethink the narrative that populates it. One fact remains: Quebec's Bill 101, by mandating that Québécois citizens' bodies produce French, demonstrates the importance of bodily ability both to law and to culture.

Counter-arguments to such a reading may certainly be presented. One could argue that the survival of a nation's culture is not solely or even largely reliant on language-related abilities and that the ensuing forms of communication – that is, productions of architecture, art, film, literature, the media, and music – can preserve and testify to the culture in question. However, without the bodily abilities to comprehend and to communicate such artifacts, cultural productions would be unable to continue to take life and, thus, to perpetuate the represented culture referenced in *loi 101*. In the most implausible circumstances of a community completely void of abilities to communicate through language, its cultural documents would risk being relegated to the archival spaces of a collective consciousness.

With respect to Quebec and a hypothetical total loss of communication in French (which could at the very least be read as a feared effacement of such an ability without necessarily implying the nation's loss of that ability), politicians and others have argued that these same sorts of documents would be replaced by those of another culture. Individuals who produced some of the aforementioned cultural works in, for example, the 1960s and 1970s did refer directly to the questions of language and bodily ability within the context of cultural heritage and nation construction. Michèle Lalonde testifies to the bond between preservation of a cultural, national identity and the ability to produce language in her aforementioned "Speak White." The title of the poem alone accomplishes such work: it evokes language and subjugation by recalling the now nearly extinct race-based Canadian slur, "speak white." The expression could be and was directed at anyone who did not speak English and, therefore, who did not live, or appear to be of, the anglophone norm. Furthermore, in the poem's own call to slander what it presents as the slur's Canadian-anglophone origins, its title emphasizes the bodily ability to speak – and thereby to speak a language – as the means through which identification is realized and which the Québécois must now refuse by *not* speaking "white."[14]

Still another counter-argument to the centrality of bodily abilities to law and culture could be that a nation's legislation regarding language learning and language production governs not the citizen's abilities but, rather, the citizen's duty to learn and to produce the designated language. In other words, the duty and not the ability is situated at the forefront of the legislation. It is true that the wording of the bill speaks to the obligation to preserve cultural heritage through the expansion of French education and thus production, as evidenced in the preamble of *loi 101*. However, the premise of such an obligation denotes, even within the most common-sense paradigm, the possession of the bodily abilities to learn and to produce the language. As demonstrated above, language cannot be produced and thus reproduced without the abilities to do so. Because the duty specified by the law requires the production of language, this duty and its production are conceived in a manner that speaks of the citizen's abilities to produce language. Even in counter-cultural productions, citizens find themselves defined not solely in terms of linguistic production but also in terms of the abilities to be used to refuse undesirable and arguably abnormal(ized) linguistic reproduction.

CONJOINMENT AND HISTORIES
OF ABNORMAL PRODUCTION

In order to highlight the necessity of such reproduction in the citizen, *Les têtes à Papineau* assigns its protagonists the conjoined body that, in Western traditions of abnormality, is a quintessential trademark of various forms of production. Certainly the constructs of language and the abilities to produce it surface in the protagonists' abilities to speak two languages. Each language is produced primarily by each of the two heads. In order to understand how the characters are associated with sociocultural normative constructs as well as with production, I study here the ways in which the lives of Charles and François speak to forms of economic (including financial) production typically associated with displays of bodily abnormality and always dependent on the body's abilities. Before discussing the connection to production-oriented spectacles of bodily abnormality where bodily abilities were positioned within varied spectrums as extraordinary, I want to look at the long-standing association between conjoined twins and the abnormal upon which the novel depends.

Documented preoccupation over the exceptionality of conjoined twins, and in particular the origin and the meaning of their presence, has existed in the West at least since Antiquity. It is believed that, in Ancient Greece, the presence of such "monsters" signalled the arrival of good or ill from the gods, who had fallen silent, as well as forms of production to come (Garland Thomson, "Introduction," 3). Since the early modern era, science and medicine have catalogued conjoined twins, speculating on what their physical and metaphysical origins might be. In the first paragraph of *Des monstres et prodiges* (1574) [*On Monsters and Marvels* (1982)], Renaissance surgeon Ambroise Paré articulates his thoughts on the meaning of monsters (which include conjoined twins). In addition to stating that monsters are outside the course of nature, Paré also writes that such soma often signifies misfortune to come: "MONSTRES sont choses qui apparoissent outre le cours de Nature (et sont le plus souvent signes de quelque malheur à advenir) comme un enfant qui naist avec un seul bras, un autre qui aura deux testes, et autres membres, outre l'ordinaire" [MONSTERS are things that appear outside of the course of Nature (and are usually signs of some forthcoming misfortune), such as a child who is born with one arm, another who will have two heads, and additional members over and above the ordinary] (3; 3). Isidore Geoffroy Saint-Hilaire, said to be one of the founders of modern teratology, further expanded scientific studies through detailed reclassifications of corporeal human anomalies, including with respect to forms of conjoinment, in *Histoire générale et particulière des anomalies de l'organisation chez l'homme et les animaux* (1832) [*General and Particular History of Structural Monstrosities in Man and Animals*].[15] He also factors into *Les têtes à Papineau* in reference to the long tradition of the scientific classification of bodies, particularly those that did not adhere to scientific norms (131). In various scientific ways, conjoined twins were regularly considered *lusus naturae* – aberrances or freaks of nature.

The West of the nineteenth century, particularly the United States, moved conjoined twins into new arenas: they became more prevalent on the stages of circus sideshows, where they were sources of amusement, as well as in literature and newspapers, where they were objects to consume and to study. Historically speaking, the most famous examples of conjoined twins, both in the United States and abroad, are Chang and Eng Bunker, to whom the expression "Siamese twins" is accredited (Wu 29–30). Whether in ancient or in modern times, what seems to fascinate onlookers is not solely how conjoined twins – with the Bunkers as one example – came to exist but also how they were able to coexist and how the two individuals managed the abilities of the body that housed them. It was never just a question of what the twins were: it was also a question of what the twins were able to do – or, at the very least, what abilities the viewers believed their bodies to possess based on what spectators were allowed to see and the narratives they reproduced. Clearly, the reproduced human body that did not adhere to normative constructs of corporeal structures, which in this case is the conjoined twin, attracted attention for a variety of reasons. Each of these reasons focused on forms of production, be they biological, supernatural, or financial. As the history of Chang and Eng Baker shows, certain cases would become celebrated.[16]

Les têtes à Papineau recalls all such discourse of production and abilities relating to conjoined twins in the self-narrated and self-composed version of the life that Charles and François deem "bicéphale." One such form of production for conjoined twins is rooted in the body's overall ability to capture attention due to an appearance understood across the centuries as freakish (scientific or performative), an appearance to which abilities are always connected. In recognizing these traditions, Godbout's novel provides the reader with a physical description of the protagonists. This description is not only of conjoined twins but also, as records from Paré through Saint-Hilaire to the Mayo Clinic ("Conjoined Twins") demonstrate, of an exceptional if not implausible example of conjoinment: "Nous n'avons, de naissance, qu'un seul cou, un seul tronc, deux bras, deux cannes, un organe de reproduction. Cela nous tient ensemble. Ensemble. Nos deux têtes prennent racine à la hauteur de la trachée-artère, de guingois, de ghingoua, mais à même le cou. Comme les deux branches d'un V victorieux. Elles sont autonomes. Pas que pour les émotions ! La pensée. La voix. La salive aussi" [By birth, we have only one neck, one trunk, two arms, two legs, one reproductive organ. They hold us together. Together. Our two heads take root just above the windpipe, askew and askance, but of the same neck. Like the two arms of a victorious V. They are autonomous. But not only for emotions! For thoughts. Voices. Saliva, too] (15–6). Painting all elements of Charles and François (except for the heads) as shared, Godbout's novel provides a rare if not fantastical example of conjoined twins – one that steps outside the patterns of one bodily site of connection and that makes the reader contemplate whether such twins come from the realm of the real or not, all the while knowing that these particular twins are fictional.[17] Furthermore, by presenting them, in their own words, as a scientific wonder, the text, much like a sideshow barker, works to convince the reader of the Papineaus' body's uniqueness through its abilities. Theirs is a form that moves from the intellectual ("pensée") through the physiological ("salive") and includes the sensory-motor ("voix"). The demonstration of these three arenas intends to fascinate the reader by showcasing the protagonists' extraordinary ability to cohabitate as well as to share nearly all bodily abilities.

The protagonists' presentation of themselves echoes the ways in which they recognize their engagement in various displays of their body. It also points to the ways in which such displays reproduce the history of enterprise and profit common in freak shows and how their success depends on their bodily abilities. The twins identify this phenomenon in their bilingual word play, which intends to demonstrate to the reader their extraordinary translinguistic abilities: "Freak show. Fric chaud" [Freak show. Fast dough] (106). In addition to recognizing that their body generates money, Charles and François demonstrate how broadly referenced institutions and their respective discourses inform this phenomenon by literally tapping into their body. Such use of of the corporeal structure is true even of their newborn body, which is kept in the hospital after their mother's discharge. They undergo weeks of inspection and study on the part of various hospital administrators and health care practitioners as well as a series of readings by winners of the week of "poésie nationale" [national poetry]. Their biologically produced body comes to signify a site of study and a repository worthy of reverence (and, for some, the monster that signalled a union to come), even though they deemed themselves, retrospectively, "Grands Prisonniers des Arts, de la Science et de la Nation" [Great Prisoners of the Arts, of Science and of the Nation] (50–1).

Financial gain also plays a role in the public nature of Charles's and François's first days of life. During the same hospital stay, the administrators lose no time organizing revenue-generating events such as symposia thematically related to conjoinment and a "semaine des physiciens" (physicians' week). The Papineau twins also receive a delegation in the name of Albert Einstein. Even the federal government capitalizes on the symbolic potential of the twins by putting their effigy on a postage stamp (53). The agents of such activity around the protagonists proclaim to have the twins and their conjoinment as its focus; the real focus, however, is on how the twins' conjoinment and their ability to coexist can advance the agents' goals – the making of profit. In sum, the twins become what they themselves call "une Entreprise" [an Enterprise] that, for many – and in numerous ways – reproduces financial gain (53).

Although some of the displays of Charles and François are the result of the efforts of external agents, others appear to be a gesture of agency on their part: recognizing the profits of such reproduction, they choose to demonstrate themselves. In freak discourse such moments may be read to suggest a reclaiming of agency, whereby freak performers profit from the display of their bodies and, thus, from the industry.[18] An early example in the protagonists' life is their childhood friendship with the Fontaines, a family of small people who live in a house built in proportion to their bodily size and dubbed the "Palais des nains" (Dwarf Palace). Their claiming of agency and, thus, profit comes as they regularly open their home to viewers willing to pay a fee: "Leur logis était ouvert aux passants curieux. La famille Fontaine … le père nain, la mère naine et les enfants menus acceptaient comme allant de soi que l'hérédité leur avait joué un vilain tour. Ils gagnaient leur vie, impassibles, avec ce défaut de structure. Ils assumaient leur programme génétique" [Their residence was open to curious passers-by. The Fontaine family … the dwarf father, the dwarf mother and the tiny children took it for granted that heredity had dealt them a bad hand. Unfazed, they earned their living with this structural defect. They accepted their genetic programming] (77). Couched in a scientific discourse within which laws of nature determine the body's form but not the mind's capacities, this citation reveals how the Fontaine family possesses the wherewithal to accept its corporeal structure and, in true enterprising fashion, to profit from it. Business increases when the four-year-old protagonists come to visit, a development that inspires the Fontaine father to announce their presence: "En visite aujourd'hui: les Têtes à Papineau" [Visiting today: The Papineau Heads] (79). With such examples, the text demonstrates precisely how the body can possess the ability to reproduce simply by being seen, especially if one type of freak body coexists – even if only for an afternoon – with another.

As the Fontaine family's existence generates revenue, it also appears static – almost unproductive of anything other than revenue, particularly as the family members accept their "programme génétique" in the staging of bodies and lodging. I discuss the importance of similar statements concerning the scientific determination of abilities later in this chapter. Here, I maintain that such stasis, although willed, runs counter to the movement Charles and François come to embody with their rise to global fame in various circles. Speaking from experience but not from his prodigious nature as a non-normative individual, the Fontaine father tells the protagonists they could one day realize a certain reproduction, which they summarize in their own words: "Nos deux têtes nous mèneraient aussi loin que nous voulions" [Our two heads would take us as far as we wanted to go] (79). Such increasing fame reflects not only their ability to profit from their freakishness but also the profits their abilities will bring them as future celebrities. For example, in consultation with their father, they collectively accept *Paris Match*'s offer to be the topic of a photo-essay on conjoined twins, in which they are compared to Chang and Eng Bunker (107–8). As objects, Charles and François would and do increasingly fascinate not only the general public but also specific audiences; as subjects, they feed such fascination by placing themselves both centre page and centre stage.

As time progresses, the protagonists turn to where the money, fame, and pleasure increasingly appear: from articles in credible journals in medicine and psychology; from talks on stages of universities in Belgium, England, and France; and soon after on their own talk show, where they demonstrate their renowned abilities for language and rhetoric in what they call their "discours dialectique" [dialectic discourse] (107–8). Such presentations find particular value not simply in the protagonists' ability to perform their individuality but more so in the coexisting individuality of their linguistic abilities, which they willingly demonstrate. Within the multi-layered system of reproduction, their body's ability to produce profit because of its physical appearance goes hand in hand with language production as coexisting abilities, as shown in Charles's mastery of English and François's of French.

THE PUSH AND THE PULL OF THE CITIZEN'S ABILITIES

Coexistence of abilities in extraordinary characters such as Charles and François may take on greater meaning when conjoined twins are read as a metaphor for the identity of the citizen as well as for the ability of citizens to coexist successfully. Furthermore, such coexistence may or may not be read as the fulfilment of a citizen's obligation to reproduce the nation. The notion that more than one head can successfully form a united state might recall, for example, the frontispiece to Thomas Hobbes's *Leviathan* (1651), where many heads coexist best when controlled by a central and overarching head of government, theoretically resulting in a harmonious state.[19] Cynthia Wu's work on the conjoined Bunker brothers might also be read in this way, particularly for her discussion of their reappearance in mid-nineteenth-century illustrations and essays. Wu argues that these documents spoke to a nation's "many-headed" union during a period of civil unrest, war, racial strife, and new waves of immigration (30).

As citizens, Charles's and François's relationship to the community may also be read as organically coexistent. Here it is possible to conceptualize the protagonists as mutually distinct yet collaborative forces drawn to one another and dependently productive of community, which recalls Jean-Luc Nancy's work. In *La communauté désoeuvrée* (1986) [*The Inoperative Community* (1991)], Nancy discusses the necessity of attraction in community by adapting the theory of clinamen, the natural attraction between atoms, to describe the attraction of individuals in a community: "On ne fait pas un monde avec de simples atomes. Il y faut un *clinamen*. Il faut une inclinaison ou une inclination de l'un vers l'autre, de l'un par l'autre ou de l'un à l'autre. La communauté est au moins le *clinamen* de l'"individu"" [One cannot make a world with simple atoms. There has to be a *clinamen*. There has to be an inclination or an inclining from one toward the other, of one by the other, or from one to the other. Community is at least the *clinamen* of the "individual"] (17; 4). In addition to speaking metaphorically of social cohesion, this *clinamen* – this attraction, this pulling-towards, and this coming-together – is, according to Nancy, a physical and therefore *natural* foundation of the operative community and, thus, of being-together.

Just as *clinamen* may be a metaphor for social cohesion, so it is possible to reason that the sustained fusion of the two embryos of which conjoined twins are formed – a fusion that generated such twins and that is therefore biological – is a similar metaphor. Such cohesion and dependence within difference are in ways more optimal than their separation. With an echo of Maurice Merleau-Ponty's chiasmic association and a nod to Mireille Rosello's theory of *contamination* as a coming together of differences and a successful basis for community, the corporeal formation and lived cooperation of the Papineau twins prior to their meeting with Dr Northridge testifies to a pluralistic and very real and fully abled coexistence: "I exist *with* you; you exist *with* me." What is more, the atom attraction at the base of Nancy's hypothesis and represented in the novel's protagonists is born of abilities – the biological abilities to reproduce and the intellectual and imaginative abilities to create characters such as the Papineau twins.

An example arises again in Charles's and François's ability to compose a narrative together despite their differences of opinion. It represents their potential to be good citizens who cohabitate and who, especially through language, embody such cohabitation. It also suggests the capacity to work together while maintaining an individuality that is anchored in and produced through linguistic abilities. These abilities are always prodigious.

One set of capacities that reappears throughout the novel, and that informs the linguistic production of the protagonists as cohabitating citizens, is heightened cognitive skills, which I read as a type of intellectual ability. They play a key role in the identification of the protagonists as neonatal citizens as they emphasize their presence and importance from the first day of their existence. However, the reader is shown not only how their cognitive abilities are heightened but also – because of their age – how they are extraordinary. Clearly a fascination with Charles's and François's ability simply to coexist prefaces all this. Various scenes evoke in other characters, and quite possibly in the reader, familiar questions with respect to conjoinment billed as freakery: How *do* the twins do it? How *can* they always live together? How is it productive? To this list, it is possible to add: how do they speak, converse, write, and communicate through language?[20]

A poignant example of Charles's and François's coordination of their abilities may be seen in their description of the line of gawkers outside the hospital nursery, a scene that encompasses both the gawkers' reactions and the protagonists' judgment of them: "Les curieux firent la queue comme au cinéma … Les foules sont souvent bêtes … Pour un peu ils auraient confondu nos têtes avec des reliques sacrés! … Ils [les spectateurs] étaient vieux et laids. Ils puaient le tabac. On entendit des rires nerveux, des soupirs stupides, des: 'Regarde! Regarde! Tabarnac as-tu vu ça! Calvaire qu'y sont laids!' D'autres *morons* se penchaient sur nous. Des milliers de *morons* unicéphales" [The onlookers lined up as if at the cinema … Crowds are often idiotic … It was as if they almost thought our heads were sacred relics! … They {the spectators} were old and ugly. They reeked of tobacco. We heard nervous laughter, bewildered sighs, expressions like: "Look! Look! Fuck did you see that! Fuck, 're they ugly!" Other morons leaned over us. Thousands of unicephalous morons] (45). Clearly the protagonists' intellectual ability to judge arises in this scene: as the crowd critiques the newborns' physical appearance, the twins critique the crowd for its inferior "unicéphale" intelligence. In addition to calling the reader's attention to the variations of point of view within Quebec (as well as to norm-centred contemplation of corporeal variation), this scene also plays on the adage that two heads are better than one. From the first few days of their lives, Charles and François are capable of comprehending how events such as the spectacle of their nursery-based life and abilities are showcased as central to the identification of the citizen-to-be. And they accomplish such acts individually yet together.

Although such abilities contribute to the prodigious personae of Charles and François as well as demonstrate their extraordinary position within the intellectual abilities spectrum, the abilities that draw the most attention are those that are linguistic, be they the production of language, the comprehension of language, or both. To demonstrate the centrality of such abilities, the novel relies yet again on the iconically freakish body of the conjoined twins, showing it to be a space mappable by languages and related abilities. An earlier citation referring to the distribution of the heads clearly demonstrates a spatial conceptualization: "Vues de face, Charles est à gauche, François, c'est la tête de droite" [Viewed from the front, Charles is to the left, François is the head to the right] (23). If taken allegorically for the representation of anglophone and francophone Canada, and if the novel is understood as a charting of such history, the heads of the protagonists can be said to be atlases for the onlooker, with Charles to the west and François to the east. Such distribution is further reinforced by the distinction of the protagonists' linguistic abilities, with, for example, Charles having a greater command of English: "Charles parle anglais 'sans accent'" [Charles speaks English "without an accent"] (96). A citation from the end of the novel continues the linguistic distinction in a letter (in English) to the protagonists' editor explaining the unsurprising post-surgical loss of the French language: "French speech was in the left side of François's brain" (155).

The novel never offers any indication that either Charles or François cannot speak both French and English; however, in these references (the latter of which further underscores the physiological attachment to linguistic abilities), it becomes clear that these languages do have primary points of reference in the conjoined state and in the Québécois context: Charles, English; François, French. The protagonists refer to themselves as "un parfait bicéphale *bilingue*" [a perfect bicephalous *bilingual*] (96 [emphasis in original]). With two languages as well as the previously discussed autonomous "pensées" and "voix" inhabiting the same body, and with English to the left (west) and French to the right (east), the twins personify Canada, with Quebec to the east and, thus, orientalized.[21] They also embody Quebec, where, including in Montreal, anglophones may be said to live more in the west and francophones more in the east. At the very least, Charles and François represent the citizens' abilities to speak the languages within the context of the nation, and their relationship with such abilities becomes central to their identity as coexisting citizens.

At the same time that the freakish conjoinment represents the abilities of citizens with regard to coexistence, it also shows that such a metaphorical reading can and does reveal a push and a pull in a different direction. The representation of such diverging paths heightens the differences and emphasizes the fracturing union as the protagonists' distinct abilities are accentuated. The transformation is situated amidst the conflicting sociocultural expectations of the citizen that the protagonists represent. Their previously successful union becomes one that is unable to reproduce the nation because of the linguistic cacophony of its citizens. Amidst all this, the reader sees and knows how the twins' coexistence and, thus, their coexisting abilities came to be articulated as disharmonious: Northridge's proposed intervention. Such influence is especially remarkable as the twins' preparation for the operation is what, in a significant way, leads to the writing of the *journal*. The twins' now incongruous abilities become, after the first conversation with Dr Northridge, viscerally apparent to the protagonists. From that point forward, they come to view themselves as condemned to conjoinment.

The end result is undoubtedly the amalgamation that Northridge advocates, one that he proposes as a liberation of the conjoined and that the novel reveals as a further formation of the twins. Alice Dreger's *One of Us* (2004) helps us to think even more deeply about such questions of identity, particularly with regard to each twin's individuality and the potential for its denial. Focusing largely on cases from the United States, Dreger flushes out the dialogue through her readings of biographies, especially of living conjoined twins. Most important, she argues that many conjoined twins do not feel that their corporeal union encroaches upon their individuality and, at the same time, she claims that the medical profession has manufactured a narrative about an individuated individuality. Ultimately, Dreger posits that "conjoinment does not automatically negate individual development and expression, any more than other forms of profound human relations do," and that most sets of conjoined twins have had otherwise largely peaceful, cooperative coexistences (40). She concludes that "people who are conjoined appear to share the same nature (genetics) and nurture (environment), yet end up as unique individuals" (40). Such a phenomenon is not exclusive to the United States or to the West: as websites and the Western media testify in their efforts to gain audiences and to speak to progress, socioculturally specific discourses about surgical separation exist throughout the world, as evidenced in recent surgeries performed on infants and children from Algeria, Cameroon, China, and India.[22]

In its playful representation (and mockery) of the ignorance of the situation's complexity, Godbout's text undertakes philosophical reflections on the nature and constitution of the individual. Such wonderings appear even in everyday moments. Consider, for example, the twins' debate with the box office staff of a movie theatre over how many tickets they would be required to purchase: "– Ce que vous nous vendez c'est une place assise … non? – Oui, mais vous êtes deux. – On ne peut pas s'asseoir sur *deux* chaises! – Vous êtes *deux spectateurs*. – Je vous promets qu'un seul regardera. L'autre fermera les yeux. – Bon. Dans ce cas." [You're selling us one ticket … right? – Yes, but there are two of you. — We can't sit in *two* seats! — But you're *two spectators*. — I promise you that only one of us will watch. The other will close his eyes. — Fine. In that case.] (85–6).[23] In direct correlation with the novel's title, *Les têtes à Papineau*, the commentary of the movie theatre employee comes to serve as a reflection upon what constitutes, or rather who constitutes, citizens and the facile acceptance of a unicephalous hegemony. Furthermore, the citation also demonstrates an emphasis on abilities: two heads signify double the abilities to watch, listen, and so forth, and, as such, they challenge further the employee's notion of the individual, which finds its pairing in the citizen.

These successfully coexisting abilities are transformed into failure at the hand of Northridge's operation to their conjoined narrative. The capacity to reproduce – to produce a language, and thus citizenship, and thus a cohesive nation – is precisely what Northridge works to move along the spectrum and thus to render it as a pejoratively conceived disability in need of effacement. Charles and François come to embody a new state of ability, yet in varying degrees. This transformation in ability finds prominent articulation in their announcement to their parents of the decision to undergo the amalgamation surgery: "nous ne savons plus vivre côte à côte" [we no longer know how to live side by side] (68). In sum, they no longer know – no longer possess the ability – to exist together and, thus, have succumbed to Northridge's operation.

FIRST OPERATIONS

Even though the anglophone Dr Northridge and his surgical procedure haunt the pages of the novel as metaphors for an anglophone hegemony that divides and diminishes, other forms of medicine and operation constitute a part of the Papineau twins' chronological existence. Such acts inform the protagonists' identities at the same time as they create a space within which to demonstrate their abilities.

Like many other fictional characters and like many humans in the "real world," the existence of the Papineau brothers begins with an operation born of medical treatment and biological reproduction: vaginal delivery. As with respect to the gawkers outside the hospital nursery, the protagonists present again as profoundly intellectually capable when they observe their first viewers' reactions in Dr Pilotte and his medical staff: "C'est donc les yeux ensablés de sommeil, la bouche ouverte tête de stupeur et le cœur battant que l'accoucheur et les deux infirmières virent apparaître notre première tête suivie de son écho. … [D]ès que nous sommes apparus l'une des deux infirmières fut saisie d'un fou rire aigu. L'autre jeune femme, et le médecin pardessus le marché, se virent plutôt paralysés. Cloués sur place … Ils nous offraient les masques de la peur et du rire" [It was with sleepy eyes, mouths agape from stupor and beating hearts that the obstetrician and the two nurses saw our first head appear followed by its shadow … As soon as we appeared, one of the two nurses was overcome by shrill, mad laughter. What's more, the other young woman and the doctor found themselves rather paralyzed. Stock-still … They offered us masks of fear and of laughter" (41). It would be unfair to say that the medical staff should not be startled by the appearance of a two-headed newborn, especially given that the fictional birth in the semi-realist novel is historically contextualized in 1955, a period when, unlike today, medical technology could confirm only if a woman were pregnant and not the contours of the nascent form in the womb. Although the protagonists' detailed personal recollection of visual and corporeal reactions at the time of their birth is a technical impossibility, the fact that they do remember the events and, specifically, the reactions – silenced or laughing mouths, stunned appearances, immobilized or paralyzed bodies – bears witness not only to their exceptional abilities as newborns but also to the impact of science and medicine on their body. In other words, the obstetrician and the attending staff play an important role in the novel's account of the operation of normality, for their faces, controlled by their minds, which, in turn, are informed by normative sociocultural scientific narratives, identify the protagonists as abnormal as well as temporarily yet adversely disabling for the moments of madness and paralysis they realize.

The medical gaze turns to a discursive diagnosis that works to include the narrative of religion in the operation of normality, revealing how agents often work together multiple narratives in such acts. The procedure is none too surprising given the location of a Roman Catholic hospital, as the embodiment of a pre-Quiet Revolution omnipresent Roman Catholic Church, in which the befuddled physician summons the chaplain: "Ses paroles (les premiers mots que nous entendîmes!) authentiques et historiques furent simples: 'Au secours, monsieur l'abbé!' cria donc l'accoucheur … L'abbé arriva précipitamment … prêt à administrer les derniers sacrements. Mais, quand il vit cet enfant qui gigotait devant lui comme un morceau de cauchemar, il ne put y croire. Mystère? Miracle? Supercherie? Pendant de longues minutes l'élite canadienne-française – médecin et curé –

nous contempla dans un silence incrédule" [His genuine and historic utterance (the first words that we heard!) was simple: "Help, Father!" cried the obstetrician ... The chaplain arrived hastily ... prepared to administer the last rites. But, when he saw this child who writhed like something out of a nightmare, he could not believe what he was seeing. Mystery? Miracle? Trickery? For a few interminable moments, the French-Canadian elite – doctor and priest – stared at us in an incredulous silence] (42). As members of and metonyms for the influential sociocultural components of "l'élite canadienne-française," the same men play a significant role in distinguishing normal from abnormal with regard to physical and spiritual health. Such identification is best referenced in the priest's first words to the mother of the children: "Madame ... Dieu ...... voulez-vous que nous priions ensemble pour le salut de cet enfant?!" [Ma'am ... God ...... do you want to pray together for the salvation of this child?!] (42). Here the staring faces of medicine and religion transmit a concern for saving the newborns from abnormality.

RHETORICALLY SEVERING (HALF-)MEN

The twins' extraordinary abilities, however, are eventually to be cut off in an operation that is based upon, and that builds upon, narratives of citizen and nation that differ from what the Papineau story has revealed thus far. Northridge serves also as a metonym for a normative discourse, a French-effacing English-language culture, as he proceeds brutally with the undoing of the ability-charged coexistence that Charles and François represent. *Les têtes à Papineau* reveals his tactic: to rhetorically brainwash then surgically and permanently alter the minds of the twins so that they perceive of their once largely harmonious coexistence as disharmonious. In order for Northridge to realize his goal of undoing the successful *clinamen*, he must surgically efface the twins' extraordinary abilities, particularly their linguistic abilities, and thus their cultural and ethnic reproduction. This being the case, the novel makes of the protagonists precisely what they spotlight as the recurrent subject in the writings of many a scribe: "Un sujet aussi inévitable que la problématique de la langue ou le pénible portrait de l'homme colonisé canadien-français" [A subject just as unavoidable as the problematic of language or the painful portrait of the colonized French-Canadian person] (27).

Before Northridge can proceed to the surgical operation, however, he must first conduct the discursive operation: he seeks to impart to Charles and François that, as they are currently somatically constituted, they are not whole and, thus, not normal. Northridge uses a double-blow rhetoric that presents their state of being as pejorative and abnormal. Half-men in the eyes of the administration and science, they would be considered half-citizen and half-human. Northridge's discourse constitutes a state of existence akin to a negatively charged state of disability that, through surgery, he proposes to correct and render normal: the twins would have a normal and therefore whole body – one head, one brain – that would make of them one normal person. His solution is ultimately a second birth into a normative sociocultural understanding of the body.

The final surgical operation that the twins undergo serves as a portrayal and prognostication of what many a sovereigntist feared the 1980 referendum's results could one day realize: a cultural, if not ethnic, cleansing of the French-speaking population that elicits, in certain respects, the subject state of a historically colonized population. However, the vote was an issue to be decided by citizens of Quebec who, by 1980, had fashioned themselves into autonomous individuals capable of voting for their own future. That vote finds itself indirectly yet overtly represented in a surgical discourse that intensifies the effect of the novel's message about the results. It suggests the incising, bleeding, and potential loss of life that any such surgery implies – particularly one that focuses on the operative procedure to amalgamate two heads into one – all of which are realizable through the act of cutting and captured in various forms of the verb "to cut" ("trancher"). The debate encapsulated in, and the solution proposed by, the referendum is also represented in the protagonists' family's own deliberations over the cutting of the surgery, best articulated in the words of their younger sister, Bébée: "Et si nous tenions un référendum? ... Pour trancher la question?" [And if we held a referendum? ... To cut to the chase?] (145–6).

The protagonists' explanation of the procedure early in the novel also points to the vote's severity as, in keeping with the novel's overarching ironic tone, it contextualizes it in reductive terms: "vidanger la moitié droite de la tête à Charles et la moitié gauche du cerveau de François pour ensuite trancher les deux crânes au laser, de bas en haut, comme on ouvre un melon d'eau mûr" [to drain the right half of Charles's head and the left half of François's in order to cut open the two heads via laser, from top to bottom, like the cutting open of a ripe watermelon] (23). The twins' choice to compare the surgery to the act of preparing fruit trivializes the historically unprecedented and surgically impossible procedure, noting it as some kind of everyday occurrence. As such, the comparison realizes a marked reduction that ironically underscores and intensifies the severity of an operation intended not only to significantly alter the nation, as the referendum stood to do, but also to drastically transform the bodies and the being symbolized by the culturally and ability-charged twins: "Le couteau de Northridge va nous trancher dans l'*être*" [Northridge's knife is going to cut to our very *being*] (28).

These same rhetorical representations of the 1980 vote also have meaning within the present discussion of citizenship, abilities, and Northridge's operation to the related narratives. They are particularly reinforced in the ways the novel emphasizes the formative power of external agents with regard to discursive manipulations that tend to advance a norm-centred sociocultural narrative. In a process Leslie Fiedler refers to as "creations of artistic fancy," the power is initially underscored in the twins' playful comparison between the operation Northridge proposes to events in horror films or tales of monsters (such as Dracula) (Fiedler 22; Godbout 20). As Charles and François clarify for their reader, Northridge seeks the unique with the intent to transform: "Il cherche des cas exquis. Des malformations rares. Il veut transformer le monde" [He seeks out choice cases. Rare malformations. He wants to transform the world] (19). However, Northridge's power as a doctor and, specifically, as a surgeon specializing in several practices arises in large part from the honours he has received and the care of famous and, at times, infamous patients, including the exiled and ailing Shah of Iran: "Il est diplômé, si l'on peut dire, de la célèbre Clinique Mayo. C'est un cas intéressant: cette clinique est célèbre parce que des gens célèbres y amènent leurs viscères. De là la rate du shah. ... Northridge a réalisé cette opération chirurgicale [du shah] tout en sachant que le tyrannien était condamné. C'est un artiste" [He is degreed, if one can say so, by the famous Mayo Clinic. It's an interesting situation: this clinic is famous because famous people come with their entrails in tow. Hence the Shah's spleen ... Northridge carried out this surgical operation {of the Shah} all the while knowing that the Tyrannian was condemned. He's an artist] (14). Such fame and accomplishments, which, the novel suggests, involve sidestepping ethics and politics in the pursuit of success – particularly in the field of medicine, which officially seeks the optimal and so-called normal functioning of the human body – become part of the means by which Northridge's case wins over Charles and François. They are both individuals otherwise represented as intellectually discerning who, attuned and accustomed to the urges of and for fame, surrender to the skilful and cutting rhetoric that the artful surgeon uses to present his case – a rhetoric that the twins come to internalize and Charles to admire (24, 20).

Northridge's conversation with the protagonists in the first chapter – the only face-to-face conversation he has with them – provides the clearest example not only of the surgeon's aforementioned intentions but also of the rhetorical procedures he uses to achieve his goals. Referring to both medical and legislative narratives of the norm-based individual, Northridge works to convince Charles and François of the need for the surgery in order to rectify their abnormal state and to provide them with a normal one. In comparison with the twins' initial operation at birth, when all of their faculties were not yet developed (but nonetheless extraordinary), Northridge's manipulations occur when the twenty-something twins' intellectual abilities are, according to their *journal*, fully functioning and when they are legally able to decide if the surgery is what they need.

Individual need, then, becomes the means by which Northridge begins to present his argument, focusing on the potential for newness and normality that is alive in the present as opposed to the past: "Cela ne nous aiderait pas beaucoup … de savoir d'où viennent vos ancêtres et si on les comptait comme passagers à bord du voilier de Jacques Cartier! Même les origines génétiques de votre dédoublement ne se révéleront pas très importantes, au plan médical. Ce qui compte c'est le présent, et de savoir si nous serons en mesure de vous offrir une vie normale" [It would not help us much … to know where your ancestors came from and if they were counted as passengers on board Jacques Cartier's ship! Even the genetic origins of your doubling up will not prove to be very important in the medical context. What matters is the present, and to know if we will be able to offer you a normal life] (19). When the ever-sceptical François asks Northridge why he wishes to perform the surgery and if their existence bothers him, he replies: "Pour votre bien! … On ne peut pas passer sa vie à moitié ceci et cela. Savez-vous la place que vos deux têtes vous permettent de revendiquer? Pour la science et pour l'administration, Messieurs Papineau, vous n'êtes que des moitiés d'homme" [For your own good! … You can't spend your life half here and half there. Do you understand the position that your two heads allow you to claim? In the eyes of science and of administration, Masters Papineau, you are only half-men] (21). In the space of two pages, Northridge makes his case by cutting out the history, and even the genetic heritage, used in nation-building in order to emphasize norm- and present-based references to the field of medicine and to government. In this manner, Northridge operates his version of the aforementioned narratives to impart to the protagonists the notion of a greater medical and federal cause that only whole men can realize. Here Northridge's words echo those of Lennard Davis on the theory of the "homme moyen." In *Enforcing Normalcy* (1995), Davis writes of the nineteenth-century French statistician Alphonse Quetelet, who proposed the concept of the "average of all human attributes in a given country," which became, "paradoxically[,] a kind of ideal, a position devoutly to be wished" (26–7). The ideal for any country, Quetelet's "average man" corresponds directly to Northridge's "whole man," which is the standard by which the surgeon measures Charles and François. To be such men, Charles and François must be fashioned anew and must think of the new.

Northridge's argument operates most notably on the premise that individuality brings about happiness and fullness and that such individuality can only arise from freedom from restraint. His theory attunes itself to claims similar to those teased out by Dreger's previously discussed research of actual conjoined twins and the efforts to separate them. She maintains that contemporary cultures tend to perceive conjoined twins as a problem in need of resolution, as individuals in need of freedom: "conjoined twins are trapped in such a way that makes a happy, normal life impossible. Only surgical separation could truly make them free" (7). Based largely on democratic republics such as the United States, Dreger's project is relevant to a novel such as Godbout's, in which the plot, *personnages*, and peripeteia are largely inspired by the 1980 referendum operated by the people of Quebec (who comprised a potential nation).

Furthermore, it can be posited that the notion of newness that resonates in Godbout's novel and in Dreger's work as historically and fundamentally linked to larger political and cultural movements to liberate *le peuple* also underscores the realization of the rising of a new individual. *On Revolution* (1965), Hannah Arendt's analysis of efforts to achieve similar goals, emphasizes the "new" for the people as well as for the individual: "the idea of freedom and the experience of a new beginning should coincide" (21–2). That newness also applies to the individual's faculty, which I equate with types of capacity or ability, when Arendt writes that such a transformation requires the "experience of man's faculty to begin something new" (21–2; 27).

Such indications are not found so much in *Les têtes à Papineau*'s references to Quebec's Silent Revolution as in what it portrays as the refusal and effacement of efforts to maintain minority cultures. These efforts are apparent, for example, in the attempts to endorse individuality and not a Papineau- (and therefore French-) based collectivity. Underscored by the novel's structure of nine chapters, which represent the nine months of gestation, Charles's endorsement of separation in the fourth chapter, "quatrièmement" ["fourthly"], emphasizes individual newness in terms of rebirth: "il ne s'agit pas de rendre l'âme, il s'agit de renaître. De devenir *celui* que nous aurions dû être" [It's not about the spirit passing on, it's about being reborn. To become *the one* we should have been] (70 [emphasis added]). Here Charles's own rhetoric, which echoes Northridge's, reinforces portions of the goals highlighted by Arendt: the fervour to free, to form, even to sculpt the new one (the "celui" of the novel), or "the eagerness to liberate *and* to build a new house where freedom can dwell" (28 [emphasis in original]). The new house is the normatively rebuilt *celui* – the one, the unicephalous body – that Northridge will produce of Charles and François.

The power of Northridge's rhetorical operation manifests itself in its self-interiorization, which causes a certain shift along the spectrum of intellectual abilities. At the end of the same chapter, the protagonists reveal how Northridge's rhetoric intends to assuage their fears: "Il ne fera rien qui puisse nous déplaire. Il n'est pas là pour nous détruire. Il est très conscient aussi que nous avons chacun notre vision du monde. Il ne veut pas nous anéantir. En réalité il croit que s'il réussit son intervention nous serions plus heureux. Heureux" [He won't do anything that will displease us. He's not here to destroy us. He's also very conscious of the fact that we each have our vision of the world. He doesn't want to wipe us out. In reality, he believes that if his operation succeeds we would be doubly happy. Happy] (24). The style of the citation, and in particular the use of the third-person singular pronoun *il* at the beginning of every sentence, suggests (along with the novel's ellipitical and undermining repetition of "Heureux") an automaton-like repetition of Northridge's rhetoric and, thus, an initial brainwashing of the twins, who have put Northridge's ideas at the heads of – *en tête de* – their sentences. Or at the very least of Charles's, whose hopes for the surgery's outcome harmonize with those of Northridge, as revealed by the ever-sceptical François: "rien de ce qu'il a vécu à ce jour ne l'intéresse. Il voudrait même n'avoir aucun passé. Il désire devenir un homme neuf" [nothing that he has lived up to this day interests him. He would prefer not even to have a past. He longs to become a brand new man] (22). Charles immediately confirms François's statement: "Je ne crois pas aux traces … nous avons payé assez cher, il me semble, notre filiation aux Papineau. Je ne veux plus avoir de père ni de mère. Nous serons conçus par laser cette fois" ["I don't believe in traces … we've paid quite dearly, it seems to me, for our affiliation with the Papineaus. I no long want to have a father or a mother. This time, we will be conceived by laser] (22).

What makes Charles's agreement with Northridge regarding the need for a new, whole man a case of rhetorical duping is not simply robotic repetition. Rather, what reinforces the transformation is the absence of any other such statements in the series of life events that the protagonists recount prior to their meeting with Northridge. As discussed, the conjoined existence they detail in their journal of "évolution" always demonstrates the harmonious sharing of all things and events as well as the non-suppressed existence of individuality. Only in the fourth chapter, is there evidence of a transformation that *Les têtes à Papineau* leaves unaddressed. It manifests itself in the twins' inability to explain the change, an indication that, as Northridge hopes, they may already have stopped inquiring into the past: "nous ne savions pas vraiment ce qui nous arrivait depuis quelques mois" [we really didn't know what was happening to us for the past few months] (68). Nevertheless, given the change in Charles's opinion, which appears to be as new as Northridge wants the twins to be, *Les têtes à Papineau* suggests that Northridge's arrival in Charles's and François's lives represents the Foucauldian penetration of a looming institution – here the English-language culture – into the mind of the individual. Such presence pushes Charles to operate himself discursively within the confines of the dominant ideology and later influences his position within the spectrum of linguistic abilities. The discursive shift is witnessed in moments of the twins' initial discussion of the surgery with their parents: "On se gêne … et nous en avons assez de partager le même territoire" [We get in each other's way … and we've had enough of sharing the same territory] (68).

Just as Northridge uses ardent rhetoric in order to singularize the protagonists, so other agents use equally strident commentary in an effort to arrest the severing of the union and, thus, to operate Charles and François. The commentary often materializes in hyperbolic statements that work to paint Northridge's work as either against an organically constituted collectivity or akin to fascist designs that counter the reproduction of the nation. When the protagonists inform their parents, Marie Lalonde and Alain-Auguste, of the proposed surgery and their intent to pursue it, they are, not surprisingly, vehemently opposed. A thinly obscured representation of Michèle Lalonde, Marie objects to any separation and/or effacement of her children, particularly of their heads, which speak for themselves. Initially believing separation to be the procedure, she claims, in rather phallocentric rhetoric anchored in abilities to biologically reproduce, that the twins' union is natural and not to be disturbed: "Je ne veux pas voir l'une de vos têtes sur le corps d'un étranger. Votre père vous a plantés, il n'est pas question de vous transplanter" [I do not want to see one of your heads on the body of a stranger. Your father planted you, transplanting you is not even a question] (69). The legacy of the father's abilities should not be interrupted but, rather, should live on in and through his sons.

Their father's words, however, point to the processes of selection and selective inclusion reminiscent of strains of fascism, which, in certain historical contexts, has direct connections to bodily ability. Initially, Alain-Auguste's articulation makes the novel's recurrent connection between culture, nation, and the mind resoundingly clear and undeniably dependent on normative constructs of singularity: "Ein Kultur, ein nation, ein head, Ein Führer! Ya?!" [One Culture, one nation, one head, One Führer! Yes?!] (69). Here the hyperbolic reference equates Northridge's surgery with the exterminationist practices of Hitler and his efforts to build a like-minded nation of one body and one mind. As such, their father's claim decries one form of nation-thinking at the same time that it advances another: his own conceptualization of a nation that includes, at the very least, two cultures that he wishes to be preserved but that to him avoid norm-based constructions: "n'allez pas céder au syndrome du monde ordinaire" [do not give in to the syndrome of the ordinary world] (71).

Certainly such imaginings of the nation are, as many works on community have put forth, continuously subjective and selective with regard to decisions concerning what narratives and what peoples make the cut. However, when their father's allusion to the Nazi ideology of nationhood and citizenship is studied more closely along with the relationship between bodily ability and identity, the work of David Mitchell and Sharon Snyder on the Third Reich's eradication of unsightly bodies comes to mind. In the continued effort to advance the socioculturally constructed Aryan race, the Nazi regime worked to eradicate abnormal bodies, or the bodies that were not and never could be Aryan because of a specified anatomical deficiency or physiological inability. These same bodies are today considered to be disabled or of a physical form significantly removed from prescribed sociocultural bodily norms (*Narrative Prosthesis* 188). Justified through such a discourse of norm-centred bodily ability (and, at times, a discourse of intellectual ability), the Nazi rhetoric that Alain-Auguste recalls speaks very clearly to the question of ability that is at the heart – or the head – of the cerebral matter of Charles and François. Northridge wishes to cut that organic mass in two in the sociocultural reconstitution of the whole man and, thus, the citizen. The most determinant ability that Northridge operates, and the ability upon which hinges the reproduction of culture and the nation, is the production of language.

TERMINAL CUTS TO LANGUAGE

The representations of language production in *Les têtes à Papineau*'s discussion of sociocultural coexistence and effacement ground themselves not only in the bodies that reproduce the language and culture but also in the abilities of those bodies to reproduce the cherished and natural resource. The connection between language and culture in arguments for nationhood recalls the centrality of language and its production in historical efforts at forging an identity for Quebec as a francophone community and thus as a nation. In this light, efforts at maintaining community depend in fundamental ways on the spectrum of linguistic abilities that produces language (specifically, the French language) as well as on the preservation of such production. Linguistic ability, then, becomes central to identity, especially to the identity of the citizen. The citizen and her linguistic abilities, in turn, become the primary vehicles for realizing the reproduction of the nation.

Such questions are clearly exemplified in the Papineau twins. This is not simply because of their decision to undergo surgical amalgamation and to risk losing certain abilities; rather, it is because of the ways in which Northridge speaks of the operation to create the "new man" and its crucial relationship to abilities governed by the head. From such an ability-informed perspective we can answer the question asked at the beginning of this chapter and that Charles and François raise in their *journal*: "est-ce que la citoyenneté est attribuée à la tête ou aux jambes?" [is citizenship attributed to the head or to the legs?] (96).

There are many moments in the novel that highlight the importance of intellectual ability as it is seen as connected to, and part of, linguistic abilities. Extraordinary, these abilities sit in a particular and valorized position on the related spectrum of abilities. The novel's title, *Les têtes à Papineau*, emphasizes intellectual ability in two ways. First, through the substantive *têtes*, the title highlights the core of all bodily ability, the epicentre that informs the entire body how and when to use all of its abilities. For example, in talking about how they have learned to coordinate their shared body in order to walk, the protagonists affirm a scientifically accepted supposition by emphasizing the increased need to use and coordinate ability: "Il fallait qu'en une fraction de seconde l'ordre partît de nos cerveaux vers les jambes, les orteils, le talon. Car chacun de nous contrôle la moitié du corps, du côté opposé à sa tête" [It was necessary that, in a fraction of a second, the order went from our brains to our legs, our toes, our heels. Because each of us controlled half of the body, the side opposite its head] (73). Second, the title evokes an idiomatic expression related to Quebec's historical efforts at linguistic and cultural preservation: "ça prend pas la tête à Papineau (pour comprendre ça)! [It doesn't take a genius (to understand that)!]" Still in use today and most often used in the negative, this expression is based upon the legendary sophisticated intelligence of Louis-Joseph Papineau, who was known for his active opposition to the nineteenth-century expansion of English, particularly in Bas-Canada. In the novel, even the presumed ancestor of Charles and François, and thus of Quebec, suggests the importance of both language and intellectual ability.

Emphasis on the ability to produce language, and in various forms, also appears throughout the novel. Certainly, the protagonists' abilities to produce the spoken and the written word, as well as their heightened capacity to do so, demonstrate the centrality of linguistic ability to their identities. Their writing of the *journal* is perhaps the most emblematic representation of their abilities. It may even be assumed that their interest in such a creation has genetic implications and is thus – like French for the Québécois – of the body: their father, Alain-Auguste, who "planted" them, is himself a journalist who demonstrates an affinity and passion for composing text. He also reveals "une propension à … produire de nouvelles réalités" [a propensity … to produce new realities"] (32). Throughout their *journal*, the protagonists choose to refer to him most frequently as "A.A.," the nickname he used in signing off on the works he composed (32, 45). The protagonists' birth announcement is a prime example of his ability to create with language: "Il aurait pu demander à un collègue de le remplacer. Il n'en fit rien. Nous étions un fait divers en or, il mit ses émotions de côté, dans le tiroir de gauche, et plongea avec une belle objectivité professionnelle sur le clavier de son dactylographe Underwood" [He could have asked a colleague to replace him. He did nothing of the kind. We were a golden human interest story, he put his emotions to the side, in the drawer to the left, and plunged upon the keyboard of his Underwood typewriter with an impressive, professional objectivity] (46). The twins, whether in person or via the computer screens and keyboards set before them in their pre-operative hospital room in Vancouver, continue their genetic legacy in the discussions with Northridge stitched throughout the novel.

Whereas such abilities find themselves overtly showcased, they also become covertly targeted by the operation that aims, ultimately, to efface French-language abilities and, thereby, French-language culture. Northridge's initial conversation with the protagonists seems sincere for, in telling them of the normalizing benefits that produce the "new man," he also warns them that some loss of ability may occur: "Il se peut … qu'après l'opération vous ne puissiez plus écrire du tout. Vous le savez?" [It's possible … that after the operation you will no longer be able to write at all. You're aware of this?"] (22). As the above discussion of the "new man" reveals, François passively resigns himself to Charles's goals, while Charles, enlivened by the desire to be born anew and to be rid of the Papineau heritage, shows a total disregard for the potential loss of the ability to write: "Ca m'est égal!" [I don't care!] (22).

What comes through as a facile acceptance of an invasive English-language hegemony in the character of Northridge appears even more distressing in the character of Charles, whose indifference to language production is expressed in his willingness to arrest, if not destroy, the ability to produce language that is explicitly connected to French.

Only a page after this potential loss is revealed, Charles and François discuss with Northridge the connection between the surgeon's life and the French language. The details are revealed in the story of Northridge's biological mother, Germaine Beaupré, whose presence expands the novel's discussion of sociocultural identity, language, and the ability to realize their reproduction. A francophone from Manitoba, Germaine was preparing to become a nun; however, in an act painted as her resistance to the anglophone "grand Tout confédéral" [the great confederate Whole], she had sex with the train conductor of the "transcanadien" [transcanadian] and conceived the future Dr Northridge (18). As the novel continues to demonstrate, not surprisingly, Germaine's plan, like all others that aim at francophone linguistic perpetuation, comes undone when she places the child in an orphanage from which an anglo-Catholic family adopts him. Shortly after the placement, she dies, and, a year later, the Northridge family relocates to a resoundingly anglophone Vancouver (19). The sole recognition of his biological mother – his signature of "Gregory B. Northridge" – provides testament to his theory that searching in the past is of no use to the present. By cutting off all but the "B" and ensconcing it between two names of English origin, Northridge has confined the abnormal, incomplete, and now historical francophone Beaupré to a controlled, if not muted, existence.

What the discussion of Northridge's mother also suggests is the controlling of an ever-looming, ever-genetic francophone history through the willed crushing of the ability to produce the French language. As the protagonists discuss Northridge's mother, Charles begins to align himself with the surgeon's theory, particularly in his response to François's focus on the past: "– Un jour, dit François se tournant vers le docteur, vous reconnaîtrez le Beaupré qu'il y a en vous. – Et vous souhaiterez l'étrangler! ajouta Charles" [– One day, said François turning towards the doctor, you'll recognize the Beaupré that's in you. – And you'll want to strangle it! added Charles] (22). Charles's powerful use of the verb *étrangler* [to strangle] suggests a repressed hostility that may echo one that Charles suggests Northridge could hold towards his mother. However, of more direct relevance here is the connection between effacement of ability and production of language and culture. The throat, as home to the larynx, or the "voice box" and, thus, an integral part of speech production, ultimately becomes the target of attack. Charles's explicit reference to "Beaupré" as linguistic signifier of Northridge's personal connection to such effacement intensifies the alliance with Northridge's plan to make the new and whole man. It also suggests that French language ability, connected to the throat, persists as a corporeal menace to the very essence of the individual. In such light, Charles's exclamation further suggests that, for the transformation to occur, all past and present French-language abilities must be decimated – with almost no regard for the operation's brutality and almost no apology for its severity.

Notwithstanding its references to linguistic abilities and the events surrounding the 1980 referendum, *Les têtes à Papineau*'s most telling representation of linguistic abilities arises in, as the novel's title suggests, the operation's emphasis on the head and, thus, the brain. If the explanations of the operation are examined closely, it becomes apparent that the impending loss of language ability of which Northridge warns stands to manifest itself through the loss of French language ability. Such a loss appears clearly predictable given Northridge's plan for the cerebral hemispheres, which is to empty out the right half of Charles's head and the left half of François's head. When meeting with their parents, Charles regurgitates Northridge's explanation but with the emphasis on which parts of the brain will be kept: "l'hémisphère droit de François et mon hémisphère gauche formeront notre nouveau cerveau" [François's right hemisphere and my left hemisphere will form our new brain] (70).

Most apparent in the twins' explanation are the recurrent gains of the newness that the operation stands to afford them with the "nouveau cerveau" [new brain] – gains that become increasingly recognizable as the ones that Charles favours more than François. If the domain of science is again brought into the discussion, as the novel regularly highlights through Northridge's elaborate tests and espousals of medical advances, it can only be noted that the removal of the left hemisphere of François's brain foretells the loss of the linguistic abilities to produce French. The left hemisphere of 70 to 95 percent of humans is documented as being primarily responsible for the production and comprehension of language, notably Broca's area and Wernicke's area (but also other areas) (Grodzinsky and Santi 474–5; Blank 1835–36). Looking at the Papineau narrative, where science and culture meet in the narrative of the citizen and where narratives are continuously operated, it becomes apparent that François is most recurrently and primarily associated with everything pertaining to Quebec and French and, thus, with the linguistic abilities of Quebec. As the protagonists themselves indicate, François produces language and rhetoric in a stereotypically, historically connected French and, by extension, Quebec manner: "Charles trouve ces jeux de mots [de François] particulièrement idiots. Le côté gaulois de François l'horripile" [Charles finds this wordplay {of François} particularly stupid. The Gaulois side of François exasperates him] (17).

Here the novel reveals how operations target the termination of specifically French linguistic abilities and, thereby, the elimination of a spectrum. Northridge's explanation of the surgical operation, particularly his decision not to specify that most language skills in many individuals reside in the left hemisphere of the brain but, rather, to suggest that the protagonists *might* lose only the ability to write, further discloses both his intentions and his agility as a rhetorical manipulator. His operation of the narrative he presents to the protagonists is reinforced through the strategic choice of the respective hemispheres, which come not from the sides of the head that will ultimately be brought together – François's left and Charles's right – but from the sides that will realize francophone cultural decapitation. In sum, Northridge's proposed operation emphasizes the death of the abilities to comprehend and to produce the French language and, thus, the death of their importance in the inferred continuous war between French and English over the body of Quebec.[24]

WHEN FREAK BECOMES MONSTER

As *Les têtes à Papineau* reveals the operation to be a procedure that Charles relentlessly pursues and to which he leads his brother and himself, as it returns repeatedly to the question of language and the ability to produce it within the context of the nation, and as it waxes recurrently ironic and warns consistently of opposite intent, the operation's outcome is what the reader suspects it will be: a new individual who no longer possesses the ability to articulate or to comprehend the French language. Once again, the novel speaks directly to the ways in which language ability and production inform the composition of the nation, the individual, and the citizen. The final chapter, which unveils the fruits of Northridge's work, also reveals how the related operations afford not clarity or solution but, rather, new possibilities that are to be read not as freakish but as differently and thus pejoratively monstrous.

The novel's structure foretold such a coming, or such a birth, through its nine chapters of gestation. The last chapter, written in English as a letter, opens by reinforcing a new English (and federal) rather than an old Quebec context through the date "July the 1st" – Canada Day (155). But perhaps just as important is the fact that the character whose voice is heard is neither Charles nor François. It is a new protagonist in the singular, a new individual and, thus, a new citizen who has almost no recollection of the twins and who has acquired the ability to "speak right" and, to reference Michèle Lalonde once more, to "Speak White." With the creation of Northridge's anglophone whole man, the novel's final chapter returns once again to the metaphorical representation of the English defeat of Quebec and the French ability that, as the chapter's title "enfin" ["at last"] suggests (and as alluded to by the numerous elliptical appearances of the same word throughout the novel), has been anticipated.

The transformation takes form in the words of the new protagonist, Charles F. Papineau, who has written to the former protagonists' editor, whose location on rue Saint-Dénis is equally telling, at the very least for the fact that a portion of it has been a hub of the francophone intellectual elite since the 1960s. The letter serves as official notice that this anglophone individual cannot honour the publishing contract for Charles's and François's *journal*. Expressing himself in his "new" language, rendered in italics as indication of both a foreign and an invasive language, Charles F. (of Northridge's English present) distances himself from the protagonists' past as well as from French: "*I am truly sorry I can't honor the publishing contract Charles and François Papineau had previously signed with your house. As you must have learned from Dr. Gregory B. Northridge, it is impossible for me to write the last chapter of the book in* your *language*" (155 [reverse emphasis added]).[25] Breaking the contract, he recuses himself from the protagonists' French-language obligations and the French-language abilities that had previously inhabited the body.

In addition to displaying the new individual, the chapter continues the novel's emphasis on the brain as the centre of all language-related ability by confirming earlier suspicions about the combining of the two heads and the two brains: the new protagonist cannot comprehend and produce French because "*French speech was in the left side of François's brain*," the side that Northridge had always proposed to remove (155). The brain, largely responsible here for such abilities, is irrevocably manipulated. Furthermore, in keeping with the novel's ironic tone, the chapter, through a change in the font, confirms as unsurprising the loss of such ability and the attainment of passivity that Northridge realized: "*It was a shock for the* entire *surgical team when it became clear that once beheaded 'Les Têtes' were replaced by a unilingual individual. So be it*" (155–6). Here Northridge's nine-chapter operative mission for the unilingual unicephalous Charles F. recalls the Terror of Robespierre that, through the multiple beheadings at the end of the French Revolution, eliminated through execution all abilities of the individuals who did not adhere to the philosophy of "une volonté UNE [ONE will]."[26]

The new individual's place of employment – "Computer Science Center, English Bay, Vancouver, B.C." – continues to blatantly criticize the produced re-formation in tandem with references to hubs of informational activity and the comprehension and production of programmed languages. The nods to anglophone culture ("English Bay," "Vancouver," and "B." for "British" in "British Columbia"), along with the connection to computers as hubs of information that process and neither think nor live, underscore Northridge's operative re-programming: Charles's and François's now altered hubs of linguistic abilities as well as their extraordinary intellectual abilities, which brought them much recognition, have been operated into a near humanless mind that processes only English in anglophone lands.

Most notably, the last chapter of *Les têtes à Papineau* emphasizes the loss of the entire gamut of abilities to produce the French language and thus to reproduce Quebec culture. The writing of French – and not writing in any language, as Northridge had speculated – has disappeared. The new protagonist affirms he is unable to write the book's final chapter (which is the reader's final chapter and thus concludes the reader's book) in the now exteriorized editor's language, which is French: "*it is impossible for me to write … in your language*" (155). Writing now occurs not only in the English language but also – as the typically anglophone signature of "*Charles F. Papineau*" mimics the French-strangling name of "*Dr. Geoffrey B. Northridge*" – in English style (155–6). With the novel's usual dose of irony, the chapter also highlights the loss of French speech. Moved along the spectrum of linguistic abilities, the new protagonist explains his new inability to reproduce French words in speech and to comprehend French, in-cluding the few remaining French voices he hears from what is likely the prosodic right side of François's brain: "*when I hear the words, I cannot reproduce them. It is as though they were a mesmerizing speech!"* (155). And the last paragraph of the letter transmits the loss of the ability to read French: *"Of course if you were kind enough to send me the diary in translation, I promise you I will study it and send you some feedback"* (156).

Such aspects of the re-creation of life that posit the brain as the centre of such activity and that realize the re-formation of bodily ability recall literary works of other periods, one of the most notable being Mary Wollstonecraft Shelley's *Frankenstein; or, The Modern Prometheus* (1818). The similarity appears not only in the parallel roles of science and medicine but also in the male desire to be a progenitor that Marie-Hélène Huet discusses in *Monstrous Imagination* (1993). The phenomenon is evident in both Shelley's Victor Frankenstein, as Huet argues, and in Godbout's Gregory B. Northridge, as shown here. In a statement of sociocultural supposition, *Les têtes à Papineau* makes an explicit and general comparison early on: "Les Britanniques ont toujours eu un faible pour les histoires de vampires et de châteaux hantés piqués sur des sommets brumeux. Gregory Northridge nous a affirmé qu'il avait voulu … faire notre connaissance. Il appartient à cette famille de scientifiques lunatiques qui ne réunissait, au siècle dernier, que les soirs de pleine lune. Il y a chez lui, quand il se déplie lentement pour se lever, un côté Dr Frankenstein dans le geste" [The British have always had a weakness for stories of vampires and of haunted castles perched on foggy mountaintops. Gregory Northridge affirmed with us that he had wanted … to make our acquaintance. He belongs to that family of quirky scientists who would only come together, a century ago, on nights of the full moon. When he rises slowly to a standing position, there's a Dr Frankenstein side in his movements] (130).

The resemblance also arises in Shelley's and Godbout's use of monsters and operated abilities to provide a warning. In Shelley's work it is a warning about the exploitation of the individual during the period of the Industrial Revolution; in Godbout's novel, it serves as a warning about the individual and the culture in a post-referendum, revolution-inspired era in which the reduction of both is the potential consequence of the expansion of another culture, language, and set of abilities. Here, then, Northridge – as a metonym for the penetrating expansion of English-language culture that seeks to disturb and to refashion abilities – becomes what François describes as a "sculpteur inquiétant" [disturbing sculptor] (143). In this light, it is possible to see how the final chapter and, indeed, the entire novel warn of a new individual and the possibility of damages to language – where French has only an occasional, mesmerizing, yet incomprehensible, presence – and its related abilities. As such, *Les têtes à Papineau* uses the operated heads of Charles and François, and the operative outcome that is Charles F., to recall the prognosticative function of "monstres" that Paré outlines and that was discussed above: "signes de quelque malheur à advenir" [signs of some forthcoming misfortune] (3; 3).

Les têtes à Papineau contains many such warnings. I have already discussed the poignant, revelatory scene in which, with regard to the pursuit of one culture, the protagonists' father compares Northridge to Hitler. There is also Northridge's explanation of aspects of the procedure, which repeatedly points to the intended goals and is prefaced by his hope ("nous espérons" [we hope]) for the success of a never-before completed operation (132–3). And there is the twins' own observation that, by not revealing on computer screens the same text to both protagonists when one of them wrote on his own, Northridge's use of the keyboards and monitors through which they engaged in dialogue with him had already been operating the dissolution of their union: "Il est en train de nous opérer, dit François, puisqu'il a trouvé une façon de scinder notre discours" [He's in the process of operating on us, said François, as he's found a way to split our discourse] (95). Even genre change – from the *journal* to the letter discussed above – signals transformation. Indeed, Bellemare reads it as a sign and thus as an "explication du changement" [explanation of change] within the text that is mirrored in the operation (*Jacques Godbout, romancier* 195). Suggesting the author's "prise de position ferme au plan linguistique" [firm position on linguistic matters], Piette proposes the letter as a means of dissociation: "L'effet de lecture est donc d'associer le lecteur québécois francophone au journal intime et de le dissocier de la lettre finale (l'anglais servant de repoussoir)" [The effect of reading is therefore to associate the francophone Québécois reader with the diary and to dissociate him from the letter at the end (with the English serving as a foil)] (126).

Yet the most specific warning of the creation of monstrosity appears in the novel's eighth chapter, in which François pens his own prognosticative imagining of the operation. In his text, he speaks specifically of the "nouveau monstre" [new monster] that he fears Charles and he will become after the surgery (145). Concretely, the "monstre" that François concocts preoperatively signals a malformation that announces the state of the post-operative individual: because the required left half of his own cranium was too small to contain the left side of Charles's brain in this fictional version, François's own creation must now wear "une calotte" (a skullcap) made of glass to cover the reconstructed brain (144). Here it is also possible to think of François's version as a reference to craniometric studies and thus to the classifications of intelligence of the human species (e.g., Samuel George Morton's 1839 study, *Crania Americana*): François's brain reads as smaller and, therefore, as having inferior abilities, leaving the right side of his head too small to house the right hemisphere of Charles's brain.

The reference to the "monstre" can be read further to extract a larger message within the sociocultural debate of language, culture, and nation, where the search for independence conceived of in present terms can lead to loss of culture and of abilities. As discussed within Quebec's historical context, the novel foretells that the results of the 1980 referendum (59.56 percent against, 40.44 percent for) paint French as lesser than English and thus as worthy of elimination. François himself refers to the monster in similar terms when he writes of what the protagonists' dreams may provoke: "Il se peut ... que nos rêves cèdent la place à un nouveau délire, tout simplement. Et puis je n'ai plus vraiment envie d'écrire qu'une seule phrase en épilogue : 'Je ne veux pas mourir,' et François, la main hésitante au-dessus du clavier ajoute, songeur: 'mais je sais que c'est inutile. Le processus est enclenché comme un vote de grève,'" [It's possible ... that our dreams will make space for a new frenzy, basically. And so I really only have a desire to write one single sentence for the epilogue: "I do not want to die." And François, his hand hesitant over the keyboard, added pensively: "but I know that it's useless. The process is set in motion like a vote to strike"] (145). The ultimate vote born of the referendum points to a new state, which François likens to a new frenzy: as the mind of François essentially dies by the scalpel, the language and the culture of the French disappear by the vote, which – as the majority of Quebec people reject even the consideration of sovereignty-association and concede to cultural submission – is already under way.

Warnings of the new "monstre," however, speak most specifically to the individual citizen of such a nation; they also appear very clearly in reference to the brain and its spectrum of linguistic abilities – abilities that Charles F., for all intents and purposes, lost. More specifically, the warnings portray François as the representation of an individual who used his spectrum of linguistic abilities. He speaks to Charles at the same time as he writes the final words of his imagining of the operation: "et François, la main hésitante au-dessus du clavier, ajoute songeur" [and François, his hand hesitant over the keyboard, added pensively]. As the novel continues to show, the individual citizen's identity remains conceived in the varied linguistic – physical and intellectual – abilities to produce language that François realizes while existing in a state of interdependence – a state that he fears to lose but accepts as disappearing. Conversely, the ability to comprehend and to produce language appears as central to the comprehension and the production of the individual capable of existing in interdependence. *Les têtes à Papineau* suggests, then, that operations that eliminate such a state may result in François's new "monstre": not the freak that the protagonists were in their successfully conjoined state and in Northridge's scientific eyes but, rather, the monster, as alternate and pejorative translation of "monstre," who is ultimately mutilated and brainwashed into reproducing anglophone culture. What comes to life is the frightening monster – but here it is the unilingual monstrosity that Godbout's novel portrays as the ultimate threat to Quebec, the monster that Quebec has brought upon itself: "*Both heads wanted so much to be normalized. Well, there is no one left to blame for what happened, is there?*" (155–6).

The twenty-first century state of Quebec, with a less than 10 percent anglophone population, reveals that the concern and frustration expressed in *Les têtes à Papineau* about language, nation, citizenship, and identity are no longer as palpable as they once were for the francophone population. However, the novel predicts that Quebec, in the form of the new and monstrous protagonist, will remain reminded of past abilities that it chose not to protect – particularly the emotive content of speech in the right hemisphere of François's brain, out of which voices "*still occasionally break through*" (155). *Les têtes à Papineau* can be said to demonstrate how the spectrum of linguistic abilities required for the production of language remains not only an integral part of the debate on language, culture, nationality, and, especially, citizenship but also a fundamental component of the culture that human beings live and reproduce.

INTERLUDE TWO

In his final chapter of *On Monsters: An Unnatural History of Our Worst Fears* (2009), Stephen Asma asks his readers to consider future monsters and, thereby, the future of monsters. As his epilogue shows, Asma in no ways suggests (or, for that matter, believes) that monsters will ever disappear. They are as much a creation of and by the self as they are of and by society. One of the aspects that Asma's last chapter evaluates concerning the future of monsters is the technological means by which they and concepts of them may surface: the varied forms of scientific operation that alter somatic development as well as genetic constitution. Reflecting upon the meeting of "epistemological categories or taxonomies of nature" and biotechnology, he states that the latter "has given us the tools to move creatures around on these continua" (269).

Readers of *On Monsters* know that Asma discusses monsters in their historical and scientific contexts. For example, he refers to Etienne Geoffroy Saint-Hilaire's classifications of bodies and logic of monsters along with his son Isidore's use of the term "teratology" to map out what he proposes as new scientific developments in the classification of anomalies. Readers also know that he looks at the ponderings about what technology could lead to (e.g., Mary Shelley's literary imagining regarding Frankenstein's monster). To expand such discussions, Asma asks the readers of his final chapter to consider actions taken by members of contemporary societies concerning the bodies of, for example, their children and to think about whether or not these actions may be monstrous and/or whether the operated bodies may be monsters.

One of the examples relevant to *Operation Freak* is that of a six-year-old brain-dead child named Ashley. According to Asma, her parents decided to have her body drastically altered through the use of technology in order to stunt her growth, to "keep her small and easily transportable," and, according to the parents, to improve "the quality of life for their daughter" (269). Each of the operations altered Ashley's various bodily abilities: "A team of doctors administered a two-year regimen of intense estrogen, which closed her growth plates and shrank her height by over thirteen inches. In addition, Ashley's uterus was removed to guard against future menstrual cramps, and also pregnancy if she were to be raped. Finally, Ashley's breast buds were removed because she 'has no need for developed breasts since she will not breast feed,' her parents argued, 'and their presence would only be a source of discomfort to her'" (269). Ashley's procreative abilities were clearly targeted, definitively removed from the realm of her existence.

However, Ashley's overall physiological capacity to grow and to develop was also fully arrested. Remaining as omniscient as any author might, and referencing the critics of such acts, Asma avoids judging the parents' decision, claiming: "we can expect to see more of this somatic redesigning in the future" (269). Reading the parents' statements in the spirit of *Operation Freak*, it becomes possible to understand how they identified and then, through operations, re-identified their daughter and her existence in terms of her body's abilities. Most notably, because of her loss of cognitive abilities, her varied spectrums of bodily abilities would be conceived anew. These same abilities would be read in accordance with relevant sociocultural constructs of gender, enabling her parents out of their care for her to project that a potential rapist would identify Ashley as a female and, thus, as a candidate for brutal violation. It took various forms of operations to bring the story of Ashley's body and its abilities first to Asma's attention and then to that of his readers.

3

Regenerating Family Fortune:
Incising Orders of Gender and Procreation
in Tahar Ben Jelloun's *L'enfant de sable*
and *La nuit sacrée*

Il y a le corps, c'est très important, parce que nous venons d'une société où
le corps est hyperprésent et hypervalorisé
[The body is very important, because we come from a society where the
body is hyperpresent and hypervalorized]

Tahar Ben Jelloun, Arabies

En facilitant l'acte de reproduction, la main humaine semble ainsi avoir
"tranché juste"!
[Facilitating the act of reproduction, the human hand seems to have "cut
correctly"!]

Malek Chebel, Histoire de la circoncision

As represented across the pages of Tahar Ben Jelloun's *L'enfant de sable*
(1985) [*The Sand Child* (1987)] and *La nuit sacrée* (1987) [*The Sacred
Night* (1989)], the novels' protagonist is always and forever operated for
reasons of production. The protagonist's reproductively frustrated
father decides to first rhetorically and later performatively operate his
child's gender from female to male in order to produce an heir he
names Ahmed. Oum Abbas, the profit-focused proprietor of the *cirque
forain* nestled at the city's boundaries, digitally operates the protagonist's genitalia in order to produce the cross-dressing performer Zahra,
who will, in turn, produce revenue. Five vengeful sisters of the protagonist forcibly and surgically alter her female genitalia in order to, as
they claim and use as their justification, reproduce the non-female

order that their father had first produced, which thereby reproduces the order intended within the Arab-Muslim community. Repeatedly operated beyond all constructs of normality into the freak of culture, one character's words – from his version of the protagonist's adventures – summarize well such a lived process: "Ahmed n'est pas une erreur de la nature, mais un détournement social" [Ahmed is not one of nature's mistakes, but a social deviation] (*L'enfant de sable* 160; *The Sand Child* 124).

Although such operations aim at production and speak of gender, their recurrence points to an unexplored reason why the body in these two novels remains a site of operation and source of reproduction: the body's physiological ability to reproduce as linked to financial production. Most notably, the two novels begin and continue because of operations born of the body's perceived socioculturally norm-based biological ability to reproduce.

The novels continue to demonstrate this emphasis through the expansion of norm-based conceptualizations of (particularly) the female body's ability to reproduce. Inevitably, the result is the creation of *fitna*, or disorder, which, as a sociocultural phenomenon, corresponds directly to the freak of culture. Like the norm-perturbing *monstre*, the appearance of *fitna* within the sociocultural context eventually provokes anxiety regarding the protagonist's actual ability to procreate. As the body's gendered capacities to reproduce inform here the notion of *fitna*, it is possible to see the means by which the spectrum of procreative abilities forms an integral part of the identification of the protagonist. It also becomes apparent how such inscriptions of ability and disability are arbitrary. Because the operative processes cause the protagonist to move between categories of gender and within the spectrum of reproductive abilities, I refer simultaneously to both of the character's first names, Ahmed/Zahra, throughout the chapter.

To give substance to my claims, I begin by discussing how fictional oral narrative holds a central and reproductive role in *L'enfant de sable* and *La nuit sacrée*. I then explore how gender is explicitly connected to the fictional narrative as well as to the Arab-Muslim master sociocultural narratives that inform the process of identification. I focus on how biological production is specifically addressed and clearly operated not only in Ben Jelloun's novels but also in the aforementioned sociocultural narratives. I concentrate first on how these master narratives spell out the gender of male (virile) and female (passive) in terms of biological reproduction, and how they are reinforced as well as expanded to include the economic and specifically financial production from the *cirque forain* performances. I then investigate the historical acceptance of the operated eunuch (also a "détournement social") within Arab-Muslim sociocultural structures and how this reveals the arbitrary foundation of related sociocultural narratives. By examining next the operations to genitalia (real or phantom) that Ahmed/Zahra endures at the hands of the family, I disclose how fundamentally important bodily abilities are to identification processes. Although only certain of the represented operations are regular sociocultural practices in the geographical region of Morocco (and, by extension, the Maghreb), they all serve as pain-ridden tropes that draw attention to areas of specific bodily abilities. In the end, I reveal how the operation of normality remains a constant in processes of writing and of identification (at least as exemplified in these two novels of Ben Jelloun), how norm-based sociocultural narratives of gender and bodily ability are part of such operative rewriting, and how the operation of such normatively conceptualized narratives realizes reproduction in its multiple forms as it demonstrates the malleability, and thus movement, of bodily abilities within spectrums.

NARRATIVES, ABILITIES, ISLAM

As many critics insist, and rightly so, Ben Jelloun's novels are texts that delight in imagining the unusual. For example, due to his creation of scenes and characters that are neither clearly "real" nor clearly "imagined," it is possible to consider his work to be inspired by, and to contribute to, the genre of fantastic literature. Such a concept of the recurrently fantastic imagery in Ben Jelloun's literature may be read alongside Tzvetan Todorov's *Introduction à la littérature fantastique* (1970) [*The Fantastic: A Structural Approach to a Literary Genre* (1973)], particularly his discussion of hesitation: "il faut que le texte oblige le lecteur à considérer le monde des personnages comme un monde de personnes vivantes et à hésiter entre une explication naturelle et une explication surnaturelle des événements évoqués" [the text must oblige the reader to consider the world of the characters as a world of living persons and to hesitate between a natural and a supernatural explanation of the events described] (37–8; 33). Most of Ben Jelloun's dreamlike scenes in *L'enfant de sable,* which are read as intertexts of Jorge Luis Borges or of characters speaking with other characters whom they may or may not have dreamed (up), are a repository of elements that the readers may attempt, if Todorov's claim is accepted, to explain as either natural or supernatural as they work their way through the narratives.[1] The very distinction of natural/supernatural implies a sociocultural formation of the reader that hinges on what appears of the natural, or everyday, realm and what does not. Such a distinction is not a way of excluding but of identifying events and characters, thereby predicating identification on difference as it is contained in a narrative and as it is informed by the world around the reader.

While Todorov's work invites reflection upon the reader's engagement with the fantastic in Ben Jelloun's work, critics of Ben Jelloun also encourage consideration of the strange, particularly as it relates to the characters. Mustapha Marrouchi writes quite clearly of the same subject when he states: "Ben Jelloun has the gift of making his characters strange" ("My Aunt" 331). Here Marrouchi refers not simply to the fact that Ben Jelloun's characters look or appear strange but also to the fact that they act strangely. Such a claim is possible with respect to Ahmed/Zahra's epistolary correspondence, which, depending on the reader, may or may not be a self-composed and, thus, imagined series of letters to what appears to be a love interest, all of which may appear a "strange" way of identifying oneself. Here again the distinction that Marrouchi makes functions similarly to Todorov's in that it infers, intentionally or not, a process of identification within two distinct yet interrelated contexts: (1) what appears to be strange and what appears to be normal in the narratives being read, and (2) the sociocultural narratives that enable the reader to make such a binary-based distinction. At the very least, the reader's attention is drawn to the presence of such spaces in an effort to determine, if not what is real and what is fantastic, then how the two spaces work together and why they might be together. Because of the multiple representations that may evoke notions of the strange, Ben Jelloun's works seem to issue a call to the reader to consider the various spaces, a call that may well be the hesitation of which Todorov himself writes.

Discussion of reflection on the supernatural and on the strange, of the reader's identification of such states, and of the centrality of narratives to such identification points to ways in which the reader manipulates, or operates, a literary work through normative paradigms. By asking for consideration of the spheres into which the reader may place an event or a character, I highlight the plurality of narrative spaces involved in and operated for such identification. Such a conclusion is relevant not only to the characters in a literary work but also to the sociocultural phenomena of identification that novels such as those of Ben Jelloun often represent and that the reader contemplates. One element that factors prominently into sociocultural reflection upon Ben Jelloun's work is the presence of Islam and its tenets, which exist in various narratives, be they written, lived, or both.

In *Coran et Tradition islamique dans la littérature maghrébine* (2002) [*The Qur'an and the Islamic Tradition in Maghrebian Literature*], Carine Bourget develops a discussion of imagery in Ben Jelloun's work reminiscent of Todorov's distinction of negotiated narrative spaces. Specifically, Bourget highlights a movement, and an interdependence, between what can be considered two religious spaces referenced in the representation of Sufism in Ben Jelloun's novels, particularly *L'enfant de sable* and *La nuit sacrée*. Her careful analysis demonstrates that these works highlight both the insistence on the individual (and thus on the individual's mystical pursuit of innate knowledge) and the emphasis on community (*Umma*) and the collective and continued realization of Islam and its laws (54). Bourget, like Todorov, underscores the role of the individual in interpreting narrative in both of these spheres, only with Bourget the narrative solely influences the "real" (be it of the individual or the *Umma*), which is composed of individuals working to perpetuate or reproduce Islam.

Emphasis on the multiplicity of Islam's narratives and agents, as well as the agents' reading of the narratives, also appears in other projects, such as those of Malek Chebel, Fatima Mernissi, and Patrick Bannerman.[2] Like many scholars of Islam, Chebel speaks of Islam in ways comparable to narrative, using the spellings "islam" and "Islam" in *L'esprit de serial* (1988) [*The Spirit of the Seraglio*] to distinguish between two interpretations of Islam that exist in the French language. The editors' notes for the 1988, 1995, and 2003 editions clarify that "islam" encompasses the official, religious, or juridical executions of Islamic order and that "Islam" refers to the global Islamic community at large, which includes the varying global practices and interpretations of the Islamic faith.

In *Islam in Perspective* (1988), Bannerman discusses distinction of space in similar terms when he addresses the order of operation of the principles as moving from Allah to the individual. Guidance comes first from the general principles (the Qur'an) and second (at least throughout most of Sunni Islam, of which the Maghreb is part) from the Prophet's application of these principles (the Sunna, the hadith). However, it is the duty of the believers – and particularly those accorded juridical powers – to provide specific interpretations as they operate power and the related narratives (34, 22). Their applications are the interpretations of the aforementioned order within specified sociocultural contexts, and they may in some cases distinguish themselves from those held by members of the larger Islamic community. Such a chain of interpretation demonstrates that there exists an element of plasticity with respect to Islam in that those who govern must determine how best to apply the general principles. Their acts of jurisprudence (*fiqh*) can be influenced by and adapted to the historical context of each situation provided they remain consistent with (or at least claim to be consistent with) the Qur'an and other works relevant to Islamic law. Souad Eddouada's words on *fiqh* in the Moroccan context underscore not only its largely historical conservative tendencies in the interpretation of Islamic law since the 1957 naissance of the nation-state but also the pliability of the related master narratives, which, through their interpretation, "impl[y] the non-accessibility to the original text, which invalidates the idea of an authoritative single reading" (59).

In *Beyond the Veil* (1975) [*Sexe, idéologie, Islam* (1983)], and again, in a slightly modified 2003 excerpt in "The Meaning of Spatial Bodies," Mernissi speaks to a somewhat similar distinction in her detailed emphasis on the two universes of Islam.[3] Drawing categorical distinctions between these two universes, she categorizes one as the (predominantly male and male-governed) community of believers (*Umma*) and the other as the (predominantly female but male-governed) domestic unit; one as having to do with religious faith and its related activity, the other with sexuality; one as having to do with the mind, the other with the genitals (*Beyond* 81–2; *Sexe* 155; "Meaning" 490–1). Unlike Bourget, Bannerman, and even Chebel, Mernissi does not suggest an elasticity with regard to the passage of the individual between two spheres; rather, she regularly demonstrates such movement as unacceptable to the larger community, which favours a rigid boundary, arguing that the occasional violation of that boundary results in disorder, or *fitna* as it is later discussed (*Beyond* 81; *Sexe* 151). Eddouada provides a slightly different spin with respect to the nation-state's historical efforts to build and maintain a notion of collective will. She argues for the centrality of women, which ultimately perpetuates the imbalance to which Mernissi alludes: "Women hold a central place within a presumed coherent Muslim family and society. Their inequality in relation to men is defined within a meaning of justice proper to a 'coherent Muslim community'" (62).

Mernissi's work helps to flush out my discussion of reproduction (especially in a Maghrebian and specifically Moroccan context) with arguments that ardently emphasize the centrality of gender, the sexual body, and biological reproduction to Islam's two universes. She maintains that there exists a strategic and essentialist interpretation of the sexualized body or of sexual beings upon which the simultaneous division of the two universes hinges and that also perpetuates Islam. Perpetuation, however, does allow for these sexual beings to come together in order to engage in biological reproduction. It is useful to note that, in "The Meaning of Spatial Boundaries" (2003), Mernissi underscores reproduction by moving the word "procreation," which, in the 1975 version was parenthetical, to a post-colon centre stage: "men and women are supposed to collaborate in only one of the tasks required for the survival of society: procreation" (491).[4] In what could be argued to be the only blending of the universes in Mernissi's otherwise strict categorization, she reveals biological reproduction as the one way in which the narratives of the two gendered universes are operated together. The goal is the reproduction of Islam, which is not only a religion but also what Bannerman calls "a legal system, an ethical system, and principles of social behavior" (19).

The operation of multiple narratives, then, proves recurrent in processes of identification, be it identification of strange characters in fantastical novels or of human bodies in sociocultural structures. Within the sociocultural context under examination, the narratives speak about the abilities of the human body and the ways in which they are intended and used to reproduce Islam both as a religion and as a community of individuals with goals that, at times, are contrary to, even as they take advantage of, the religion itself. Mernissi as well as Chebel (particularly in *Le corps en Islam* [Chebel 1999] [*The Body in Islam*]) highlight the myriad ways in which the human body and its abilities occupy much space in Islam's master sociocultural narratives, particularly with regard to the Arab-Muslim Maghreb.[5] More specifically, their works help us to understand how the Arab-Muslim Maghrebian and, specifically, Moroccan human body as represented in Ben Jelloun's two novels is conceived and therefore identified in gendered terms that posit biological reproduction as a human ability.

The same texts also help us to think anew the operability and thus malleability that surfaces in *L'enfant de sable* and *La nuit sacrée*, particularly on the part of operating agents who call upon and thereby operate multiple sociocultural narratives to frame and justify their operations to the body. Ultimately, both the bodies and the narratives become, as Chebel writes, "une sorte d'archive vivante qui permet à l'observateur, des siècles après, de mesurer le degré d'acculturation de la société où il est immergé" [a sort of living archive that allows the observer, centuries later, to measure the degree of acculturation in the society in which he is immerged] (*Le corps* 35). It is the narrative of Ben Jelloun's novels that attests to such operability not only in its content, which follows the life and the body of Ahmed/Zahra, but also in its structure.

"HOMME" AND THE OPERABILITY OF NARRATIVE

One of the primary means by which *L'enfant de sable* and *La nuit sacrée* begin to transmit normative operations is through the adaptations to narrative that form the novels themselves.[6] One might argue that the novels are narratives about narrative, be it the narrative of gender, of ability, or of narrative itself. The explicit references to multiple narrators and, more, to the numerous relocations of narration emphasize such operation because they reveal how any narrative is never singularly static but is always multiply operated, even disrupted.

Odile Cazenave (1991) speaks quite cogently on the topics of gender and narrative transformation. What is of particular interest in Cazenave's discussion is that the production of what she considers to be the protagonist's ambiguous identity is presented in terms of reproduction for she writes of "how ambiguity in gender and identity is reproduced in the text" (437). On one level, Cazenave's words invite a consideration of what such reproduction means not just for the formation but also for the repeated formation of identity. Her emphasis on such a reading is suggested in the prefix "re-" and is also apparent throughout the novels as multiple characters seek to identify Ahmed/Zahra through norms of gender. Later, I look at how bodies of characters (specifically the protagonist's) and of narratives are multiply operated within such an identification process. For the time being, however, my focus is on the ways in which narratives themselves are multiply and repeatedly operated and how such operations not only contribute to but also echo the goals of reproduction demanded of ability-rich characters who are here considered to be freaks of culture. The goal of such narrative operation is not to reproduce the master narrative in its integral form but, rather, to use it in order to reproduce the goals individuals pursue, whatever those goals might be.

Ben Jelloun's novels demonstrate many such operations. The abundance of critical discussion that exists on these two novels often hovers around the narrative contributions by multiple characters and their debate over the veracity of the version recounted. Critics often discuss the implications of the multiple narrators (including the protagonist) who recount Ahmed/Zahra's extraordinary tale. They also explore how the tale becomes a salient example of working the gender narrative within a Maghrebian Arab-Muslim context as well as within the theoretical context that, elsewhere, is explained as the doing of gender (Haycs *Queer* 165; Butler *Undoing* 30). For example, in *L'enfant de sable*, the first and primary individual to operate the tale is the *conteur* (the taleteller); later, the members of the audience that encircle him, and eventually individuals in cafés after his disappearance, propose or contest existing versions of the protagonist's narrative. With the *conteur* typically considered the master and centre of the tale, such a multifaceted process may be read as destabilizing the singularity of the *conteur*'s tale and, thus, any one tale or any one voice.

The "Préambule" of *La nuit sacrée* shows Ahmed/Zahra reclaiming the narrative and recounting the entire second novel, thereby both troubling the tradition of the *conteur* and perpetuating it by becoming a *conteuse* (a storyteller who is a woman). The protagonist's actions explicitly frame the narrative as a response to and a continuation of the constructions in *L'enfant de sable*. As such, the same actions move the narrative further away from a central version of a singular narrative towards one informed by all of the narratives about the protagonist, which now span two novels. Marc Gontard's words in *Le moi étrange: Littérature marocaine de langue française* (1993) [*The Strange I: Moroccan Litterature in French*] summarize how such multiplicity underscores the narrative plurality that is fundamental to the operating of narrative normality: "Une telle technique permet donc à Ben Jelloun de faire éclater le monologisme narratif traditionnel et d'instaurer dans son récit une narration plurielle et contradictoire avec le renversement de la hiérarchie narrateur/narrataire" [Such a technique then allows Ben Jelloun to explode traditional narrative monolinguism and to introduce in his narrative a plural and contradictory narration with the reversal of the narrator/narratee hierarchy] (15). Here Gontard's analysis of Ben Jelloun's technique reveals the author's work as, in part, the execution of Roland Barthes's theory of reading (*S/Z*): multiple narrators realize plurality of narrative within the novels through their rereading and reimagining of Ahmed/Zahra's story.

The reproductive effect of operating narrative becomes even clearer when the representation of the *conteur* and his work is examined more closely to show how he operates it to realize his own goals and how the narrative is operated. As Mohammed Berrada explains, a *conteur* (a *rawi*) is, within the tradition of storytelling and especially by the circle of listeners that surrounds him (*halqa*), considered a master of his craft and also an artist (26, 21). Berrada also states that one of the primary goals of the *conteur*'s work is: "enrichir la mémoire collective" [to enrich the collective memory] (26). Analyses such as Gontard's might tend to encourage the assumption that the *conteur*'s tale, with a presumably singular narrative voice, remains static. However, it is not likely that this is Gontard's intention. He speaks of taletelling in Ben Jelloun's novels in terms of a narrative device and a metaphor of voice, arguing that the recounted tales work to expand the notion of a fixed collective memory and to enrich its thematic and sociocultural content. It is also important to consider that the permanence of the tale does not appear as a manifest staple of a tradition in which the *conteur* seeks, among other things, to win over an audience in order to subsidize his life. Rather, as Berrada maintains, he often refashions the tale in order to win the audience and, in doing so, occasionally retraces history: "Cette ré-écriture de l'histoire s'enrichit à travers les âges, les époques et les générations … [Les événements du passé] n'ont jamais cessé d'être sujet à de nombreux remaniements et à l'intégration de nombreux éléments historiques" [This re-writing of the story enriches itself throughout the ages, eras, and generations … {The events of the past} have never stopped being subject to numerous modifications and to the integration of numerous historical elements] (27–9).

How the novel's *conteur* operates narrative to reproduce his goals of credibility and profit appears most evidently in the content and the composition of the preliminary chapter of *L'enfant de sable*. Its title, "Homme" ["Man"], and its content point to the operations of gender and bodily ability that I address later in this chapter.[7] However, "Homme" also reveals how narrative is susceptible to the operations that realize reproduction as well as to the fact that more than one agent operates the narrative. It begins from a third-person point of view that centres on a detailed physical and psychological portrait of a male individual of multiple abilities. The reader assumes the character is the reason for and centre of the novel. In part, this is because of the chapter's title, "Homme," which is also assumed to refer to the character's identity; in part, it is because of the substantive in the novel's title – *enfant* – whom the reader supposes refers to an earlier version of the character described in the first chapter, making of this presumed man the novel's protagonist. The reader might also infer that the point of view is that of a seemingly omniscient third-person narrator who establishes the portrait of a character the reader might take to be Homme.

However, fourteen paragraphs later, the reader is shown how change and movement in narration are integral to the novel and how more than one narrator is the agent of such operations. Immediately after the portrait of the character thought to be Homme, two different narrative voices appear and a question is posed about the portrait – "Et qui fut-il ?" [And what had he been?] – swiftly followed by a short two-sentence paragraph from a different omniscient point of view, which reveals the *conteur* as the individual asking the question of his audience (12; 5). After these two shifts, the *conteur* takes back the narration for almost two pages, during which he addresses his audience about the complexity of the tale. Then the omniscient narrator returns to conclude the chapter by describing how the *conteur* and his audience, after the former's final word for the day, disperse. By such marked changes in narrative voice, the chapter entitled "Homme" signals that multiple voices are a regular, albeit imbalanced, component of narrative, that such polyvocality is part of operated narrative, and that a single, unoperated narrative – even within a chapter – cannot exist.

The representation of multiple narratives goes further to reveal the marriage of oral and written narratives that are involved in such operations, a marriage that many critics and theorists argue is typical of postcolonial Francophone literature.[8] Yet the postcolonial context does not always take control of Ben Jelloun's novels as the protagonist interacts within myriad contexts, which, although transmitted in French, have little to do with the history of the French colonial presence in the region. Nevertheless, the oral and written traditions remain central to the novels. With the *conteur* in the first chapter of

L'enfant de sable, the novel acknowledges the oral narrative tradition the *conteur* embodies: he is, as Berrada reminds us, "la source de transmission de la culture populaire et d'un certain savoir, ayant une relation avec l'histoire et le passé du pays" [the source of transmission of popular culture and of a certain knowledge, which is connected to the history and the past of a country] (26). However, within the *conteur*'s explanation of his encounter with and recounting of the tale that feeds Ahmed/Zahra's narrative, the chapter reveals that what he recounts comes from the contents of the character's journal, which he claims to possess, and that the two forms of narrative must therefore come together (*L'enfant* 12). In other words, the chapter, and by extension the novel, demonstrates how the cultural tradition of orality is to a degree a reproduced written work. It also reveals how such multiplicity as is represented in the two narrative forms always exists in the operation of narrative.

The representation of the *conteur*'s engagement with the tale also suggests not only how narrative is operated and therefore multiple but also how, because of the work of any *conteur*, the tale is to be manipulated and varied. To recount the tale, the *conteur* does not even open the "livre du secret" [the secret book] that he claims is the source of his portrait. Instead, he affirms that he has learned the tale by heart – "j'en ai appris par cœur les étapes" [I have learned the stages of it by heart] – revealing that he is just as reliable as are the pages in the journal (13).[9] However, in that same sentence, the *conteur* states that the journal, as the "livre du secret," encourages neither static nor unchanging states of being but, rather, invites a journey down "le chemin du livre" [the road of the book] (13; 5–6). In so doing, he reveals the existence of at least two narratives: (1) that written in the journal and (2) that which the *conteur* constructed as he journeyed down the path of the book. The resultant version that the *conteur* produces points to that variation and change that comes with the reproduction of narrative from multiple narratives – here, that of the character retold by the *conteur* – despite his claim to authenticity.

Such multiplicity is expanded in numerous ways, one of which includes the very shifting of the narrative and that results from invitations to compose it. In *L'enfant de sable*, such an operation appears in the representation of the fictional narrative as collectively manipulated, particularly in the participatory and inscribable gestures that relocate the narration. One example appears in the blank pages of the journal that, early on, the *conteur* asks his listeners to fill in (41–3;

27–8). Yet another arises in the fatigued *conteur's* handing over of inkwell, pen case, and a now-effaced journal to his audience in *L'enfant de sable*'s concluding moments (209; 165). Movement of narrative also surfaces in the *conteur's* confession that he formed the Ahmed/Zahra narrative by adapting the story of an Egyptian-named Bey Ahmed – a story he was asked to take possession of and to recount – to a Moroccan sociocultural context (207–8; 164–5). The second novel, *La nuit sacrée*, further advances the collective memory project embodied by the *conteur,* and it does so by shifting the narrative to an entirely new narrator – the protagonist.

The *conteur's* claim to authority reveals more than multiplicity of narrative: it points to the intents and motivations that are prevalent in any operation of narrative. As demonstrated, the *conteur* works to valorize his craft by placing himself at the centre of it, telling his listeners that he has the individual's journal and thus access to the origin of the narrative. The *conteur* also presents himself as one to be believed, as a quasi-religious figure who is capable of guiding others through what promises to be a spiritual journey. He also proclaims that the journal that contains the story has illuminated him, and thus, as Cazenave similarly maintains, he becomes *the* one to be believed: "Ce livre, je l'ai lu, je l'ai déchiffré pour de tels esprits. Vous ne pouvez y accéder sans traverser mes nuits et mon corps. Je suis ce livre. Je suis devenu le livre du secret" [I have read this book. I have deciphered it for others. You can gain access to it only by traversing my nights and my body. I am that book. (I have become the secret book)] (Cazenave "Gender" 446; *L'enfant* 12–3; *Sand* 5).[10] By legitimizing his own narrative (as well as his own body) through both textual and spiritual substantiation, the man who is the *conteur* aims to operate his narrative as the unique (if not supreme) means by which the audience understands the character. Similar to what Eileen Julien says of the role of the griot in many Sub-Saharan African novels, here the *conteur* offers his message "when and to whom he wishes to proffer it and is designed to suit the needs of the authority he serves" (14). The difference in Ben Jelloun's novels appears in a slight modification, where the authority the *conteur* serves is his own.

Still, despite the air of dependability arising from the *conteur's* efforts to sell his authority, he reveals his motivations: (1) to avoid losing his credibility and thereby his audience to other storytellers, a transition that both the final chapter of *L'enfant de sable* and the first chapter of *La nuit sacrée* represent as a result of failing abilities to tell tales, and (2) to earn his living, as the final paragraphs of the first chapter of *L'enfant de sable* reveal: "avant de partir, un gamin lui remit un pain noir et une enveloppe" [Before he left, a small boy handed him a loaf of black bread and an envelope] (14; 6). Preparing to leave the public square after his day's work, the *conteur* receives the compensation that allows him to continue his storytelling. As such, it is clear how the *conteur* operates narrative in order to reproduce not simply the creative tradition of his profession but also – and equally so, as the bread and envelope are his only identifiable compensations – the economic tradition of livelihood. Indeed, the chapter entitled "Homme" demonstrates how the winning of food and the funds one might presume to be in the envelope motivates agents such as the *conteur* to operate narrative and thereby to reproduce the payments. It also outlines the ways such motivations, along with multiple narratives and multiple voices (or, agents), factor into not just any operating of narrative but (as "Homme" also speaks to gender and disability) the operating of normatively charged bodily abilities throughout their respective spectrum.

OPERATING GENDER AND ABILITY IN "HOMME"

Emphasizing his authority to operate narrative is not the only means the *conteur* uses to realize reproduction. He also accomplishes his mission through the manipulation of gender and ability that point first to the operating of sociocultural normality. As already discussed, the *conteur*'s motivations are revealed in the concluding chapters of *L'enfant de sable* upon his return to the narrative. How he operates gender and ability comes not in self-recognition but, rather, in a vision he has of another character, Fatima, the epileptic and crippled cousin turned wife of Ahmed/Zahra. During this encounter, the disabled Fatima – who no longer struggles with epileptic seizures (but who is never clearly identified as no longer being epileptic or crippled) – utters these words to the *conteur* on how he selected and discarded her: "Je suis celle que tu as choisie pour être la victime de ton personnage. Tu t'es vite débarrassé de moi" [I am the woman you chose to be your hero's victim. You soon got rid of me] (205; 162). Her words explain how the *conteur*'s version of Ahmed/Zahra's life unfolds, in part, because of Fatima: once the protagonist begins to benefit from the knowledge of the disabled, exploited Moroccan woman, she dies.

However, it is in the chapter entitled "Homme" that the *conteur* begins to operate characters in terms of bodily abilities as he paints the portrait of the unnamed character who has chosen to live in near total seclusion. In an unnamed individual who is to be taken as a disabled "homme" (man) and thus likely the chapter's Homme, gender and ability are shown to be equally fundamental to the *conteur*'s process of reproduction, particularly as they shift away from implied norms. For example, the *conteur*'s description of Homme highlights the character's bodily state as a series of acquired conditions identifiable as a variety of abilities (some of them readable as disabilities) that have shifted into reduced states and that span various spectrums of human abilities: emotional, intellectual, physical, and multiple combinations between the three. Within the chapter, the abilities are categorically classifiable as a limit. The *conteur*'s very first words describing Homme's prematurely aged face emphasize an overall declining shift: the reader learns of a "profonde blessure" [deep wound] that transmits a negatively charged, reductive representation (*L'enfant* 7; *Sand* 1).

One of the most telling examples of the representation of reductive, or even eliminated, bodily ability comes when the *conteur* describes Homme's gait: "sa démarche était devenue celle d'un handicapé" [his walk had become that of a handicapped person] (10; 4).[11] The *conteur* also reveals that Homme experiences unrelenting nervous tics and the inability to control his body, both conditions that further distance the character from being a controlled, strong, and virile man (10; 3). Allergens take on a new role for Homme: "Il avait dévélopé ces allergies: son corps, perméable et irrité, les recevait à la moindre secousse, les intégrait et les maintenait vives au point de rendre le sommeil très difficile" [He had developed allergies; his body, permeable and irritated, reacted to the slightest attack, absorbed it, and maintained it in all its intensity. Sleep became impossible] (8; 2).

Homme also acquired a painful hypersensitivity to light, portrayed in a manner that foreshadows the cutting narratives and blades to come: "Il évitait de s'exposer à la lumière crue … La lumière du jour, d'une lampe ou de la pleine lune lui faisait mal: elle le dénudait, pénétrait sous sa peau et y décelait la honte ou des larmes secrètes. Il la sentait passer sur son corps comme … une lame qui lui retirerait lentement le voile de chair qui maintenait entre lui et les autres la distance nécessaire" [He avoided light: daylight, lamplight, even the light of the full moon. Light laid him bare, penetrated beneath his skin, revealing his shame and unshed tears. He felt it pass over his body like … a blade slowly tearing away the veil of flesh that maintained the necessary distance between himself and others] (7; 1).

Invariably, Homme is represented as largely weakened. By reference to his new position within various spectrums of ability, he therefore does not measure up to the portrait of what the reader would assume him to have been prior to this chapter: a normal, virile man. Ridha Bourkhis's discussion of the following citation of Bernard Chanfrault accurately summarizes the role of such an operated body in Ben Jelloun's work: "c'est d'abord un corps blessé, brisé, fracturé; c'est le corps de l'immigré, de l'exilé, de l'exclu, du déraciné" [it's above all an injured, broken, fractured body; it's the body of the immigrant, the exiled, the excluded, the uprooted] (275–6). From this perspective, it is possible to understand Homme's body and, therefore, the secluded Homme as an injured, broken body, at the very least exiled or excluded from society as well as from norms of bodily abilities.

The fact that the character's new states of varied abilities are acquired raises questions of cause and, ultimately, of agency. One significant operator who has no contact with Homme's body but who has significant access to Homme's narrative is, again, the *conteur*. As has been shown, the *conteur* is a master at operating narrative in order to gain his audience and, thus, his living: "Vous ne pouvez y accéder sans traverser mes nuits et mon corps. Je suis ce livre" [You can gain access to it only by traversing my nights and my body. I am that book] (12–3; 5). Such a statement is further highlighted by the previous reference to the last chapter of *L'enfant de sable,* in which the *conteur* confesses that his story of Ahmed/Zahra is in fact an adaptation of the tale of an Egyptian named Bey Ahmed. Such operations, along with the use of a disabled Fatima, reveal (1) that the *conteur* operates characters and their abilities to reproduce for his own benefit and (2) that operating characters is a regular part of narrative in Ben Jelloun's two novels.

However, the text also reveals that other agents have pursued the character, causing the acquired shift in abilities and other marks, such as "quelques rides verticales, telles des cicatrices creusées par de lointaines insomnies" [a few vertical lines like scars dug long ago by sleepless nights] (7; 1). The reference to the agents appears clearly yet vaguely when the *conteur*, through a rhetorical operation to maintain his audience, explains how Homme feels about the possible loss of his self-exclusion: "Il serait projeté nu et sans défenses entre les mains de ceux qui n'avaient cessé de le poursuivre" [he would be thrown naked and defenseless into the hands of those who had constantly pursued him] (7; 1). The chapter's only mention of the agents, here the multiplicity at the heart of operation, rings through in the demonstrative pronoun "ceux" [those]. Furthermore, the substantive "mains" [hands] and the locution of ongoing intent ("n'avaient cessé de le poursuivre" [had constantly pursued him]) foreshadows the means by which said agents operate throughout the novel. The notion of pursuit in the infinitive "poursuivre" reinforces a certain subjugation on the part of the character who is pursued and expects to be operated, despite any former expressions of agency that may have generated such pursuit. As such, the text highlights the role of multiple agents in the operative act as well as the importance of the abilities of a gendered individual, particularly as the agents' pursuit alone – with no referenced physical contact – has already altered the character's abilities into Chanfrault's and Bourkhis's aforementioned "corps fracturé" [fractured body] (276).

Although the chapter reveals the externality of primary operating agents (and thereby underscores their multiplicity), one other moment points to a more local source. In the same sentence from which the above citation is taken there appears a subtle suggestion that the character's own comportment fed the desire for the pursuit that may (and does) lead to operations. The continuation of this citation suggests why the agents pursued the character: "de leur curiosité, de leur méfiance et même d'une haine tenace; ils s'accommodaient mal du silence et de l'intelligence d'une figure qui les dérangeait par sa seule présence autoritaire et énigmatique" [with their curiosity, mistrust, even hatred, because they found it difficult to bear the silence and intelligence of his face. Its overbearing, enigmatic presence] (7–8; 1). Far from an explicit explanation of the cause of the pursuit, the character's authoritarian and enigmatic presence are nevertheless at the base of the motivation for the agents' pursuit, making the character an unwilling minor agent but an undeniably major factor in the operated state of ability.

At the same time that the chapter reveals the operation of gender and ability through the character's acquired altered abilities and the agents who contribute to the operations, it also exposes how the narrative of Man, with Homme as a man, is as operable as is the narrative of the chapter and how the centres of such narratives are alterable and therefore arbitrary. As previously mentioned, the character's host of abilities, including the disabilities within the *conteur*'s tale, is to be taken as a negatively charged limit caused by the pursuit of others.

However, the chapter itself complicates this reduction. The previous decentring of narrative that is explicit in the structure of the chapter "Homme," and that is continued in the operations to traditional narrative and narrative voice throughout *L'enfant de sable*, tells the reader that a new means for thinking narrative *and* identity exists. In other words, because the chapter title refers to a normative typology and because the character to whom the title refers is categorically and largely pejoratively disabled, the reader is advised that the norm of Man – for this chapter and thus for this novel – has been operated into a new conceptualization. Man is reproduced by multiple narratives, including those of varied spectrums of bodily abilities and the operations performed on them. Such a reading is further advanced if we look again at the chapter's title: it is neither "Un homme" ("A Man") nor "L'homme" ("The Man"), either of which would suggest a specific individual – and thus *the* specific (yet unnamed) individual in the chapter – through the use of either the indefinite or the definite article. Instead, the chapter is entitled "Homme," thus referring to the aforementioned typology, even the category of identity known as "Man," which can include not only Homme but also the *conteur*.

Such a reconceptualization of the chapter entitled "Homme" does not serve to posit Man, or, more specifically, Maghrebian Arab-Muslim Man, as, for example, disabled; rather, it accomplishes several tasks. It works to demonstrate the impossibility of a singular, unoperable, central narrative of Man by destabilizing the norm of Man as only able-bodied. By extension, it shows how narratives – be they of literature or of identity – are like the bodies they reproduce: operable and therefore not possibly static. Furthermore, the chapter presents manhood not as explicitly biologically congenital but, because of the narrative and bodily operations, as discursively *and* corporeally acquired.

Indeed, the "true" identity of the first chapter of *L'enfant de sable*'s unnamed character, which the *conteur* provides in the following chapters, reinforces such a conclusion. This character is the biological woman Ahmed/Zahra, a body that never possessed the penis of Man and that eventually and traumatically loses the clitoris of Woman. What becomes apparent is the production of a character who, due to multiple operations, must always lose the bodily part symbolized by either of the protruding articles ("Un" or "Le") excised from the chapter's title, thereby allowing the operated title to encapsulate the multiple normative operations that Ahmed/Zahra lives. Furthermore, the version of Man that the chapter and its title offer prepares the reader for the remainder of Ben Jelloun's two novels: a series of enforced operations grounded in normative narratives of gender and ability, of which forms of reproduction, and specifically biological reproduction, are a fundamental component and by which Ahmed/Zahra moves throughout the spectrum of procreative abilities.

MAN, WOMAN, AND THE REPRODUCTION NARRATIVE

What are Islam's words on gender and ability, and what precisely do they say about gender and procreation? To be sure, a discourse of biological reproduction has long resided at the origins of Islam: its progenitors, Ibrahim and Hajar, were able to conceive Ishmael in the face of Sarah's initial barrenness and, by way of such a reproductive operation, beget the Prophet Muhammad. From such heritage it might even be arguable that the foundation of Islam as a faith, and its varied sociocultural interpretations around the globe, rest in large part on a premise and a precedent of bodily ability.

To begin to find answers, it is necessary to first tease out the fundamental elements of biological reproduction that exist in the corresponding Arab-Muslim norm-based master narratives of Man and of Woman and that inform the culture and the society of Morocco. In my exploration, the aforementioned work of Mernissi and Chebel are in dialogue with works such as Butler's *Bodies That Matter* (1993) and *Undoing Gender* (2004) as well as Stiker's *Corps infirmes et sociétés* (1982) in large part because of the ways in which they all theorize and deconstruct normative sociocultural conceptualizations of the body, gender and (with regard to Stiker) the concept of disability. It is true that an ability-informed discourse has already been apparent in, for example, the host of charitable organizations and disability rights groups in Morocco.[12] However, what individuals such as Mernissi and Butler say about the body, and in particular what Stiker argues, helps in thinking the question of bodily abilities that, in the present context, has not yet been engaged in theoretical terms.

Of equal importance for reflecting on the interplay between sociocultural narratives and bodily abilities is how operations, such as those depicted in Ben Jelloun's novel, provide grounds for the marginalization and/or exclusion of individuals who cannot biologically comply with them. Within the sphere of Islam alone, such excluded individuals could often be understood as *fitna*, the form of socioculturally defined disorder that must be either corrected or exterminated.[13] Moroccan interpretations of *fitna* do exist and have been explored by anthropologists, and discussion of such instances within the context of the spectrum of procreative bodily abilities discloses key ways in which *fitna* informs identification. Given the existence of such identity formation in a normative, ability-charged sociocultural context, individuals labelled as *fitna* can be read as freaks of culture. To understand the ways in which sociocultural norms guide such identification, it is important to first explore the related (and, given the novels' content, the conservative) elements in the Maghrebian continuum of Arab-Muslim narratives.[14]

To begin from the beginning, Man and Woman are to be understood within the context of a social tradition. One of the customs that helps us to interrogate such identification is the heteronormative institution of marriage and its production of family. The Qur'an holds that men and women are made to become pairs, and, if they desire to be faithful to the Prophet's tradition, they are to wed. The tradition concerns not just the union of their respective families but also its expansion through the creation of a new familial unit (Denny 268).[15] Sura 4:1, 7:189, and 53:45, among the many, reveal how such creation is emphasized through biological terminology that explains it as the joining of life forces (sperm and egg transforming into the "clot," or embryo) and thus the realization of concealed potential (offspring).[16] The different versions of Morocco's own family law, the *Moudawana*, contain similar Qur'an-based constructs in its recognition of Shari'a (or the advised path to follow in life).

Some critics argue the presence of resoundingly conservative aspects of Islamic traditions as, in part, a representation of the nation-state's Muslim population. They also maintain that it was an effort – an operation – of the post-independence government of Mohammed V to guarantee support from key conservative populations of the nascent nation-state in order to help overthrow the French colonial presence (Eddouada 57–9; Zvan 3). Mohammed V's grandson, Mohammed VI, effectuated the latest controversially less-conservative revision in 2004 to allow more rights for women with respect to marriage and divorce. However, many elements of the law – such as those dealing with childbirth and the official determination of parental filiation in Article 142 of Book 3 ("De la naissance et de ses effets") ["On

Birth and Its Effects"] – still speak to the importance of biological reproduction in the Moroccan family: "La filiation se réalise par la procréation de l'enfant par ses parents" [Filiation is achieved through procreation of the child by the parents] (93).[17] With such heteronormative language, Eddouada's pre-2004 words become a means to contemplate how revised legislation, such as the latest version of the *Moudawana*, as "an incarnation of national homogeneity," continues to enforce sociocultural norms that are driven by "a community-based politics and notions of 'common good'" (61–2).

Of further use in understanding such Maghrebian interpretations of Man-Woman unions and biological reproduction are anthropological studies of Morocco and Algeria that are focused on the period when the former was ruled by the manifestly conservative king Hassan II (1961–99). Such studies include the previously discussed work of Mernissi and of Chebel. The fact that their projects were published before or during the period when Ben Jelloun penned *L'enfant de sable* and *La nuit sacrée*, and the fact that they centre around many similar questions, helps to frame the present discussion within a historically related sociocultural context. One recurrent discussion is most certainly the hierarchical order for men and women, which Abdelwahab Bouhdiba does a fine job of capturing in *La sexualité en Islam* (1975) [*Sexuality in Islam* (1985)]: "[à] l'homme le statut majeur, à la femme l'éternelle minorité" [The man gets major status, the woman eternal minority] (140; 114).

However, such works also highlight the Father-Mother relationship, which is fundamental to Maghrebian Arab-Muslim society and that exists in the Man and Woman narratives. As Bouhdiba writes, this union holds a "position centrale et universelle ... dans [le] processus du renouvellement de la création" [central, universal position ... in {the} process of the renewal of creation] (16; 7). With respect to sexual relations in this union, Bouhdiba states: "La relation sexuelle du couple reprend et amplifie un ordre cosmique qui la déborde de toutes parts: la procréation réédite la création" [The sexual relationship of the couple takes up and amplifies a cosmic order that spills over on all sides: procreation repeats creation] (16; 8). Concerning all such relations, Mernissi writes that the individual is not expected to suppress instincts but, rather, to engage in them in a way that conforms "to the demands of religious law" [aux exigences de la loi religieuse] (1, 5).

An example of this line of thinking, which shifts the discussion from Man-Woman to Father-Mother and, therefore, heterosexual parents, comes from another work of Chebel's, *L'imaginaire arabo-musul-mane* (1993) [*The Arab-Muslim Imaginary*], in which he contemplates the influence of the Arab-Muslim imaginary on social structures. He affirms that much of what this imaginary has become is due to "la structuration inconsciente qui commande [le] rôle principal de l'édifice social, le couple Père-Mère et ses effets" [the unconscious structuring that determines {the} central role of the social edifice, the Father-Mother couple, and its effects] (51). In this statement, the connection between male and female is further underscored as one to be understood not simply as Man-Woman but more as parents of children and, thus, of Islam and its offspring. Mernissi's reading of Al-Ghazali and his explanation of the integration of sexual instinct within Islamic social order sheds further light on the importance of the Father-Mother union. Her analysis points out that, according to Al-Ghazli, all that these couples do and desire as parents would perpetuate the human race and thus the earthly and spiritual manifestations of Islam (Mernissi, *Beyond*, 2–3; Mernissi, *Sexe*, 7–8).

Inscribed in this Father-Mother obligation of biological reproduction are the aforementioned hierarchical codes of activity and passivity for Man and Woman that, with respect to Woman, have been widely discussed elsewhere.[18] What requires further examination is the discourse on the human body and its abilities within the context of these codes. With respect to the conservative narrative of Woman, Mernissi explains that a woman, as a naturally sexually active if not aggressive female, is to be kept submissive and to be the depository of life-giving forms and substances (*Beyond* 16, 2; *Sexe* 22–3, 7). Chebel's reflections also emphasize the woman's passivity in professional terms: she is "exquise lorsqu'elle est séductrice ou amante, mais cesse de l'être lorsqu'elle occupe une chaire liée à un quelconque pouvoir, prérogative masculine" [exquisite when she is a seductress or a lover, but stops being that when she occupies a professorship linked to some power or a masculine prerogative]; moreover, when she adheres to the assigned role of Woman, she is a "bonne musulmane" [good Muslim] (44). Eddouada succinctly sums up the same distinction as it has been historically lived in a post-independence Morocco guided by the *Moudawana*: "Gender difference means the man's preeminence and the woman's subordination" (60).

There are moments when Woman is understood as active, but such activity is limited to domestic life and, in particular, to being able to reproduce biologically, or *enfanter* [to give birth]. Her broader social activity remains limited. Indeed, bearing children is what aligns any woman with the order of the Woman narrative, particularly as Chebel reads this bodily ability within the parameters of the family. A woman's highest calling as well as salvation from *fitna*, as Chebel maintains, is to produce a male child: "l'enfant mâle, à naître ou déjà né, est la seule condition qui sauve la mère du chaos" [the male child, to be born or already born, is the only condition that saves the mother from disorder] (49). In the same context, a woman deemed to be sterile or unable to biologically reproduce – thus embodying the "catastrophe irréparable" [irreparable catastrophe] – can be operated into a status of "handicap" (Chebel, *Le corps*, 57–8).[19] Most certainly, a woman's reproductive inability is read pejoratively as a disability for her bodily ability blocks the perpetuation of order. In this respect, such a woman not only is but creates *fitna*. The operation of sociocultural norms on the woman's body is worthy of further exploration, and Chebel expresses this well with respect to reproductive organs and the assumptions made based on biological constitution: "Il est insidieux, au point où la biologie utérine semble devenir complice à la quête culturelle et sociale" [The point at which uterine biology seems to have become an accomplice to the cultural and social quest is insidious] (*L'imaginaire* 47).

The corresponding narrative of Man is one that emphasizes an active state or virility. In her essay, "Le désert perpétuel: Visages de la virilité au Maghreb" (1998) ["The Perpetual Desert: Faces of Virility in the Mahgreb"], Nadia Tazi demonstrates that the role of the man, as male, is to be virile, to lead, to defend, to love, to create offspring, to perpetuate the human race. In other words, the ultimate calling of Man is to be both social and productive. Tazi is careful to point out that this tends towards a superhuman model, especially in love and in war between human beings, and that a man is responsible for both maintaining and realizing the most that he can. A man is nothing short of a "Surhomme" [Superman] (Tazi 53–4). To be this, to excel in love and war, implies not simply the goal but also the ability to achieve it: each man's body must be able to wage war (real and metaphorical) in order to efface disorder as well as to make love and, thereby, as the Qur'an reveals, to create. The narrative of Man states that in his body there must reside the ability to realize this higher calling. If this is the narrative that explains Man's goals, then Tazi's reading, which exposes the binary-driven identity categories, helps to explain that a man capable of possessing this virility is truly Man and thus able-bodied (read "normal").[20] Conversely, a man incapable of such a state (which includes procreative abilities) may not be read as Man but as pejoratively disabled.

In sum, the Man-Woman/Father-Mother couple that is the product of intertwined sociocultural norms of gender and bodily ability becomes what Chebel, when discussing the heterosexual model, calls in *L'esprit de sérail* the "mode d'emploi" [manual] and the "poseur de lois" [policy maker] in Arab-Muslim society (207). To this end, the Man and Woman narratives assign very specific bodily abilities to male and female bodies, and men and women must be able to follow this "mode d'emploi" to be considered "bons musulmans." In other words, male bodies are understood to be able to do certain things that female bodies are not, and vice versa. This same categorization is based on abilities of the body that may or may not be associated with its anatomical structure but are certainly culturally assigned to specific bodies. One example (familiar to some readers): because the "normal" female body "has" ovaries, fallopian tubes, and a womb, all female bodies must bear children. In this respect, what individuals live and do would reproduce premises of bodily ability connected to gender as they appear and are operated within related master sociocultural narratives. However, as Ben Jelloun's novels reveal, the ways in which agents operate such norm-based narratives and the related bodies in order to realize their own reproduction make known the ways in which narrative is malleable and bodily abilities move within a spectrum.

THE FREAK OF FEMALE REPRODUCTION

In *L'enfant de sable* and *La nuit sacrée* not all operating agents realize as extensive a transformation of bodily abilities as is demonstrated in my discussion of Homme. Nevertheless, each pursuit, each manipulation, and each incision that I study is grounded in bodily abilities associated with the male and female genders. The affected abilities are not regularly as broad-sweeping as are those of Homme; but the operations conducted always alter bodies in ways and in places associated with procreative abilities. Yet, although the agents' method is to tap into (sometimes literally) such abilities, their ultimate aim is the realization of individual goals through operations of the related master sociocultural narratives. As previously mentioned, certain of the operations may involve Ahmed/Zahra's consensual participation; however, as Ben Jelloun's novels work to underscore the recurrently dominant exteriority of operations that realize the manipulated freak of culture, the protagonist's active engagement comes through as remarkably minimal and regularly forced.

From the outset of Ben Jelloun's two novels, the multiply operated protagonist, switched of gender and rich in abilities, was always already a freak of culture. However, the most poignant example of such operations comes in *L'enfant de sable* during Ahmed/Zahra's time as a performer at Oum Abbas's *cirque forain*. It is one of the few moments in which it is possible to discern the protagonist's connection to tropes of freak discourse as well as participation in freak of culture identification. It is also a moment in which the reproduction of the freak involves multiple agents – actively, Oum Abbas and her son Abbas; passively, Ahmed/Zahra – and master sociocultural narratives related to norms for both genders built into the performed *homme* and *femme fatale* roles. With more than one agent from society and with sociocultural norms at hand, the citation used to open this chapter – "Ahmed n'est pas une erreur de la nature, mais un détournement social" – takes on a double meaning with respect to the social (*L'enfant* 160). And, although the protagonist's time at the Abbas circus does not involve surgical operation to bodily abilities, it does involve manipulation of bodily parts: those required for the *femme fatale* performance and, subsequently, those normatively associated with procreation. Once operated, these body parts contribute to freak of culture reproduction grounded in the biological, which becomes financial. Conducted as such, the active agents' operations further decentre and destabilize the static, normative roles of gender and ability.

L'enfant de sable's chapter titles alone provide key indications of such emphasis. As with the references to gender in the chapter title "Homme," two other chapters in Ben Jelloun's novel refer simultaneously to the freak of culture and to gender: chapter 11, "L'homme aux seins de femme" ["The Man with a Woman's Breasts"], and chapter 12, "La femme à la barbe mal rasée" ["The Woman with the Badly Shaven Beard"], the latter of which was foreshadowed in *L'enfant*'s first chapter in the phrase "un visage mal rasé" [a badly shaven face] (111, 125, 7; 83, 95, 1). Such descriptions do not defy natural possibilities of the human body that fall outside of scientific norms; rather, they rely upon typical classifications of freaks, which both Bogdan and Garland Thomson reveal as historically hyped up characteristics that Western showmen used to advertise their performers (97; "Introduction" 5). The two chapter titles also underscore the importance of those particular parts of the body that agents target in their operations, resulting in reproduction.[21]

The details of the performance recounted in chapter 11 disclose more fully the means by which Ahmed/Zahra's body is operated in the name of reproduction. As mentioned above, Ahmed/Zahra does possess agency with respect to joining the circus: "J'étais disponible, décidée à me laisser faire et à laisser venir les choses. Je la suivis en silence" [I had decided to go along with her and let things happen to me. I followed her in silence] (118; 89). Clearly, a degree of self-affirmation appears in that the protagonist does decide to take part in the venture. In other scenes, Ahmed/Zahra does not refuse but, rather, agrees to perform the role of the *homme/femme fatale*. With these scenes, it is certainly possible to conclude that such a decision factors into an increasing development in the protagonist's evolving location of agency, or what Cazenave calls "the step-by-step shaping of the person" ("Gender" 441).

However, the recurrent if not the dominant presence of external powers and penetrating discourse in the two novels – forces that, according to Foucault, weave themselves into the subject's negotiation of identity – encourage a different reading (Foucault, *Surveiller*, 31–2). They suggest less control on the protagonist's part with respect to the operations. In a very general sense, Oum Abbas and Abbas appear not as dominating but as protective forces, and the circus a place in which Ahmed/Zahra finds some comfort. However, Foucault's floating, haunting power structures do find their form in the institution that is the Abbas family. Ben Jelloun's novel accentuates such a relationship, with Ahmed/Zahra's recurrent passivity evident in the presence of Oum Abbas and Abbas. Although the protagonist does decide to join their community, the circus owner and her son do indeed operate Ahmed/Zahra in contexts of gender and ability that emphasize reproduction and realize more of the protagonist's narrative.[22]

In the *conteur*'s version of Ahmed/Zahra's life at the circus, Abbas remains fundamental to such operations. He is one means by which Ahmed/Zahra, as well as the reader, learns of the ways in which the agents target specific body parts and thereby realize a fragmentation to which the titles of chapters 11 and 12 allude. The isolation of parts begins when Abbas, as instructor, explains to the protagonist what the *homme/femme fatale* performance entails and produces: "Tu te déguiseras en homme à la première partie du spectacle, tu disparaîtras cinq minutes pour réapparaître en femme fatale … [U]n vrai spectacle avec une mise en scène, du suspens et même un peu de nu, pas beaucoup, mais une jambe, une cuisse … On va travailler les gestes et les sous-entendus! … Il arrive parfois que des hommes s'excitent et jettent sur la danseuse des billets de banque" [You'll dress up as a man in the first part of the show; then you'll disappear for five minutes and reappear as a *femme fatale* … {A} real show, with proper staging, suspense, and even a bit of nudity, not much, just a leg, a thigh … We'll have to work on the gestures and innuendos! … Sometimes men get excited and throw bank notes at the dancer] (121; 92).

Abbas's instruction contains, upon first reading, a discourse of performance that relates most obviously to the act of dressing. In keeping with the representation of the freak of culture and thus *fitna*, clothing oneself gender-opposite in the represented sociocultural context contributes to the construction of the freak. As Bouhdiba explains, cross-dressing categorically violates Arab-Muslim sociocultural norms and subjects offenders to the wrath of Allah (44; 31). It is true that the actions and the events that Abbas describes are all understood to occur within the context of a spectacle that does not fully convince the viewer. The protagonist describes the particular air of illusion well in reflecting on the existence of such circuses within the related sociocultural context: "J'avais déjà entendu parler de ces spectacles forains où l'homme joue à la danseuse sans se faire réellement passer pour une femme, où tout baigne dans la dérision sans réelle ambiguïté" [I had already heard of those circus shows in which men dress up as female dancers without really passing themselves off as women, in which there is an atmosphere of derision, without any real ambiguity] (120; 91).

However, there is still an element of passing required of the performance in order for it to be profitable. Jarrod Hayes (2000) offers a complex discussion of the scene that speaks, not directly to the issue of cross-dressing, but, more largely, to the element of crossing genders through performance. More specifically, he writes of the successful passing and performing of gender that decentres the related master narrative: "In a way, Ahmed repeatedly reveals his/her history of dressing and passing as a man on the stage of a freak show. Yet what is revealed here is less important than how it is performed; that Ahmed's anatomy is unwomanly by male standards will matter less than 'les gestes et les sous-entendus.' An audience of men decides what constitutes a good performance; for the good performance satisfies *their* desires" (169). Here Hayes, in the spirit of Judith Butler, argues that gender is an arbitrary construct and can be performed. A good performer – no matter how "unwomanly" the body may be – can convince viewers that a "femme fatale" dances before their eyes. The content of chapter 11 furthers the same argument by revealing that the performer's body does not need to be that of a woman to offer a successful *femme fatale* performance: Ahmed/Zahra both muses over Bou Chaïb, the man renowned in Morocco for female impersonation, and reveals that Malika, the existing performer the protagonist is to replace, is a man (119–20; 90–1). Similarly, the demonstration of such success, as Abbas points out, is the financial gain, the bank notes that the male viewers toss at a performer.

Hayes is certainly correct to focus on the importance of performance here, for Ahmed/Zahra becomes, as stated in chapter 12, "la principale attaraction du cirque forain" [the main attraction of the circus] (126; 96). However, in emphasizing the performance of gender and its related normative foundation, Hayes does not delve into the norms of physical ability and the impossibility of passing that surface in the discourse of the *femme fatale* performance alone. Based on the protagonist's success within a context in which the shows are known for derision and lack of ambiguity, one could argue that Ahmed/ Zahra not only entertains well but also, given life experiences as a man and the biological body of a female, plays the roles better than any other performer. To do this, the performer must possess the body parts that normally animate the performance narrative as well as the physical ability to use the listed parts to execute bank-note winning choreography. As the Abbas citation shows, the performance will involve "gestes" and "un peu de nu, pas beaucoup, mais une jambe, une cuisse." Ahmed/Zahra does possess the required body parts and, as the continued performances in later scenes reveal, is physically able to use them as required. The performance of the *femme fatale*, then, is one born in, and reproducing of, a whole bodily ability that is normal for the role. Ahmed/Zahra is chosen because of the body parts and the physical and even metaphorical bodily ability they possess, which, when used for performance, realize financial reproduction. To be sure, the body's total sum is literally of its parts.

Thinking the norms of gender and ability for the *femme fatale* role as isolated to that role is too limiting. For, as Hayes argues, gender

alone is conceived with respect to sociocultural norms that the performer's audience recognizes and, if convincingly excited, rewards.
According to the present argument, the *femme fatale* role is built upon
two distinct yet interrelated norm-based narratives: (1) the sexually
active *femme fatale* as the embodiment of sociocultural disorder and
(2) the sexually passive woman as the personification of sociocultural
order. John Esposito states that, as found in the hadith, the woman is
one of the greatest incarnations of *fitna* for man because of her presumed link to seduction, which can lead to the chaos and disorder of
fitna itself if the man gives in (87). Mernissi's project allows her to
delve deeper into such questions of embodying *fitna*: she demonstrates how, historically, a woman – and especially one who has "experienced sexual intercourse" [celle qui a fait l'expérience de la relation
sexuelle] – is repeatedly thought in terms of an active sexuality that
defines the nature of her aggression (11–2; 24–6). Mernissi reads feminist Kacem Amin's preliminary reflections on such questions in
order to further examine the following premise: *fitna* is "the connotation of a *femme fatale* attraction which makes men lose their self-con-
trol" [l'idée d'une *femme fatale* dont le pouvoir séducteur fait perdre
aux hommes la maîtrise d'eux-mêmes] (and to which they are "naturally" inclined to give in), and this is what men should flee (3–4; 10).[23]
Defined as naturally sexually aggressive, the woman is, as well as creates, *fitna* simply by existing.

Binary opposites, the tropes of the sexually passive and the sexually
active woman, serve as a means by which Arab-Muslim men can guide
themselves within a conservative Arab-Muslim Maghrebian society.
As the former is to be thought in terms of her biologically reproductive ability, which reproduces Islam's family, the latter is to be thought
of in terms of reproducing *fitna*, which destroys that same family. As
such, both tropes share the fundamental trait of reproduction and, as
such, are valorized in terms of a sexualized physical ability to reproduce. More specifically, the presumed abilities associated with their
reproductive organs – particularly the vagina, as portal to said organs
– become the primary means for operating their bodies with respect
to reproduction.

With a resounding emphasis on organs of biological reproduction
being revealed, Abbas's and Oum Abbas's respective pointing to particular body parts takes on greater meaning. Almost unbeknownst to
him, Abbas's highlighting of the partially exposed leg and then the
thigh – the body parts that lead the viewers' eyes and minds to the

vagina – assumes a metonymic position with respect to the sexualized physical ability of reproduction. And yet, because Abbas lets it be known that the successful performance must include such exposed and presumably functioning body parts and can lead to and thereby produce bank notes, his instructional operation of Ahmed/Zahra bears witness to the interplay of biological and financial reproduction in which they meld together to realize the Abbas family's financial goal. The same argument can be made for why Oum Abbas pursues Ahmed/Zahra and makes the protagonist part of her *cirque forain*. Her words and actions, specifically her digital penetration of the protagonist's vagina, reveal her intent to employ someone other than the men who can simply perform the *homme/femme fatale* act: she desires an individual who has a female anatomy and who can reproduce the role.

However, Oum Abbas's claim has not only financial motivation but also religious substantiation. The circus owner posits her pursuit within a discourse of Islam that, as discussed earlier, emphasizes the sexualized physical ability in its master narrative of Woman. Upon finding the protagonist, the circus's proprietor quickly stakes her claim: "Un des compagnons du Prophète m'a mis sur tes pas. Cela fait longtemps que je suis à ta recherche … Je te connais … Tu vas me suivre!" [One of the Prophet's companions has sent me after you … I've been looking for you for a long time … I know you … You will follow me!] (117–8; 89).

Here again the novel recalls the typically Western history of freak culture enterprise, where, as Saartje Baartman's life (see chapter 1) and Guy de Maupassant's tale "La mère aux monstres" (1883) ["A Mother of Monsters" (n.d.)] demonstrate, exploitative entrepreneurs toured extensively in search of the ultimate spectacle. But Ben Jelloun's work provides a Maghrebian Arab-Muslim context: by stating "un des compagnons du Prophète m'a mis sur tes pas," Oum Abbas states that individuals who are connected to, and therefore metonymic of, Islam speak of Ahmed/Zahra in reference to their normative, order-based narratives. Given the recurrent weight on Maghrebian Arab-Muslim constructs of gender in Ben Jelloun's novels and the aforementioned efforts to maintain such roles as well as to efface the *fitna* that comes to exist due to gender-crossing, one may suppose that the "compagnons" learned of the switch (or of the show) and thus speak of Ahmed/Zahra as a form of disorder with regard to the crossing of genders that Islam expressly forbids.

Oum Abbas's words do not work to perpetuate such a normative discourse; rather, they point to how the circus proprietor has evoked to her benefit an Islamic narrative by affiliating herself with a level high enough to enable her to speak with such presumably revered and holy individuals. The same moment may also suggest an already apparent overlap between narratives of religion and economy, the sacred and the secular. Indeed, the former, preferring to see the *fitna* that is Ahmed/Zahra contained within a circus at the margins of the walled city, may have recounted the protagonist's narrative to the latter, who as the circus proprietor is likely known as another "mère aux monstres." The scene may also reveal Oum Abbas's own proclivity to adapt narrative, claiming (perhaps falsely) religious assistance in what she presents as a quest. Regardless of the possible intent, the scene ultimately demonstrates how Oum Abbas, as agent, clarifies her authority with regard to the operations that she and her son conduct as well as to her own ability to operate: she appropriates a holy, normative narrative that, in the interest of the reproduction of which Abbas spoke, she operates. It also indicates that Oum Abbas, although likely not considered by conservative Arab-Muslims as one of the faithful, operates in terms of master sociocultural narratives and, thereby, how the latter play a crucial role in her selection of performers for a resoundingly Arab-Muslim audience.

The norm-based narratives of performer, of *femme fatale*, of Woman, and thus of Islam become the paradigm within which Oum Abbas thinks Ahmed/Zahra's body and bodily abilities. More specifically, it reveals how she, like her son, operates the body parts that reproduce the freak of culture and financial compensation. Prior to taking the protagonist to the *cirque forain*, Oum Abbas, as a woman of industry, must determine that the rumoured goods are in fact good. Her verification culminates in the immediate physical examination of Ahmed/Zahra's body: "Ses mains tâtaient mon corps comme pour vérifier une intuition. Ma poitrine minuscule ne la rassura point, elle glissa sa main dans mon séroual et la laissa un instant sur mon bas-ventre, puis introduisit son médium dans mon vagin" [Her hands roamed over my body as if to verify an intuition. My tiny breasts did not reassure her; she slipped her hand into my trousers and left it for a moment on my sex, then inserted her middle finger] (118; 89). Breast and genitalia are the goals of this pursuit, but not within a context that transmits sexual desire on the part of Oum Abbas. Rather, it is an operation that Oum Abbas conducts with respect to her own narrative as well as with respect to the undercurrent of the sociocultural normative narratives of gender and ability that inform her own.

It is also an operation that reveals how biological reproductive ability becomes the means by which Ahmed/Zahra's body is identified as being of value. This becomes especially true with respect to body parts associated with the Arab-Muslim woman's normative role in biological reproduction: they are read as the source of life that, in the strict enforcement of the same narrative, should be able to reproduce the family that is Islam's community. Handling these parts of the body (and especially the vagina), Oum Abbas identifies Ahmed/Zahra's body not only as that of *a* presumably reproductive woman but also as that of *the* reproductive woman she seeks. Putting her finger in the protagonist's vagina, Oum Abbas completes her search by touching the bodily site normatively associated with female fecundity. Her search for the *femme fatale* produces the financial *femme féconde*.

The Abbas family's emphasis on various body parts rather than on the whole body discloses a further aspect of objectification beyond spectacle and profit. It speaks to the undercurrent of identification born of operation, and Barthes's words from *S/Z* help to think this process even further. In his reading of La Zambinella, the castrato in Honoré de Balzac's *Sarrasine*, Barthes speaks of how agents understand the character's body as a "corps … déchiqueté" (dissected body) that they eventually transform into a "corps rassemblé" (reassembled body): "le sujet … ne connaît le corps féminin que sous forme d'une division et d'une dissémination d'objets partiels" [the subject … knows the female body only as a division and dissemination of partial objects] (108; 111–2). Sarrasine, sculptor, protagonist and primary agent, reassembles such division of partial objects into a body that is "fictif" [fictive], that he claims to love, and that therefore serves the purposes of the agents' own operated narrative (109; 112).

With respect to Ben Jelloun's novels, the notion of dissecting and reassembling can be taken one step further. Both Oum Abbas and Abbas only understand the protagonist in normative, reproductive, female terms relating to the parts that reproduce. It is through such understanding that they operate Ahmed/Zahra into reproducing the money they seek. As such, Ahmed/Zahra and Balzac's la Zambinella (whom the equally operative Cardinal Cicognara goes to great lengths to keep in his possession and thus maintain as a stage performer) are not only bodies understood as parts but also bodies understood as vessels of financial reproduction.

Above all Oum Abbas's and Abbas's operations of Ahmed/Zahra reveal the fundamental importance of normative biological reproduction in the operations that agents conduct in the name of reproduction. The agents' alteration of narrative and their manipulation of body give shape to the freak of culture who reproduces according to their will and their goal of turning a profit. Such an unfolding of events demonstrates how agents modify the norms of gender and ability associated with biological reproduction to shift into and affect spaces, events, and (especially) people close to them. As I now go on to demonstrate, the same operations become an effort to gain and maintain power, with agents having as their intent the alteration of bodily abilities in the name of gender. The same moments involve both surgical and discursive operations that highlight the scarring impact of the acts as the protagonist is moved within the spectrum of reproductive bodily abilities.

EUNUCHS AND THE REPRODUCTION OPERATION

Just as the master sociocultural narratives of Man and Woman are repeatedly posited as the Arab-Muslim template, so another narrative of gender is conceived for a group of individuals who do not fit under Man or Woman. More specifically, it pertains directly, and has historically been defined in relationship (but not consistently opposite), to the norm-based reproductive functions of Man and Woman. This narrative refers to the eunuch, an individual formed of a castrated male body and whose mention typically conjures up – particularly for the Western viewer of paintings such as Ingres's *L'odalisque à l'esclave* (1842) [*Odalisque with Slave*] and films like Julien Duvivier's *Pépé le Moko* (1937) – the image of a sultan's palace guard. Reproduction became fundamentally factored into their work as guards, particularly as protectors of harems. Some historians report that eunuchs' duties to the harem, as first conceived in Persia, were ultimately assigned to the castrated individuals because of their lack of body parts and their related bodily abilities. Such a distinction transformed eunuchs into the presumably perfect preserver of equally presumed female fertility (Scholz 198).

However, from an Arab-Muslim sociocultural perspective, eunuchs were more than palace guards. As studies such as Shaun Marmon's *Eunuchs and Sacred Boundaries in Islamic Society* (1995) demonstrate, they were privy to great amounts of power and respect, serving often as counsellors to sultans, occasionally as interim leaders of government, and regularly in the initial assignment that some obtained as guards to holy sites like the Ka'ba in Mecca, the Dome of the Rock in Jerusalem, and the Prophet's tomb in Medina (14).[24] Their presence was plentiful, with one notable case in the Maghreb. The Meknes court of Moulay Ismail Ibn Sharif (1672–1727), the sultan who fought the Ottoman Turks three times and won independent governance of the region that would eventually constitute a significant portion of today's kingdom of Morocco, was estimated to have between one thousand and two thousand eunuchs. Approximately three hundred were of SubSaharan African origin and were intended to guard the women of the harem (Gomez 38; Léon 25). The presence of the eunuchs, as Marmon works diligently to prove, spanned nearly eight hundred years (31–3). Piotr Scholz's *Eunuchs and Castrati* (1999) concurs with the time span, even extending it by claiming that the historical study is not yet complete due to the eunuchs who were still guardians in Mecca, Medina, and Jerusalem at the time his work was published (200). In sum, eunuchs were commonplace in certain lands regularly associated with Islam, respectfully greeted at holy sites, as Marmon indicates, and at times dutifully feared in and around the palaces of Meknes, as Father Dominique Busnot's early eighteenth-century historical report from his mission contends (94–9; 74). Such a history arises from the singularly incising operation of the genitalia at the male source of biological and, therefore, human reproduction.

How could such inclusion come to be, when the Arab-Muslim master narratives of gender and ability and their dogmatically conservative enforcement valorizes men capable of reproduction?[25] Such a body, which finds no home amidst the norm-based order of either the Man narrative or the Woman narrative, and with the role of guard for very prized spaces, could have typically amounted to *fitna*. One reason for the acceptance of the eunuch is found in the arguments related to the geographical location of the castration. Categorically speaking, the eunuch is a being repeatedly crafted within a context outside of what the Prophet established should render him, as Marmon writes, "wrought in the context of ordinary profane time" and therefore a violation of Arab-Muslim order (79). However, because the variations of castration were reportedly conducted outside the geographical reach of Islam and were performed on non-Muslims, the eunuch's presence in Arab-Muslim lands was not in violation of principles of unacceptable innovation (*bid'a*) within Islam but more an allowable creation (*ibtikar*) or introduction (*huduth*) (Scholz 198; Marmon 79–80).[26] With this rhetorical loophole, the castrated individuals were frequently brought into Islam's lands as, for example, purchases made during Arab invasions or diplomatic gifts at court in Arab-Muslim territories (Chebel 37; Grosrichard 184; Scholz 199). The geographical exteriority of the originating surgical act became one means for justifying the eunuch's extensive interiority, making an argument for the eunuch as *fitna*, or freak of culture, futile. Such logic leads to the conclusion that, primarily due to the absence of a rupture with a normative sociocultural narrative, the eunuch could not be considered a freak of culture.

Another central explanation for the eunuchs' inclusion in the Islamic master narrative involves their simultaneously symbolic and real abilities and how these were useful to courts, caliphs, and other seats of power. As the list of posts they held demonstrates, it is clear that both Islamic communities and Arab-Muslim states found eunuchs useful. Depending on the type of post held, this usefulness played itself out in a variety of ways.[27] However, it is important to remember that the primary reason eunuchs stepped into such roles had to do with their symbolic and literal lack of reproductive ability. In the presence of men (e.g., sultans) who wanted their powers of conquest and conception to be known and preserved, eunuchs offered corporeal affirmation of what they were seeking. Clearly, agents of power incorporated the eunuch into their network of sociocultural customs.

In this context of supposedly fixed abilities and power, it is useful to note that the roles the eunuchs held did not always remain entirely subservient. A good number of them negotiated their way into increasingly powerful roles. Clearly, castration had not rendered the eunuchs powerless, for some of them were advisors to and emissaries for sultans. In certain cases they were commanders in chief, such as Mi'nis, the "Emir of emirs," who had at one point appointed the caliph Qahir (931–933) and at a later time had him executed for ineffective administration (Scholz 206–7). In manoeuvring their ways into such positions of power, eunuchs also often played pivotal roles in their own sociocultural identification, demonstrating such a process of operation to be increasingly multi-voiced and fluid. Kathryn Ringrose's *The Perfect Servant* (2003), a reflection on eunuchs at the sultan's court in Byzantium, captures the essence of what, in this context, may be considered eunuch reproduction: "Although incapable of normal biological reproduction, this group of individuals reproduced itself, trained itself, and became the repository for courtly traditions" (184). However, in most cases, given the sultan's regularly respected dominance, the eunuch's gaining of power depended on his gaining of acceptance. Such acceptance remained fundamental to a narrative in which a sultan and his palace, which symbolized earthly Islamic order, repeatedly reproduced laws intended to direct and thus to form the related sociocultural structure. This reception remained equally pertinent to how the eunuch's otherwise disorderly body, as operated within Islam, became an acceptable, integral component in the maintenance of order and power.

Such a history of Arab-Muslim operation relates fundamentally to the human body and, specifically, to procreative abilities and the body parts equated with them. Rereading the master sociocultural narrative in the name of such operations conducted on eunuchs not only valorizes reproductive *inabilities* within a system of normality but also reveals how the normality of said narrative is most certainly operated. Furthermore, the reported acceptance into Arab-Muslim culture of the surgically altered, non-Muslim bodies of eunuchs reveals – in contrast to the overall exclusion of noncompliant, operated Muslim bodies in Ben Jelloun's novels – the operability, if not fickleness, of the power structures that govern sociocultural systems and the agents who negotiate them. The eunuch is most certainly allowable as *ibtikar* or *huduth*, not unacceptable and not *bid'a*, as Ben Jelloun's two novels show. *L'enfant de sable* sums up the product of such a process: "il n'y a absolument pas de place pour celui ou celle, surtout celle qui, par volonté ou par erreur, par esprit rebelle ou par inconscience, trahit l'ordre" [there is absolutely no place for him or her, especially her, who, consciously or erroneously, betrays the established order] (154; 120).

OPERATING MAN

Of all of the reproductive operations Ahmed/Zahra lives in *L'enfant de sable* and *La nuit sacrée*, there are only two that involve any surgical component: the feigned male circumcision and the actual female genital mutilation. As the descriptions alone indicate, these are the acts that relate most directly to biological reproduction. And, as the scenes reveal, only family members conduct the operations that are most intimate and painful: the father the feigned male circumcision, the sisters the actual female genital mutilation. The scenes at hand demonstrate how agents overlook biological, even familial, connections to operate the Arab-Muslim norms of gender and ability and to realize personal goals: the reproduction of a phallocentric legacy of economics (primarily finances) and order that, born of pride and greed, ends in revenge and disorder. Dissecting discourse and brandishing blades, the familial agents despotically carve their operated narrative of ability onto bodies as acts excusable in the name of Arab-Muslim narratives that they claim to uphold but ultimately manipulate. Whereas the agents realize only the female circumcision through the cutting of Ahmed/Zahra's body, they all require the same body for both of the operations. One profoundly cutting impact of the operations is that they expose the mutable nature of bodily abilities. In the end, they emphasize the reproduction of the freak of culture as they demonstrate how the protagonist is invariably moved within the spectrum of procreative abilities.

In *L'enfant de sable*'s second chapter, "La porte du jeudi" ["The Thursday Gate"], Ahmed/Zahra's father, Hadj Ahmed Souleïmane, appears anguished by the presence of seven daughters and the absence of a son and heir. He understands his perceived lack of progeniture as a detriment to his existence in the Islamic community, as interjected by the *conteur*: "notre religion est impitoyable pour l'homme sans héritier" [our religion is pitiless for a man who has no heirs] (18; 10). However, the remaining portion of the *conteur*'s reflection shows that the root of Hadj Ahmed's ultimate concern is not the demonstration of religious faithfulness but the loss of an economic legacy: "elle [la religion] le dépossède ou presque en faveur des frères" [It {religion} dispossesses him in favor of his brothers] (18; 10). Hadj Ahmed frets that the majority of his fortune will, upon his death and in the absence of said heir, pass into the hands of his brothers, as outlined in agnatic practices of family law (18; 10; Charrad 236). He also worries that the same loathsome siblings will publicly ridicule him if the eighth child is not a boy (18; 9–10). The norms of the Man narrative weigh heavily on his shoulders for what Hadj Ahmed struggles with most, and most personally, is the self-perception of a deficiency, a reproductive disability that diminishes his virility: "Il disait que ... son corps était possédé par une graine maudite et qu'il se considérait comme un époux stérile" [He said that … his body was possessed by an accursed seed, and that he regarded himself as a sterile husband] (17; 9).[28] Here Hadj Ahmed frets over what being *unable* to have a male heir represents: a-virile, unproductive of life-giving fluids, and therefore excluded from Arab-Muslim life.

Such anxiety over biological reproduction has deep roots in the Arab-Muslim tradition (in particular the perpetuation of a patriarchal system). The story of Hadj Ahmed's potential reproductive disability recalls the previously referenced challenge faced by Islam's own originators: Ibrahim, a fertile Hajar, and a presumably barren Sarah. As such, Hadj Ahmed's gesture, which is similar to Ibrahim's and Sarah's – to find a means to biologically reproduce and to continue the lineage – unveils how norms of reproductive ability and the body continue to be the conduit for operations of sociocultural norms.

Whereas Hadj Ahmed's predecessors eventually pursued productivity through another female body, he focuses on the procreative abilities of his unnamed wife. After several attempts to locate a "cure" (and therefore focusing on the requirements of cultural norms rather than on the material lottery of reproduction), his next attempt at operation is to transfer his self-perceived incapacity to her: "J'ai compris que tu portes en toi une infirmité: ton ventre ne peut concevoir d'enfant mâle" [I realized that you carry some infirmity within you: your belly cannot conceive a male child] (*L'enfant* 21; *Sand* 12–3).[29] In so doing, Hadj Ahmed accomplishes what, in a rhetorical question, Chebel posits regarding confirmed male sterility as a pejorative disability and its transference to the most fundamental female reproductive organs: "le follicule ovarien est[-il] responsable de ce handicap?" [Is the ovarian follicule responsible for this disability?] (*Le corps* 58).

When the child's birth unsurprisingly produces a female and Hadj Ahmed's operation on his wife proves ineffective, he then follows Ibrahim's tradition of using another female body – only now it is that of the young female child that he is determined will be a boy (*L'enfant* 23; *Sand* 12). Himself void of what he considers fully functioning sexual organs, Hadj Ahmed confirms the child's imagined organs through the male circumcision ritual inscribed in Arab-Muslim sociocultural narratives (Chebel *Le corps* 173). As Chebel posits in *Histoire de la circoncision* (1992) [*The History of Circumcision*], one of the primary motivations for the operation is a twofold belief arising from undocumented "vieux mythes" [old myths]: (1) that the uncircumcised penis diminishes the male child's own reproductive capacities and (2) that circumcision has "le but de faciliter l'office de la nature" [the goal of facilitating the duties of nature], where nature refers to fecundity as the goal of all Muslims (104). Although aspects of Chebel's argument stand on an at-times questioned foundation, his discussion proves useful in that it demonstrates the passage of the cultural realm into the natural realm. By exploring the context and implications of circumcision, Chebel reveals how the operation, a sociocultural custom, has in many ways become understood as necessary to nature. Human intervention, with its intent to encourage reproduction, functions as beneficial to the agents of such intervention: "La main humaine … a ajouté à l'ordre naturel quelque chose qui ressortit directement à sa volonté propre, à son intentionnalité" [The human hand has added something to the natural order, something that falls within the domain of its self-will and of its intentionality] (105).

The realization of individual will as associated with biological reproduction is precisely and blatantly what Hadj Ahmed pursues. His acts are akin to the efforts to appropriate, or to at least approximate, the female procreative powers, a process that Marie-Helene Huet discusses in *Monstrous Imagination*. Only here, Hadj Ahmed, as father, steals the reproductive powers directly from his wife by operating the imagined penis of his biological daughter in an effort to secure his own financial reproduction and, therefore, his legacy. Such realization occurs not due to what Marrouchi rightly maintains is the entering of "the culturally charged territory of … gender passing – the attempt of women to pass as men" (331). Moreover, it materializes through an operation that is ultimately ability-crafting through constructs of gender roles. By dressing his newborn biological daughter with male genitalia – with the ultimate fabric of flesh – in a performative context intended to represent reality, Hadj Ahmed violates the sociocultural order that is reinforced by gender-driven vestiary customs (Bouhdiba 44; 31). With no historical or religious precedent for making a girl a boy, Hadj Ahmed's operation incites *fitna* because it is undeniably *bid'a*.

The performative component of the ceremony also factors into Hadj Ahmed's efforts to reproduce via operation. Much like Ahmed/Zahra's stint as the *femme fatale* freak in the *cirque forain*, the simulated circumcision of a feigned foreskin is a spectacle. It is an event that family, including Hadj Ahmed's aforementioned brothers, attends and celebrates, and it is one that must convince its viewers to accept illusion. Furthermore, the circumcision is, as a performance, doubly difficult, not only because Ahmed/Zahra has no penis but also because most members of the family have "leurs soupçons" [their suspicions] about the anatomical truth of this child (*L'enfant* 32; *Sand* 21). Disbelief must not be suspended but dispelled, and such success is what preoccupies Hadj Ahmed during the preparation: "Comment procéder? Comment couper un prépuce imaginaire? … Comment allait-il contourner la difficulté et donner encore plus de force et de crédibilité à son plan?" [What was he to do? How could an imaginary foreskin be cut off? … How could the father overcome this difficulty and promote his plan?] (31; 20). Although Hadj Ahmed does not perform the operation, he does orchestrate it. The circumcision as an operation, then, must produce, through performance, not only the child's virile procreative abilities but also an ensuing narrative whose recounting will reproduce the child's missing penis and, thereby, the legacy of Hadj Ahmed.[30] Ben Jelloun's novel harmonizes here with Chebel, who writes: "que signifie une circoncision pratiquée par le père sur la personne de son fils, sinon qu'un héritage possible (qu'il soit symbolique ou réel) se transmet à cette occasion ?" [what does a circumcision, carried out by the father on the person of his son, mean other than the passing on of a possible heritage (either symbolic or real) at the moment of the event?] (*Histoire* 124).

Where this scene distances itself from the illusion of performance is in the literal cutting required for the reproduction. As previously mentioned, Hadj Ahmed offers his index finger as the object to be operated: "Figurez-vous qu'il a présenté au coiffeur-circonciseur son fils, les jambes écartées, et que quelque chose a été effectivement coupé, que le sang a coulé, éclaboussant les cuisses de l'enfant et le visage du coiffeur. L'enfant a même pleuré … Rares furent ceux qui remarquèrent que le père avait un pansement autour de l'index de la main droite. Il le cachait bien. Et personne ne pensa une seconde que le sang versé était celui du doigt" [No, his son was presented to the barber-circumciser, the legs were spread, and something was cut. Blood flowed, spattering the child's thighs and the barber's face. The child cried … Very few people noticed that the father had a bandage around the index finger of his right hand. He concealed it very well. And no one thought for a second that the blood they had seen came from that finger!] (32; 21). The tone of this passage veers towards the comical through the *conteur*'s subtle mockery, which is implied in Hadj Ahmed's assumption that a simple bandage will cover the equally simple "quelque chose ... coupé." Yet the tone turns towards the seriously corporeal as the father's plan is carried out through the circumciser's duty – to cut the bodily member presented to him. Desperate for a reproductive, virile heir, and therefore hopelessly devoted to his reading of Arab-Muslim normative narratives, Hadj Ahmed has advanced to the point where he endures an operation that will, as the later female circumcision proves, secure the reproduction not of his financial but of his operating legacy.

The operation of the index finger encourages further reflection on how the operation is truly for the sake of *Hadj Ahmed*'s self-perceived bodily ability. It also becomes a way to understand that the surgical intervention is the means by which he seeks to operate the narrative of his own body and, therefore, find meaning in himself through reproduction. The circumcision becomes for Hadj Ahmed what Barthes refers to, in his discussion of the menace of castration, as the "index du paradigme" [index of the paradigm] (*S/Z* 104; 107). It is the means by which Hadj Ahmed thinks about and points to (with his own index finger) the narrative of Man. In other words, the operation becomes the act in which Hadj Ahmed uses his index finger to redirect the paradigm by pointing away from his reproductive freakishness, what in Barthes's terms can be called the "blessure du manque" [the wound of deficiency] (104; 107). It deviates from the narrative of Man as it points to his ability to reproduce – even if only in word and in gesture – a son.

With the circumcision performed, Hadj Ahmed has presented the object he believes created his "son." It is not his own penis, absent the "right seed," that earlier threatened to castrate his own virility.[31] And it is not his index finger as the understudy to his child's forever missing penis. It is, instead, his "indexe," his paradigm for thinking and living the norms of virility in the Man narrative. In other words, the circumcision does not prioritize the potential for biological reproduction in his produced "son," for Ahmed/Zahra is never capable of having this male bodily ability (despite the fact that, as Chebel and others highlight, this operation suggests the further formation of a man, and, as I argue, it moves the protagonist within the spectrum of procreative abilities) (*Le corps* 82). Rather, the circumcision prioritizes the reaffirmation of Hadj Ahmed's already flaccid virility, not as a man who cannot produce males but as a man who manipulates female bodies into reproducing his goals of legacy, and therefore his child, into a freak of culture and thus *fitna*.

Clearly, Hadj Ahmed's operations are his efforts to at last wield the power and agency typically symbolized by the phallus and the abilities associated with it. Given the emphasis on the child as reproduction of the father's legacy, the somatic centrality of the child in the performance of the circumcision, and the mark of the cutting, it is clear that the operation intends for the biological girl to possess normatively construed male power conceived within the context of the ability to procreate. Ultimately, that operation in the name of Man falls short of its intended goal as it realizes yet another on the body of Woman, continuing to move the protagonist throughout the spectrum of procreative abilities.

CUTTING WOMAN

The normality that Hadj Ahmed operated through his child's feigned circumcision returns in the actual pharaonic clitoridectomy Ahmed/Zahra's sisters perform towards the end of *La nuit sacrée* and in the narrative they use to justify it. Conducted as an act of vengeance, and intended to strip the protagonist of any and all sexual abilities, their operation is represented as nothing short of female genital mutilation. Furthermore, as they ground the act in Arab-Muslim norms of Woman, the sisters operate normality the same way as did Hadj Ahmed and Oum Abbas. Only here they permanently stitch it onto Ahmed/Zahra. They distinctly alter the body parts associated with abilities to biologically reproduce, and they do so by weaving cultural practices into master narratives from other world regions in which Islam is lived and practised. Impeding procreation through a transcultural operation, the sisters' act demonstrates the complex network of norm-based operations that not only target bodily ability to reproduce the freak of culture but also alter abilities into a new state.[32]

In the chapter entitled "Cendre et sang" ["Ashes and Blood"] of *La nuit sacrée*, five of Ahmed/Zahra's seven sisters identify their sibling's whereabouts after an abrupt departure and lengthy absence: Ahmed/Zahra is incarcerated for the murder of an uncle who threatened to reveal the past's secrets to Le Consul, the protagonist's blind male lover introduced earlier in the novel. Embittered by the despotism of their sibling's previous rule of the family home, which crushed their existence, these are the unnamed and thus ever-unrecognized sisters of a similarly unnamed mother, from whom their father had regularly distanced himself (*L'enfant* 17; *Sand* 9).

On a mission the sisters justify through respect of religious tenets ("L'islam, notre guide" [Islam, our guide]), they have come to deny the recognition that Ahmed/Zahra has found in sexual activity with Le Consul. They choose a crushing act similar to the life they have lived: "Mais Dieu fait bien les choses. Quand on s'égare de sa voie, Il vous y ramène à genoux, sur une plaque de fer rougi par le feu. A présent, tout doit rentrer dans l'ordre … [C]e trou on va te le boucher définitivement. On va te faire une petite circoncision, on ne va pas simuler, ce sera pour de bon, il n'y aura pas de doigt coupé, non, on va te couper le petit [sic] chose qui dépasse, et avec une aiguille et du fil on va museler ce trou … Plus de désir. Plus de plaisir" [But God provides. Whoever departs from His path is brought to kneel on a sheet of iron reddened by fire. Now order must be restored … We are going to plug up that hole forever. You're going to have a circumcision. Not fake this time, but real. Not a cut finger. No, we're going to cut off that little thing that sticks out, and muzzle that hole with a needle and thread … No more desire. No more pleasure] (*La nuit* 158–9; *Sacred* 150–1). Clearly, the vengeful sisters seek to efface sexual pleasure and exact physical pain by excising the clitoris and near closing the vagina. Their logic concurs with Janice Boddy's study of similar surgical operations in that the regularly reported effects are pain during intercourse and/or lack of satisfaction (51). Yet, in terms that echo Bouhdiba's study of sexuality, they claim that their act enforces order: "La tradition en islam est un patron culturel idéal. S'y confronter strictement nous garantit d'être dans les voies de Dieu. L'écart est égarement et erreur" [In Islam, tradition is an ideal cultural set of rules. To conform to them strictly ensures that we are in the ways of God. Departure from them is tantamount to straying into error] (11; 2). In claiming to enforce order by obliterating disorder, and in specifying the female genitalia of the sexually active unmarried protagonist as the source of such disorder, the sisters have conceived of their act by invoking certain aspects of a sociocultural narrative.

The sisters' operation echoes those discussed earlier in this chapter, and not just in the repeated reference to circumcision. Here, the premise of disorder they single out stems again from an Arab-Muslim understanding of *fitna* as personified by the sexually active woman who is not wed. The sisters' intent to shut off body parts associated with sexual intercourse, along with their reference to "désir" (desire) and "plaisir" (pleasure), speaks clearly to Ahmed/Zahra's non-marital sexual relations with Le Consul. When the sisters join them to Islam's premise of order, they frame the protagonist as *fitna*. The same argument continues through to the normal order of biological reproduction, where, as also discussed earlier, procreation remains a central purpose of sexual intercourse between married heterosexual couples. Here such reproduction factors into operation: Ahmed/Zahra and Le Consul engage in sexual acts that, in the sisters' narrative as in Ahmed/Zahra's, have desire and pleasure as recurrent goals. Reading the scene in such a light, it becomes apparent that, although the sisters did not inherit their father's financial fortune, they are the heirs of his skills in operation and they reproduce it well.

There are two ways, however, in which the sisters' operation distinguishes itself from their father's and which demonstrate a further operation to narrative and abilities. The first pertains to the sisters' operation of narrative, more specifically to the narrative of Islam they operate. Maghrebian Arab-Muslim sociocultural norms remain an integral component of their operation. By familial extension, their father's narrative also informs theirs as they vengefully reread it. But when they include the practice of female genital cutting, they surpass and expand upon their father's operating legacy. They pull from a non-Maghrebian narrative and, as Jean Déjeux writes, socioculturally integrate the excerpt (276).

In a somewhat problematic scene, Ahmed/Zahra believes – naively and categorically – that the sisters' operation arises from contemporary Sudanese cultural customs of female genital cutting.[33] This conclusion comes from Ahmed/Zahra's efforts in the chapter following the circumcision, entitled "Les oubliés" ["The Forgotten"], where the protagonist attempts to understand the sisters' motivation in a discourse that speaks directly to bodily ability: "La gardienne [de la prison] est une esclave ramenée il y a longtemps du Soudan … Ce fut certainement elle qui suggéra à mes sœurs de me rendre infirme et m'exclure définitivement de la vie" [The guard is a slave brought long ago from the Sudan … It must have been she who suggested to my sisters that they make me an invalid and expel me definitively from life] (163; 155).

Such acts of genital cutting that the protagonist understands as pejoratively disabling are not practised in all regions or by all ethnic groups in Sudan, and they are not categorically associated with individuals self-identifying as Muslim. Those that are so understood often fall into subcategories, such as circumcision to remove the prepuce, clitoridectomy, and infibulation. What Ahmed/Zahra experiences – the excision of only the clitoris and the complete stitching together of the labia to close the vaginal opening – can be read as a slight variation of a pharaonic clitoridectomy and thus an importation of an exterior sociocultural practice.[34] This transcultural operation takes on greater significance with respect to narratives and reproduction if the sociocultural difference implied in the novel is further considered: that some Islamic cultures (e.g., in Sudan) practise forms of genital cutting (and, as Chima Korieh and others argue, for reasons related to sexual customs and virginity that have specific sociocultural implications not only with respect to biological reproduction but also with respect to beauty and family reputation); and that some Islamic cultures (e.g., in Morocco) do not (121). If the discussion focuses not on the ethics of the trans-Islamic distinction of such sociocultural practices but on the distinction itself, then the multilayered representation of the sisters' operation can be understood as revelatory of the agent's equally complex operation. Reaching beyond the borders of Morocco and through the frontiers of another country, the sisters aim to give birth to their vengeance through the discursive and surgical transcultural operation that makes of Ahmed/Zahra a freak of *cultures*.

The second means by which the sisters' operation moves away from the father's and further decentres the already decentred narrative of Ahmed/Zahra is by cutting the protagonist's body in order to cause movement within the spectrum of abilities. By aiming to alter the ability to engage in pleasurable sexual activity through an operation to the genital region, their act takes on both symbolic and corporeal relevance in that it impedes the biological reproduction that the body parts represent and that their father worked to perpetuate. The following citation from the chapter entitled "Cendre et sang" ["Blood and Ashes"] shows how the sisters' vengeful operation – immediately following the sociocultural contextualization provided by one of the sisters – intends to cause pain for both the protagonist and the reader:

> Deux de ses compagnes me ligotèrent les mains sur la table glacée. Elles me déchirèrent mon saroual et levèrent mes jambes en l'air. L'aînée me mit un chiffon mouillé dans la bouche. Elle posa sa main gantée sur mon bas-ventre, écrasa de ses doigts les lèvres de mon vagin jusqu'à faire bien sortir ce qu'elle appelait « le petit chose », l'aspergea d'un produit, sortit d'une boîte métallique une lame de rasoir qu'elle trempa dans l'alcool et me coupa le clitoris. En hurlant intérieurement je m'évanouis.

Des douleurs atroces me réveillèrent au milieu de la nuit ...
Mon sexe était cousu. (159–60)

[Two of her companions tied my hands to the icy table. They tore
off my saraoul and lifted my legs. The guard, who knew the place
well, showed them two hooks in the ceiling and brought them
some rope. My legs were held apart, tied on each side. The oldest
stuffed a damp rag into my mouth. She put a hand on my belly
and crushed the lips of my vagina with her fingers until what they
called "the little thing" came out. They sprinkled it with something, took a razor blade from the metal box, soaked it in alcohol,
and cut off my clitoris. I fainted, screaming inside.

Excruciating pain woke me in the middle of the night ... My
sex was sewn up. (151)]

The same body part that Oum Abbas only digitally operated for the
financial reproduction of her *cirque forain* is here cut off from any
reproduction, and the related procreative abilities are at the very least
symbolically shifted to a new position within the spectrum. Closed,
Ahmed/Zahra's vagina can neither receive nor give forth the life that,
as discussed earlier in this chapter, Arab-Muslim narratives emphasize
as essential to Islam's earthly presence and thus to order. The potential disorder of the newly altered bodily ability also gives way to male
anxiety (similar to the anxiety of the father) even after the stitches
have been removed. Ahmed/Zahra learns that Le Consul had obses-
sively asked health care staff at the prison about potential perturba-
tions of reproductive ability (167; 158). His question further proves
the value (and male ignorance) of such gendered ability in the conservative, norm-based phallocentric Arab-Muslim narrative that Ben
Jelloun's novels recurrently evoke.

With such closure to biological reproduction, the sisters' act runs
contrary to the narrative they recount at the same time as the operation reproduces *fitna*: by prohibiting said reproduction it realizes further deviation from Arab-Muslim and, specifically, Moroccan sociocultural norms of gender and ability. Cutting (off) the ever
unmentionable "chose" and stitching closed the troublesome "trou,"
they, like their father, craft their own disorder-squashing normality
through an operation of the Father's master narratives, their father's
own similarly crafted narrative, and Ahmed/Zahra's body. Operated
beyond all operations, Ahmed/Zahra's body becomes yet again *bid'a*:

the embodiment of unacceptable sociocultural innovation that, shifted to a position of disorderly bodily abilities, is fundamental to the reproduction of the freak of culture. And the scars, along with the abilities moved throughout the reproductive spectrum, remain a written corporeal reminder of the power of operation.

INTERLUDE THREE

Haiti's calamitous 12 January 2010 earthquake tragically killed hundreds of thousands of Haitians and injured many more. Some doctors from various parts of the globe, who had successfully arrived in the devastated regions of the nation, determined that the most efficient cure for profoundly injured limbs was amputation.[1] Many mainstream media outlets tended to emphasize the surgical procedures as life-saving efforts to preserve an individual's existence, particularly that of those who were trapped by rubble. However, the same media organizations and other news forums, along with reports by specialists in social work and medicine and by scholars of the humanities, revealed a different perspective: many of the amputations might well have been hastily conducted on a portion of the estimated two thousand to six thousand individuals (some in "execution," or "guillotine," style) and thus produced unnecessary disabilities and, potentially, subsequent amputations.[2] The over-arching concern was that the removal of the limbs added challenges to previously normative able-bodied Haitian individuals who would now be disabled and find their livelihoods challenged, if not arrested, by the demands of daily living.

The significantly augmented rate of amputation and the resultant increased level of disability, along with the remarkably short domestic supply of prosthetics (which are intended to help restore some of the lost abilities), would become part of the new ways that Haitian citizens would be thought globally and would think locally as they and their nation worked towards its rebuilding. Many Haitian advocates for the disabled, advocates who are themselves disabled and working with the Christian Blind Mission (CBM), recognize the post-

12 January increase in demographics of the disabled as a means for not only rebuilding public structures to include disability access but also rebuilding the national ideology of disability from one of shame to one of equality.

Anne Luze Denestant, a hairdresser who lost her arm and thus one form of livelihood, has begun working alongside other members of CBM to advocate for greater rights for the disabled. Denestant and other working women similarly disabled are now, in the public sphere and the private sphere, both thinking anew and newly understandable within the context of their altered abilities – in some cases for the better and in some cases for the worse.[3] Such a woman, the "poto mitan" (pillar) or the "fanm vayant" (woman of valour) in Haitian creole, must think differently. And they are thought differently in terms of what they might one day produce, be it for themselves, their family, their community, or their country.[4]

$$4$$

Witchy Ways: Transregional Mutilations of Race and Supernatural Abilities in Maryse Condé's *Moi, Tituba sorcière … Noire de Salem*

Quel était ce monde qui avait fait de moi … une paria?
[What kind of a world was this that had turned me into … an outcast?]

Maryse Condé, Moi, Tituba soricière … Noire de Salem

The gods, monsters, and ghosts spawned by racial terminology redefined the supernatural. What colonists called sorcery was, rather, an alternative philosophy.

Joan (Colin) Dayan, Haiti, History, and the Gods

A witch's work speaks of bodies and abilities. At least that's what Maryse Condé's *Moi, Tituba sorcière … Noire de Salem* (1986) [*I, Tituba, Black Witch of Salem* (1994)] conveys in the life it imagines for a largely historically elided enslaved individual who practises supernatural healing arts. The novel's title points to such aspects with its emphasis on Tituba's assigned body colour ("noire" [black]) and a designated name for her abilities ("sorcière" [witch]). As the novel unfolds, readers learn how remarkably important Tituba's body is to the transregional formation of identity that she lives and, thus, how crucial bodily abilities are to identification. A slave for more than half of the novel, she lives the iconoclastic experiences of her historical counterparts – social and psychological denigration, forced manual labour, and beatings.

Tituba is also a multiply charged signifier of economic reproduction. As an enslaved or emancipated "black witch" moving across the forests of Puritan Massachusetts and the plantations of Barbados, Tituba's body comes to symbolize a transregional evil. Her skin colour, "à peine rougeâtre" [far from being light] is a product of her Ashanti mother's rape by an English sailor while sailing across the Middle Passage (18; 6). As such, it represents her biological formation across the races, and, in the context of economic endeavours realized by the colonial machine, results in her inclusion in the "black" race. Many critics have discussed how such aspects of Tituba's identity symbolize, among numerous options, rebellion against oppression through anticolonial or antipatriarchal counterdiscursive strategies, or Condé's own conceptualization of an ambiguous, impermanent creolization arising from blended narratives.

Yet *Moi, Tituba* contains various unexplored ways in which the already racially charged, economically conceived protagonist is identified in relationship to bodily abilities. Such moments are themselves further informed not only by master sociocultural narratives of race and economics but also by those of healing and spiritual practices. Labouring at times as a slave and regularly healing the enslaved, Tituba – body, mind, and soul – is often identified in terms of her abilities to produce treated or healed bodies who find solace in her care but who continue to exist as vessels of labour. Agents use such activity to identify her in terms of her abilities and, as a result, shuttle her discursively through the spectrum of what I call supernatural abilities. Specifically, Tituba's capacities to heal are discursively mutable but supernaturally untouchable. In this process, the agents perceive both her body and her being as at times benevolently abled and enabling and at times (and more often than not) as malevolently disabled and disabling.

The agents' repeated efforts to use and to control her abilities arise from what those abilities are able to reproduce and how it benefits them, be it through labour and the economy or through embodiment of evil and society. Furthermore, the agents' efforts – discussed here as operations to both Tituba and to master sociocultural narratives – make it evident how such ability-charged constructions of identity occur and how, when mixed with constructs of race, they constitute a complex identification process. The course of action is realized from operations most notably to the body, which are always visual and frequently penetrating and mutilating. To realize their goals, the agents operate norm-based master narratives of religion, law, and economics that speak of bodies in the context of race and abilities, with the latter being at times physical but, more often, supernatural. Most certainly, they operate the narratives for their own profit.

As, at times, an agent of such operations, Tituba recounts from a retrospective point of view the entire series of ability-focused operations that reproduce her identity and her narrative. She works to reveal the operations that made of her the exotic witch, a moniker she labours continuously to redefine or at least clarify as *guérisseuse*, or healer. The point of view from which she recounts the agents' operative use of narratives – and, to a degree, the novel's blending of narratives – parallels the agents' own operations of narratives and bodies. Throughout the novel, Tituba contemplates such an identificatory process, providing a term that defines the result of sociocultural intervention when she asks, "Quel était ce monde qui avait fait de moi … une paria?" [What kind of a world was this that had turned me into … an outcast?] (81; 49).[1] Together, Tituba's uses of her varied abilities as a black slave and especially a healer, the operations conducted on and in her, and the narratives created by and related to her are what reveal the perpetually present role of the spectrum of supernatural abilities in processes of her identification. An exotic witch operated discursively and physically across the Caribbean Basin (and especially the Lesser Antilles) and the North American continent, Tituba is the transregional freak of culture.[2]

In this chapter I discuss the ways in which *Moi, Tituba* reveals such an identification process. I begin by exploring how various narratives inform Tituba's identity. Specifically, I examine how the novel and narrative voice show that agents – including Tituba – use discursive operations to realize profit. To understand the context in which narratives connect to certain abilities in the novel, I then explore documents that discuss supernatural healing arts from varying periods and regions of mainland North America and the Caribbean Basin (considered here as one model of transregionality). I also provide a means for discussing such arts in terms of physical, intellectual, and spiritual abilities that are of the entire body and that are dependent on, and at times referred to as, *connaissance*. I also look at how Tituba's recounting of her identification process reveals a very similar interpretation of these supernatural abilities and her body. From there, I examine how Tituba's ability-charged existence closely resembles that of historical freaks of culture, specifically for how she is staged, used, marginalized, and constructed as exotic. Many of these experiences, including the novel's final and fatal mutilation, are the penetrating operations conducted on Tituba's body and in the name of her abilities. They demonstrate the mutual importance of race and bodily ability in efforts to reproduce profit as they highlight Tituba's discursive movement within the spectrum of supernatural abilities that these identity categories simultaneously inform. As it reveals the impermanence of any bodily ability and the transregional dialogue between cultures and narratives, *Moi, Tituba* also expands Judith Halberstam's (1995, 1) argument that "identity and humanity become skin deep" to say that identity and humanity become skin and ability deep.

OPERATING TITUBA NARRATIVES

Tituba's name does not always immediately conjure an image. To gain a better awareness of who she is, listeners most often require a few details: a black slave in Salem inculcated with "voodoo" and interrogated in the 1692 witch trials; a character in Arthur Miller's play, *The Crucible* (1953). At this point, the image of an ignorant, uneducated, almost "primitive" black being confessing crazily to kinship with the Devil (who speaks through a cow) comes to mind – a representation best concretized in Miller's stage directions (*"Negro slave … in her forties"*) and in the following passage: "Devil, him be pleasure-man in Barbados, him be singin' and dancin' in Barbados … (*A bellowing cow is heard*) … Aye, sir! That's him[!] … take me home, Devil! Take me home!" (Miller 7, 113). Even in this preliminary glimpse, Tituba's portrait depends significantly and historically on her body's relationship to both colour (*Negro*) and to spirituality ("Take me home, Devil!").[3]

Scholars and activists have made efforts to clarify what they deemed as unclear in such representations of Tituba. Recent historical research aims at revealing how only one element of this particular tradition is verifiable: Tituba's enslavement. Others, such as her racial origin and her practising of a malefic "witchcraft" (whether English magical folklore, rituals of the Caribbean said to be "voodoo," or a mixture of the two), have either been overturned or reevaluated through the investigation of a variety of historical documents as well as assumptions regarding Caribbean culture. Perhaps the most extensive historical analysis is Elaine Breslaw's *Tituba, Reluctant Witch of Salem: Devilish Indians and Puritan Fantasies* (1996), which calls for an overhaul in recent contemplations of Tituba.[4] She speaks of a rethinking of the previous perspectives in order to take into consideration the geographical displacement and the physical appearance of bodies living in and passing through the Caribbean (92). Breslaw studies trial depositions alongside other documents to reveal Tituba as more than a confessed witch. Moreover, she aims to show that Tituba was a smart if not cunning individual, a woman who consciously confessed to the accusations in front of members of the colonial judicial system in order to cheat certain death (117). Breslaw also makes a strong case for Tituba's biological origins as Arawak and not African, and she then hypothesizes the impact of such origins on Tituba's work as a slave accused of witchcraft. Historically grounded, Breslaw's work cannot go much beyond Tituba's sale in April 1693, after her thirteen-month imprisonment whose purpose was to compensate for her incarceration fees, as she disappears forever from official written records.

However, history is not the only field interested in refocusing the lenses used to view Tituba's body. Certain literary works have zoomed in on Tituba's life, and critics of these works have proposed multiple interpretations of the ways in which, as well as for what, Tituba serves as a metaphor. One reading that addresses Tituba's racial representation and demonstrates its alteration over time is Chadwick Hansen's 1974 article, "The Metamorphosis of Tituba, or Why American Intellectuals Can't Tell an Indian Witch from a Negro."[5] The transformation, Hansen argues, occurs over the course of centuries and appears in the pages of literature. It started when Tituba was first documented in written works, described as an "Indian woman servant" in the 1692 arrest warrant; but then it morphed into the depiction of her as half-Negro/half-Indian in, among others, Henry Wadsworth Longfellow's dramatic text *Giles Corey of the Salem Farms* (1868). The culmination would be her representation as "Negro slave" in Miller's *The Crucible* (1953), which quickly transmits a racial categorization of "black" (Breslaw 110–11; Hansen 6, 10).

Tituba's more recent representations fall in line with a series of works that aim to recover authenticity or, at the very least, agency either for: women of colour, as witnessed in works thematically comparable to *Moi, Tituba*, such as Maya Angelou's *I Know Why the Caged Bird Sings* (1969), Alice Walker's *The Color Purple* (1982), and Toni Morrison's *Beloved* (1987); women from varying regions of the world, as in Mariama Bâ's *Une si longue lettre* (1979) [*So Long a Letter* (1981)], Assia Djebar's *Femmes d'Alger dans leur appartement* (1980) [*Women of Algiers in Their Apartment* (1992)], and Nawal El Saadawi's *Woman at Point Zero* (1975); or women as mystics or witches, as in Marion Zimmer Bradley's *The Mists of Avalon* (1979) or Gregory Maguire's *Wicked* (1995). With respect to Tituba, Anne Petry's *Tituba of Salem Village* (1964) cannot be forgotten, particularly because it recounts through third-person narration and a series of interior monologues the events in Tituba's life leading up to and including the witch trials.

As readers of Condé's work know, *Moi, Tituba* offers the only full (and mostly fictional) representation of Tituba's life, from her conception into earthly matter to her ascension to the spiritual realm. Published in 1986, it is the only such imagination of Tituba to date, and many interviews with Condé point to the reasons she chose to write Tituba's tale. Notable are her conversations with Françoise Pfaff, in which Condé reveals that, in writing the novel, her research proved Tituba to be an individual scandalously "rayée de l'histoire" [crossed out of history] (Condé, "Retour," 91; Condé, "Return," 60). Condé's delight in the writing process, and the lightness she attributes to aspects of the plot, are apparent. However, amidst such statements, readers learn that Condé's frustration with absence of information on Tituba is born of two sources: (1) Condé's own experiences after arriving in California and (2) Condé's claim that no official written narrative of a figure viewed as pivotal to Salem's events of 1692 as Tituba exists outside of the depositions from the trials. For Condé, the claimed scarcity of records implies a lacuna in the official memory of the community. This, to her, was blatantly racist and her inspiration to write the novel: "ce qui m'avait interpellée, c'était le racisme à l'égard de cette femme noire qu'on avait complètement oubliée … Tout cela m'a paru révoltant et j'ai eu le désir de donner une vie à cette occultée, à cette oubliée" [I was mainly interested in the racism affecting this Black woman, who had been completely forgotten … All of this seemed revolting to me, and I wanted to give a life to this obscure and forgotten woman] (91; 60).

VOICE OF NARRATIVE

The implications of race are of profound importance for the present discussion, in part for their further connection to the bodily abilities used for labour and for healing, which many of *Moi, Tituba*'s characters, as operating agents, supposed for Tituba. However, Condé's statement on the racist negligence in written historical documents with respect to Tituba's life, as well as her creation of a full-life narrative for the overlooked individual, demonstrates, at least from the author's perspective, the central place that narrative holds in the novel and in its representations of race and, I would add, ability. Even historians such as Breslaw speak in terms of sociocultural narratives as they liken the tale of Tituba to a process of "creative adaptation" that involves the "transformation of a set of Puritan beliefs and rituals under the influence of a Caribbean culture" (Breslaw 134).

History itself has a particular place with respect to *Moi, Tituba*. In an interview with Ann Armstrong Scarboro, Condé has in no uncertain terms stated that it "is not a historical novel" (200). Nevertheless, historical moments and narratives as they pertain to the disciplines of history and literature run rampant through her work. They also show the long trajectory out of which contemporary ability-charged identities are born, thereby speaking to the present as well.

For these reasons, if for no other, history will inform my approach to Condé's novel. Examples of the varied historical narratives that populate *Moi, Tituba* include: historical documents about Tituba and slavery; oblique references to Condé's personal life (particularly as a subject of onlookers' gawking); intertextual references, such as the inclusion of Hester Prynne from Nathaniel Hawthorne's *The Scarlet Letter* (1850) or the Afro-Caribbean folklore tales that Tituba tells; and the imagining of Tituba's full-life narrative. The presence of such narratives, the movements across them, and the working together and adapting of them into one cohesive transnarrative text correspond to the similarly worked yet differently aimed series of bodily operations in the novel. Historical and fictional agents within the novel, and from across geographical regions, conduct the operative acts with respect to perceived and presented notions of Tituba's race and abilities.

Certainly in the rather serious reading of *Moi, Tituba* unfolding here, the cautions that Nicole Simek as well as Condé herself invoke against taking the novel too seriously should be remembered, given, for example, the recurrent moments of playfulness and parody that frequently appear in Tituba's at times self-undermining voice (Simek 39; Condé "Retour" 90; Condé "Return" 60; Condé "Afterword" 212).[6] I acknowledge such observations and also encourage the recognition of such parodic play, which is itself an operation of the tone and the intent of a text. However, *Moi, Tituba*, like much of Condé's commentary on racism with respect to Tituba, also pushes in very clear ways for the serious reading of narrative. Condé herself states that, in writing the novel, she "hesitated between irony and a desire to be serious" ("Afterword" 201). Marie-Denise Shelton's remarks on Condé's novel speak of how narrative is mobile as well as multiple as it writes certain histories: "With this novel Condé displaces the narrative beyond boundaries, across borders, in an attempt to reconstruct personal and collective history" (720). In other words, the narrative in Condé's novel, as well as the identity arising from it, is not containable – it moves around and about. The narrative and the identity are also multiple and occur multiple times in the recounting of the histories of the individual and the community (which, for my purposes, lean more towards Condé's "desire to be serious").

Although my discussion of the operations to narrative focuses on their multiplicity and their effect, it does not solely address author intent. Specifically, I examine how operations to narrative – including but not primarily certain gestures by Condé – occur explicitly within the novel and how they play a central role in the identification of Tituba. One of the most noticeable means by which narrative is operated and by which characters obtain their profit is though voice, be it the voice of the narrative or the voice of a character.

The reading of voice in the discursive operations to narrative resemble Roland Barthes's theory of the *opérations* of text in that each operating agent, with her own voice, produces her own text.[7] Yet, such operations are also thought in relation to the normative sociocultural histories that inform *Moi, Tituba* and that are represented in a colonial, religious, and transregional context. These recountings inform the narratives, and their voices are read here in ways that echo Edouard Glissant's discussion of national literature and its functions: as "désacralisation" [demythification], which is "démonter les rouages d'un système donné" [to dismantle the internal mechanism of a given system]; or as "sacralisation," which is "rassemblement de la communauté autour de ses mythes" [reuniting the community around its myths] (*Poétique* 329–30; *Caribbean* 99–100). Given that Tituba moves across regions and falls into various narratives, it becomes possible to think the voice in and of narratives and literature not solely in the context of the nation but also across regions. *Moi, Tituba* is then one example (among many) of Condé's efforts to destabilize myths and mysteries of transregional histories. Dawn Fulton's words on Condé's work underscore this tendency: "the gesture of demystification marked her career early on" (17).[8] Such a statement carries great weight with respect to the crucial role of narrative voice (in particular Tituba's voice) in that it troubles the myths and mysteries of race and bodily abilities but also of narrative itself.

Before even beginning *Moi, Tituba*'s first chapter, readers learn exactly how voice connects to the operations of narrative when Condé emphasizes this rapport by operating herself into the narratives of

Tituba. In a preface that reads as the first page, Condé playfully claims to have received the tale from Tituba first-hand: "Tituba et moi, avons vécu en étroite intimité pendant un an. C'est au cours de nos interminables conversations qu'elle m'a dit ces choses qu'elle n'avait confiées à personne" [Tituba and I lived for a year on the closest of terms. During our endless conversations she told me things she had confided to nobody else] (7; iii). Such a statement, particularly the use of the verbs "dire" and "confier," alludes to an intergenerational tradition of oral narrative represented in the novel through the tale-telling that Tituba, her mother, and even her grandmother reproduce in a lineage of which Condé now becomes a part (14; 3–4).[9] However, Condé's inscription is, as her conversations with Pfaff suggest, a self-confessed *clin d'oeil* regarding the author's inspiration to write and, thereby, to imagine (and playfully so) the text: "L'inspiration 'surnaturelle' existe puisqu'on a soudain envie d'écrire à propos d'une créature totalement imaginaire qu'on n'arrive jamais à rencontrer, qui n'existe pas" ["Supernatural" inspiration does exist in a sense, since you suddenly feel like writing about a totally imaginary creature whom you have never seen or met, and who doesn't exist] (Condé "Retour" 89; Condé "Return" 59).

Condé's playfulness and creation with her voice can then be read in terms of narrative operations as her *own* supernatural abilities – where the preface may well refer to, for example, the archival research on Tituba and to the personal reflections on both of their lived experiences.[10] The operations arise from Condé's intentional blending of narratives during the writing process, in which she playfully alludes to creation, which Carla Peterson explains as follows: "Pour raconter l'histoire des Africains dans le Nouveau Monde, l'écrivaine a recours à l'adaptation, à la substitution, à la contrefaçon même, tout comme cette population asservie qui peuple son roman" [In order to write the story of Africans in the New World, the writer has recourse to adaptation, to substitution, to counterfeiting even, just like the enslaved population that fills her novel] (101).

The operations also suggest a certain authority over the narrative and its voice, which allows Condé to realize a work that she herself believes should be read not simply in the context of its historical references to the Americas and slavery: "Je voulais montrer que les intolérances, les préjugés et le racisme dont Tituba est victime, existent encore dans l'Amérique contemporaine. *Moi, Tituba, sorcière ... Noire de Salem* est un roman d'aujourd'hui, ce n'est pas du tout un roman historique" [I wanted to show that the intolerance, prejudice, and racism that victimized Tituba still exist in contemporary America. *I, Tituba, Black Witch of Salem* is not a historical novel, it's about the present] (Condé, "Retour," 96; Condé, "Return," 64). Simek maintains that Condé's fictional work, like literature in general, is plastic enough to make it "a vital means for elucidating the present" (68). Condé herself writes in similar terms of the reproductive potential of the novel in *Le roman antillais* (1977) [*The West Indian Novel*]: it is a way of finding in the "passé l'image du présent" [past the image of the present] (15). Kaiama Glover's words on narrative and voice, as readable in the preface as well as the novel's epilogue, bring clarity to the discussion of authority and temporality: "Condé foregrounds this precise question of narrative authority in *I, Tituba* by positing and then stepping categorically away from generic conventions. She bookends 'Tituba's' account with clear assertions of her own authorial voice, keeping the reader very much unbalanced with respect to a 'her-story' that both formally and thematically straddles the past and the present" (101). Clearly *Moi, Tituba* must also be understood in relationship to its contemporaneous, if not timeless, commentary on the operation of narrative.

The narrative voice of *Moi, Tituba* – and the voice *of* Tituba – emphasizes how such operations pertain most evidently to the human body by detailing numerous harmful operations to characters' bodies, including the protagonist's own body. As such, the text accomplishes yet another goal Condé puts forth in her conversations with Pfaff: "j'écris … toujours pour provoquer les gens, pour les obliger … à regarder des choses qu'ils n'ont pas envie de regarder" [I write … to provoke people, to force them … to see things they don't want to see] (Condé, "Vie," 50; Condé, "Plural," 30). Recounted in retrospect, the novel makes readers see first-hand the forced operations, such as exploitation, mutilation, rape, and beatings, that were typical of the institution of slavery at the core of the colonial endeavour but that, as Condé and others insist, can be read as manipulations that are also relevant to contemporary contexts.

Of course, trusting the words of Tituba as her own *conteuse* gives reason for pause. As Gerald Prince regularly and wisely asks, can the words of any first-person narrator – and especially one who is the protagonist – be trusted?[11] All comments on the novel as parody aside, I suggest that, given Tituba's retrospective admissions of occasional manipulation of text, use of irony, and disregard over whether she cares what readers think of her words, her words can be taken quite seriously. Such an interpretation becomes further plausible given that Tituba, in telling her tale, has an interest in setting certain records straight by making her story known and creating a history for herself. It is this effort that speaks most directly to the questions of narrative and voice, particularly regarding how the words of her tale reveal processes of identification grounded in race and bodily ability.

Condé did, of course, say that her novels force readers to see what they do not wish to see. In my reading, the unseeable is the operative acts that characters like Tituba endure. Narrative voice is one of the primary means for confronting readers with the physical and psychological pain of such operations because it renders them increasingly subjective and therefore personal as it situates them within Condé's own version of history. One such moment appears in the first words of the novel, when the reader learns that an English sailor raped Tituba's Ashanti mother: "Abena, ma mère, un marin anglais la viola sur le pont du *Christ the King*, un jour de 16** alors que le navire faisait voile vers la Barbade. C'est de cette agression que je suis née. De cet acte de haine et de mépris" [Abena, my mother, was raped by an English sailor on the deck of *Christ the King* one day in the year 16** while the ship was sailing for Barbados. I was born from this act of transgression. From this act of hatred and contempt] (13; 3). Obviously, Tituba did not witness the violent and penetrating operation that her mother suffered; however, the protagonist uses her voice to testify to the aggression that her mother lived, an aggression regularly realized through, and often at the sight of, the slave's body, and that was told in turn to the protagonist. Such testimonial produced in the words of the fictional Tituba reveals how the body becomes and remains the recurrent vessel in the discourse surrounding such narrative operations as well as how the sight of the body leads to and culminates in penetrating, mutilating operations of it.

However, the first-person narration does not simply create voice and emphasize the body and its centrality to narrative. A form of testimonial intermingled with commentary, Tituba's narrative voice also underscores perspective by highlighting cultural practices and experiences (in this case represented as historical) and, thereby, making known the text's own ability to reveal differences in practices. Such recounting recalls Glissant's theory of the production of narratives as a means of maintaining the existence of not only peoples but also of their sociocultural practices.[12] One of Lydie Moudileno's arguments concerning the writing in Condé's novels posits that the recounting, as Glissant reads it, works as an echo and a product of the plantation, a concept Glissant posited in earlier work as the "culture populaire du temps du système des Plantations" [popular culture of the era of the Plantation] (Glissant, *Le discours*, 310).[13] Recounting was what many slaves had done for centuries in order to survive the atrocities of their production-based existence – atrocities that realized the plantation's own reproduction. In speaking of the narrative practice of cultural reproduction, Moudileno speaks metaphorically in terms of reproductive abilities when she refers to the plantation and its potential for fecundity as a "matrice" [womb] (145).

One of the recurrent means by which *Moi, Tituba* emphasizes perspective through sociocultural reproduction involves the telling of tales that are of Afro-Caribbean origin. Recalling the adventures of many characters known for their extraordinary abilities, both Tituba's mother and Tituba herself recount stories theorized as necessary to their ability to survive physical labour in the houses or on the plantations where they work (14, 70; 3–4, 42).[14] To recount, the storyteller must of course use her voice. However, that is not what is of greatest importance here; rather, what is of importance is the fact that Tituba uses her voice as narrator to regularly underscore the Afro-Caribbean origins of the tales and, in so doing, to turn the reader's attention towards a specific sociocultural perspective.

Another means by which voice creates such perspective appears in Tituba's revealing the origin and, more specifically, the benevolent intent of her malevolently represented abilities as a *guérisseuse* (healer). The knowledge behind Tituba's faculties had been passed on for generations, and it finds its way into her existence through Man Yaya. Peterson maintains that such acts were part of Condé's intended representation of Tituba: "insister sur le fait que son savoir ésotérique est celui d'une guérisseuse qui se place au service de son peuple" [to insist on the fact that her esoteric knowledge is that of a healer who puts herself at the service of her people] (101).[15] Like the tales, the narrative voice reveals to the reader through Tituba's explanation that such practices – especially those of healing – are neither abnormal nor evil. Rather, they are of another cultural background and their goals are palliative. Together the tales entertain and distract whereas the healing practices offer care if not cure.

In addition to underscoring perspective, narrative voice in *Moi, Tituba* highlights agency through the representation of multiple agents who use their voices to transmit and to operate narrative. At times, such operations aim to enhance the narrative through strategic references to extraordinary bodily abilities. Specifically, Tituba's contemplative narration discloses how agents of all backgrounds use discursive and rhetorical procedures to operate narratives in order to realize reproduction for their own profit. One example appears in Tituba's reference to the recounting of the myth of Ti-Noël, the escaped slave who counters and foils slavemasters' plans, whose tale members of the Barbadian slave and maroon communities keep alive. Ti-Nöel is never the "vieillard" (old man) who, based on the passage of chronological time, Tituba supposes he would be: "Depuis le temps qu'il vivait dans les imaginations, ce devait être un vieillard" [He had been living in everyone's imagination for so long that he must have been an old man by now] (221; 143). Instead, Tituba shows that he remains what the members of the communities want and need him to be: a legend they reproduce in order to maintain hope and, in certain ways, a saviour, a liberating and extraordinarily able-bodied individual. They emphasize abilities ascribed to the young and the indomitable, and thereby remove from him any potentially limiting or even disparaging character traits or physical qualities: "on lui prêtait jeunesse et audace et on se répétait ses hauts faits: 'Le fusil du Blanc ne peut pas tuer Ti-Noël. Son chien ne peut pas le mordre. Son feu ne peut pas le brûler. Papa Ti-Noël, ouvre-moi la barrière!'" [he was said to be young and bold and his exploits had become household legends: The white man's gun cannot kill Ti-Noel. His dog cannot bite him. His fire cannot burn him. Open up the gate, Papa Ti-Noel] (221; 143).

The most obvious manifestation of agency resides in the attribution of voice to Tituba. The gesture appears explicit even in its first and perhaps clearest form, the novel's title, *Moi, Tituba sorcière ... Noire de Salem*. Peterson speaks of such representation as an "affirmation de volonté" [affirmation of will] and as a "prise de conscience radicale" [radical awareness] (102). However, it is Isabel Carrera Suárez who speaks of it in terms of a discursive strategy: "The main strategy is that of giving the voice and the text to Tituba herself, presenting her as author of the narrative ... The agenda of recovering her story is explicit in the narration, as Tituba herself describes at length her fear of being forgotten in history" (147). Through such a realization of self, Tituba shows, in addition to her fears, the ways that she also operates narratives – including master sociocultural narratives – with the intent to profit from her actions.

One example of this type of operation appears in the production of vengeance, which Tituba wishes to exact on Susanna Endicott, her second mistress. As the mistress of John Indian and (by marriage) of Tituba, Susanna, in an effort to maintain control over Tituba's enslaved body, aims to intimidate her with presumed knowledge of her past: "N'as-tu pas été élevée par une certaine négresse Nago, sorcière de son état et qui s'appelait Man Yaya? … John Indien est-il au courant de tout cela?" [Weren't you brought up by a certain Nago witch called Mama Yaya? … Does John Indian know about all this?"] (48; 26). Here Susanna works to manipulate Tituba by referring to the very bank of supernatural abilities that are associated with the protagonist as well as by inferring how they – as the purportedly clandestine craft of a "sorcière" (witch) – might prove problematic if exposed.

Tituba's own operation of narrative with respect to this moment in the novel becomes apparent when she later recounts how she conversed with Man Yaya regarding how to use her supernatural abilities in order to avenge herself. During the conversation, Man Yaya reminds her that a certain master narrative of their craft exists, explaining to Tituba the philosophy behind their abilities: "Ne te laisse pas aller à l'esprit de vengeance. Utilise ton art pour servir les tiens et les soulager" [Don't let yourself be eaten up by revenge. Use your powers to serve your own people and heal them] (51; 29). In this one moment, Tituba highlights how she operates narrative for her own benefit as well as how the discursive operation alters the master narrative of supernatural abilities. She moves it away from what she had previously iterated ("J'étais faite pour panser" [I was born to heal]), only to later operate it again after her death as she returns to the philosophy of Man Yaya and those before her: "Car, vivante comme morte, visible comme invisible, je continue à panser, à guérir" [For now that I have gone over to the invisible world I continue to heal and cure] (26, 268; 12, 175).

As much as the narrative voice funnelled through Tituba becomes the means by which she admits to her own operations, it also emphasizes the operative acts that external agents conduct, the ways in which their profit-centred operations cut deeply, and Tituba's awareness of the operations. In Susanna's same efforts to control Tituba, she relies upon and repeats to her what she learned from her friends about the protagonist's rearing: that Man Yaya was, as reread through the colonial lens, a witch and not a healer. Where the narrative discloses Susanna's capacity for operating narrative to her own benefit is in

Tituba's description of Susanna during her catechism lesson, the same interaction referenced above. Susanna uses her knowledge of Man Yaya as leverage: "Susanna Endicott eut un sourire qui signifiait que toutes ces arguties étaient de peu de poids … Son sourire s'aiguisa et ses lèvres minces et décolorées palpitèrent: – John Indien est-il au courant de tout cela? … Elle rebaissa les yeux sur son livre" [Susanna Endicott smiled as if all these niceties bore little weight and went on … She smiled knowingly and her thin, colorless lips fluttered. 'Does John Indian know about all this?' … Her eyes dropped back to her book"] (47–8; 26–7). Through a knowing smile and a subtle gaze at the book Tituba knows to be Susanna's sacred text, and thus physical testament to a master sociocultural narrative of religion, Susanna demonstrates her authority. In this one moment of operation, she allows three narratives to come together to benefit herself: the narrative of Man Yaya, which she learned from her friends; the narrative of slave labour so deeply woven into the colonial project that slaveowners such as Susanna worked to perpetuate it through efforts to save "savage" slaves with catechism lessons; and the narrative that a Christian-informed colonial enterprise maintained through spell-casting witches who embodied, by partaking in a calamitous "commerce avec Satan" [commerce with Satan], a threat to the religiously and culturally charged hierarchy (48; 27). The words on Susanna's lips and at her fingertips are the tools she uses to conduct such rhetorical procedures in her operation of Tituba and the sociocultural narratives used to identity her as a slave of questionable abilities.

Through these examples, it becomes clear how voice is one of the primary means by which agents conduct their discursive operations in Condé's novel as well as how it presents the operations to the reader. Condé, Tituba, and the operating agents in the novel all use their various voices to adapt existing master narratives to reproduce their individualized and collective goals. The various narratives – the historical, the contemporary, the racialized, the healing, the colonial, the Christian (and, as shown later, the Puritan of New England colonies) – are what the agents operate together and what Tituba relates. What the reader is left with, it seems, is similar to what Julie Nack Ngue wisely observes about truth and history with regard to other works by Condé: "The reader … is left to assume that Condé espoused another sort of truth – subjective, contingent, fragmentary, contradictory – a truth without norms or rules, a truth which may allow for the production of new composite histories" (*Critical* 75). However, through Tituba's recounting of such operations, voice relates – with its own dose of operation – how she is defined in terms of what her racialized, spiritualized, and even vilified body is said to be able (and not to be able) to do within and across regions (as she moves from Salem to Barbados and back).

SPEAKING OF RACE

What are the master narratives, then, that guide and inform such representations of Tituba as they relate to the spectrum of supernatural abilities and their relationship to constructs of race? And how can they be spoken of within the context of a pariah or a freak of one culture when two geographical spheres are represented and multiple historical periods are referenced? The answer appears in the novel itself and the narratives it contains: those that formed the colonial system and that, in many ways, continue to inform many of the nation-states born of such a system.[16] Thinking of the novel's geographical spaces as representations of contemporary regions, it becomes apparent how depicting the operations that reproduce Tituba as a freak of culture also speak metaphorically of the sociocultural narratives of race and bodily ability. More specifically, it helps to demonstrate how at least some members of these regions identify themselves and other individuals through the sociocultural narratives that they operate. Fulton expresses similar thoughts with respect to Titubua's social marginalization in one of the novel's historical contexts: "While [Tituba] faces the most ostensible forms of social exclusion in the racist communities of colonial New England, she is no less an outcast in her native land of Barbados or even among her fellow slaves" (40). Because Tituba, as both a character and a narrative, resides in yet moves across such cultural and geographical spaces, she can eventually come to be understood as a transregional and transcultural freak of race and bodily abilities. As if by design, the protagonist's name nods to this role: in the simple past tense, *elle tituba* – she moves and stumbles between the narratives and the cultures that work to operate her.

Understanding more fully the operative context within which Tituba as a freak arises requires a second look at the various master sociocultural narratives in the novel. The narratives are implicitly connected to the forms of reproduction that the external agents pursue in their operations. To borrow the words of Moudileno, who describes the composition of the cast of writer/characters in Condé's series of

Guadeloupe-based novels, Tituba (and virtually any other protagonist of Condé's fiction) is a character who has been "soumis[e] à des déterminations historiques, sociales et culturelles" [submitted to historical, social, and cultural determination] (144). Ylva Hernlund and Bettina Shell-Duncan concur: "As bodies move through … different domains, they become subject to regimes that intersect in varied and sometimes contradictory ways" (3). With Moudileno's qualification in mind and Hernlund and Shell-Duncan's emphasis on the body, the discussion of *Moi, Tituba* becomes more productive when conducted across several disciplines that address the varying physical, labouring abilities Tituba demonstrates as a slave and her supernatural abilities as a healer.

From the eighteenth century to and beyond the decolonization of the 1960s, writers, politicians, and everyday citizens worked, with varying degrees of fervour, to challenge the discursive representations and lived operations of the colonized black body. In *The Invention of Africa: Gnosis, Philosophy, and the Order of Knowledge* (1988), V.Y. Mudimbe's inquiry into the origin and existence of an African philosophy depends on the history of colonial developments. In particular, he explores how the nineteenth- and twentieth-century scramble for Africa contributed to the forming and deforming of the African continent of the 1980s. His discussion of the normalizing long-term impact of external, Western operators on the lands and peoples of Africa, without ignoring the contribution of indigenous populations to such operations, remains relevant today.[17] Mudimbe offers proof of his argument by discussing how the colonizers obtained their goals through "the domination of physical space, the reformation of *natives'* minds, and the integration of local economic histories into the Western perspective" (2).[18] Mudimbe states that these complementary projects form what might be considered the colonizing structure, an entity that "completely embraces the physical, human, and spiritual aspects of the colonizing experience" and that can be said, at least here, to envision the reproduction of the empire (2).

Mudimbe's words on Western anthropological descriptions of the "primitive" in relation to colonial development take on increased importance for my argument as it suggests the reproduction of social identity as informed by multiple sources: it is "ideological … and concerns the relationship between an individual's projection of consciousness, the norms exemplified by one's society, and the social or the scientific dominant group" (17). Later, I demonstrate the accuracy of Mudimbe's quote with regard to describing Tituba's encounters with the individuals who operate the master sociocultural narratives and her body's. Here, however, Mudimbe's reading of the primitive as a key factor in the establishment of the superiority of the white race and in the justifying the development of European structures in "'virgin areas'" becomes pivotal. It demonstrates not only the now long-standing critical reading of the central need to reproduce the primitive but also the identification of the primitive in relationship to the master sociocultural narrative used to "assign to things and beings both their natural slots and social mission" (17). Certainly Mudimbe's words speak to the civilizing mission that he and many others continue to discuss as the recurrent means by which European empires operated the populations they came to govern and, in many cases, to sell. Not surprisingly, one goal of such operations was to reproduce a narrative of a primitive who, as both discursive construct and living body, helped an empire to realize its intended profits. The resultant flourishing would be both economic and ideological, and it would come from the "physical, human, and spiritual aspects" that fuelled such colonial projects.

Within the French colonial enterprise and its importation of African bodies to the Caribbean Basin, the historical significance of the *corps nègre* (black body) as a physical non-intellectual, even non-human, body speaks (much as does Mudimbe's work on the primitive) to similar (if not the same) forms of reproduction. The body, in the context of Condé's novel, includes all variations of skin colour, as exemplified not only in the novel's title *Moi, Tituba sorcière ... Noire de Salem* but also in characters' recurrent references to Tituba's "rougeâtre" skin colour. Despite the variation, she is always a "négresse" [Negress] (33; 16). There is also the self-assigned descriptor of "à peine rougeâtre" (due to the English sailor who raped her Ashanti mother), which places Tituba within the twentieth- and twenty-first century terminology of *métisse* (mixed race).[19]

First and foremost it must be noted that the enslaved bodies of African descent residing in the lands of the French colonial empire when slavery was legalized (from the early seventeenth century until, at least officially, the final abolition of slavery in 1848), and constituting the majority of the African-descended population, were legislatively and juridically not human. Article 44 of the first version of the *code noir* (1685) (*The Black Code*) reads: "Déclarons les Esclaves être meubles" [We declare slaves to be chattel].[20] As the founders of Negritude put forth in the 1920s and 1930s, and as Aimé Césaire decried later in *Discours sur le colonialisme* (1955) [*Discourse on Colonialism* (1972)], the black body read as *nègre* remained, generally speaking, both a constantly negotiated yet perpetually needed signifier of the ability to produce manual labour.[21] It was also an acceptable and accepted symbol of a categorically misunderstood if not dismissed *civilisation nègre* (black civilization) with little to no intellectual worth. As other works of Césaire's, like *Cahier d'un retour au pays natal* (1939), demonstrate, *le corps nègre* was commanded to be physically able and condemned to be intellectually disabled.[22] Colonial discourse even worked to render such cultural distinctions inalterable and, thereby, as Francis Affergan's work (1991) on similar forms of colonial discourse's perpetuation of hierarchization shows, prohibits (even as it proposes) assimilation (22–3).

In *The French Atlantic Triangle* (2008), Christopher Miller testifies to the strategic use of racially charged terminology such as *nègre*. One poignant example appears in his discussion of eighteenth-century dramatic texts, in which he comments on slavery. He focuses on how playwrights such as abolitionist Olympe de Gouges composed their own works, at times strategically employing racially charged referents such as *sauvages* (savages), *esclaves* (slaves), and *nègres* in descriptions of characters. Miller argues that revised versions of her works, such as *L'esclavage des noirs* (1792) [*Black Slavery*], demonstrate signs of strategic operations in which "sauvages" become "nègres" (125). Given Gouges's political positioning, such a gesture appears to be an attempt to bring the audience directly into the then contemporary debates about slavery and efforts at abolition. However, Miller points out that, in the earlier version of *L'esclavage*, entitled *Zamore et Mirza* (1788) [*Zamore and Mirza*], the terminology was "written all over the play but between the lines and with confusion" (126). Such representation, Miller argues, demonstrates how "eighteenth-century ideas of race were somewhat fluid" when compared to those of the mid-nineteenth century, particularly in the years following Arthur de Gobineau and the Saint-Hilaires (123).

Miller does caution against a facile conflation of eighteenth-, nineteenth-, and twentieth-century conceptions of race. As an example, he highlights the slippery use of terminology in the eighteenth century, which moved between multiple references of racial categories and enslavement ("it is as if slavery *were* race here"), as opposed to the more concretized reference to groups of different racial categories in the later nineteenth century (124). Within the late eighteenth-century context, Miller points out how Gouges's use of such terms and rhetorical operations in the later version of the play maintained a master-over-slave hierarchy of which the *nègre* was certainly a factor (126, 131, 128). Most directly, he states, based on his reading of Gouges's own commentary on the newer version of the play, that the text "does encourage submission [of slaves], and it does tread softly on the question of actual abolition" (131). Miller's discussion reveals that, even at the doorstep of the burgeoning new definitions of the individual and one of the most notable modern efforts at liberating and theorizing Western humankind – the French Revolution of 1789 – the construct of the *nègre* as part of the French colonial empire, remained both fluid and problematic. Specifically, it persisted in the hearts and minds of liberty- and equality-minded individuals as an unintentional means of maintaining subjugation and of ignoring the very real traffic between Africa and the Caribbean.

Where Miller's work speaks of enslaved black bodies, others speak of the black body in terms of physical abilities and what such an ability-charged body could, would, or should reproduce. In *La force noire* (1910) [*Black Force*], French army general Charles Mangin argues that an exceptional physical ability to engage in battle resides in the very physiology of the black body due to a supposed constant engagement in war throughout the existence of the *race nègre* (225–6). His goal was to justify the deployment of troops from the colonies (notably from West Africa), composed of bodies he maintained were biologically and culturally programmed to wage war, in France's military operations. Focusing on abilities to engage in battle, Mangin's argument testifies to the continued operation of narratives of race and ability that work to include in the colonial discourse of the black race the capacity to fight – a very valued capacity at a time when European nations were desperately competing to reproduce their empires.

Throughout *Femmes des Antilles* (1998) [*Antillean Women*], Gisèle Pineau and Marie Abraham speak in part about the value of marketed black bodies (specifically, enslaved female bodies) to the narratives used to realize production: "chacune des parties du corps" [each of the body parts] were measured and evaluated to determine "l'étendue des profits" [the extent of profit] (64). Many of the body parts to which Pineau and Abraham refer have themselves, because of their associations with the black body, been read in relation to (and thus seen as revelatory of) abilities.

The racialized body's connection to abilities continued to appear in the sciences. Lennard Davis's *Bending over Backwards* speaks of how, well into the twentieth century, the black body corresponds directly to the notion of parts. Davis shows that, in contemporary scientific circles, there is a polemic about race and fundamental body "parts" – that is, DNA – with some researchers maintaining that certain genetic predispositions to disability are specific to established racial or ethnic categories (15).[23] The nineteenth-century expansion of craniometry as a science by which to measure human intellect also gives evidence to scientific categorization. It includes work by Samuel George Morton in the United States and Georges Vacher de Lapouge in France. Etienne Geoffroy Saint-Hilaire's assessment of Saartje Baartman, the "Hottentot Venus," also culminates in primate-like comparisons and, thus, the demarcation of a lesser intelligence.

The "Hottentot Venus" concept serves as a transition to another example of the body's abilities – sexual capacities – as discussed by Sander Gilman in *Difference and Pathology* (1985). Gilman studies the iconography of black sexuality (particularly black female sexuality) as frequently read in one of its salient icons of the nineteenth century: the large buttocks and presumed large genitalia of Baartman and the other women identified by scientists as "Hottentot Venus." According to Gilman's summary of earlier work by eighteenth-century French naturalist Buffon, such body parts signalled a "lascivious apelike sexual appetite" on the part of black women (83). In *Black Venus* (1999), T. Denean Sharpley-Whiting probes the records of Georges Cuvier, the French anatomist who examined and later dissected Baartman, and provides findings similar to Buffon's. She notes how the dissection was what Cuvier believed revealed the "hidden secrets" (and thus "missing links") in existing research on varied species and of sexuality (26–7).

As a barometer of abnormal sexuality, Gilman argues, Baartman's and other similarly racialized bodies became the contrapuntal yet operative means by which norms of sexual activity were reproduced for white women, who were placed higher in a racial hierarchy than were black women. The unread yet richly inscribed genitalia of the black women were now encoded not only as corporeal sign but also as biological catalyst of the ability to fulfill a lascivious sexual appetite. As a result, the body for which the genitalia served as synecdoche became the embodiment of heightened and deviant sexual abilities. More specifically, the body and the genitalia became the sign

for abnormal psychological behaviour and, therefore, abnormal apti-
tudes or capacities that form and inform sexual practices and that, today, can be thought in terms of a disability (83).[24]

CONNAISSANCE AND THE CORPOREAL PRACTICE
OF SUPERNATURAL ABILITIES

Such conventionally conceived Western notions of bodily abilities are
linked in various ways to what the body is able to produce and,
through operation, reproduce: intelligence, sex, labour, and disability,
to name a few. Cumulatively, they speak to what Paul Gilroy, in
Against Race (2000), proposes as a rethinking of "race" that is not
strictly limited to postcoloniality and that informs efforts to de-
essentialize the use of such terminology as well as to explore contexts
not strictly limited to colonial or postcolonial conditions.

However, there were and are other abilities that agents of Western
sociocultural structures often associate with the black body through
discursive and, at times, mutilating operations: non-Western healing
capacities, here referred to as supernatural abilities in accordance with
Tituba's role as a *guérisseuse*. Already the body of slaves, seen as dark
and often black, had been read as evil within cultures informed by
European Christian traditions that linked malevolent spiritual forces
to darkness, as evident in the discussion of Puritan traditions.[25]

I want to speak of the ways in which such practices are associated
with the racialized body and how they may be and actually have been
read as bodily abilities. This is not an effort to argue that the varied
systems of practices are essentially the same; rather, it is a gesture towards recognizing the ways in which bodies and abilities are an
integral part of various practices. As a result of the random blending
of individuals and spiritual practices from various regions of Africa
and their encounter with the spiritual practices of indigenous populations and the religious customs of the colonizers, such spiritual
disciplines are said to have adapted to or transformed slave trade
environments spanning the Caribbean Basin.

Today, there are many syncretic religions that include supernatural
abilities in their practices, such as Haitian Vodou, Louisiana Voodoo,
Obeah, Santería, and Umbanda. Each practice contains its own set of
rituals and rules, certain of which focus on and engage the wholeness
of the human body (mind, body, soul).[26] At times, these religions are
also associated with evil (much as in *Moi, Tituba*). The distinctions

between good (or "healing") and evil (or "harmful") have numerous origins, some of them within the slave communities. However, what resonates is a connection due to a common experience. According to Patrick Bellegarde-Smith, supernatural practices may have different names but they all possess similarities arising from the encounter with slavery (27).

Much of the research conducted to date argues that most forms of supernatural abilities demonstrate varied origins in SubSaharan African traditions due to the surviving enslaved individuals who adapted to their new environments. Some studies argue that the blending was caused by the historical influx of African bodies across the Middle Passage. In *La parole des femmes* (1993) [*The Women's Word*], Condé acknowledges a similar blend in the francophone regions of the Caribbean: "les esclaves arrivaient aux Antilles avec tout un tissu de croyances et de pratiques qui tant bien que mal s'intégraient à la religion catholique imposée. En Haïti, cela donne le vodou. Dans les petites Antilles, le quimbois" [slaves arrived in the Caribbean with a host of beliefs and practices that more or less integrated into the imposed Catholic religion. In Haiti, this gave way to Vodou. In the West Indies, *quimbois*] (48–9).[27]

The African-origin slave population was not the only sociocultural group in the Lesser Antilles to have observed such practices and to have blended their own with indigenous practices. Historical studies posit that the indigenous populations, the Carib and the Arawak, engaged in spiritual and healing practices that also focused on body, mind, and soul. In *Les petites Antilles avant Christophe Colomb* (1984) [*The Lesser Antilles Prior to Christopher Columbus*], Christian Montbrun traces the geographical and anthropological history of Guadeloupe and the Lesser Antilles in general, including the rituals associated with the "coutume et croyance" [custom and belief] of the Carib populations. Each branch is said to have practised localized versions of the rituals, and certain of these practices, such as initiations and funerals, would involve a majority, if not all, of the bodies in the community (120, 123, 130).

In *Tituba, Reluctant Witch of Salem*, Breslaw argues that similar trends existed in the late seventeenth-century Arawak population of South America as well as in the African slave population of Barbados, especially with regard to spiritual and healing practices that she speaks of in terms of religion: "Both groups believed that sickness and misfortune were brought by supernatural forces and could be cured by magical means; religious ritual was closely associated with medical practice" (50). The incorporation of the body in the use of such abilities is associated with the supposition that these practices involved trances on the part of the supernatural healer (122, 129). Breslaw implies that practices of the indigenous populations and those of African-based origins could well have blended in the first years of contact, when members of both sociocultural groups were made to work together and before most of the indigenous population disappeared. Phillipe Delisle (1996) suggests a similar coming together of practices in the French Lesser Antilles of the nineteenth century: with the influx of Chinese and East Indian populations in the decades after France's 1848 abolition of slavery, certain elements of the religious practices of the newly arrived groups – especially the Hindus, whose faith included a universe filled with "forces occultes, de sorciers et d'exorcistes" [occult forces, of medicine men and exorcists] – eventually blended with existing practices (76).[28]

As the developing and contemporary versions of the blended practices recall individuals' operations to such spiritual and healing narratives, the spiritual practices themselves are concerned with a mastering of the body as a conduit for human existence. As such, they can also be said to speak to capacities of the human body, and recent work on contemporary practices provides a means for thinking about the relevance of bodily abilities to spirituality. In his discussion of practices that likely informed those of colonial Barbados, Jerome Handler writes that they concentrated on the connections between body, mind, and spirit and, thus, encompassed "the whole person" (60). Christiane Bougerol's study of the *voyant-guérisseur* in Guadeloupe reveals how supernatural abilities are "innés" [inherent] to bodies of individuals predisposed to them, and how they sometimes manifest themselves as physical illness in those who refuse to accept their calling (134). Guérin Montilus writes that particular body parts, such as the head and feet, as points of entry and exit, are most associated with abilities to engage in the practices of Haitian Vodou, (or, as he spells it, "Vodun"). He also emphasizes the importance of the entire body: "The notion of person as a symbol of and for human consciousness … is distributed throughout the body as a whole" (2).

More specifically related to Condé's Tituba as a *guérisseuse noire* are the bodies of the healers – be they a *manbo* of Haitian Vodou, a *pai-de-santo* of Santería, or, in the increasingly more obscure tradition of the French Lesser Antilles, a *quimboiseur* (or, as captured in works such as Patrick Chamoiseau's *Texaco* (1992), a *guérisseur*).[29] The traditions of the francophone Caribbean islands speak most acutely to the topic represented in Condé's novel. Some studies of the practices in the French Lesser Antilles distinguish between *quimboiseurs*, who are more inclined to malevolent uses of their abilities, and *guérisseurs*, who are more inclined to benevolent uses. However, Dan Boghen and Miriam Boghen, whose work is based largely on interviews in 1972 with Martinicans, maintain that any such rigid distinction is rhetorical at best, even in contemporary Antillean practices. They claim that practitioners, whatever their titles or their intent, use many of the same techniques in their treatment of the individual (240). Bougerol offers a similar argument, even giving more of a healing role to the *quimboiseur*, whom she depicts as the *voyant-guérisseur* (133–4). To be sure, the *guérisseurs*, or healers (as I refer to them collectively), were understood to be individuals who were particularly skilled and therefore most capable of negotiating such abilities and – as identified in Haitian Vodou – the *konesans* associated with them (Michel 37).

Terminology for referring to the supernatural abilities is also specific and provides further means for thinking these abilities in the context of the human body's abilities. For example, Boghen and Boghen use expressions such as "dons" (gifts), "talents," and, most often, "pouvoirs magiques" (magical powers) to speak of the abilities of *guérisseurs*, *quimboiseurs*, and similar practitioners.[30] Such terminology refers to the abilities to communicate with spirits as well as their *connaissance* (which, orthographically at the very least, recalls the *konesans* of Haitian Vodou) with regard to healing through the use of plants (240–1). Similar distinctions exist in Christine Bastien's words on the *guérisseurs* of Mali (whom she identifies in ability-charged discourse as "doués de voyance" [gifted with clairvoyance]), which refer to their *connaissance*: "Le terme revient sans cesse dans le discours des guérisseurs et désigne, dans son ensemble, un savoir qui élève l'homme non seulement au-dessus du commun des mortels, mais aussi au-dessus des autres créatures" [the term reappears constantly in the discourse of healers, and it designates in general a knowledge that raises the individual not only above common mortals, but also above other creatures] (23, 31). A similar reference appears in Bougerol, where "don" works much like *connaissance*: "Tout *quimboiseur* soutient que son don est 'naturel,' c'est-à-dire qu'il lui est conféré par Dieu" [Every *quimboiseur* maintains that his talent is 'natural,' that is, that it is imparted upon him by

God"] (134).[31] Despite any distinctions, *konesans* and *connaissance* systematically sum up the spectrum of spiritual and healing abilities that is manifested and manoueuvred through the use of the whole human, mind and body.

REVIEWING THE SUPERNATURAL

The titles and the normalized connection between the body and such abilities within these respective cultures have often had little impact on the views of individuals and cultures not conversant in such capacities. The practices and the individuals able to engage in them often became signifiers of an abnormal, malevolent ability. In many cultures, "voodoo" still denotes evil or affiliations with the demonic, particularly regarding the casting of malefic spells and engagement in bodily possessions (Benedicty 240). Serialized television dramas produced in, for example, the United States can testify to contemporary fictional depictions that dangerously reiterate such connections with respect to similar spiritual practices.[32] Bellegarde-Smith's work on Haitian Vodou discusses similar representations in non-fiction, particularly the mainstream media (21). Such claims can be said to arise from the ways that some agents perceive the spiritual disciplines as working outside, and therefore in violation, of the Western religious, medical, and legislative doctrines that feed the related master sociocultural narratives.

Historically speaking, it has been documented that individuals who benefited from colonial communities and who resided in proximity to supernatural healers at times lived in fear of being poisoned by them. As a result, they often associated all such spiritual practices with antisocial behaviour and nascent slave rebellions. Although these feelings existed in the Caribbean-bordering regions of North America, they appeared most pronounced in the Caribbean islands, where slaves of African origin significantly outnumbered slaveholders and landowners of West-ern European origin. The eventual effect was that such agents of power often misrepresented the spiritual narrative in its entirety, operating it into one of evil in order to enhance motivations for their own protection and profit.

Historians like Handler detail such identification in Barbados, where he demonstrates how slaveholders and law enforcement agents would work to suppress the existence of such spiritual practices if they were felt to disturb order (61, 70, 75, 77). Martinique also witnessed similar developments, particularly in the early nineteenth century as colonizer fears grew over the enslaved population's presumed wish to reclaim the rights that they had briefly tasted just after the 1789 French Revolution and especially after the first abolition in 1794 (Delisle 62–3). To address the concerns, agents such as lawmakers, members of the clergy, and law enforcement officials represented the practices that their master narratives substantiated as beyond their control. They made of them practices to fear and, if necessary, efface – practices uniquely beyond their sociocultural norms.

The most frequent means of arresting such concerns materialized on the bodies of the individuals able to execute the supposed *pouvoirs magiques*. The *oungan*, the *quimboiseur*, and other spiritual healers would be understood as the ultimate receptacle of the spectrum of such healing abilities. In the narratives of the Western imagination, their corporeality was operated into being synonymous with such feared corporeal capacities. It must be recognized that members of the spiritual healers' own cultural groups are depicted as fearful of them. The beginning sections of Chamoiseau's *Texaco*, set in late twentieth-century Martinique, depict Texaco's residents as cautiously and perhaps fearfully approaching the cave of the area's *guérisseur*, Papa Totone (37–8). At times such worry was born from a spell that was thought to impart harm or death. However, it is also recorded that people have reacted with reverence towards such extraordinarily abled individuals. Various historical studies have found such speculation in slaveholders' records of the slave communities' reception of such practitioners as well as in contemporary testimony from various Antillean populations (Brereton 103–5; Fisher 105–8; J. Handler 63–5).

Within Western sociocultural structures, however, the aforementioned agents identified the highly able-bodied spiritual healers as well as those falsely associated with them in the same two ways that they identified the practices themselves: (1) as bodies able to realize profit for the agents of power and therefore normatively able-bodied within the terms of the sociocultural structure or (2) as bodies able to disrupt profit and therefore deviantly abled or disabled (and, for the agents, disabling) within the terms of the same structure. The first reading arises due to the benefits that the agents perceived such healing abilities could provide, specifically for ailing slave bodies. Not being part of the master narrative, these benefits often needed to be sought on the sly.

Contemporary fictional works perpetuate such pursuits. For a US cultural representation, consider the first season of Alan Ball's HBO television series, *True Blood* (2008). Set in southern Louisiana, an alcoholic and repentant African-American Christian woman, Lettie Mae Thornton, seeks a healer's abilities to put her back on the path to good faith as well as, in a later episode, to a life of alcohol-free and therefore fully functioning abilities ("Burning House of Love"). This same representation of marginalized spiritual practices bears traces of exotic freak spectacles through the "healer" – a bead-wearing, spell-casting black woman named Miss Jeannette, who practises only at night out of an abandoned bus located far out in the country. As could be guessed, the plotline also teases out a connection to the reproduction of financial profit: Lettie Mae's daughter, Tara, who also sought treatment and paid large sums of money for it, eventually learns that Miss Jeannette is in fact an everyday drugstore employee feigning what can be thought of here as *connaissance* in order to make ends meet ("I Don't Wanna Know").[33]

What such contemporary fictional representations revisit is the identification phenomenon that some of the historical agents, most notably slaveholders, practised. In a small number of cases, slaveowners and members of their families benefited from the healer's abilities. Jean-Claude Fignolé is one of many authors who details such a phenomenon in his novel *L'aube tranquille* (1990) [*Tranquil Dawn*], with the curing of the plantation owner, Wolf (97).[34] Certainly slaveowners were not the only agents to be aware of the healers' abilities. Historical studies demonstrate that physicians often knew and used the same herbal practices as healers and that some physicians willingly recognized the healers' advanced knowledge and abilities (J. Handler 62). However, both historical and fictional narratives seem to indicate that, of the non-slave community, it was primarily the slaveowners (white or "person of colour") and their staff who would come into contact with the healers. The motivations for such contact grounded themselves in the reproduction slaves realized, most specifically in the ability to cure, or at least compensate for, a slave's acquired illness or disability – for an ill or injured slave meant a hit to economic reproduction. As Handler states in quite Glissantian terms, the overarching goal was to restore "the fitness of the labor force and its economic productivity" (58). In such cases, the agents willingly stepped outside the master narrative to seek out the healer whom they knew to possess the needed abilities. Although some may have taken part in the spiritual practices themselves, their choice typically followed that of their slaves, who, either out of sincere belief in the practice, solace in sociocultural familiarity, or expression of cultural agency, chose healers of their own community.

The second means of identifying the bodies of supernatural abilities occurred in terms of deviant abilities. In this context, such abilities may be understood as negatively charged disabilities as the bodies were not able to produce what enforcers and operators of master sociocultural narratives expected of them. These same agents determined which spiritual practitioners were to be avoided or, in extreme cases, eradicated, a phenomenon that often resulted from the agent's determination that the abilities were no longer safe or of use. Ball's and Fignolé's works demonstrate an undeniable hesitancy on the part of individuals who choose to come into contact with healers, in large part due to the fear of the supernatural abilities used to realize healing.

Similar fears of the same abilities have existed for centuries within Western consciousness. Joan of Arc's final representation – and the burning of her living body – is one such example. Even the century prior to the debut of the slave trade and related transatlantic cultural contact demonstrates a certain emphasis on such traditions. Cora Fox speaks to such representation in her discussions of sixteenth-century English treatises on witchcraft, and Amy Graves Monroe explores the rhetoric informing and informed by the supernatural in sixteenth-century Genevan texts. If said capacities appeared to menace goals of reproduction (be they economic, religious, or otherwise), or if their misrepresentation became a useful means to gain or shift power, agents holding or attempting to hold power would often assign nomenclature such as, "witch" or *sorcière*, and thereby operate the narrative. The events in late seventeenth-century Massachusetts are the textbook example of the power of such operations. As Breslaw emphasizes, the denunciation of individuals as witches and the ensuing Salem Witch Trials of 1692 were in many ways less about the eradication of "evil" and more about the strategic gaining (or maintaining) of power in a small Puritan community (xix–xx).[35]

Such baptism was far from the only means by which an individual's suspected deviance with regard to ability would be identified: the body itself was the bearer of traits and bore the brunt of treatments.

In the Puritan New England colonies, the work of Cotton Mather claimed it was possible to identify such aberrance by examining the accused witch's body and locating specific marks, such as a "preternatural Teat" (229). As Joan of Arc's fate recounts, the most extreme form of identification in the name of such abilities (supposed or real) would be not only fatal but also, like the spectacle of whippings that slaves frequently endured, public and in certain ways prophetic – an operated body that speaks of what is and is not to be reproduced and therefore of what abilities do and do not belong.

Within the context of the Caribbean slave populations, processes of identification with respect to the spectrum of supernatural abilities appear to have varied. Indeed, individuals such as *manbos* and *guérisseurs* could become targets of similar naming or maiming processes if slaveowners and law enforcement officials felt that the individuals were an antisocial threat. Some would also have suffered the same fate as their European and North American counterparts, including but not limited to the variety of punitive acts operated on the human body (whippings, maimings, hangings) (Delisle 63–5).[36]

However, as discussed earlier, such concerns were ultimately grounded in worries over the reproduction of the plantation economy. Wanting to avoid obstacles to the profit from such reproduction, many slaveowners accepted the healers' extraordinary abilities, which, in turn, regenerated the highly desired able-bodied slaves of the plantations. Through their interaction with both the healthy body and the ill or injured body, the supernatural practitioners were, in multiple circumstances, associated with varied spectrums of bodily abilities. In an interesting contradiction, the black bodies of the healers would be read as less cataclysmic and more justifiable than their accused cousins to the north, and possibly closer to being a "normal" human than either the "white witch" or the "black slave" would ever be. Simultaneously read as beneficial and as "ill-abled" (if not disabled) with regard to the master narrative, regularly moved between the two ability-charged categories of identity, and constantly considered an exotic spectacle of a primitive nature, the indelibly marked bodies of the healers in all their operated states can be considered freaks of culture, and frequently the pariah, within these norm-based narratives of race and bodily ability. Condé's Tituba bears witness to all such events as she recounts her tale of a black woman determined to heal through the use of her supernatural *connaissance*.

TITUBA AS FREAK

Tituba's connection to sociocultural abnormality falls shy of more familiar freak discourse associations as lived by the characters in Ben Jelloun's and Godbout's novels. There are no circuses with sideshow performances, and there is neither a celebrity-making nor a celebrity-seeking element for Tituba. There are no displays of bodies in exhibits erected for the purposes of gawking at and profiting from individuals who sit amidst an "authentic" environment, as Bancel et al. discuss in *Zoos humains* (2004). And yet there are stages, there is gawking, there are performances, and there is legend in Tituba's tale, a story based most obviously on the attention-grabbing fact of her being a slave who escaped hanging. The colonial institution of slavery and its hegemonic legacy can also be thought as a display of *monstres* (echoing Dayan's "kingdom of grotesques" and "the greatest of oddities) or of "subhuman" beings like the "paria" (as Tituba calls herself) (Dayan, *Haiti*, 232, 234). The slaves' abilities to conduct physical labour were showcased and regularly observed by the overseers in the field, by slaveowners peering through windows, or by slaveowner families watching through doorways. Each of these elements and many others inform the ways that Tituba's associations with race and with supernatural abilities feed a transregional freak-of-culture status and thereby connect her to Fiedler's "absolute other" and to Garland Thomson's "extraordinary" (*Freaks* 17; "Introduction" 1). They also harmonize through their showcasing of the monstrous or the pariah with Condé's own words regarding how she prefers her fictional works to begin: "you have to start with a kind of shock" ("Afterword" 199).

Tituba's sexual proclivity alone might create one such shock, particularly as it echoes the presumed sexual abilities of historical exotic freaks of culture, such as Saartje Baartman. Tituba dedicates significant amounts of time to reflecting on her desires for men, her struggles with those desires as they affect her life (as the spirits of her mother and Man Yaya constantly remind her in reiterations of the question, "Pourquoi les femmes ne peuvent-elles se passer des hommes?" [Why can't women do without men?]), and her active sexual life with men (31; 15–6).[37] In such a context, it would be possible to explore further Tituba's connection to the hyper-sexual abilities of the "Hottentot Venus" phenomenon, which Gilman has already delineated.[38] Such a discussion could be particularly fruitful given one of

Tituba's decisions early in the novel: she is the only non-white character who, out of her love-camouflaged desire for John Indian, chooses to enter slavery to marry him, relinquishing a freedom rarely won (36–7).

To situate the novel within the broader implications of the operated *monstre de la culture*, it is necessary to first focus on the notions of uniqueness and singularity often associated with either the historical or the contemporary freak and how the novel attributes similar traits to Tituba within the context of her abilities. Her body's physical appearance alone – the "rougeâtre" colour and the acquired scars from beatings – makes her no more unusual than many of the maimed or whipped slaves she works to heal (18, 145; 6, 91–2). However, the accumulation of physical traits certainly gives her an undesirable status on the post-trials post-governor's pardon slave market, where she is examined, and next to impossible to sell to pay for her release. Tituba also becomes a slave whose body, in its misshapen form and within the narrative of slave bodies, represents limited if not lack of labour production and, thus, a workforce that can be read for negative connotations of disability. A similar phenomenon of rejection for exceptional if not unnerving corporeality also occurs when, in her effort to join in on the *Bless the Lord*'s journey to Barbados, the ship's captain nearly turns her away for her physical form (209; 135).

Tituba herself reveals how other characters in both Barbados and Salem often gawk at her. Early in the novel, Barbadian slaves unfamiliar with her because of her seclusion but familiar with the reputation of her mentor, Man Yaya, hide upon her approach and then stare as she passes by (25–6; 11–2). During the trials, she is one of the centres of attraction upon which all eyes focus (165–6; 105–6). As she arrives in the Massachusetts colony and as the accusations of witchcraft begin, Tituba reveals how numerous uses of the term *curiosité* (curiosity) describe her status as gazed upon, particularly by the Puritan community. Tituba also stands upon stages or in other venues intended to display her body where all eyes focus on her, be it during the trials, where she performs on the "estrade" [platform] her false and forced confession; as she is displayed in the prison cell during the efforts to sell her as the only way to pay for her release; or near the novel's end, when she, like many before her, stands upon the "potence" [gallows] just prior to being hanged (161, 166, 187, 263; 102, 106, 120, 172). In such cases, the sight of her body can be said to give way to an attraction to the now repulsive transregional exotic, reinforcing both an inability and ability in the viewers: the inability to *stop* staring at the unusual body and the ability to *keep* gawking insatiably and "contemplatively at the marvelous phenomena" (Garland Thomson, "Introduction," 2).

Tituba's true claim to fame, in Barbados and in the Massachusetts colony, and the reason eyes are on her arise from her abilities as a supernatural healer. According to the novel, she is the only *guérisseuse noire* in Massachusetts. Upon her return to Barbados, slaves celebrate her arrival due to the unique legend built around her – one that contains her mother's supposed (but unrealized) murder of a white slave-master and her own ability to cheat the death sentence accorded to many others (she was the only black individual) during the trials in Salem (220; 142). Although the novel's temporal markers might suggest that she is barely thirty years of age, she is also frequently referred to as "mère" (mother), an epithet that she supposes is a reference to her body's appearance (prematurely aged by operations) but that soon becomes associated with the care that she provides to the enslaved in the tradition of Man Yaya (220, 231; 142, 150).

To add to her list of freakery, Tituba is the only healer in Barbados, before and after her enslavement, represented as living in her own domicile and not using her abilities to realize harm. Her only conversation with a plantation-dwelling *quimboiseur* underscores her tendency to heal: in listening to her tale of the Salem trials, he states that he would have decimated the white residents of the Massachusetts colony (228–31; 148–50). This scene also signals one of the novel's many references to the care that women often exercise more than men, a distinction, and presumably an exception, rehashed in the scenes of Tituba's jail cell life in the Massachusetts colony with Condé's playfully added Hester Prynne, protagonist of Hawthorne's *The Scarlet Letter* (152; 96). However, in the present context, Tituba's conversation with the *quimboiseur* also operates within the distinction between *guérisseurs* and *quimboiseurs*, which holds that the latter are mostly seen as malefic and the former are only concerned with healing.[39]

Such fame earns Tituba the contestable appellation that, as discussed earlier, many agents assign to individuals working or associated with the same abilities as hers and that follows her across the regions: *sorcière*. This use of the term does of course have strong associations with feminist discourse, such as in Hélène Cixous and Catherine Clément's *La jeune née* (1975) [*The Newly Born Woman*

(1986)] and, in the context of *Moi, Tituba*, Shelton's article "Condé: The Politics of Gender and Identity" (1993). Individuals practising the supernatural healing arts have also been identified as icons of rebellion against the colonial plantation order. However, as the outlining of such nomenclature reveals, "*sorcière*" here refers to sociocultural implications of race and supernatural abilities. A term such as "witch," or *sorcière*, which implies malefic intent or dealings with devils, was not one that individuals with abilities like Tituba's and who resided in colonized regions of the Caribbean and the Americas typically chose to self-identify. In addition to the very real difference between the languages of slaves and slaveowners and, thus, the lack of awareness of such terminology, the infliction of harm and the individual's ability to reproduce such states were not always primary goals. Throughout Tituba's reflections upon her life story and her overarching goal to heal, she appears to accept the title of *sorcière*, if only due to her recognition of the futility of rejecting it.

The clearest indication of the term's use and of Tituba's (utter) acceptance of it appears in the novel's title, *Moi, Tituba sorcière … Noire de Salem*. However, the term also appears throughout the text. Tituba certainly finds herself baptized in the same manner, and for the same reasons, as her historical counterparts. Her first encounter with the term occurs at the dance at Carlisle Bay, where she performs what Man Yaya has instructed her to do in order to make John Indian love her.[40] As she scratches John Indian's smallest finger with her nail, he cries, "Aïe ! Qu'est-ce que tu fais là, sorcière ?" [Ow! What are you doing, little witch!] (33; 17). First believing the accusation is playful, she subsequently realizes the implications of the word "sorcière":

> Qu'est-ce qu'une sorcière?
>
> Je m'apercevais que dans sa bouche, le mot était entaché d'opprobre. Comment cela? Comment? La faculté de communiquer avec les invisibles, de garder un lien constant avec les disparus, de soigner, de guérir n'est-elle pas une grâce supérieure de nature à inspirer respect, admiration et gratitude? En conséquence, la sorcière, si on veut nommer ainsi celle qui possède cette grâce, ne devrait-elle pas être choyée et révérée au lieu d'être crainte? (33–4)

> [What is a witch?
>
> I noticed that when he said the word, it was marked with disapproval. Why should that be? Why? Isn't the ability to communi-

cate with the invisible world, to keep constant links with the dead, to care for others and heal, a superior gift of nature that inspires respect, admiration, and gratitude? Consequently, shouldn't the witch (if that's what the person who has this gift is to be called) be cherished and revered rather than feared? (17)]

The cherishing and reverence that Tituba feels should be demonstrated for her "faculté" (ability) appears eventually in the hearts of most of the slave community, particularly in that of Barbados upon her return. Such respect comes in part from Tituba's eventual description of her mission as one of healing (26; 12). Yet, as Tituba quickly and repeatedly learns and reveals to the reader, the term *sorcière* is regularly and repeatedly "entaché d'opprobre" (marked with disapproval) because it appears to threaten master sociocultural narratives, even if the individual's abilities work to the benefit of the same narrative and its agents. Such change in perspective is an operation that Tituba lives, as demonstrated on the part of her third mistress, Elizabeth Parris: once the accusations of witchcraft begin, she accepts more fully the community's evil-fearing Puritan narrative, which defines Tituba's work as evil (112, 115; 70, 72).

As with any *monstre de la culture* construct, a connection between Tituba and some form of reproduction exists. Here, it does so not only within but also across regions. During her time as a slave, Tituba is crucial to economic reproduction because of the cheap labour that she provides and the profit that she realizes for others. Because of Tituba's initial desire to be with John Indian, her second mistress, Susanna Endicott, does not even have to purchase her, and thus the "free" labour that Tituba produces brings Susanna an almost double profit.

Other moments of reproduction surface when Tituba finds herself confronted with the realities of biological procreation, herself becoming pregnant twice but never giving birth. Such abilities of her body link her directly to the reproduction of slaves and, thereby, the increased reproduction of the plantation workforce. Not wanting her first unborn child to live what she or any other child of colour had endured, Tituba induces an abortion. Operating her own body, she takes part in a phenomenon, not uncommon among enslaved women, whose purpose is to arrest the profit of such reproduction, a phenomenon frequently appearing in fictional representations of both undocumented and documented slave histories.[41]

STRANGE ABILITIES

Despite such connections between body and ability, the reproductive abilities of a body identified as a female slave are not the most poignant means for reading Tituba as a freak of culture; rather, the most poignant means are her abilities as a supernatural healer. Tituba's service as a *guérisseuse* regularly requires her to use her whole body. It might even be possible to say that Tituba operates her own body: she uses her head to choose spells and treatments, and she uses both her head and the rest of her body to conjure spirits and to concoct remedies. Her use of such abilities speaks to what Maude Adjarian says of Tituba's "natural knowledge": "It provides them [black colonials] the means to ease the physical and emotional manifestations of the daily brutalities visited on them and gives them what they need to survive what colonial culture cruelly enacts on their bodies, minds, and spirits" (244). Such thoughts also resonate in Simek's examples of cultural hybridity, as exemplified in, for example, Tituba's abilities to crossbreed plants to improve the efficacy of her practices (34).

However, the realization of such cultural practices also involves Tituba's use of her body's physical abilities and her *connaissance*. Throughout *Moi, Tituba*, it is apparent how Tituba uses her whole body to realize supernatural healing practices and, most notably, her physical and intellectual abilities to gain access to the spiritual. One example is the mention of the plants in the Massachusetts colony that are unknown to her and the knowledge that she gains of their abilities to comfort or to cure. This knowledge is part of the *connaissance* that Tituba acquires from the spirit of Judah White (afterlife friend of Man Yaya) while in Boston prior to arriving in Salem, and she uses it as she gathers needed doses to produce her treatments (84–6; 51–2). A direct reference to *connaissance* as linked to the abilities to choose and gather plants appears when Tituba is once again in Barbados. When Man Yaya refuses to help the protagonist because of her sexually charged ulterior motive in providing protection to Christopher, leader of the maroons, Tituba uses her own intellectual faculties to find the plants necessary for such a plan: "Je devais compter sur les seules ressources de mon intelligence et de mon intuition. Je devais parvenir seule à cette connaissance plus haute" [All I had to count on was my intelligence and my intuition. I had to arrive at this higher sphere of knowledge on my own] (229; 148).

The moment that best exemplifies Tituba's use of her entire body in the practice of supernatural abilities occurs while she is in Salem and she calls to Man Yaya and her mother for advice. The moment involves a range of abilities, her own as well as those of her two spiritual guides: they must, as Man Yaya advised her before her departure for the Massachusetts colony, "enjamber l'eau" [cross the water], an ability that the novel represents as difficult even for those in the spiritual realm (52; 30). Where this activity becomes directly connected to Tituba's *connaissance* and her abilities is in the way that she first demonstrates her awareness of the animals in the village when summoning forth her guides, selecting not one of her own chickens as the offering to local spirits but, rather, the star sheep "à la robe immaculée" [that had an immaculate coat] of neighbour Goody Hutchinson's flock (133; 84).

Because the contact with Man Yaya and Abena involves the intense use of so many of her abilities, the encounter requires Tituba (who asks the animal to forgive her and to transmit her message) to mark her body with the blood of the sacrificial lamb. After, she spends a lengthy amount of time prostrate on the cold ground and in prayer:

> Je lui tranchai le cou d'un geste net, sans bavures … J'oignis mon front de ce sang frais. Ensuite, j'éviscérai la bête … Je fis quatre parts égales de sa chair que je présentai aux quatres [sic] points cardinaux …
>
> Après quoi, je demeurai prostrée tandis que prières et incantations se bousculaient dans ma tête. (134–5)

> [I slit his throat in one quick movement … I anointed my forehead with the fresh blood. Then I gutted the animal … I divided its flesh into four equal parts, which I presented to the four cardinal points …
>
> After that I remained prostrate while prayers and incantations buzzed in my head. (85)]

Because of the involvement of her intellectual, physical, and spiritual capacities, the scene reinforces the need for the whole body to use such abilities and, thus, the centrality of these abilities to supernatural practices.[42]

Tituba's abilities, which are grounded in her *connaissance* and which necessitate the use of her whole body, are the ones that lead consistently to various forms of penetrating and mutilating operations and that, because they move her throughout the spectrum of supernatural abilities, demonstrate abilities as alterable.

AN OPERATED BODY EXOTIC

The operations that Tituba endures see the light of day because of the varied goals of operating agents from across various lands, socio-economic structures, and ages. One such source arises from Tituba's work as a slave – as it is read in a colonial master narrative built upon a hierarchy of the races, executed in the Americas and the Caribbean Basin in ways that are transregional, and realized through the commands and the abilities of her body. Tituba herself speaks of the benefits that slavemasters and others, ready to dominate the world, extract from the bodies of slaves and their abilities: for her, they are benefits realized "grâce au produit de notre sueur" [with the sweat of our brows] (260; 170).

How the use of her body and others' suspicions of such use ties in to the designation of the exotic lies in the ways in which Tituba works as well as entertains the children of the Parris household in Salem Village and the particular demands they make upon her. Her race and, especially, her supernatural abilities become major components of a perceived transregional sociocultural exoticism that echoes a frequent if not primal element of the identity of historically documented "primitive" freaks of culture.

Such notions of the exotic are not quite the same as the notion of the exotic that depends on the creation of an overwhelming sense of the foreign with a hint of danger. William Schneider demonstrates how, in exoticizing displays of bodies, skin colour, along with physiognomic legends, sumptuary customs, and methods of defence employed by dominated cultures were exploited to present a more "native," or barbaric, side of those cultures, which was encapsulated in exotic (and therefore abnormal) bodies (136).[43] To viewers, these bodies were considered sources of fascination and were sought solely for viewing pleasure and, in the tradition of the zoo, for education.

In "Le frisson sauvage: Les zoos comme mise en scène de la curiosité" ["The Savage Shudder: Zoos as Staging of Curiosity"], Eric Baratay explains this thirst for the exotic: "Le public veut des bêtes curieuses, sauvages, féroces, bien différentes des espèces européennes, pour se dépayser et rêver aux contrées lointaines" [The viewers want strange, savage, and ferocious beasts, much different from the European sort, in order to remove themselves from the familiar and to dream about faraway lands] (33).[44] In their introduction, the editors of the collection in which Baratay's article appears, *Zoos humains* (2004), theorize the spectacles as human zoos (as the title suggests) and maintain that they served the three distinct functions "distraire, informer, éduquer" [to entertain, to inform, and to educate] (Bancel et al. 13).[45] As such, the bodies in the displays were, although of great entertainment value, nothing more than objects; they were, in the viewers' eyes, inferior, "savage" bodies in need of civilizing and were better off separated from the general public in locked cages or enclosed displays. They were also the means by which the viewers could identify themselves as civilized and, therefore, as normal.

Tituba's exotic body represents much more than the physical savagery and barbarism that patrons of such attractions dared approach. It symbolizes a living and present source of both fascination and fear. Unlike those in spectacles isolated by stages, fences, or gates, Tituba's freak of culture body lives among its historical and fictional viewers. As Marion Starkey writes in her insightful yet at times riskily anachronistic historical study *The Devil in Massachusetts* (1949), Tituba's body, during the trials, was "marked ... by her exotic coloring" (33).

In Condé's representation, Tituba's exotic body represents to the girls of Salem Village what the bodies in the human zoos signified to their viewers: a source of both distraction and education. Before the girls' convulsions and the subsequent trials begin, the children are enticed by the exoticism that they believe Tituba's body contains. Abigail Williams and Betsey Parris, the niece and daughter, respectively, of Tituba's second master, Samuel Parris, and who were also in Barbados at the time of Tituba's purchase, already experienced part of what Baratay called the "contrées lointaines." Tituba herself recognizes the impact of the supposedly exotic Barbadian culture on the girls' lives in a comment with intertextual connections to earlier literary conceptions of exoticism, such as Charles Baudelaire's "L'invitation au voyage" (1861) ["Invitation to the Voyage" (1982)].[46] Tituba explains: "les jours qu'elles y avaient coulés, avaient été faits de luxe et de volupté" [the life they had spent there was composed of luxury and voluptuousness] (101–2; 63).

However, Tituba's exotic body represents more than just *luxe* and *volupté*. As teller of strange tales, it symbolizes and educates about unimaginable fantasies of far-away lands. It also encapsulates very particular abilities, ones these two girls and their friends in Salem Village come to demand of it as labouring slave and exotic performer: "– Tituba, chante-nous une chanson! – Tituba, raconte-nous une histoire … Raconte-nous celle des gens gagés!" [Tituba, sing us a song! Tituba, tell us a story! … Tell us the one about the people in league with the devil] (99; 61). To a degree, Betsey and Abigail already know Tituba's exotic potential from the tales of her homeland that she recounted to them while sailing from Barbados to Boston: "ceux d'Ananse l'araignée, des gens gagés, des soukougnans, de la bête à Man Hibé qui caracole sur son cheval à trois pattes" [those of Anancy the Spider, people who had made a pact with the devil, zombies, *soukougnans*, and the hag {Man Hibé} who rides along on her three-legged horse] (70).[47] Such potential for entertainment is most certainly not unique to Tituba. Other fictional works depicting the Americas – one thinks of Margaret Mitchell's hyperbolic representation of the "mammy" in the antebellum United States in *Gone with the Wind* (1936) – suggests how slaves were expected to entertain children and were ordered by children to do so.[48]

However, the children's insistence on being told tales of the "gens gagés" ("Leurs histoires favorites étaient celles des gens gagés" [Their favorite stories were about people in league with the devil]) reveals how their demands indicate their connection between Tituba's exotic "dark" body and the extraordinariness of her supernatural abilities (97; 60). The connection is further established when they ask questions about the practising of said abilities, such as regarding the deck of tarot cards Abigail acquires ("-Crois-tu qu'on puisse lire dans l'avenir avec cela ?" [Do you think we can read the future with these?]) or the palm of the hand ("-Et là, là, peut-on lire dans l'avenir ?" [And there, do you think you can read the future there?]) (111; 69–70).

The children's requests also replicate all the other commands in the novel as they morph into demands for an objectified body to serve according to its abilities. Tituba highlights the precise nature of their orders: "au lieu de me solliciter, elles m'ordonnaient" [instead of asking me, they ordered me] (99; 61). And yet, as the story of the historical Tituba tells, such rhetorical operations of her bodily abilities in Condé's novel, which demand that they reproduce entertainment, never remain so seemingly innocent as assumed with regard to children. For *Moi, Tituba*, and in particular Tituba's recounting of such operations, reveal how agents never perceive her supernatural abilities with any consistency. Moreover, they seek to pull from them what they find useful, an extraction that, as Tituba shows, results in penetrating and disfiguring operations to her body. The end result of the agents' manipulation is the rendering of Tituba as permanently, pejoratively disabled.

OPERATIVE COMMANDS OF THE SUPERNATURAL

In addition to unveiling her extraordinary exotic status across sociocultural structures, Tituba's tale reveals to readers the many ways in which agents across the same transregional, colonial space operate her supernatural abilities in order to realize profit. Certain of the operations are discursive only, whereas others are both discursive and corporeal – the most extreme of which penetrates her body and her mind.

What remains common among the operations is that they all rely upon assumptions of supernatural reproduction attached to Tituba's identity. She herself summarizes the process well when speaking of the word *sorcière*: "Chacun donne à ce mot une signification différente. Chacun croit pouvoir façonner la sorcière à sa manière afin qu'elle satisfasse ses ambitions, ses rêves, ses désirs" [Everyone gives that word a different meaning. Everyone believes he can fashion a witch to his way of thinking so that she will satisfy his ambitions, dreams, and desires] (225; 146). Placing the commanding activity within a continuum of possibilities open to everyone, Tituba's words demonstrate how such operations are not limited to one party or even region; rather, they constitute a transregional social phenomenon that singles her out from all others of her sociocultural status and makes of her a freak of culture.

All of the operating agents within the novel make such demands directly of Tituba across the regions; yet each does so by choosing which supernatural abilities associated with Tituba's identity are the most profit-bearing for them. One example in Salem occurs with Sarah, a fellow slave who asks for vengeance on her abusive mistress, a vengeance that could cause harm if not death and that would identify Tituba as malefic. Tituba's denial of the request emphasizes that her supernatural abilities are, as other scenes in the novel reveal, for healing. However, it is Sarah's request alone that demonstrates the agent's willingness to sidestep accepted master sociocultural narratives and to selectively adapt the narrative of Tituba's supernatural abilities for personal gain (108–10; 67–9).

The captain of *Bless the Lord* provides a clear moment in which Tituba makes it clear that her identification is directly influenced both by her abilities and by how they are moved within the spectrum. He only grants her passage once he learns of her reputation. The papers that she holds in her hands, demonstrating her freedom from official enslavement, mean nothing to the captain as, upon seeing her body, he identifies her negatively as a racialized and now post-incarceration disabled body disinclined to produce much labour. Once he learns of her reputed supernatural abilities, his identification of her shifts towards her ability to heal: in order to sail with them, he demands she provide what is needed to produce the most successful voyage: "tu veilleras à la santé de mon équipage et tu empêcheras les grains !" [you will watch over the health of my crew and ward off storms] (210; 135).

These self-serving operations have a clear impact on Tituba's (lack of) connection to community and thus on her identity. Later on in Barbados, Christopher, the leader of the maroon community that Tituba stumbles upon almost immediately after her return, also operates her abilities. Tituba explain how he asks her to give him the ultimate ability for the presumed benefit of the unfreed slaves: "Tituba, je veux que tu me rendes invincible" [Tituba, I want you to make me invincible] (225; 146). Desirous of sexual relations that are both certain and certain to diminish, Tituba uses her *connaissance* to grant his request. To no surprise, she learns that Christopher's operation of her abilities was only for his own profit, that it was an egocentric operation whose purpose was more power: he ultimately relies upon a tacit pact between his maroon community and the slavemasters, which, despite their ideological differences, assures their respective successful existence and guarantees the final earthly operation of Tituba's abilities (249; 163).

Mireille Rosello's words concerning Tituba's efforts to negotiate her freedom are relevant here and for most of Tituba's interactions with other characters. She writes that the protagonist's supernatural abilities realize no long-lasting collaborative connection between communities; moreover, because her abilities (such as being able to speak with the deceased) "fait figure de savoir inclassable, intransmissible" [are part of an unclassifiable, intransmissible knowledge], they reinforce certain divisions (*Littérature* 65). Christopher selectively uses this "savoir" – the *connaissance* – and all the related bodily abilities that Tituba possesses to underscore separation and, thereby, to gain profit.

Curiously, though, the only division that remains is not that between the maroons and the colonial forces but, rather, that between Tituba and both of those communities.

Many of the operations that Tituba endures are presented to her as a means to subvert master sociocultural narratives, and the typical impact on her abilities is to (re)define them as malefic. Yet, there are also operating agents who wish to use her abilities and, at the same time, feign a desire to reinforce such narratives. However, at some point, the transaction becomes viewed not as benevolent but as malevolent. The end result still realizes the discursive movement of Tituba's supernatural abilities within their spectrum. Such is the case with Dr Griggs, who, prior to the accusations of witchcraft in Salem, respects Tituba for her abilities and, like many of his historical counterparts, seeks her assistance (127). Once the tide begins to turn against Tituba, however, so does Dr Griggs: in diagnosing the presumably ailing, convulsive girls, he quickly avoids Tituba and pronounces the cause – in Tituba's presence – to be that of "la main du Malin" [the evil hand of Satan] (129; 81).

When in prison with Sarah Good and Sarah Osborne for alleged witchcraft – two women to whom she demonstrated compassion prior to their incarceration – Tituba explains that she witnesses them harmonize accusations against her, singling her out, and literally out of their shared cell, for being a "créature de Satan" [creature of Satan] (148–9; 94). In such scenes, the colour of Tituba's skin, which many use to associate her with the black race and, therefore, with the enslaved, becomes of further use in the designation of her abilities as an incarnation of evil within the Puritan community. Here Tituba may be considered "Satanically abled" and, therefore, pejoratively disabled. The agents who are operating the discourse of her race and her abilities – Dr Griggs, but especially Sarah Good and Sarah Osborne – do so in order to generate their own profit by dissociating themselves from her. The expanse of such identification is represented here through various strata of the sociocultural structure as the operating agents are metonyms for differing social levels: from those assumed to be higher (like Dr Griggs) to those thought to be lower (like the impoverished and beggarly Sarah Good).

Still there are other operations that target both discourse and abilities. Transmitted as orders to represent the two identity categories, the operations intend to enter Tituba's mind even as they first and forcibly penetrate her body. Prior to the aforementioned arrest, Tituba

finds herself seized and restrained in the privacy of her quarters in the
Parris household: she is the captive of three men wearing black hoods
and brandishing their choice tools of operation – fists, rope, and, most
notably, a sharpened stick.[49] More specifically, the men (one of whom,
due to his voice, Tituba recognizes as Samuel Parris) want her to con-
fess two acts at the upcoming trial: (1) that she cast a spell on the children and that (2) she worked in commerce with Satan alongside the
likes of Sarah Good, Sarah Osborne, and others, whom, as revealed
later, the hooded men want removed from the sociocultural structure
for reasons related to power (144, 200–1; 91; 129).[50] Tituba's body as a
sign of malevolent abilities remains central to the abusive men's
operation; and the operation's penetrating, devouring, and deforming
imprint on her body is suggested not only in the verb that opens the
scene ("pénétrèrent" [surged]) but also in the simile she chooses for
the assailing operators: "grands oiseaux de proie" [great birds of prey]
(143; 90).[51]

Like all similar moments in the novel, the brutality of the scene
unfolds as Tituba recounts it without hesitation. The effect is a transmission not only of the profundity and violence of the operation, particularly with the sharpened stick intended for vaginal penetration,
but also of the multi-nuanced and forced role of reproduction, especially after Tituba's initial refusal to regurgitate their narrative:

> L'un des hommes se mit carrément à cheval sur moi et commença
> de me marteler le visage de ses poings, durs comme pierres. Un
> autre releva ma jupe et enfonça un bâton taillé en pointe dans la
> partie la plus sensible de mon corps en raillant:
> – Prends, prends, c'est la bite de John Indien ! (144)

> [One of the men sat squarely astride me and began to hammer
> my face with his fists, which were as hard as stones. Another lifted
> up my skirt and thrust a sharpened stick into the most sensitive
> part of my body, taunting me: "Go on, take it, it's John Indian's
> prick" (91)]

The pleasure that the holder of the stick seems to derive in his sexually charged locution could call for a reading of implied and real
sexual abilities. More specifically, the scene could lead to a reading of
the operating agent's presumption of hypersexual abilities for the
black race, as discussed earlier with respect to the body of Saartje

Baartman and also as examined in Frantz Fanon's *Peau noire, masques blancs* (1952) [*Black Skin, White Masks* (1967)].[52] Given the novel's resounding representations of men's abuse of women, the evocation of gang rape in the scene under discussion speaks to the violent advance of phallocentric narratives across cultures and genders as well as the novel's own narrative.[53]

However, the details of the scene reveal more about operation, ability, and identity. On the one hand, the agents seek to acquire power in the reproduction of the master sociocultural narrative, which they find beneficial, by forcing a false confession grounded in Tituba's supernatural abilities. On the other hand, the presence of penetrating violent operations, as revealed in the agent's commentary and also in John Indian's reaction ("ma femme torturée … ma femme violée" [my tortured wife … my ravished wife]), reveals how Tituba's identity hinges on her presumed race as well as her physical bodily abilities (145–6; 92).

Clearly, the encounter is unlike the requests for healing discussed earlier, either historically (when slavemasters sought *quimboiseurs*) or in a contemporary context (when transactions are enacted between patient and supernatural healer). Here the agents demand a false confession that is rooted in Tituba's associations with race and bodily abilities and that serves their interests in gaining power. Condé's *Moi, Tituba* revisits the effort to represent a power struggle that involves clandestine, abusive efforts to gain or maintain power through the operation of both discourse and body. In so doing, it reveals the importance of bodily abilities not only to Tituba's identity but also to the master sociocultural narratives of race and ability that inform her identity and that the operating agents intend to reproduce as they selectively expel members of the community.

The employment of such violent and penetrating operations as those that appear in the first chapter of *Moi, Tituba*'s second section highlight one means of gaining power at various turns in the novel. Of course, such scenes evoke a timeless violence against women all the while situating it withing the colonial tradition of slavery. Moments from the first chapter of the novel's first section also echo Tituba's torture scene not only in placement but in content: Tituba's mother's rape by an English sailor, which eventuates in Tituba's conception; the attempted rape of her mother by their first master, Darnell Davis, and the defensive stabbing for which her mother is hung (13, 19–20; 3, 7–8).[54] The violent acts constitute an operative tradition wherein one sociocultural narrative penetrates the other in order to perpetuate and thus reproduce itself, squashing reciprocally penetrating efforts at self-defence while demonstrating disregard for the woman's biological ability to procreate.

This notion of reproduction is further accentuated in the twice-violated region of the body that, as cited above, Tituba designates as the most sensitive part of her body ("la partie la plus sensible de mon corps"). As mentioned, the agents operate Tituba a second time for continuing to refuse to reproduce the narrative with which they penetrate her body: "Alors, de nouveau, ils s'acharnèrent sur moi et il me sembla que le bâton taillé me remontait jusqu'à la gorge" [So they pounced on me again and it seemed as if the sharpened stick went right up to my throat] (145; 91). The agents shove the sharpened stick further into Tituba's body through the orifice directly connected to biological reproduction and making her feel as if it has penetrated her throat. Here the stick functions as an obvious metaphor of the phallocentric narrative that appears to nearly touch the bodily area able to produce speech – the throat – out of which the agents want their narrative to be reproduced. To get there, however, they choose to operate the bodily area symbolically and corporeally associated with a woman's procreative abilities, her genitalia and her vagina.[55]

Although Tituba reveals how and why she does eventually concede to the hooded agents' request after counsel with Hester Prynne and John Indian, she never wholly acquiesces to their reproductive intentions. The novel's epilogue continues and expands this depiction: by revealing Tituba's post-death spiritual ability to care for and motivate others across regions in the battle against the domination of penetrating sociocultural narratives, it reveals her intent to remain true to her work as a supernatural healer. Moreover, it demonstrates a unique characteristic of her supernatural abilities. Although agents operate narratives and bodies to profit from these abilities and, in so doing, operate what they produce as well as the ways in which others perceive them (i.e., where they sit within a sociocultural spectrum), the abilities themselves are unaffected. Conversely, as the supernatural healer works to cure or to alleviate illness and injury or to use her body's capacities to conduct her work, the body's centrality to the use of the abilities – at least in the earthly realm, as viscerally reinforced through scenes of torture and pain – remains clear. Ultimately, such operations reveal how several spectrums of abilities factor into the identification process that Tituba lives and, as heavily foreshadowed, dies.

EXECUTING MUTILATION

Whereas the operations in the name of race and supernatural abilities may be penetrating to the body, they can also be maiming and disfiguring, like the beating of Tituba's face during her torture scene. A similar example is the stoning she suffered at the hands of the Puritans outside of the eventually torched house of Benjamin Cohen d'Azevedo, the Brazilian Jew who had purchased her from prison but who, as time passed, secured her freedom in compensation for her supernatural gifts to the family and prepared her passage on the above-discussed *Bless the Lord*. A collective operation, the Puritans' act left Tituba's body swollen and wounded with the feeling of being completely broken (206; 132–3). Despite her professed intention to heal, Tituba reveals how she remains the malevolently abled transregional freak of culture who is inevitably transformed into the dangling strange fruit.

The presence of similar operations to other enslaved characters' bodies, particularly in Barbados, becomes an equally revelatory factor in the race- and ability-informed identification processes. They emphasize to what extent race and bodily abilities in general are intertwined in such processes, particularly as Tituba comes into contact with them. They also heighten the emphasis on Tituba's own supernatural abilities to heal (particularly the enslaved) and her dedication to such abilities, in the name of which she lives the ultimate disfiguring operation of her body – hanging. As the novel eventually shows, that fatal operation haunts her in both Massachusetts and in Barbados and, thus, throughout the text because of her associations with certain constructs of race and supernatural abilities that are often policed and punished.

Revisiting relevant aspects of the historical context of such treatment helps us think through its complexities and its realities as they appear in *Moi, Tituba*. The gratuitous torture of slaves did, invariably yet variedly, exist in the French colonial empire. In its official intent to curb the excessively mutilating or exterminating treatment of slaves, the *code noir* did allow for punishments of slave bodies that most certainly altered these bodies and their abilities. For example, Article 38 defines what is allowed with respect to fugitive slaves absent for two months: "il aura le jarret coupé" [he shall have his hamstring cut], a mutilation that not only retards the ability to ambulate and thus to flee but also reduces the capital worth of the labouring slave (*Code noir*; *Black Code*). Similarly, British colonial legislative powers worked not to halt but, rather, to curtail such treatment in islands such as Jamaica, where the Consolidated Slave Act, 1784, provided a limit of thirty-nine lashes of the whip (Stoddard 386).

Early eighteenth-century letters from French ministers of the Caribbean colonies to the respective governors of those colonies articulated continued efforts to police slaveowners' debilitating punishments of slaves (including those suspected of witchcraft), such as the cutting of legs or, ultimately, execution (Gisler 106). Many of the letters included statements similar to the following, which, as a reapplication of the *code noir*, worked to prevent slaves from wanting to flee their enslavement and thus to continue realizing reproduction of labour: "Il convient à la vérité d'empêcher la violence des maîtres à l'égard de leurs esclaves ; mais il est nécessaire aussi de contenir les esclaves dans la dépendance où ils doivent être et de ne rien faire qui puisse leur donner sujet de s'en écarter" [It is in truth to stop the violence of the masters with respect to their slaves; but it is also necessary to maintain slaves in a necessary dependence and to do nothing that can give them cause to remove themselves from it] (107).

Condé's novel reveals at many a turn Tituba's reflections on the maiming of bodies, especially after she works to alleviate suffering or to promote healing. Almost as a response to the *code*, she states: "Notre esclavage n'est pas terminé. Oreilles coupées, jarrets coupés, bras coupés" [I have forgotten that our bondage is not over. They are lopping off our ears, legs, and arms] (161; 102). However, such maiming also appears with respect to slave labour. The individuals whom Tituba treats have "membres labourés par les moulins" [limbs crushed by the mills] (231; 150). Regardless of the specific reason, the novel's depiction of these events underscores such mutilation as a form of injustice. It also continues to connect Tituba, as embodiment of supernatural abilities, to bodies read not just in terms of mutilation but also in terms of the entire spectrum of physical abilities.

One such example appears towards the end of the novel, when the severely whipped body of a young slave, Iphigene, arrives at Tituba's domicile. She describes him in the following manner: "Il avait reçu 250 coups de fouet sur les jambes, les fesses et le dos, ce que son organisme, affaibli par un séjour en prison – car c'était un insolent, un récidiviste, une mauvaise tête de nègre dont on ne parvenait pas à mater le caractère – n'avait pas pu supporter" [He had received 250 whiplashes on his legs, buttocks, and back, and his body, weakened by a spell in prison, had collapsed. The boy was a hardened offender and nobody could tame his insolence] (244; 159). Near death, virtually immobile, carried in by fellow slaves, Iphigene's disfigured body symbolizes in two respects the pejoratively disabled slave: (1) it is now no longer able to work (after much time previously working, as captured in the image of his "main … déjà déformée et calleuse" [hand … already rough and distorted"]) and (2) as Tituba's sardonic summary of the reasons for his whipping reveals, it is now no longer able to reproduce the master's narrative (245; 160).

And yet it is Iphigene's brutally whipped body, negatively disabled in the eyes of the colonial agents of power, that becomes the catalyst for the final operation of Tituba's ability- and race-charged identity. In the preceding chapter, Tituba explains how she learns from the slaves she visits and treats what the *planteurs* and the *contremaîtres* suspect: that the interplantation movement of a non-enslaved black individual is a clandestine effort to initiate a rebellion. Their perception of Tituba, to which I add Tituba's likely malefic position within the spectrum of supernatural abilities, makes her the embodiment of a rebellious force that is able to disable their colonial economy. As a result, they are after her "peau" [skin] (231–2; 150).

Only two pages prior to the introduction of Iphigene, Tituba tells her reader that, surprisingly given her body's age (or experiences), she is pregnant from her sexual relations with Christopher (242; 158). After Iphigene has had time to recover and they settle into domestic life, Tituba reflects on the care and future of her unborn child. Her recounting indicates that she speaks to Iphigene of a dream to bring drastic change to the current sociocultural structure, suggesting an optimistic belief that they could work together to realize liberation, especially for future generations (247; 161).[56]

Already rebellious and contemplating similar ideas, Iphigene is eager to begin such a transformation through a full-island rebellion against the slavemasters: he and many others will set fire to the plantations in the hope of killing off the individuals who strive to maintain the colonial narrative of slavery, which is both ability- and race-informed. Although Tituba does at times regret her initial encouragement of the revolt, and although she does attempt to convey to Iphigene how the act will make them like their violent masters ("Devons-nous devenir pareils à eux?" [Do we have to become like them?]), she finds herself unable to convince Iphigene of the need to use her supernatural abilities to contact the spirits and to request their counsel before taking action (248, 251; 162, 163).

Not surprisingly to a reader of Condé accustomed to the recurrent thwarting of any slave's expression of subjectivity (particularly that of a woman slave), the insurrection fails. Betrayed, Iphigene and Tituba are arrested, and law officials beat Iphigene into another state of profound, negatively charged physical disability: he can barely stand, can hardly see, and can no longer speak (262; 171–2). Of course, Tituba's impending punishment of hanging – the final earthly operation she will have – is to be expected. There are certainly key, well-developed scenes of hangings that mark Tituba profoundly concerning the fate of other women characters: Tituba's mother for stabbing her master in self-defence; an elderly woman in Boston accused of practising witchcraft; and a suicidal and pregnant Hester (20–1, 81–2, 174; 8, 48–9, 111). The night before the arrest, the simultaneous occurrence of two events foreshadow Tituba's fate. The first is the death of a rabbit that she discovers is pregnant while gutting it. The second, in an echo of punishments allowed by legislative texts as well as of operations that Tituba endured, is her accidentally dropping the knife and cutting her left foot at the discovery of the rabbit's unborn offspring, a penetration that shifts her physical ability to ambulate within the spectrum and later deters her chances of fleeing arrest (256, 261; 167–8, 171). Even the novel's opening epigraph, taken from the work of sixteenth-century Puritan poet John Harrington ("Death is a porte whereby we pass to joye; / Lyfe is a lake that drowneth all in payne") announces that (Tituba's) death is to come (9; vii).

Tituba's hanging of course realizes the mutilation of her body and its earthly abilities. It also gives way to a series of operations that, one final time, move her supernatural abilities within a discursive spectrum. Tituba's final reflections on her last moments of human existence demonstrate how agents operate narratives from across the regions of Massachusetts and Barbados in order to effect the fatal enforcement of an ability-informed juridical normality. Such working of the narrative means, of course, that Tituba finds herself reacquainted with the term *sorcière*, ushered out of the mouths of agents who are surveying the scene of execution: "-Eh bien, sorcière! Ce que tu aurais dû connaître à Salem, c'est ici que tu vas le connaître!" [Well, witch, what they should have done to you in Boston, we're going to do here!] (262; 171).[57] His words come to fruition: the punishment also involves a reworking of all charges ever brought against her – not only the failed revolt in Barbados with which she is associated but also the accusations from the Salem trials – as well as new claims fabricated for her hanging.

To demonstrate the existence of such an operation, Tituba summarizes the executioner's words. They explain the hanging as a punishment that she had "échappé" (escaped) at the same time as they distort the events that she has already detailed throughout the novel: "J'avais ensorcelé les habitants d'un village paisible et craignant Dieu. J'avais appelé Satan dans leur sein, les dressant les uns contre les autres, abusés et furieux. J'avais incendié la maison d'un honnête commerçant [Benjamin Cohen d'Azevedo] qui n'avait pas voulu tenir compte de mes crimes et avait payé sa naïveté de la mort de ses enfants" [I had bewitched the inhabitants of a peaceful, God-fearing village. I had called Satan into their hearts and turned them one against the other in fury. I had set fire to the house of an honest merchant who had decided to disregard my crimes, but who had paid for his lack of judgment with the death of his children] (263; 172). Clearly, Tituba's listing of the events in a courtroom style and void of exclamations demonstrates her lack of emotion and, hence, her lack of surprise at the time concerning the narrative operation. Nevertheless, her statements demonstrate that the North American colony's governor's pardon of judgment against those accused of witchcraft in the Salem trials was overlooked (186, 210; 119, 135).

Tituba's words also reveal that the blame for the fire that community members set to the d'Azevedo house (in protest of a domicile in which there was a prospering living together of "Juifs et ... Nègres" [Jews and niggers]) was reassigned to her (206–7; 132–3). Thus, the Barbadian slavemasters and law officials operate Tituba's narrative to recast her racially charged supernatural abilities as utterly uncontrollable and counter-productive to the transregional sociocultural structure that they wish to preserve. Adjarian's words are useful here: "Tituba is privy to knowledge not actively pursued, defined and *controlled* by the colonizers. She is thus a threat to both white masculine and colonial privilege, that is, to the New World order named into existence by white European males" (244).[58] By positing her crimes within a tradition of supernatural abilities that are already regularly and selectively manipulated into being malevolent, the operating agents make of Tituba a discursive freak of *cultures* – two culturally similar yet geographically distinct world regions.

As the executing operation allows the agents to rewrite Tituba's freak body and its supernatural abilities as evil and therefore counterproductive, the final product provides them with a corporeal warning of the abilities no other person or slave should possess if she or he wishes to adhere to the master sociocultural narrative. Certainly, in the context of Condé's novel, these particular agents, as arbiters of the law, would not necessarily need a particular narrative to justify their act. Any narrative that they operate is the narrative that reigns, even if it is a narrative that they themselves manipulate.

However, what is worth noticing here is that the scene demonstrates the regular interdependence between narrative and body – specifically, bodily ability – in such operations and how one can reproduce the other. As Tituba knows all too well, her hanged body will serve – just like her mother's, the elderly woman's, and those of the many others publicly executed before her for the same reason – as a visible reminder to any onlookers that certain acts, as well as the spectrum of supernatural abilities (including the *connaissance*) that enable one to conduct such acts, are fatally condemnable.[59] The hanging then becomes an operation intended to connect disobedient ability-charged bodies to reproduction in two ways: (1) as unable to produce anything of their own volition (including Tituba's unborn child) and (2) as able to produce everything that their newly mutilated state – where tongues protrude and necks bend to the side, permanently – can transmit.

This particular notion of reproduction, which is culturally crafted, literally grows into a notion that alludes to nature. Standing upon her last earthly stage, Tituba reflects upon the scene: "Autour de moi, d'étranges arbres se hérissaient d'étranges fruits" [All around me strange trees were bristling with strange fruit] (263; 172). A similar expression precedes this, during Tituba's days of the Salem accusations and threats of execution: "Quel beau fruit, les arbres du Massachussets porteront !" [What a magnificent fruit swinging from the trees of Massachusetts] (120; 75). The novel's intertextual reference to the song "Strange Fruit" (1939), written first as a poem by Abel Meeropol and most famously performed by Billie Holiday, is certainly a reference that spans centuries of similar processes of identification (in the case of Merpool's poem, the lynchings in the United States). However, in the present transregional context, the reference also speaks to the ways that the operated bodies, as strange spectacles, are now differently able in their mutilated state to reproduce the master sociocultural narrative so dependent on constructs of race and bodily ability.[60]

At the same time that "étranges fruits" echoes the objectification that slaves repeatedly lived, the notion of strangeness also recalls the varied ways in which Tituba has constantly been identified as monstrous, marginal, malefic, and therefore freakish. As an object to be eaten, strange fruit also recalls the construct of the racialized exotic that attracts the children of Salem to her and incites them to consume her. And, as an object of abilities, the unusual object underscores the construct of the "thing" that is associated with abnormal phenomena or is itself a phenomenon, the same thing that is also the slave. Here, dangling above the stage-like gallows, Tituba's hung body is repeatedly identified as the difficult black slave, the exotic *sorcière*, and the rebellious free person of colour hidden beneath the clothes of the *guérisseuse*. The self-proclaimed pariah becomes and remains the ability-charged transregional freak of culture.

Conclusion

Désormais il nous devient possible ... de distinguer quelle combinaison monstrueuse a dû réellement exister, quelle autre n'est que le produit bizarre et
irrégulier d'une supercherie ou d'un jeu de l'imagination.
[From now on it becomes possible for us ... to distinguish which monstrous
combination really did exist, and which one is just the bizarre and irregular
product of trickery or of a play of the imagination.]
Isidore Geoffroy Saint-Hilaire, Histoire générale et particulière
des anomalies de l'organisation chez l'homme et les animaux

When Michael Jackson died on 25 June 2009, the world seemed focused both (and once again) on his body and on its abilities.[1] The
"King of Pop," globally renowned for his self-designed and, from some
perspectives, "freakish" lifestyle as well as his extraordinary ability to
perform, was suddenly depleted of all bodily abilities and subjected
to the coroner's knife. The related news reports showcased Jackson's
death as well as the coroner's report, which, once public, laid bare private details of his body and its altering abilities, which had long been
under scrutiny.[2]

One of the more notable capacities would be his body's altered ability to produce pigmentation, or vitiligo, as demonstrated in the
patches of light and dark skin most clearly distinguishable on his
chest, arms, and face. Television news broadcasts, newspapers, and websites also honed in on the now-unearthed operations that Jackson's
body had endured in response to his transforming abilities: tattoo
work on his scalp, presumably chosen due to the body's reduced ability to produce hair; the multiple injection sites on his body, some due
to the administration of propofol to help him with his diminished
ability to sleep, others speculated as passageways by which varied substances were introduced in order to assuage his body's decreasing abil-

ity to tolerate pain. Such details, along with the disclosure of his "alarming" thinness (62 kilograms at one hundred and seventy-five centimetres tall) and his tattooed eyelids and lips, moved Michael Jackson's identity from the freakish and perverted individual once suspected of victimizing children to the pitiable individual victimized not only by external forces but also by his body's transformed abilities. Previous concerns (particularly in the United States, where his identity seemed the most troubling) about his gender, his sexuality, his race, and perhaps even his ability to biologically reproduce seemed all but forgotten now that the autopsy revealed that Jackson's suspected conditions appeared fundamentally related to his bodily abilities.

Yet, under the vivisecting eyes of the media, such abilities could not be at rest, even when Michael Jackson's body was.[3] The reports seemed to imply that the fact that a body as altered as Michael Jackson's could still perform, or could even function for that matter, was astonishing. And it drew people in. The tone of many a broadcaster's voice capitalized (and almost literally so) on the state of his bodily abilities: it would transmit either awe over the presumably waif-like and withering body that could still cast a spell over any audience or sadness over the loss of such an extraordinarily abled body. A new claim to Jackson's fame had now become the ways in which his body had become unable to exist; how it was, in negatively charged ways, disabled. The operation by the coroner made apparent the means by which extraordinary, diminished, and faded bodily abilities informed and inform the identity of a man already and continuously conceived in terms of sociocultural constructs of race, gender, and sexuality in the United States. Freakishly hyperbolic with regard to identification processes, Michael Jackson's identity remains regularly informed by the aforementioned identity categories in conjunction with the spectrums of bodily abilities across which his body was constantly negotiated.

This brief exploration of the representations of Jackson's premortem and postmortem abilities serves as another reflection on the connection between spectrums of bodily abilities and related identification processes. Michael Jackson has long been considered eccentric, extraordinary, and freakish for his boundary-breaking choices in the personal, the professional, and the global arenas. These same ways of thinking about Michael Jackson occur differently in the various regions of the world where his name and legend appears. Furthermore, his identity has experienced repeated shifts within normative constructs of identity such as gender and race. However, it was upon death, when people could (finally) gain access to his body, that his identity was assessed in terms of bodily abilities heretofore undisclosed, an operation that finds some of its precedents in those ardent efforts to identify the historical bodies of Cyparis, the Dionne quintuplets, Saartje Baartman, and the Bunker brothers. The bodies of the latter three of this group would succumb to varying forms of autopsy in a final effort to articulate the abilities that did (or, in the end, did not) inform their identity as well as where these individuals sat within the related spectrums of ability.

When assessments of disability and inability meet assessments (made throughout Jackson's life) of celebrated extraordinary abilities, rigid dichotomies conceived in terms of ability are destabilized. What begins to appear is the permanently shifting construct of identity that moves along spectrums of bodily abilities lived by such identified bodies. Furthermore, the levels of abilities associated with Jackson and his identity are no longer solely understandable in terms of a binary opposition like disability/non-disability. Instead, Michael Jackson's reported and remembered range of abilities – the inabilities, the disabilities, the diminished abilities, and the extraordinary abilities – demonstrate once again how identity is conceived within spectrums as well as how abilities, narratives, and identity are forever operable. Although they open bodies in order to identify what makes them work, operations are neither the singular nor the ultimate identificatory gesture. Nor are they the way by which bodily abilities enter into the identification process. Bodily abilities are always already present in identity as well as in human existence. The operations are just one means through which such identification occurs and spectrums of abilities become increasingly evident.

It is for these and related reasons that Michael Jackson, a non-Francophone (and non-francophone) individual, leads off my concluding remarks. The operations to Jackson, as well as those performed on the characters studied in this book and on the individuals spotlit in the interludes, mirror each other for the repeated emphasis and presence of bodily ability. The characters' stories also demonstrate the inherent, predictably unpredictable movement within spectrums that inform the identity formation of any and all individuals regardless of their position in the world. Simply speaking, bodily ability informs all identities and all master sociocultural narratives, and certain individuals are selected as models of who does and does not belong. Jacques

Godbout's Papineau twins essentially narrate how a range of linguistic abilities (including intellectual and physical abilities) are crucial to the reproduction of the citizen of a nation as well as of a federal state. Ahmed/Zahra, in Tahar Ben Jelloun's two novels, is the model for how procreative abilities coincide with sociocultural constructs of gender within the realms of religion and the family. Maryse Condé's Tituba recounts how supernatural abilities are woven together with narratives of race in the identification of individuals within transregional cultural and economic spheres.

The movement of Tituba is, like the errances of Cyparis and Michael Jackson, what most clearly characterizes the shuttling across spectrums of abilities that all individuals encounter in the operation of identity. Agents constantly probe Tituba's body as they alter the meaning of her supernatural capacities (while her actual abilities remain unaffected); the operations depend not only on the sociocultural sphere through which she passes but also on the need for social or financial gain on the part of those who surround her as she walks her exotic witchy body across many stages. Members of Ahmed/Zahra's various families repeatedly (dis)place the protagonist's procreative abilities in ways that benefit only the operator and never the operatee, a series of gender-bending manipulations nuanced by the time spent performing as the Abbas's *homme/femme fatale*. Authority figures regularly reshape Charles and François, the truly dynamic duo of many performative discourses, within the realm of language, hoping to produce what one surgeon finally does: a linguistic citizen machine incapable of remembering plurality but capable of producing the *one* history of a citizen and, by extension, of a nation.

The agents' operations to the freak characters, who are as extraordinary as Jackson and Cyparis, realize a recurrent reproduction that ultimately hinges on the body's ability to produce. Like the surgically separated young Moroccan sisters of Interlude 1, the amalgamated Papineau brothers are intended to usher forth a somatic signifier of individualism and citizenship that is selectively and socioculturally normative. Akin to Ashley of Interlude 2, Ahmed/Zahra undergoes operations that, ultimately, never generate human heritage but always fertilize familial fervour. Tituba, similar to Anne of Interlude 3, finds herself operated in an arena of healing through contact with agents representing sociocultural narratives of varying regions that, in varying ways, seek profit through corporeal transformation.

Both the operation and reproduction depend extensively on the readings of and the writings on bodily abilities. Such words come in the form of narratives: the master sociocultural narratives but also the narratives that the main characters populate and produce. Narrative proves itself to be just as malleable as bodily abilities. Certainly the operating agents demonstrate how master narratives – be they economic, medical, religious, juridical, or legislative – are pliable and therefore impermanent: but the narratives of the novels themselves underscore such transformability. As Charles and François edit their *journal*, Tituba modifies her *récit*; and Ahmed/Zahra's tale embodies narrative operation as multiple narrators recurrently shift the direction of the text. In such light, narratives and bodily abilities come to mirror each other for they find themselves equally alterable, shifted throughout spectrums of possible productive positions.

Grosso modo, *Operation Freak* demonstrates the operative interplay between narrative, identity, and the spectrum of bodily abilities in identification processes from around the world. In so doing, it offers not only another means for understanding the complex and unending production of identity but also a way to think about negotiations of ability and narrative as the global means of operations continue to cross-pollinate and multiply. Again, an example arises from the earthquake of 12 January 2010, which has become a means by which Haitian disability rights activists are working to advance equality for all. They are aiming to bring their country into compliance with their own law concerning integration of the disabled and with the nation's status as a signatory of the 2009 United Nations Convention on the Rights of Persons with Disabilities ("Handicapped Struggle"). Josué Joseph, a spokesperson at the Secretariat of State for Integration of Persons with Disabilities, which works with many of Haiti's organizations for the disabled, has stated that the advancement of such changes can begin to allow the disabled of Haiti to come out of their hiding places. Joseph claims that, where disability was once assumed to be a contagion and largely associated with poverty, it may now be associated with any class because individuals of all social levels have experienced amputation or injury and thus disability. Recognizing the impermanence of bodily ability, Joseph states: "January 12 proved that we are all potential [sic] handicapped" ("Haiti's Disabled"). Dramatic works such as Frankétienne's *Melovivi ou Le piège* (2010), which depicts a conversation between two characters locked in a structure consisting of post-natural disaster debris accumulation, offers the chance to contemplate what and how, after such transformation, individuals are able to create through their linguistic abilities.

With the 2004 modification of the *Moudawana* in Morocco granting more rights for women, one might also speculate that the heir-producing *fait divers* out of Morocco that motivated Ben Jelloun to compose both *L'enfant de sable* (1985) and *La nuit sacrée* (1987) might not resurface. However, because debate remains over the edited family law for the amount of rights it offers (too many or too few), might further operations occur to both the law as narrative and to the abilities of the bodies it addresses? Or might parents decide that the new law affords them untapped opportunities to alter procreative bodily abilities in the name of profit-centred reproduction? How might the newly accorded rights be distributed to Azizah and Saeedah of Interlude 1? And in what ways is their ability-targeted operation – an act argued to enhance the existence of the twins as individuals and that may or may not ease their transport – different from that of Ashley's of Interlude 2? What will Azizah's and Saeedah's own stories reveal one day about their spectrums of abilities and how their ability-targeted operation did or did not afford them rights within the family of Morocco? Some speculative answers within a relatively similar sociocultural context already seem to appear in Slimane Benaïssa's *Les colères du silence* (2005), a novel about post-surgically separated male conjoined twins living in the margins of society in a relatively contemporary Algeria. Questions of the ability-charged operated woman in a "new" Morocco merit further exploration, and Valérie Orlando has begun to do so in *Francophone Voices of the "New" Morocco in Film and Print* (2009).

Although the rhetoric of the freak of culture is not at the forefront of such current examples, I maintain that ability-charged forms of identification that adopt and adapt narratives will continue to exist. They always do. As Franck Collard and Evelyne Samama (2010) show, identification in terms of spectrums of bodily abilities and the sociocultural norms attached to them has been occurring in various part of the world for centuries. The operations may or may not result in the apparent construction of freaks of culture, although Bancel et al. (2004) argue convincingly that spectacles of ability-identified individuals will continue to exist. Nevertheless, it is certain that such identity formation will reproduce itself for as long as individuals occupy and use their bodily abilities and for as long as agents work to make profit from bodies, abilities, and narratives.

Operation Freak, then, is unable to "heal the world," as Michael Jackson himself wished to do. But it most certainly provides – in the novels of Jacques Godbout, Tahar Ben Jelloun, and Maryse Condé and through the narratives of various world regions – a means to think about identity and the world, the bodies and narratives that constitute them, and those who choose to operate them.

Notes

INTRODUCTION

1 Sources state that there were two other identifiable survivors: most documentation, like Alfred Lacroix's *La montagne Pelée et ses éruptions* [*Montagne Pelée
and Its Eruptions*]) and Simone Chrétien and Robert Brousse's *La montagne
Pelée se reveille*) [*Montagne Pelée Wakes Up*], identify Léon Compère (Léandre),
a shoe-maker (301–2; 192–3); only a few reference Havivra Da Ifrile, a
young girl ("How Volcanoes Work"). As these two individuals saved themselves by escaping Saint-Pierre shortly after the eruption, Cyparis's story
seems to have became the most intriguing as he was the only one who
survived while still in the city (aside from the handful noted to have lived
just a short time longer after the eruption, as documented by, for example,
Lacroix in text and in image, 281–99). Montagne Pelée would in that year
have several more eruptions of the same kind, which Lacroix dubbed *nuée
ardente* (and which is still the term volcanologists use today to discuss
similar eruptions). These explosions caused further devastation to the same
or neighboring regions especially on 20 May and 30 August, the latter of
which affected an area of 115 square kilometers (45 square miles) and killed
an additional 1,000 people. Nearly all of the historical studies referenced in
the present project indicate that such an eruption had not been recorded
since the modern colonization of Martinique, and that further research
suggests that the Caribs who inhabited the island prior to European presence
were said to know of montagne Pelée's potential and to refer to it as "the
mountain of fire" (Lacroix; Chrétien and Brousse; Scarth; Soter).

2 Peter Morgan's *Fire Mountain* is the only contemporary historical study that
focuses almost entirely on the life of Cyparis and events informing it.
Through field research in Martinique, Morgan's project provides a useful

snapshot of the historical and contemporary legacies of Cyparis as well as a collection of historical images of or incorporating Cyparis.

3 Cyparis also appears in several works of fiction: Raphaël Confiant's *Nuée ardente*, Daniel Maximin's *Soufrières* [*Sulfurers*], Luc-René Tabar's "Le maudit miraculé" ["The Miraculous Convict"], and *Cyparis, seul au monde* [*Cyparis, Alone in the World*], Mylène Wagram and Tabar's dramatic adaptation of Tabar's text. All translations here and throughout the present project are, unless otherwise specified, the present author's; titles of texts without a date signal the absence of an existing translation and do not appear in the bibliography.

4 See Figure 137 in Lacroix and Photo 22 in Chrétien and Brousse, as well as the numerous historical and contemporary on-line images.

5 Martinique's governor, Louis Mouttet, perished in the eruption.

6 An abridged copy of this letter, along with copies of related archived documents, is available at stpierre1902.org. Other sources, including Tabar's "Le maudit miraculé," contain a full reproduction of Mary's letter (29–35). The original letter is in the Archives départmentales de la Martinique in Fort-de-France, as noted by Dominique Taffin, "Le pays."

7 The websites listed as sources are only a handful of the many that rehash similar details. The second referenced source is a significant transcription of the letter of Père Mary, also cited in the present section. The variety of texts in the following paragraphs also relates many of the same details.

8 In addition to the then contemporary printed works like Mary's letter and Lacroix's *La montagne Pelée et* mentioned above, Cyparis's skin and the placement of his burns became the somatic text testifying most palpably to the legitimacy of his survival.

9 Mary writes that he saw Cyparis "racontant ingénuement son histoire à la foule qui l'entourait" [naively recounting his story to the crowd that encircled him], a statement that shows, among many things, Mary's evaluation of Cyparis's abilities to narrate as well as the crowd's interest in hearing him recount his tale.

10 Lacroix's work also testifies to racially charged colonial discourse still alive in the early twentieth century. His reference to the other aforementioned survivor, Léon Compère (Léandre), as a "cordonnier" (shoemaker), includes no reference to race. Lacroix's identification of Cyparis emphasizes the juridical context, given his reference to the latter's now-famed imprisonment. However, his statement also identifies Cyparis as a "nègre," a term ripe with its obvious long-standing pejorative connotations (among which may be included a range of deficient and excessive abilities) but that some might

argue should be translatable here as "Negro," given the scientific nature of Lacroix's work (299–302).

11 Kennan's work exists in translation as *Le désastre de la Pelée*.

12 In a short piece on Cyparis's treatment, Thierry Lefebvre swiftly claims that Kennan's assessment of the healing tends on the spectacular. Lefebvre seeks to undo such representation by providing a presumably logical explanation of the progress in pharmacological discourse, thereby linking Cyparis's narrative to the contemporary scientific (678–9). Kennan's manner of writing about Martinique and about Cyparis does exude in many passages an exoticizing, objectifying tone (for it is certainly the travel narrative that accentuates the curiosities of a "country"). However, it also appears to provide observations helpful in tracing the progression of Cyparis's and of Martinique's narrative, and for this reason the work merits further exploration the least of which should be historiographical. Furthermore, Lefebvre's assessment of Kennan, which comes from the French translation of 2002, misinterprets Kennan's passage about Cyparis's healing that in no identifiable way transmits it as spectacular. One of the more credible contemporary studies of both montagne Pelée and Cyparis comes from Morgan's *Fire Mountain*. Working within a historical context, Morgan revists the events through a detailed exploration of a variety of documents – including Kennan's above-referenced work as well as Lacroix's – as he traces as much of Cyparis's own story including that of his geneaology and the historical production of his varied names (227–8). Morgan's project also offers through the reading of various documents perspectives from Martinicans of other parts of the island (notably Fort-de-France) on the moments and days after the eruption as well as details on the subsequent eruptions of the same year that decimated neighboring villages like Morne-Balai, Morne-Capot, Ajoupa-Bouillon, Morne-Rouge, and nearly all inhabitants (including Père Mary). For further studies (and of varying quality), see again Chrétien and Brousse's *La montagne Pelée*, as well as Gordon Thomas and Max Morgan Witt's *The Day the World Ended*, Alwyn Scarth's *La catastrophe* [*The Catastrophe*], Léo Ursulet's *Le désastre de 1902 à la Martinique* [*The Disaster of 1902 in Martinique*], and Ernest Zebrowski, Jr.'s, *The Last Days of St. Pierre*. In *Essais de mémoire*, Philippe Ariès provides reflection on 1902 as a means for examining memory as related to such events, but includes no reference to Cyparis.

13 The description finds itself strikingly repeated in the Barnum and Bailey poster created for billing Cyparis as "Ludger Sylbaris" or "The Most Marvellous Man on Earth"; for reproductions of the image, see Chrétien

and Brousse, Morgan *Fire*, and "The Barnum and Bailey." See, also, the adaptation of the poster for Wagram and Tabar's *Cyparis, seul au monde*.

14 Based on existing research, references to Cyparis in French-language texts seem to have dwindled after his engagement with Barnum and Bailey.

15 Nearly all of the projects cited and referenced here systematically agree that the records on Cyparis's life after 1903 are virtually non-existant. The varied accounts, and especially those that push his fall from fame, as well as events that could have led to the reported stabbing and the assumed expulsion from the circus bring into question whether or not Cyparis's life was really saved by the eruption.

16 Use of the term "intellectual" with respect to abilities differs from discursive practices in regions such as the United States, where expressions such as "mental retardation" and "intellectual disabilities" are used. Moreover, its presence in *Operation Freak* refers to the full spectrum of intellectual abilities, which include but are not limited to clinically or culturally classifiable intellectual disabilities, assesments of intelligence, and references to skills needed to engage in a profession, trade, or craft. For discussion of the terminology (including the changing of the name) in the US context, see, for example: Schalock, et al., "The Renaming"; and the website for the American Association on Intellectual and Developmental Disabilities (aamr.com). Uses of the same expression, as well as variations of it along with terminology for different yet related theoretical, educational, and scientific conceptualizations (e.g., "learning disability" in the United Kingdom), appear in other parts of the world. In French, related expressions may include "déficience intellectuelle," "incapacité intellectuelle," and "handicap mental." These appear in journals such as *Revue francophone de la déficience intellectuelle* [*Francophone Journal of Intellectual Disability*] and are used by the Union Nationale des Associations de Parents, de Personnes Handicapées Mentales et de leurs Amis, France [The National Union of Associations of Families, Mentally Handicapped Persons, and their Friends, France]. They are also used by l'Institut québécois de la déficience intellectuelle [the Quebec Institute of Intellectual Disability] and research centres such as the Institut Cochin in Paris and organizations such as the Canadian Association for Research and Education in Intellectual Disabilites. They also appear in conferences, such as the 2008 conference in Morocco entitled "The Socioprofessional Integration of Individuals with Intellectual Disabilities" at the Mohamed VI National Centre of the Disabled.

17 Godbout's novel remains untranslated, and, because of the strategic use of French and English in the narrative, it is in ways untranslatable.

18 For broader discussions of the field, see, among others, Beniamino, *La fran-cophonie littéraire* [*The Literary* francophonie]; Moura, *Littératures francopho-nes et théorie postcoloniale* [*Francophone Literatures and Postcolonial Theory*]; or Tétu, *Qu'est-ce que la francophonie?* [*What Is* la francophonie?]. One of the many recent participants in this debate is Subha Xavier, who has developed a theory grounded in concepts of migrant literature that she has presented at various conferences, including "Mémoire, diasporas, et formes du roman francophone contemporain" ["Memory, Diasporas, and Forms of the Con-temporary Francophone Novel"], sponsored by the Department of French Studies, University of Waterloo (29 April 2011). See also her article, "Mehdi Charef and the Politics of French Immigration."

19 Again, unless otherwise stated, all translations are mine.

20 Publications related to *littérature-monde* have appeared. Le Bris and Rouaud, *Pour une littérature-monde* [*For a World Literature*]; Hargreaves et al., *Trans-national French Studies*. See also Deblaine, Abdelkader, and Chancé, eds., *Transmission et théories des littératures francophones* [*Transmission and Theories of Francophone Literatures*].

21 Songolo maintains that, for example, the (now decade-old) increase in tenured US faculty positions in *la francophonie* attests to its rise in popular-ity. However, a home for this body of literature – a body understood as non-European French-language literature – is often contested and inconsistent within the "global" academy because the field is seen at times as temporary and even as dangerous to existing departments of French or literature (7).

22 See Davis, *Bending over Backwards* (especially "Who Put the 'the' in 'the Novel'?"), and Quayson, *Aesthetic Nervousness*.

23 See both Garland Thomson's introduction to the collection *Freakery* and her own study, *Extraordinary Bodies*.

24 See, among others, Swan's "Disabilities, Bodies, Voices"; and Davis's *Enforcing Normalcy*.

25 Such spectral conceptualizations of identity also find an echo in Benítez Rojo's theory of the polyrhythm in Caribbean cultural production (see *Repeating Island*, particularly the introduction). With intersecting rhythms and no fixed centre, such production implies movement that is connected to, for example, body language and the ability to walk (well) (18).

26 Dayan's work also serves a similar discourse. When, in the preface to her recent monograph, *The Law Is a White Dog*, she interrogates populations understandable as the disenfranchised, she underscores the need to bring the notion of continuum (including, for example, that between past and present) into discussions of identification. Similarly, the question of bodily

abilities permeates her work. In the same project, Dayan employs concepts
of disability to speak of such processes in a context that references what she
terms "negative personhood" (xii-xiii). Dayan's earlier work, *Haiti, History,
and the Gods*, speaks very clearly of the varied abilities – physical and
spiritual – that Jean-Jacques Dessalines was said to possess and for which he
is remembered (see the sections entitled "Dessalines, Dessalines Demanbre"
and "Dismemberment, Naming, and Divinity").

27 See also Murray's "Autism Functions" and *Autism*.

28 One of the notable exceptions and now frequent references is Stiker, *Corps
    infirmes et sociétés*, first published through Aubier Montainge (1982) and
    now in its third edition through Dunod (2005); it has also existed in
    English translation since 1999 as *A History of Disability* (U of Michigan P).

29 See, for example, the afterword in Eagleton, *Literary Theory*.

30 For examples of certain of the preliminary works, see Davis, *Enforcing
    Normalcy*; Linton, *Claiming Disability*; and Mitchell and Snyder, *Body and
    Physical Difference*. Recent projects include Murray, "Autism Functions" and
    Autism; and Siebers, *Disability Theory* and *Disability Aesthetics*. For inter-
    sections with other categories of identity, see Garland Thomson, *Extraordi-
    nary Bodies* (with particular emphasis on representations of women); and
    McRuer, *Crip Theory*. With respect to literature of metropolitan France, see
    Berberi's various articles exploring the uses of disability and impairment in
    nineteenth-century literature, including her most recent, "Rhapsodist at
    Mid-Century." Collard and Samama recently released *Handicaps et sociétés
    dans l'histoire: L'estropié, l'aveugle et le paralytique de l'Antiquité aux temps
    modernes* [*Disabilities and Societies of History: The Cripple, the Blind, and
    the Paralytic from Antiquity to the Modern Era*], a collection of historical
    studies of varying world regions that run through the late eighteenth
    century.

31 See Quayson, *Calibrations* and, especially, *Aesthetic Nervousness*. See also
    Barker, *Postcolonial Fiction and Disability* (2012) and "From Narrative
    Prosthesis to Disability Counternarrative," and Amanda Morrison's
    "Cuerpos latinoamericanos: La discapacidad fundacional en la novela
    hispanoamericana 1847–1958" ["Latin American Bodies: Disability as
    Foundational in the Latin American Novel 1847–1958"]. My use of "the
    West" (and its derivatives) aligns itself with Glissant (1981; 1989), who
    defines it as a project and not as a space (14; 2).

32 For Nack Ngue, see again *Critical Conditions* as well as her essays (notably
    "The Body of Survival" and "Colonial Discourses").

33 An increased understanding of the historical ideology of bodily ability in a
    developing French colonial empire should also include the study of any

discourse pertaining to the bodies and abilities attributed to the range of ethnic groups consolidated under the reign of Louis XIV and his systematic, even normalizing, efforts to produce a cohesive identity for the kingdom.

34 See Flaugh, "Of Colonized Mind and Matter."

35 See, for example, Sharpley-Whiting, *Black Venus*; and Gilman, *Difference and Pathology*. Saartje Baartman is but one example among many of individuals from varying world regions and varying historical periods brought to Europe, specifically France, and exhibited within a context either of "scientific" (e.g., ethnographic) abnormality or of cultural performativity. French explorers and colonizers of the sixteenth century captured various peoples of the New World and brought them to the court, where these individuals became spectacles and, at times, slaves. The display of difference took on a larger scale, especially for France's kings and queens; such spectacles included the parade of costumed individuals, the replication of presumed customs (with recognition of cannibalism), and the creation of villages constructed in what were believed to be an authentic reproduction of various New World populations (such as the Tupinamba from regions of today's Brazil). See, for example, Jaenen, *Friend and Foe*; and Dickason, "Sixteenth-Century French Vision of Empire."

36 Buck-Morss's reading of Sala-Molins's *Le code noir* provides a useful understanding of "meubles" as "moveable property" (32). See also Dayan's reading in *Haiti*.

37 See, for example, Gagné, *King's Daughters and Founding Mothers*.

38 The French translation of Garland Thomson's introductory essay to *Freakery* proposes *monstre culturel* as the equivalent to "freak of culture" (Thomson, "Du prodige à l'erreur," 44). While there is perhaps little denotative difference between *monstre culturel* and *monstre de la culture*, the latter responds directly, in a reappropriative gesture, to historical French terminology such as *merveille de la nature* and, to a lesser degree, *bizarrerie de la nature*.

39 When the term appears in the novels, it refers most often to a character's monstrous psychological or social comportment.

40 The most notable thus far is Bancel et al., *Zoos humains*, whose essays primarily explore the presence of colonized individuals in displays in Western Europe and the United States. As more thoroughly explained in chapter 1, two editions of *Zoos humains* exist in the original French, with some differences between them. I reference and cite the 2004 publication.

41 It must be noted that the novels were published in the 1980s by authors who, although of different regions of the world, were living primarily in geographical regions (Quebec, the United States, and France) where the above-mentioned critical discourses of the body, and in a nascent manner of

the freak and of disability, were rising to the surface. Such an intersection of author, sociocultural region, and ideological shift may seem to suggest an external cultural influence on their writings of the body. However, they do not impose one specific culture or discursive strategy on the varied socio-cultural contexts that they represent; rather, the authors have chosen to detail the ways in which characters, as individuals existing within the repre-sented regions, find themselves and their bodily abilities operated by agents who hold the reins of such discourses.

42 Bancel et al. (*Zoos humains*) along with Castillo (*Baroque Horrors*) and the previously referenced Chemers (*Staging Stigma*) continue to help us think through the varied reasons for the presence of displays and spectacles in different time periods, geographical regions, and stylistic traditions.

43 See, again, Garland Thomson's introduction to *Freakery*. See also Fiedler. *Freaks*; and Bogdan, *Freak Show*.

44 See, for example, Yvon Bellemare's work on Jacques Godbout, Carine Bour-get's and Jarrod Hayes's work on Tahar Ben Jelloun, and Mireille Rosello's and Christopher Miller's work on Condé.

CHAPTER ONE

1 It may come as no surprise that Chebel's approach was developed during his professional work in psychoanalysis. The fact that he completed his work in Paris and has continued to write from France about the Maghreb and, specifically, about his homeland, Algeria, have resulted in claims that his work is irrelevant. See, for example, Nidhal Guessoum's critique ("Une histoire déformée de la Raison en Islam" ["A Deformed History of Reason in Islam"]) of Chebel's *L'islam et la raison: Le combat des idées* (2006) [*Islam and Reason: The Battle of Ideas*].

2 *Operation Freak* follows Garland Thomson's lead by using "freak discourse" (see the introduction to *Freakery*).

3 Because of its historical positioning in Montaigne's editing process and its ensuing content, the 1588 edition remains central to the present study.

4 See also Glidden, "Face in the Text"; Boyle, "Montaigne's Consubstantial Book"; and Lyons, *Before Imagination*.

5 Other readings of the *boiteux* and the *boiteuses* include Davis, *Return of Martin Guerre*; and Renner, "Monstrous Body of Writing."

6 Be it to demonstrate his own human nature or to draw in his reader, Montaigne strengthens his argument by including himself in the group of gawkers: "Car, par la seule authorité de l'usage ancien et publique de ce mot, je me suis autresfois faict à croire avoir reçu plus de plaisir d'une

femme de ce qu'elle n'estoit pas droicte, et mis cela en recepte de ses graces" [For by the sole authority of the ancient and public use of that proverb, I once made myself believe that I had received more pleasure from a woman because she was not straight, and credited that to the account of her charms] (1034; 791).

7 See also Diprose, *Corporeal Generosity*. Nietzsche, like Montaigne, wrote of human nature in a manner that demonstrates a wry awareness of the realities of the human body. Their changes in health shifted their bodies away from constructed norms of sociocultural abilities. Furthermore, their writings demonstrate how illness alone, as Nack Ngue (*Critical Conditions*) argues, alters abilities and therefore informs not only identity but also the writing process.

8 See also Stone, *Culture and Disability*.

9 In addition to the UN General Assembly's *Convention on the Rights of Persons with Disabilities and Its Optional Protocol*, disability rights representation also exists in forums such as the Organization of African Unity's *African Charter of Human and People's Rights* (chapter 1, article 18 [4], 1982) as well as in the *Inter-American Convention on the Elimination of All Forms of Discrimination against Persons with Disabilities*, adopted 7 June 1999 by the Organization of American States. Research into the application and efficacy of the latter two enactments as they relate to cultural production has yet to be conducted in any significant manner. Within the context of the French nation-state, see also the loi du 11 février 2005 ("Loi 2005–102") whereby the French government works to assure more extensive access to and maintenance of rights for the disabled in all of its departments through the establishment of Maisons départementales des personnes handicapées. For the overseas departments of French Guiana, Guadeloupe, Martinique, Mayotte (a department effective March 2011), and Réunion, this may allow for reflective incorporation of relevant sociocultural and geopolitical criteria without teetering towards risky applications of cultural relativism. However, such questions are yet to be explored.

10 See also Nack Ngue's *Critical Conditions* for her incorporation of Dayan's work.

11 As a demonstration of the long-term awareness within metropolitan France of the dismemberment of slaves and the value placed on their body's abilities, see Jean-Michel Moreau's drawing (with the following excerpt: "C'est à ce prix que vous mangez du sucre en Europe" [It is at this price that you eat sugar in Europe]) for the mutilated sugar mill slave of Surinam in chapter 19 of Voltaire's *Candide*.

12 The translation, completed by J. Michael Dash, is only one of several

selected essays from *Discours*. See Mardorossian's commentary on the need for a full translation in "From Fanon to Glissant."

13 See again Miller, *French Atlantic Triangle*, particularly his discussions of the work of Césaire as an attempt to reimagine the lines between West Africa, the Caribbean, and France.

14 See, for example, the calls to action and commentaries of the Liyannaj Kont Pwofitasyon (LKP) [Stand Up Against Exploitation] and the Confédération générale du travail de la Martinique (CGTM) [General Confederation of Labour in Martinique]. Note that, particularly since February 2009, they have spoken (largely metaphorically) not only of submission and objectification but also of the amputation of powers and a resulting overall immobility. See, notably, "Préparons activement la mobilisation générale à compter du jeudi 5 février" (n.d.) ["Let's Actively Prepare for the General Mobilization of Thursday 5 February"] by the CGTM and "Contre la peur et l'agenouillement" (5 October 2009) ["Against Fear and Subservience"] by the LKP.

15 See also the edited collection by Reeser and Seifert, *Entre hommes.*

16 Emphasis in the original and the translation.

17 The citation from the English is found on Tremain's page 5; however, the citation here is from the 1978 translation as Tremain's source includes one difference in punctuation. Also, Tremain does not cite the original French.

18 References such as "notre société" (our society) reveal Stiker's end-goal: to discuss the epistemology of disability and impairment thought in French society (*Corps infirmes* 30; *A History* 32). It is not until the third edition (2005) that Stiker adds a chapter in which he proposes a means for discussing "une nouvelle théorie du handicap" [a new theory of disability] grounded in psychoanalytic notions of liminality. In addition to providing a useful outline of four existing theories of disability, Stiker aims (as the note for the third edition explains) to enliven the debate. He has a second book (2006) that explores literary representations of disability from the sixteenth into the twentienth centuries.

19 The two terms collapse into "disability" in the 1999 English translation, which speaks to certain theoretical trends with respect to disability; it should be noted, however, that some disability studies specialists writing in English make the same distinctions as did Stiker for both similar and different reasons. For developments in terminology, see the transformations traced by Barnes and Mercer in *Disability*. To draw the same distinction in English and to make Stiker's terminology clear, I use only literal translations for the discussion of his work.

20 It is worth noting that, to a significant degree, Garland Thomson's study revolves around the specific emphasis on bodily ability in the United States with regard to the Americans with Disabilities Act, 1990. However, her theory of normality as a cultural construct remains general – general enough to be adapted to other cultures.

21 To bring back an earlier citation, Garland Thomson maintains that "the 'physically disabled' are produced by way of legal, medical, political, cultural, and literary narratives that comprise an exclusionary discourse" (*Extraordinary* 6). In the past few years, the question of eugenics has been playing an increasing role in Garland Thomson's research. See, for example, Garland Thomson *Staring*.

22 Davis argues in the same project that the nineteenth-century Western novel is, in a period that witnessed significant developments in science (with an emphasis on cures), profoundly linked to disability, health, and normativity. In the chapter entitled "Who Put the 'the' in 'the novel'?", he posits that, in large part, the novel rose because it presented protagonists who were removed from or clashed with a norm, along with their ensuing experiences, and that readers yearned to consume either the consequent struggle or reconciliation. Davis's claim needs to be further explored in comparison to, for example, French novels of the seventeenth and eighteenth centuries. However, a very fruitful conversation could be realized by reading his work alongside Prince's "Towards a Normative Criticism of the Novel" as well as with Beniamino's "Langue et norme littéraire" ["Language and Literary Norms"] in *Francophonie littéraire*.

23 See, for example, Paré, *Des monstres et prodiges*.

24 Of related interest on various forms and contexts of exhibits (of the human but also of the non-human) are Clair, *Human Curiosities*; Hamon, *Expositions*; and Mauriès, *Cabinets de curiosités* [*Cabinets of Curiosities*].

25 See also Gordon, *Why the French Love Jerry Lewis* and *Dances with Darwin* for more on the role of ethnicity and medical conditions such as epilepsy in the development of popular entertainment in nineteenth- and twentieth-century France.

26 Because the English version of the introduction is radically different in content and in organization from the original French, the translation for this citation is my own.

27 Eighteenth- and nineteenth-century scientists also worked to establish a hierarchy of the races that sought to associate, among other things, certain types of abilities with specific racial categories that were established or that various scientists were in the process of establishing. See, as examples, Gobineau and the Saint-Hilaires.

28 For an analysis of historical documents detailing the civilizing mission, see Francis Affergan's chapter, "Inclusion et exclusion" ["Inclusion and Exclusion"], in *Critiques anthropologiques* [*Anthropological Critiques*].

29 See also his article, "Le Freak, C'est Chic" for an earlier reflection on the topic that offers additional perspectives.

30 In a British context, see Durbach's *Spectacle of Deformity: Freak Shows and Modern British Culture*.

31 There is no explicit reference to Genette's theory of hypertextuality or to his hypertext; however, the parallel is worthy of further exploration.

32 The Hippocratic Oath (including its many versions translated into different languages for different cultural contexts) functions as a historically institutionalized promise to, among other things, ethically care for the body while treating it. Steven Miles's *The Hippocratic Oath and the Ethics of Medecine* offers just one example of the oath's historical and contemporary interpretation in the practice of medicine and the practitioner's engagement with patients.

33 *The Deliverer from Error* has also appeared as *Deliverance from Error* (as in the translation of McCarthy).

34 Lennard Davis has already begun work on ability-charged readings of Hippolyte and the few portraits of him that are informed by the intersections between "capitalism, material life, culture, and fiction" ("Constructing Normalcy" 27). Davis teases out how characters in the novel, depending on their interests in profit and production, perceive Hippolyte as healthy and productive or as unhealthy and unproductive and, thus, in need of a cure. Davis's highlighting of such varied sociocultural understandings of bodily ability within one cultural context speaks to my discussion of the spectrum of bodily abilities. Consider, in particular, this reflection from Davis's same essay: "Hippolyte's disability is in fact an ability, one which he relies on, and from which he gets extra horsepower, as it were" (Davis 20). Davis's argument could be taken farther with an exploration of Gustave Flaubert's personal history, particularly his upbringing at the hands of his father, Achille-Cléophas Flaubert, a surgeon in Rouen. It is also worth looking at Flaubert's own meticulous research and incisive method as they appear, for example, in his search for *le mot juste* (the right word).

35 See, for example, Sartre, *Huis clos* [*No Exit*]; or Camus, *La peste* [*The Plague*].

36 See, among others, Zola, *Germinal*; or Maupassant. "La mère aux monstres" ["A Mother of Monsters"].

37 For Fanon, see the aforementioned *Peau noire, masques blancs*. With respect to Foucault, see, for example, Miller, "Toward a Post-Foucauldian History of Discursive Practices."

38 Emphasis added.

39 When Foucault speaks of the means by which deviated or abnormal subjects can come back to the normal, he argues that the institutionalized practice relies upon the individual's confession – the detailing of childhood or of the personal story. Caputo and Yount explain that such recounting leads to the production of the subject, a process conducted within a context of, and therefore dependent upon, norm-based power relations associated with the institutional environment that oversees such confession (6).

40 See Benjamin, "Work of Art in the Age of Mechanical Reproduction"; Hennessy, *Materialist Feminism and the Politics of Discourse*; Jameson, *Postmodernism*; or Marcuse, *One-Dimensional Man*.

41 See, among other projects, Taylor, *Sources of the Self*; and Kruks, *Retrieving Experience*.

42 In the first volume of *Histoire de la sexualité*, Foucault discusses the history of capitalism's development when he explores the development of the discourse on modern sexual repression – an exploration that, especially in its discussion of reproduction, speaks to what I propose in this section: "à l'époque où on exploite systématiquement la force de travail, pouvait-on tolérer qu'elle aille s'égailler dans les plaisirs, sauf dans ceux, réduits au minimum, qui lui permettent de se reproduire?" [At a time when labour capacity was being systematically exploited, how could this capacity be allowed to dissipate itself in pleasurable pursuits, except in those – reduced to a minimum – that enabled it to reproduce itself?] (12–3; 6).

43 See Butler, *Bodies That Matter*; and Cixous, "Le rire de la méduse" ["The Laugh of the Medusa"].

INTERLUDE ONE

1 See Dreger, *One of Us*.

2 Prior to this book's publication, for "King Abdulaziz Medical City," the Kingdom's website for the National Guard Health Affairs listed on its "Department of Surgery" page a category entitled "Achievements" under which was listed "Twin surgeries." Emphasizing the operations as humanitarian acts, the Kingdom also established a website named *Conjoined Twins* dedicated entirely to surgical individuation (6 January 2010). See also "Siamese Twins and Separation" and the related blog postings.

3 "72 Hours after the Successful Separation."

4 "Moroccan Twins Aziza [sic] and Saeedah Leave the NGHA."

5 With regard to the Cameroonian twins Pheinbom and Shevoboh, who were operated upon on 21 April 2007, an April 2010 update by Ngwa Niba,

"Cameroon's Conjoined Twins Help Spread Islam," emphasizes two details: (1) further delays in full realization of the twins' individuality, including the wait to return to Saudi Arabia for prosthetic legs and the completion of the ability to individually ambulate, and (2) the sociocultural context of their home village, Babanki Tungo, where they were once feared as a curse but are now valued as a blessing. As the title reveals, the article even goes so far as to suggest that Pheinbom's and Shevoboh's successful operation at KAMC and their return to the village is responsible for the spread of Islam due to the Saudi government's establishment of an Islamic centre (including a mosque and primary school) and the steady conversion of several community members (with the twins' parents being the first to make the change) of the predominantly Christian community. For the BBC's original report on Pheinbom and Shevoboh, see "Joy as Cameroon Twins Separated."

CHAPTER TWO

1   See, for example, Bellemare, *Jacques Godbout: Le devoir d'inquiéter* [*Jacques Godbout: The Duty to Disturb*] and *Jacques Godbout, romancier* [*Jacques Godbout, Novelist*], Galéry "*Les têtes à Papineau*: Comment peut-on être québécois ?" [*Les têtes à Papineau*: How to be Québécois?], Piette, "Les langues à Papineau: Comment le texte national se fait littérature" ["The Papineau Languages: How the National Text Becomes Literary"]; and Sadkowski, "Questioning National Identities."

2   As indicated in chapter 1, my intent is not to rely solely on Foucault in this or in any other specific theoretical position. Despite such statements, it would be entirely possible to conduct a Foucauldian analysis of the text in order to demonstrate that the protagonists, influenced by the power that Dr Northridge holds as representative of clinical knowledge and authority, are – or Charles is – disciplined into believing that they are deviant and therefore being convinced to alter their bodies. Such a subjugation of the disciplined soul penetrated by power relations demonstrates the possibility of rereading the *tête-à-tête* as the condemnation of the minds, not the heads (and thus their bodies). François's subtle, quiet resistance to Northridge does, however, trouble too simple a reading. Nevertheless, the notions of corporeality and condemnation, as implicit within the protagonists' statements, are revisited later in the chapter in a somewhat different context. As the protagonists' narrative speaks of a menace to Quebec's laws on the use of French, a Foucauldian reading of this particular scene could be furthered with arguments about agents of medical (specifically psychological) expertise who invade and alter the medical and judicial institutions: "L'expertise

médicale viole la loi dès le départ" [Expert medical opinion violates the law from the start] (38; 41).

3 The reference to intellectual abilities aligns itself with the explanation provided in chapter 1.

4 Emphasis in the original.

5 See Paterson's discussion of postmodernism's mid-1980s rise in *Postmodernism and the Quebec Novel*, originally published in French as *Moments postmodernes dans le roman québécois*.

6 See Piette for a more extensive discussion of the journalist as inventor and embellisher in Godbout's literary works and essays.

7 Due in part to this rebellion, the Parliament of the United Kingdom passed the Union Act, 1840, whose controversial and contested article 41 mandated the erasure of the use of French in, for example, the writing of legislation and which, thereby, intensified the long debate over the use of language.

8 See, for example, Maillet's allegorical novel, *Pélagie-la-charette* [*Pélagie*], which testifies to the ramifications of such eviction.

9 Mainstream internet sources, such as a Daily Kos wiki page, "Quebec Sovereignty Referendum" (17 April 2006), hypothesized that, had the PQ taken the majority in the then projected 2007–08 general elections in Quebec, it would have pushed for another referendum within eighteen months of taking power. On recent activities, see most notably Bernard Drainville's 19 February 2010 letter, "Lettre à Lucien Bouchard: La course vers la souveraineté" ["Letter to Lucien Bouchard: The Race for Sovereignty"] originally published on *Le Devoir.com* but also listed on the "Actualité" page of the PQ website.

10 Since the inception of *loi 101*, the Quebec government enacted *loi 178* in 1988 to allow for an increased representation of English in some public signage and advertisements (Bourhis and Landry 110–1). In 2008, Pauline Marois made efforts to rewrite *loi 101* to allow for increased instruction of French in schools and to encourage its use in small businesses.

11 Recognition of the anniversaries of *loi 101* prove the continued efforts not only to preserve the language, the culture, and even the legislation but also to demonstrate the expanded ethnic base of Quebec, as with the celebration for the bill's twenty-fifth anniversary. One striking example includes the televised advertisement "Charte de la langue française: 25 ans et pleine d'avenir" ["Charter of the French Language: 25 Years and Full of Future"], a performance of Yves Duteil's song "La langue de chez nous" ["Language from Our Home"] by individuals chosen to represent Québécois of various ages, ethnic backgrounds, regions, and social levels. A link once existed for "Le Jour anniversaire de la Charte de la langue française" ["Anniversary Day of the Charter of the French Language"].

12 See Dubuisson and Nadeau, *Etudes sur la langue des signes québécoise* [*Studies on Quebec Sign Language*]; Gaucher, "Le citoyen sourd: Du mouvement social à la communauté identitaire" ["The Deaf Citizen: From Social Movement to Group Identity"]; and Veillette *État de la situation de la langue des signes québécoise : Rapport de recherche et pistes de solution proposées par l'Office des personnes handicapées du Québec. Synthèse* [*The Current State of Québécois Sign Language: White Paper of the Office of Disabled Persons of Quebec. Synthesis*].

13 The findings are located on a Wikipedia page for LSQ. More work needs to be done to follow through on the relationship between citizenship and the deaf community, including how members of the latter might feel about such linguistic divides and their own relationship with *loi 101*.

14 For contemporary musings on the multi-layered history of the racial slur, see *Debates of the Senate (Hansard)*; and Zolf, "Speak White."

15 The only translation to date of Isidore Geoffroy Saint-Hilaire's work is of the title as located under his name in the online version of the *Encyclopaedia Britannica*. His research is in part a response to and continuation of works of his father, Etienne Geoffroy Saint-Hilaire, such as *Philosophie anatomique: Des monstruosités humaines* [*Anatomical Philosophy: Human Monstrosities*].

16 Multiple births (triplets, quadruplets, and beyond) function in a similar manner. Historically speaking, Canada contributed to this industry of production with the Dionne Quintuplets, who, in the seven years after their 1934 birth, attracted 3 million visitors to their state-sanctioned observatory in northern Ontario. They are also explicitly referred to in *Les têtes à Papineau* with respect to the amount of attention they, like Godbout's protagonists, received in printed text alone (97). See Berton, *Dionne Years*, for one version of their life history, including discussion of concerns that the children might be anglicized while under the state's care. See also evidence of scientific fascination in the detailed studies of the Dionnes' development during their residency at the Defoe Nursery, published in Blatz et al., *Collected Studies on the Dionne Quintuplets*.

17 One similarly documented case appears in Paré's figure 13, only here the heads correspond to aspects of the body relating to the male and female genders (17; 19).

18 Bodgan, among others, proposes that such choices are the product of profit-hungry parties who sought out such legendary bodies and placed them on stage (13–4). See also Bancel et al., *Human Zoos*. Chemers's *Staging Stigma* touches on the question of exploitation but looks more deeply at the question of the choice of freak performers.

19 See, among many examples, the cover of the Oxford World's Classics 1998
    edition of the text.

20 See Grosz, "Intolerable Ambiguity," and her framing of similarly posed ques-
    tions, including those related to sexual activity ("How do they do *it*?") (64).
    See also Blyn, "From Stage to Page," for her distinction between spectacle
    and carnival in written literature, particularly her work on spectacle in liter-
    ature that she identifies as "freak fictions."

21 Here a reading of Said's *Orientalism* may be more fully developed, includ-
    ing with regard to the ways that Quebec represents a mysterious yet objecti-
    fied space.

22 While the United States is arguably the largest proponent of such an ideol-
    ogy, globalization via media and internet could be argued to disseminate
    the awareness of such surgeries. The rhetoric of such reports often addresses
    the procedure in a manner that supports norm-centred ideals of indepen-
    dence as well as scientific progress. Consider the following examples, with
    fuller narratives at *ConjoinedTwins.med.sa*: the Kingdom of Saudi Arabia's
    extensive reporting on numerous cases of successful surgical separation of
    twins (primarily from the Kingdom but also from regions such as
    Cameroon, Morocco, The Philippines, and Poland) conducted at King
    Abdulaziz Medical City (see Interlude One); Russo's 2008 reporting for ABC
    News, which bears traces of a discourse of independence and progress in
    her article on two-year-old Lakshmi Tatma from India (who, in 2007, under-
    went surgery at Sparsh Hospital in Bangalore for removal of a parasitic
    twin); and Emma Morton's 2010 report for the United Kingdom's the *Sun*
    on the "surprise" appearance of a parasitic twin. What requires attention in
    further exploration of such cases is the level to which Western ideology has
    informed the decisions to individuate as well as the degree to which the
    correlating sociocultural contexts demonstrate an ideology (if any) of such
    individuation.

23 See also Thomspon, *Mystery and Lore of Monsters*, especially the chapter enti-
    tled "The Psychology of Monsters: The Law of Monsters," for commentary
    on the allocation of individuality (126). Contemporary discussions similar
    to these continue to occur, including with respect to conjoined one-year-old
    twins. See Jacoby, "Airline"; and Martin, "Delta Requires Two Seats."

24 The notion of the war finds other references in *Les têtes à Papineau*, notably
    in François's likening of the surgery to a bloody, violent battle in the chap-
    ter entitled "huitièmement" ["eightly"] as well as in the opening reference
    to the facility with which Northridge was affiliated – the "Institut des anciens
    combattants de Vancouver (BC)" ["Veterans Institute of Vancouver [BC]"]
    (Godbout 145; 13). For more on the relationship between disabled veterans

and the Western state and society, as well as the fate of such veterans in nation-states of frequently shifting power regimes, see Gerber's edited collection, *Disabled Veterans in History*.

25 As the novel works continuously to present a general anxiety about English-language invasion, whether from anglophone Canada or from the United States, the letter demonstrates a hint of a non-Canadian English and thus a further external contaminant in the spelling of "honor," which does not respect the standard Canadian English spelling of "honour."

26 Varying historical interpretations of the citation can be found in, for example, Archibald Alison's *History of Europe from the Commencement of the French Revolution in 1789, to the Restoration of the Bourbons in 1815*; Edme-Bonaventure Courtois's *Papiers inédits trouvés chez Robespierre, Saint-Just, Payan, etc., supprimés ou omis par Courtois* [*Unpublished Texts of Robespierre, Saint-Just, Payan, etc., Removed or Omitted by Courtois*]; or Ernest Hamel's *Histoire de Robespierre, d'après des papiers de famille, les sources originales et des documents entièrement inédits* [*History of Robespierre, according to Family Papers, the Original Sources and Documents Wholly Unpublished*]. For more information on Robespierre, *la Terreur*, or the French Revolution of 1789, see Laurent Dingli's *Robespierre*; Jean-Philippe Domecq's *Robespierre, derniers temps* [*The Last Days of Robespierre*]; David Jordan's *The Revolutionary Career of Maximilien Robespierre*; Jean-Clément Martin's *La Terreur: Part maudite de la Révolution* [*The Terror: The Accursed Part of the Revolution*]; and Anne Simonin's "The Terror as a Legal Fiction."

CHAPTER THREE

1 For one critical reading among others on the presence of Borges (through style, content, and character) in Ben Jelloun's novel, see Fayad, "Borges in Tahar Ben Jelloun's *L'enfant de sable*."

2 With respect to the Maghrebian narratives under discussion, although all interpretations of such categories are not identical in Algeria and Morocco, their frequent similarities allow a careful combination in order to decipher the fundamental concepts at play in these processes of identification and their related narratives.

3 In this chapter I consider Mernissi's source text to be the original 1975 English text and use it as the base for the discussion. The 2003 text reveals minor changes to the distinction between the two universes, and these tend to take the emphasis off of sexuality and place it on domesticity. Citations from the 2003 edition are referenced only if they differ from the earlier edition and only if they inform the discussion (in such cases, page number

references are for the English original, then the French translation, and then the English republication). I do not make references to the revised edition in the English, released in 1987 with a new introduction; however, I have included it in my bibliography.

4 The citation in the original English reads as follows: "Members do not partake in any unifying task together (except procreation)" (*Beyond* 82); the French translation places the concept in a dependent clause: "A l'exception de la procréation, hommes et femmes ne sont pas censés collaborer aux tâches que requiert la survie de la société" (*Sexe* 158).

5 Chebel's *Le corps en Islam* was first published in 1984 as *Le corps dans la tradition au Maghreb* [*The Body in the Maghrebian Tradition*].

6 See "Operating Narrative: Words on Gender and Disability in Two Novels of Tahar Ben Jelloun" (2009) for my preliminary discussion of this topic.

7 For the most part, I follow the existing English translation of the two novels. However, later in this section I explain the reason for the change from the English "The Man" (1). A handful of similar variations appear as well.

8 In addition to Glissant, *Poetics of Relation*; and Moura, *Littératures francophones*; see also Julien, *African Novels*, for an intelligent discussion of the complexity of orality and in particular how her argument works to undo essentialist interpretations of orality as it appears in African novels.

9 The bracketed clause in English was not carried over from the French.

10 The parenthetical sentence in English was not carried over from the French.

11 As I show in chapter 1, "handicap" and all of its variants, along with "infirmité" and its derivatives, are the terms that in French disability studies equates to the term "disability." In this instance only, I follow what the translator chose.

12 Bargach, *Orphans of Islam*, includes a list of long-standing charitable organizations for a variety of disabilities that should be compared to recently formed rights-based associations such as the Association Provinciale des Amis de l'handicapé (2003) (Provincial Association of the Friends of the Disabled) and the Collectif pour la Promotion des Droits des Personnes en situation de Handicap (2005) (Collective for the Promotion of Rights of the Disabled).

13 Originally referring to the testing of a metal with fire, *fitna* has come to signify a testing of the believers through persecution, enchantment, or seduction in which the Qur'an (sura 8:36–40) calls for them not only to refuse but also to put to an end. Such tests are often those of the flesh, tests that lead the believer astray. Thus, these tests demonstrate how closely *fitna* is linked to the human body (Newby 63; Esposito 87).

14 As established earlier, use of the term "conservative" for Islamic practices,

regions, and so on is largely informed by the concepts outlined in Bannerman's *Islam in Perspective*.

15   See also Hewer, *Understanding Islam*.

16   For a more extensive list of related sura, see the introduction in Chebel, *Le corps en Islam*.

17   At Mohammed VI's instruction, Morocco's government also issued the publication (in Arabic as well as in French, "en espérant permettre d'élargir la diffusion de ce guide aux lectrices et lecteurs francophones" [in the hope of enabling a wider distribution of the guide to its female and male francophone readers]) of a "guide pratique," or practical guide, for interpreting and applying the new version of the law both within the familial structure and within spheres of jurisprudence. Given the recurrent connection of the *Moudawana*'s articles to Islamic law alone, the document might also be read as a demonstration of the former's continued adherence to Shari'a. Such a conclusion is especially noteworthy given that, with the revised version, Mohammed VI proposed to modernize Morocco by rereading what I understand as master sociocultural narratives. An unofficial English translation of the entire Moudawana exists under the heading "The Moroccan Family Code (*Moudawana*) of 5 February 2004 on the website for Human Rights Education Associates (hrea.org); however, the translation here is my own. Further reflection upon such questions should also take into consideration Mohammed VI's proposed changes to the Constitution (and the changes to some of his powers) that would, as he argued, make Morocco a constitutional monarchy. The changes were put to a referendum on 1 July 2011 and voted on by just over 98 percent of voters (see Oberlé's "Maroc: Plébiscite confirmé pour la nouvelle Constitution" ["Morocco: Plebiscite Confirmed for the New Constitution"]). For additional reflection on the legislation, see Orlando, Hebouche, or Zvan.

18   See Amer, "Uncovering the Meaning"; and Lazreg, *Eloquence of Silence* and *Questioning the Veil*.

19   In this context, it is possible to consider these mid-1980s Moroccan French-language novels as testimony to how gender and disability were lived in Morocco. Neither women nor the disabled would be understood as deserving of rights or capable of independence, even during Morocco's gradual adoption of a rights-based model of government in this same period. Until the 2004 changes to the Moudawana, which included according women many rights equal to those of men with respect to marriage, women had virtually no say in polygamy or divorce. The disabled have also often been viewed as bodies in need of charity. See Bargach, *Orphans of Islam*.

20   See also Hayes, *Queer Nations*.

21 One may claim that such chapter titles function as Ben Jelloun's own efforts to attract readers to his texts – that is, through an artificial insertion of Western cultural referents to the freak. However, the consistent insistence on operation and sociocultural norms in the two novels is revelatory. It demonstrates that such authorial choices – read here as of the text – operate metaphorically for the typically hidden and damaging operations that reproduce freaks of culture in any country, including Morocco.

22 In the spirit of the novels, the character Salem later operates the *cirque forain* adventures to develop his own ultimately tragic ending. His version does involve cutting the protagonist's body in the fatal rape scene that he proposes: the protagonist, in an act of self-defence against an Abbas turned violently and sexually exploitative, places razor blades between the buttocks in order to wound or kill the sodomizing rapist (*L'enfant* 143; *Sand* 110–1). Although Salem's version could be read as a continuation of the exploitative operations of the Abbas family, the goal realized in Ahmed/Zahra's exertion is the non-alteration of procreative abilities. For that reason alone, the scene does not target the bodily region directly related to reproduction.

23 The French translation of Mernissi's work singles out via footnote a linguistic distinction in Amin's text – that "femme fatale" appears in French in his work composed in English – without providing any speculation as to what such a distinction might suggest (10).

24 The familiarity if not permanency of eunuchs finds greater proof in Marmon's study of written records dating from 1435. They indicate that Sultan Barsbay's appointment of a non-castrated male to the post of chief eunuch at Muhammad's tomb was considered a violation of tradition (42–3). See also Malti-Douglas, *Power, Marginality, and the Body*, for a reading of bodily abilities: the blind man was reputed for his enhanced sexual abilities ("the most virile of people") and the eunuch for his heightened clarity of sight and, thus, insight ("the one whose vision is the most correct") (226).

25 Such classification extends even to sexual intercourse, as Scholz demonstrates in reference to sura 2:25: eunuchs could be read as excluded even from Islamic afterlife and, thus, not as Muslim men. This is because castration prohibited them, as holders of male bodies, from following the holy directive in the afterlife of having sex with the "chaste virgins" (20). The question of eunuchs in the afterlife is debatable. However, the notion of sexual activity is not: Ringrose, Grosrichard, and others, as well as the online discussions at www.eunuch.org, reveal the contradiction and obvious conclusion that, although the eunuch was not (and is not) capable of biological reproduction, he was certainly capable of many kinds of sexual activity.

26 Marmon, *Eunuchs and Sacred Bodies*; Scholz, *Eunuchs and Castrati*; and

Chebel, *L'esprit*, provide extensive detail on the types of castration lived by the eunuchs (all external genitalia, testicles only, penis only, etc.), some of which were reportedly used to determine the status and, therefore, the duty and hierarchy of the eunuchs. This often resulted in a multifaceted hierarchy based on skin colour.

27 Grosrichard argues that their distribution of duties was especially evident in the writings on fully castrated black eunuchs (184–5).

28 This self-perception of deficiency in his a-virile daughters is comparable to what Barthes, in *S/Z*, proposes as the response of Sarrasine when he learns of and contemplates la Zambinella's castration and thus envisions the feared, ablating act of loss (104).

29 Such representation can be read to speak to the hadith-based ideology in the Sunan of Imam Abu Dawud that Allah has appointed a cure for every disease and that Muslims should always seek such treatment (Sunan Abu Dawud 1469:3865). Some members of the Islamic community include infertility within this range of disease. However, the same passage also corresponds to the trap of which many scholars of disability studies speak: disability as a trope for the passive, unproductive individual, either incapable of conforming to, or longing for a "cure" that will release them into, a normative state. See Davis, *Bending over Backwards*; and Garland Thomson, *Extraordinary Bodies*. On practices of men reassigning reproductive infertility to women, see, among others, de la Cruz et al., "History of the Penis."

30 While the *conteur*'s narration proposes other possibilities, such as replacing Ahmed/Zahra with a male child, Hadj Ahmed knows he must present the protagonist for circumcision, if only to resolve the question of the child's age and appearance. Chebel's specification of the typical age for circumcision as between three and five concurs with a detail specified only later in *La nuit sacrée* regarding the feigned circumcision: "Je devais avoir trois ou quatre ans" [I must have been three or four] (Chebel, *Le corps*, 173; *La nuit* 114; *The Sacred* 106).

31 Chebel (*L'esprit* 174) theorizes the child's own fear of castration during the process of circumcision, and Hayes (*Queer Nations*, 241–61) offers a fruitful discussion of emotional reactions to the similar prospect of castration.

32 Such readings might infer that pejoratively reductive connotations are assigned to the female and to the disabled body through the operation of the same narratives and that women are the regular and often tortured means by which both the narratives of Man and Woman are operating. With respect to gender, critics have offered strong arguments that perceive Ben Jelloun's narratives as further reductive of women for the violence that his female characters endure. See, for example, Boutkhil, "Evil Eye."

33 See Kratz, "Seeking Asylum," for a concise yet effective explanation of the
    various terms rhetorically used for such sociocultural operations, including
    her proposition to use the designation "genital modification" as an effort to
    approximate some neutrality within "the broader array of practices grouped
    together in international debate" (167, 196). See also Hernlund and Shell-
    Duncan, "Transcultural Positions."

34 This version includes the stitching together of most of the labia to form a
    small aperture, a procedure that is at times referred to as a Sudanese cli-
    toridectomy. Such acts were the focus of much global attention and were at
    the source of a decades- (if not century-) long related polemic, which
    includes the decade of the 1980s, when Ben Jelloun composed the two nov-
    els under study here (Kirby 84–5, 92). The scene from *La nuit sacrée* may
    well be argued as looking (and in ways as naively or as categorically as the
    protagonist) for possible assumptions of the Sudanese as barbarous and
    backwards, taken from a global discourse of female genital cutting that is
    itself a sociocultural narrative. Thinking in such terms reveals how operat-
    ing agents may rise to the level of the author, who, like the *conteur*, operates
    narratives to produce an incisively convincing and captivating norm-based
    tale.

INTERLUDE THREE

1 See, among others, McRuer, "Reflections on Disability," in *Disabling Postcolonialism*, a special issue of *Journal of Literary and Cultural Disability Studies*
   (October 2010).

2 Examples on both sides of the debate include: Cojean, "A Port-au-Prince, des
   amputations par milliers" ["In Port-au-Prince, Amputations by the Thou-
   sands"], *Le Monde*, 29 January 2010; Phillips, "Haiti Earthquake Creating a
   Generation of Amputees, Doctors Warn," *Guardian*, 1 March 2009; and
   Chancy, "Desecrated Bodies/Phantom Limbs." See also Munro, ed., *Haiti
   Rising*.

3 See "Haiti's Disabled"; "Handicapped Struggle."

4 See also http://www.potomitan.net/ (on the film *Poto Mitan*, 2009), which
   discusses the state of women's affairs in Haiti. The entirety of this reflection
   on amputations and normative discourse could also be connected to other
   historical periods in Haiti, when bodies were operated and mutilated by
   external forces, including but not limited to the Haitian revolution, the US
   occupation of the early twentieth century, and the Duvalier regimes (see
   Dayan *Haiti*). It is also possible to read such examples within the context of
   the greater francophone Caribbean, with events that disfigured bodies and

subsequently resulted in the transformation of abilities to produce. One such example is the discussion of Cyparis in the introduction to this book.

CHAPTER FOUR

1 Both *Le Robert* and the *Oxford English Dictionary* define "pariah" as a member of either a very low caste or of no caste – an "outcaste" – in India (originally) and as adopted in European sociocultural contexts. However, it is *Le Robert* that highlights the importance of the body to the etymology of "pariah." It states that contact with such individuals was "considéré comme une souillure" [considered a blemish]; it also provides a very telling synonym for "intouchable" [untouchable], proving through the use of a term that emphasizes physical contact with another body how the term "pariah" is inextricably linked to the body. See also the brief yet colourful history of the word "paria" in *Magazine littérarire* (1995).

2 This study's previous chapters could also have included discussion of the protagonists within varied geographical contexts as the novels do depict the characters' moving between various regions. However, because the representation of such movement in Condé's novel so clearly depicts the movement across and through sociocultural regions and so clearly demonstrates the importance of such movement to the identification processes that inform Tituba, the discussion of transregionality is most readily evident within the context of *Moi, Tituba*.

3 See Hawthorne, "Young Goodman Brown," for an example of other literary works set in Puritan factions of seventeenth-century New England and featuring a character said to represent the Devil. For one among many studies of the Salem witch trials, see Jackson, *Witchcraft of Salem Village*.

4 As a historian, Breslaw affords little space to Condé's novel. She enumerates it in an endnote among the other fictional works on Tituba, declaring it largely irrelevant to her own study because it "explores the condition of the contemporary African-American woman" (Breslaw 202n4). Breslaw's statement could be taken as correct, particularly when thinking of what Condé articulated in her interview with Scarboro: "Writing *Tituba* was an opportunity to express my feeling about present-day America … Every black person in America will tell you that racism still exists … As a foreigner and a French-speaking person, I don't suffer directly from it" ("Afterword" 203). However, the feelings that Condé conveys come from her own life. Her interview with Pfaff indicates that the novel was based, in part, on her own experiences of being viewed by many as a francophone woman of colour married to a white Englishman and frequently being marginalized at what

she then described as a small college in California (see Condé, "Vie," 39; Condé, "A Plural," 23). Breslaw's assessment seems to have missed the fact that, although the novel is not historical, it is an inquiry into historical methods of construction as well as, in its own way, into historiography. Later in the chapter I address Condé's own words on whether or not *Moi, Tituba* is historical.

5 There is a danger in so ardently disconnecting Tituba from fictional yet historically accepted African origins. Such debunking risks transferring the negative associations from one more general category of race (black or African American) to another (Amerindian). This is especially apparent in the title of Hansen's article, which was written in 1974, when the "African American" was still the "Negro." He removes the label of "witch" from "Negro" but transfers it to "Indian." Without investigating the complexities of race wrapped up in the word "Indian," Hansen's article may, in ways, rewrite what he accuses other historians of writing: "[not just] second-rate history but second-rate sociology as well" (9). In *The Making of Salem*, Robin DeRosa contributes to the conversation on Tituba's representations with regard to history, claiming that Condé is, among other things, "interested in challenging the serious academic notion that Tituba can be located at all" (115).

6 For related discussions of parody in *Moi, Tituba*, see, for example, Peterson's "Le surnaturel dans *Moi, Tituba, sorcière … Noire de Salem* de Maryse Condé et *Beloved* de Toni Morrison" ["The Supernatural in *I, Tituba, Black Witch of Salem* of Maryse Condé and *Beloved* of Toni Morrison"] and Suárez's "The Americas."

7 See, again, *S/Z*, particularly as I discuss it in chapter 1.

8 Peterson makes similar observations that Condé's creolizing form of writing "est en fait subversive et permet à Condé d'interroger les termes traditionnels selon lesquels l'Histoire de l'Ouest [sic] est écrite et l'historien porte jugement" [is in fact subversive and allows Condé to interrogate the traditional terms according to which History of the West is written and the historian passes judgment] (102). See also Wilson's "Sorcières, sorcières: 'Moi, Tituba, sorcière … Noire de Salem,' révision et interrogation" ["Witches, Witches: 'I, Tituba, Black Witch of Salem,' Revision and Interrogation'"].

9 See Scarboro's interview with Condé for the latter's comments on the parodic inclusion of the intergenerational connection (211–2).

10 Interestingly, Condé's conversation with Pfaff, in which she reveals her research, does not mention documents such as those Breslaw uncovered; her conversation with Scarboro takes a clear position: "I was not interested at all in what her real life could have been. I had few precise documents:

her deposition testimony. It forms the only historical part of the novel, and I was not interested in getting anything more than that" (201).

11 See, for example, Prince, *Narrative as Theme*.

12 See, for example, "Littérature et production" ["Literature and Production"] in Glissant, *Le discours antillais*. This essay is not included in the essays selected for the translation, *Caribbean Discourse*.

13 This citation is also from "Littérature et production." The work of Glissant that Moudileno cites in her own discussion comes from *Poétique de la relation*, notably pages 86 and 89, on the latter of which appears the verb "enfanter" (to give birth to).

14 As many of the other fictional texts that contain Tituba as a character show (e.g., Jackson's *Witchcraft of Salem Village*), the telling of such tales is repeatedly indicated as one of her pastimes in the Salem community.

15 See also Condé's interview with Scarboro (206).

16 For a discussion of similar questions in relation to theories of French Caribbean identity, literature of the French overseas departments, and their intersections in "a composite Caribbean pluralism," see Murdoch, *Creole Identity* (18).

17 The French government's early twenty-first century desire to retool the historical narrative of colonialism appeared in the loi du 23 février 2005 (Loi 2005–158) requiring the alteration of materials, such as school textbooks, to include, as stated in Article 4, the "rôle positif de la présence française outre-mer" [the positive role of the French overseas presence] during the centuries-long project of exploitation. Such a campaign produced its own polemic concerning the complex history of colonial endeavours and recalls the manipulation of narratives of and about a colonized Africa that Mudimbe discusses (Montvalon).

18 Emphasis in the original.

19 See Dayan, *Haiti*, for her discussion of Saint-Méry's and Buffon's mid-eighteenth-century racial categorization, which, in the case of the former, located both skin colour and blood on a gradated hierarchy (with white at the top) and, in the case of the latter, theorized albinism as degeneration and a "trick of nature" (238).

20 The Garrigus translation covers some but not all of the code's articles, including those referenced here (all translations are mine). For an in-depth analysis of the contradictions and inconsistencies of post-1685 government action and the *Code*, see Sala-Molins, *Le code noir, ou, Le calvaire de Canaan* [*The Black Code, or The Ordeal of Canaan*]. Dayan (*Haiti*) and Miller (*French Atlantic*) also outline how much the code was respected and, more significantly, ignored or operated largely to the benefit of white individuals; Dayan

writes further of the level of bodily operations that the code allowed: "Since slaves are construed as things without thought, then no amount of amputation, torture, or disfiguring can matter" (204). Similarly, just as Affergan argues that documents of colonial history regularly attest to a contradictory rhetoric of de/humanization, so the *code noir* speaks of certain human abilities of slaves (e.g., article 28). In explaining that any possessions of slaves were the property of their masters, the article recognizes: (1) the slaves' capacity to foster familial relations (using rhetoric not dissimilar to that concerning similar relationships of the colonizers); and (2) the incapacity to dispose of their own possessions ("lesquelles dispositions nous déclarons nulles, ensemble toutes les promesses & obligations qu'ils auraient faites, comme étant faites par gens incapables de disposer & contracter de leur chef" [which dispositions we declare null, together all the promises and obligations that they would have made, as if made by people incapable of disposing and contracting of their own accord]).

21 For a perspective on gender in this context, see Morgan, *Laboring Women*.

22 In harmony with chapter 1, the use of "intellectually disabled" with respect to the *nègre* does not seek to replace "mental retardation" with "intellectual disabilities." However, the historical, scientific, and geopolitical connections between such categories of identity have been explored in, for example, Mitchell and Snyder, "Eugenic Atlantic."

23 See, among others, Olsen, "Genetic Archaeology of Race"; and Clarke et al., "Biomedicalising Genetic Health." See also Davis's discussion of distinctions at the cellular level, particularly regarding Henrietta Lacks, her cells (labelled "HeLa" and used in the study of cervical cancer), and the eventual 1967 assignment of racialized cellular difference and its ability to contaminate (*Bending over Backwards* 15–6). See also Skloot, *Immortal Life*.

24 Gilman continues to posit that such sexual proclivities and capacities were presumed for various minority races and ethnicities throughout Europe and, thus, became a means of perpetuating social hierarchy. The same or similar attributes (as well as "specific pathologies of their genitalia") were also extended to white prostitutes as a way of justifying their control and/or exclusion (95).

25 See Dayan, *Haiti*. See also Asma, *On Monsters*, especially the chapter entitled "Torturers, Terrorists, and Zombies: The Products of Monstrous Societies," for a discussion of earlier origins of identification that connect the epidermal and the spiritual.

26 Today, the existence of such practices varies across the larger of the francophone islands: in Haiti, Vodou practitioners continue to exist as discussed in Bellegarde-Smith and Michel and in articles in *Le Monde* that recognized

their work in the days leading up to the 12 January 2010 earthquake (see Cojean, "En Haïti," 23 January 2010); in Guadeloupe and in Martinique, practitioners seem rare, almost vestiges of cultural practices slowly disappearing at the hands of globalization (see Boghen and Boghen).

27 On Vodou, see Dayan, *Haiti*.

28 See also Brereton, "Society and Culture."

29 For the purposes of my project the spelling of creole terms related to Haitian Vodou follows that practised by scholars such as Patrick Bellegarde-Smith and Claudine Michel, contributors to and editors of *Haitian Vodou*. See their essays.

30 See also Martine Coadou, *Serpent, manicou et … dorlis: Bestiaire symbolique Martiniquais* [*Serpent, Opossum and … Dorlis: Symbolic Bestiary of Martinique*] for a related discussion of the perception and representation of animals in *quimbois*.

31 Emphasis in the original.

32 Concerning Santería alone, see: "The Gift," from the third season of *Law & Order: Criminal Intent*; "Ritual," from the fifth season of *Law & Order: Special Victims Unit*; and "Curse of the Coffin," from the fifth season of *CSI: Miami*.

33 Fearing exposure, Miss Jeannette reminds Tara that her mother believes herself to be healed and that Tara's threat to reveal the facts will only disrupt such a psychosomatic cure. Such representation has a historical parallel: in his study of documents concerning the Barbadian slave population, Jerome Handler points out that slaveowners and other individuals made similar statements concerning the slaves' faith in the healing practices ("Slave Medicine," 72).

34 Daniel Maximin provides a similar portrait in the character of Miss Béa in *L'isolé soleil* [*Lone Sun*].

35 See Hawthorne, "Young Goodman Brown."

36 See also Gisler, *L'esclavage aux Antilles françaises (XVIIe–XIXe siècle* [sic]*)* [*Slavery of the French Antilles (Seventeenth to Nineteenth Centuries)*], particularly the chapters "L'Ancien Régime" ["The Old Regime"] and "La Monarchie de Juillet" ["The July Monarchy"].

37 On the implications of narcissism in Tituba's sexual meditations, see Glover's "Tituba's Fall."

38 Given the broader Americas context of the novel, further connections could be made to American pop culture references that unite sex and the freak, such as in the Rick James song "Super Freak," or that underscore freakishness and individual expression, as in Missy Elliott's "Get Ur Freak On." The video for Elliott's song could also extend the discussion of Condé's Tituba:

in addition to showcasing hip hop culture, it also weaves together numerous bodies and forms of non-us, at times exoticized, cultures (including borrowings from music and dance of India as well as words from Hindi and Japanese) in rather loose representations of spiritual or mystical practices and the afterlife.

39 In her interview with Scarboro, Condé reveals her awareness of a similar distinction in practices of SubSaharan Africa, where she had spent much time. This appears at the same time that she claims she possesses no knowledge of witchcraft as it is known in the United States and that the healing recipes she included were those she found in seventeenth-century books (206). It must also be noted that Condé's text seems at times to equate and perhaps conflate (or, in Shelton's terms, to render ambiguous) the two terms: when Tituba recognizes that she needs the help that Man Yaya refuses her, she uses *quimboiseur*, *sorcier*, and *sorcière* interchangeably to refer to the individuals who might offer her counsel or advice (Condé 229; Shelton 721). Given Condé's own statements, conflation seems unlikely. In the same interview, she also professes her questioning and at times disregard for monolithic identity categories such as "woman" and "race" as well as her recognition of the misappropriation of a typically negative term such as "witch" to someone who performs the positive work of healing. With such statements in mind, then, Condé's juggling of terms such as *quimboiseur* and *sorcière* in reference to an individual who works largely for the betterment of all could be read as the author's further destabilizing of identity categories.

40 Although Tituba and Man Yaya's manipulation of John Indian's body does not abide by the tradition of helping others physically or emotionally, it does not intend to harm anyone and is therefore not associated with what others might consider malefic practices. It could be hypothesized that the spell to control John's affections may be Man Yaya's (and Condé's) cure for the community of slave women in Barbados as it will protect them from John Indian, whom Man Yaya describes in the following manner: "On dit que c'est un coq qui a couvert la moitié des poules de Carlisle Bay" [They say that this cock has coupled with half the hens in Carlisle Bay] (30; 15).

41 One example of such a discussion, including the punitive gestures enacted upon the women for performing such acts, can be found in Pineau and Abraham, *Femmes des Antilles*. See also Dayan's *Haiti*, the section "Tools of Terror." Among the many fictional representations of a legacy of such acts, see Agnant, *Le livre d'Emma* [*The Book of Emma*].

42 In *Littérature et identité créole aux Antilles* [*Literature and Creole Identity of the Antilles*], Rosello discusses Tituba's ablity to live with the death of oth-

ers as well as her own in a lexicon that recalls both that mentioned in the above discussion of the *guérisseurs* and that of bodily abilities. In Rosello's words, Tituba is "capable d'entrer en contact avec les morts" [capable of entering into contact with the dead], and she possesses a "don" (talent), "pouvoirs" (powers), "puissances" (strengths), and "connaissances" (knowledge) (64–5).

43 The chapter entitled "Africans in Paris" from Schneider's book, *An Empire for the Masses*, has been reworked and translated into French for Bancel et al.'s *Zoos humains* and is entitled "Les expositions ethnographiques du Jardin zoologique d'acclimatation" [Ethnographic Expositions of the Jardin zoologique d'acclimation](72–80).

44 Baratay's essay was not included in the English translation, *Human Zoos*.

45 For the same reasons explained in chapter 1, the translation provided here is mine.

46 See, most notably, the refrain of Baudelaire's poem: "Là, tout n'est qu'ordre et beauté, / Luxe, calme et volupté" [All is order there, and elegance / pleasure, peace, and opulence] (13–4; 58–9).

47 The English translation provides an explanation of *soukougnan*: "literally, 'bloodsucker'; word derived from the African language of the Tukulör people, where it designates a spirit that attacks humans and drinks their blood like a vampire" (186). *Gens gagés* has here a nuanced sense.

48 For studies on the mythologizing of such figures in American cultural representations, see Clinton, *Plantation Mistress*; and Turner, *Ceramic Uncles*.

49 The English translation changes the number of men from three to four, a modification that does not appear to have been addressed critically or otherwise.

50 Breslaw's study provides a similar articulation on the historical particularities of the power struggle: "prior animosities among neighbors" (103).

51 Continued reinforcement of such referents for penetrating operations surfaces in two reappearances of the simile in the same chapter (first to ministers and second to constables) (141, 146; 89, 92) as well as in the next to last chapter of the novel (250; 163).

52 Most notable are Fanon's discussions in the chapters "La femme de couleur et le Blanc" ["The Woman of Color and the White Man"] (35–50; 41–62) and "L'homme de couleur et la Blanche" ["The Man of Color and the White Woman"] (53–66; 63–82).

53 On acts involving multiple attackers, see, for example, Sanday, *Fraternity Gang Rape*.

54 For a richer discussion of the relationship between subjectivity, narrative, and rape in the novel, see Manzor-Coats, "Of Witches and Other Things."

55 Such connections to biological reproduction regularly surface in the novel, most notably in Tituba's being conceived through her mother's rape as well as in Tituba's own pregnancies, the first of which she terminates to prevent future agents from operating her child's own body, and the second of which leads agents, because of their efforts to control her abilities, unwittingly to hang her (86, 263; 52, 172).

56 See Reyes-Santos, "Witch or Feminist," for a reading of Condé's text not only as an exploration of the relevance of feminist readings to Condé's work but also as a statement that individuals – male and female – of the same or similar socioeconomic positions should combine their efforts against oppression. For further discussion of master/slave relationships and the ideological effects of revolution, see Buck-Morss, *Hegel*.

57 The English translation provides no explanation for why it changed "Salem" to "Boston."

58 Emphasis in the original.

59 See Dayan, *Haiti*, but also Asma's discussion of Marshall's "Crane's 'The Monster'" in his chapter entitled "Torturers, Terrorists, and Zombies."

60 One of the many other intertextual references to Holiday's "Strange Fruit" appears in Agnant's *Le livre d'Emma*, a work that also explores transregional identificatory processes of women in a post/colonial island/mainland context.

CONCLUSION

1 The events of and around Michael Jackson's death are undoubtedly complex, complicated, and, for his loved ones (especially his children), difficult. Many of the expressions of sympathy, including those from some of the biggest names in the media, were undoubtedly sincere. And yet it remains undeniable that the media reports were at times slanted to attract the widest audience. In this respect, the shock value of the media spectacle must take its share of the credit for drawing the public eye in the global media race to broadcast the latest details. This is particularly true with respect to an individual as internationally main-staged and pursued as Michael Jackson.

2 Jackson's body and its abilities may well remain forever public in the internet postings of the coroner's report such as the following – a posting that allowed for my attempt at thinking about Jackson's bodily abilities: Michael Jackson Autopsy Report (16 May 2010). Other reportings of his death include: "Michael Jackson Is Dead," "Michael Jackson, 50, Is Dead," and "Le roi de la pop." A variety of projects that use Michael Jackson as a means to effect discussion include: Gates, "Reclaiming the Freak"; Haiken, *Venus Envy*,

especially the chapter entitled, "The Michael Jackson Factor: Race, Ethnicity, and Cosmetic Surgery"; Taraborrelli, *Michael Jackson*.

3 Even Robinson's memorial collection of interviews (*Vanity Fair*), mostly from the earlier years of Jackson's solo career, attempts to present Jackson in normative terms. Most notably, Robinson offers a qualifying analysis. She provides a list of Jackson's later extraordinary and, one can add based on the tone of the text, freakish moments as not so scandalous and thus as emblematic of his "pure" talent and character as a performer and human being (296).

Bibliography

Abraham, Marie, and Daniel Maragnès, eds. *Guadeloupe: Temps incertains.*
Paris: Autrement, 2001.

Abreu, Maria Leonor de. "La problématique identitaire chez Jacques Godbout." *Anglophonia: French Journal of English Studies* 1 (1997): 87–94.

Abu-Sahlieh, Sami A. Aldeeb. "Male and Female Circumcision: The Myth of
the Difference." In *Female Circumcision: Multicultural Perspectives*, ed.
Rogaia Mustafa Abusharaf, 47–72. Philadelphia: U of Pennsylvania P, 2006.

Abun-Nasr, Jamil, M. *A History of the Maghrib in the Islamic Period.* Cambridge: Cambridge UP, 1987.

Accilien, Cécile. *Rethinking Marriage in Francophone African and Caribbean
Literatures.* Lanham: Lexington, 2008.

Adams, Rachel. "An American Tail: Freaks, Gender, and the Incorporation
of History in Katherine Dunn's *Geek Love.*" In *Freakery: Cultural Spectacles
of the Extraordinary Body*, ed. Rosemarie Garland Thomson, 277–90. New
York: New York UP, 1996.

Adjarian, Maude. "Healing Life in Death through Narrative: The Power of
Womanspeak in Maryse Condé's *I, Tituba, Black Sorceress of Satan* [sic]." In
Beyond Survival: African Literature and the Search for New Life, ed. Kofi
Anyidoho, Abena P. A. Busia, and Anne V. Adams, 243–9. Trenton: Africa
World, 1999.

Affergan, Francis. *Critiques anthropologiques.* Paris: Presses de la fondation
nationale, 1991.

Affergan, Francis, Silvana Borutti, Claude Calame, Ugo Fabietti, Mondher
Kilani, Francesco Remotti. *Figures de l'humain: Les représentations de
l'anthropologie.* Paris: Ecole des Hautes Etudes en Sciences Sociales, 2003.

Agnant, Marie-Célie. *The Book of Emma.* Trans. Zilpha Ellis. Toronto:
Insomniac, 2006.

– *Le livre d'Emma*. Montréal: Remue-ménage, 2001.

Agnaou, Fatima. *Gender, Literacy, and Empowerment in Morocco*. New York: Routledge, 2004.

Al-Ghazali, Abu Hamid. *Deliverance from Error: Five Key Texts Including His Spiritual Autobiography*, al-Munqidh min al-Dalal. Trans. Richard J. McCarthy. Louisville: Fons Vitae, 1999.

– *On Disciplining the Soul* and *On Breaking the Two Desires*. Books 22 and 23 of *The Revival of the Religious Sciences*. Trans. T.J. Winter. Cambridge: Islamic Texts Society, 1995.

– *The Revival of the Religious Sciences*. al-Ghazali.org. Al-Ghazali Website, 25 February 2009. Ed. Muhammad Hozien. Web. 30 September 2009.

Alison, Archibald. *History of Europe from the Commencement of the French Revolution in 1789, to the Restoration of the Bourbons in 1815*. New York: Harper and Bros., 1842.

Amer, Sahar. "Uncovering the Meaning of the Veil in Islam." unc.edu. The Veil, January 1999. Web. 15 July 2009.

American Association on Intellectual and Developmental Disabilities (AAIDD). aamr.org. 21 August 2011.

Amiel, Denys, ed. *Les spectacles à travers les âges: Théâtre, cirque, music-hall, cafés-concerts, cabarets artistiques*. Paris: Editions du cygne, 1931.

Amin, Qasim. The Liberation of Women *and* The New Woman: *Two Documents in the History of Egyptian Feminism*. Trans. Samiha Sidhom Peterson. *Tahrir al-mar'a* and *al-Mar'a al-jadida*. 1899 and 1900. Cairo: American U in Cairo P, 2000.

Anees, Munawar A. *Islam and Biological Futures: Ethics, Gender and Technology*. London: Mansell, 1989.

Angelou, Maya. *I Know Why the Caged Bird Sings*. 1969. New York: Bantam, 1971.

Appiah, Anthony. "The Uncompleted Argument: Du Bois and the Illusion of Race." In *"Race," Writing, and Difference*, ed. Henry Louis Gates, Jr, 21–37. Chicago: U of Chicago P, 1986.

Arendt, Hannah. *On Revolution*. New York: Viking, 1965.

Ariès, Philippe. *Essais de mémoire, 1943–1983*. Paris: Seuil, 1993.

Asma, Stephen T. *On Monsters: An Unnatural History of Our Worst Fears*. Oxford: Oxford UP, 2009.

Bâ, Mariama. *Une si longue lettre*. 1979. Dakar: Nouvelles éditions africaines, 1987.

– *So Long a Letter*. Trans. Modupé Bodé-Thomas. London: Heinemann, 1981.

Bakhtin, Mikhail. *Rabelais and His World*. Trans. Hélène Iswolsky. Bloomington: Indiana UP, 1984.

Balzac, Honoré de. *Sarrasine*. 1830. Paris: Flammarion, 1989.
- *Sarrasine*. Trans. Clara Bell and others. *Project Gutenberg*. N.p., n.d. Web. 26 July 2010.
Bancel, Nicolas, Pascal Blanchard, Gilles Boëtsch, Eric Deroo, and Sandrine Lemaire, eds. *Human Zoos: Science and Spectacle in the Age of Colonial Empires*. Trans. Teresa Bridgeman. Chicago: U of Chicago P, 2009.
- *Zoos humains: Au temps des exhibitions humaines*. Paris: La Découverte, 2004. Rpt. of *Zoos humains: De la Vénus hottentote aux* reality shows. Paris: La Découverte, 2002.
Bannerman, Patrick. *Islam in Perspective: A Guide to Islamic Society, Politics and Law*. London: Routledge, 1988.
Baratay, Eric. "Le frisson sauvage: Les zoos comme mise en scène de la curiosité." In *Zoos humains: Au temps des exhibitions humaines*, ed. Nicolas Bancel, Pascal Blanchard, Gilles Boëtsch, Eric Deroo, and Sandrine Lemaire, 31–7. Paris: La Découverte, 2004.
Bargach, Jamila. *Orphans of Islam: Family, Abandonment, and Secret Adoption in Morocco*. Lanham: Rowman and Littlefield, 2002.
Barker, Clare. "From Narrative Prosthesis to Disability Counternarrative: Reading the Politics of Difference in *Potiki* and *The Bone People*." *Journal of New Zealand Literature* 24, 1 (2006): 130–47.
- *Postcolonial Fiction and Disability: Exceptional Children, Metaphor and Materiality*. Houndmills: Palgrave Macmillan, 2012.
Barnes, Colin, and Geof Mercer. *Disability*. Cambridge: Polity, 2003.
"The Barnum and Bailey Greatest Show on Earth: Ludger Sylbaris." Image Circus World Museum, Baraboo. Geology.sdsu.edu. How Volcanoes Work, n.d. Web. 5 March 2011.
Barrucand, Marianne. *L'architecture de la Qasba de Moulay Ismail à Meknès*. Etudes et travaux d'archéologie marocaine, vol. 6. Casablanca: Royaume du Maroc, Ministère d'état chargé des affaires culturelles, Division de l'archéologie des monuments historiques, Des sites et des musées, Service de l'archéologie, 1976.
Barthes, Roland. *S/Z*. Paris: Seuil, 1970.
- *S/Z*. Trans. Richard Miller. New York: Hill and Wang, 1974.
Bastien, Christine. *Folies, mythes et magies d'Afrique noire: Propos de guérisseurs du Mali*. Paris: L'Harmattan, 1988.
Baudelaire, Charles. "L'invitation au voyage." In *Les fleurs du mal*. Sec. 1, *Spleen et idéal*, 13–4. 1861. Paris: Gallimard, 1972.
- "Invitation to the Voyage." *Les fleurs du mal: The Complete Text of* The Flowers of Evil. Trans. Richard Howard, 58–9. Boston: D.R. Godine, 1982.
Beauvoir, Simone de. *Le deuxième sexe*. 1949. Paris: Gallimard, 1968.

– *The Second Sex*. Trans. Constance Borde and Sheila Malovany-Chevallier. New York: Alfred A. Knopf, 2010.

Bébel-Gisler, Dany, and Laënnec Hurbon. *Cultures et pouvoir dans la Caraïbe: Langue créole, vaudou, sectes religieuses en Guadeloupe et en Haïti*. Paris: L'Harmattan, 1975.

Beckles, Hilary McD. "Kalinago (Carib) Resistance to European Colonisation of the Caribbean." *Caribbean Quarterly* 38, 2/3 (1992): 1–14, 123–4.

Bellegarde-Smith, Patrick. "Broken Mirrors: Mythos, Memories, and National History." In *Haitian Vodou: Spirit, Myth, and Reality*, ed. Patrick Bellegarde-Smith and Claudine Michel, 19–31. Bloomington: Indiana UP, 2006.

Bellemare, Yvon. *Jacques Godbout, le devoir d'inquiéter: Essai*. Brossard: Humanitas, 2000.

– *Jacques Godbout, romancier*. Montreal: Parti Pris, 1984.

Bellhouse, Mary. "Candide Shoots the Monkey Lovers: Representing Black Men in Eighteenth-Century French Visual Culture." *Political Theory* 34, 6 (2006): 741–84.

Benaïssa, Slimane. *Les colères du silence*. Paris: Plon, 2005.

Benedicty, Alessandra. "Vodou, Ethics, and Aesthetics: Haiti and the Creole Poetics of Frankétienne, Jean-Claude Fignolé, and René Depestre." Diss. U of Wisconsin-Madison, 2004.

Beniamino, Michel. *La francophonie littéraire: Essai pour une théorie*. Paris: L'Harmattan, 1999.

Benítez Rojo, Antonio. *The Repeating Island: The Caribbean and the Post-modern Perspective*. 2nd ed.. Trans. James Maraniss. Durham: Duke UP, 1996.

Benjamin, Walter. "The Work of Art in the Age of Mechanical Reproduction." 1936. In *Illuminations*, trans. Harry Zohn, 219–53. New York: Harcourt, Brace and World, 1968.

Ben Jelloun, Tahar. *Harrouda*. 1973. Paris: Denoël, 1988.

– Interview with Amal Naccache. "Tahar Ben Jelloun, ou Comment créer français, en arabe." *Arabies* 13 (1988): 88–90.

– Interview with Catherine Argand. *Lire*, 1 March 1999. www.lire.fr. N.p. 30 September 2004.

– Interview with Gerry Feehily. "Tahar Ben Jelloun: Bound to Morocco." www.independent.co.uk. *Independent*, 3 March 2006. Web. 23 April 2009.

– Interview with M'Hamed Alaoui. "Les silences accumulés: Une interview de Tahar Ben Jelloun." *Jeune Afrique*, 16 February 1974, 36–8.

– Interview with Pierre Maury. "Tahar Ben Jelloun: Deux cultures, une littérature." *Magazine littéraire* 329 (1995): 107–11.

– Interview with Pierre Maury. "Tahar Ben Jelloun Talks to Pierre Maury."
   Banipal: Magazine of Modern Arab Literature 8 (2000): 16–7.
– *L'enfant de sable*. Paris: Seuil, 1985.
– *La nuit sacrée*. Paris: Seuil, 1987.
– *The Sacred Night*. Trans. Alan Sheridan. New York: Harcourt Brace
   Jovanovich, 1989.
– *The Sand Child*. Trans. Alan Sheridan. New York: Harcourt Brace
   Jovanovich, 1987.
Bennett, Steve. "On-Site Martinique: Sometimes It's Best to Be Drunk and
   in Jail." uncommoncaribbean.com. Uncommon Caribbean, 12 October
   2010. Web. 26 July 2011.
Berberi, Tammy. "A Rhapsodist at Mid-Century: Refiguring Disability in the
   Poetry of Tristan Corbière." *Journal of Literary and Cultural Disability Stud-
   ies* 3, 1 (2009): 51–66.
Bernabé, Jean, Patrick Chamoiseau, and Raphaël Confiant. *Eloge de la
   Créolité*. 1989. In *Eloge de la Créolité / In Praise of Creoleness*, 7–68. Paris:
   Gallimard, 1993.
– *In Praise of Creoleness*. 1990. Trans. M.B. Taleb-Khyar. In *Eloge de la Créolité
   / In Praise of Creoleness*, 69–128. Paris: Gallimard, 1993.
Bernard, Augustin. "La France au Maroc." *Les Annales de Geographie* 26, 139
   (1917): 42–58.
Bernd, Zila. "La quête d'identité: Une aventure ambiguë." *Voix et images* 12, 1
   (1986): 21–6.
Berrada, Mohammed. "Le théâtre au Maroc: Tradition, expérimentation et
   perspectives." Diss. Université de la Sorbonne Nouvelle (Paris III), 1998.
Berton, Pierre. *The Dionne Years: A Thirties Melodrama*. New York: W.W. Nor-
   ton, 1978.
Bhabha, Homi K. *The Location of Culture*. London: Routledge, 1994.
– "The Third Space: Interview with Homi Bhabha." In *Identity: Community,
   Culture, Difference*, ed. Jonathan Rutherford, 207–21. London: Lawrence
   and Wishart, 1990.
Bill 101. L.R.Q. chap. C-11 (1977, chap. 5). "The Charter of the French Lan-
   guage." Trans. n.s. oqlf.gouv.qc.ca. Office québécois de la langue française,
   n.d. Web. 4 May 2012.
Binet, Jean-Paul. *L'acte chirurgical*. Paris: O. Jacob, 1990.
Black Code, The. Trans. John Garrigus. "Code Noir." nationmaster.com.
   Nation Master, n.d. Web. 23 March 2011.
Blacking, John. *The Anthropology of the Body*. London: Academic, 1977.
Blanchard, Pascal. "Les zoos humains d'aujourd'hui ?" In *Zoos humains: Au
   temps des exhibitions humaines*, ed. Nicolas Bancel, Pascal Blanchard, Gilles

Boëtsch, Eric Deroo, and Sandrine Lemaire, 417–27. Paris: La Découverte, 2002.

Blanchard, Pascal, and Nicolas Bancel. *De l'indigène à l'immigré*. Paris: Gallimard, 1998.

Blanchard, Pascal, Nicolas Bancel, and Sandrine Lemaire. "Le spectacle ordinaire des zoos humains." *Polémiques sur l'histoire coloniale: Le Monde diplomatique*, "Manière de voir" 58 (2001): 40–5.

Blanchard, Pascal, Nicolas Bancel, and Sandrine Lemaire, eds. *La fracture coloniale: La société française au prisme de l'héritage colonial*. Paris: La Découverte, 2005.

Blanckaert, Claude. "Of Monstrous Métis? Hybridity, Fear of Miscegenation, and Patriotism from Buffon to Paul Broca." Trans. Sue Peabody. In *The Color of Liberty: Histories of Race in France*, ed. Sue Peabody and Tyler Stovall, 42–70. Durham: Duke UP, 2003.

Blank, S. Catrin, Sophie K. Scott, Kevin Murphy, Elizabeth Warburton, and Richard J.S. Wise. "Speech Production: Wernicke, Broca and Beyond." *Brain* 125 (2002): 1829–38.

Blatz, W.E., N. Chant, M.W. Charles, M.I. Fletcher, N.H.C. Ford, A.L. Harris, J.W. MacArthur, M. Mason, D.A. Millichamp. *Collected Studies on the Dionne Quintuplets*. St George's School for Child Study, U of Toronto. Toronto: U of Toronto P, 1937.

Blyn, Robin. "From Stage to Page: Franz Kafka, Djuna Barnes, and Modernism's Freak Fictions." *Narrative* 8, 2 (2000): 134–60.

Boddy, Janice. "Gender Crusades: The Female Circumcision Controversy in Cultural Perspective." In *Transcultural Bodies: Female Genital Cutting in Global Context*, ed. Ylva Hernlund and Bettina Shell-Duncan, 46–66. New Brunswick: Rutgers UP, 2007.

Bogdan, Robert. *Freak Show: Presenting Human Oddities for Amusement and Profit*. Chicago: U of Chicago P, 1988.

Boghen, Dan, and Miriam Boghen. "Notes sur la médecine populaire à la Martinique." In *L'archipel inachevé: Culture et société aux Antilles françaises*, ed. Jean Benoist, 233–48. Montréal: Presses de l'Université de Montréal, 1972.

Bongie, Chris. *Exotic Memories: Literature, Colonialism, and the Fin de Siècle*. Stanford: Stanford UP, 1991.

– *Islands and Exiles: The Creole Identities of Post/Colonial Literature*. Stanford: Stanford UP, 1998.

Bordo, Susan. *Unbearable Weights: Feminism, Western Culture, and the Body*. Berkeley: U of California P, 1993.

Bougerol, Christiane. *Une ethnographie des conflits aux Antilles: Jalousie, commérages, sorcellerie*. Paris: Presses universitaires de France, 1997.

Bouhdiba, Abdelwahab. *La sexualité en Islam*. Paris: PU de France, 1975.

– *Sexuality in Islam*. Trans. Alan Sheridan. London: Routledge, 1985.

Boulle, Pierre H. "François Bernier and the Origins of the Modern Concept of Race." In *The Color of Liberty: Histories of Race in France*, ed. Sue Peabody and Tyler Stovall, 11–27. Durham: Duke UP, 2003.

Bourget, Carine. *Coran et tradition islamique dans la littérature maghrébine*. Paris: Karthala, 2002.

– "L'Intertexte islamique de *L'Enfant de sable* et *La Nuit sacrée* de Tahar Ben Jelloun." *French Review* 72, 4 (1999): 730–41.

Bourhis, Richard Y., and Rodrigue Landry. "La Loi 101 et l'Aménagement du Paysage Linguistique au Québec." *Revue d'Aménagement Linguistique*, Hors série (2002): 107–31.

Bourkhis, Ridha. "La Connotation du corps dans l'œuvre de Tahar Ben Jelloun." *IBLA* 55, 170 (1992): 275–82.

Boutkhil, Soumia. "'The Evil Eye': Re/presenting Woman in Moroccan Literature in French." In *Representing Minorities: Studies in Literature and Criticism*, ed. Larbi Touaf and Soumia Boutkhil, 56–73. Newcastle: Cambridge Scholars, 2006.

Boyle, Marjorie O'Rourke. "Montaigne's Consubstantial Book." *Renaissance Quarterly* 50, 3 (1997): 723–49.

Bradley, Marion Zimmer. *The Mists of Avalon*. 1979. New York: Knopf, 1982.

Brereton, Bridget. "Society and Culture in the Caribbean: The British and French West Indies, 1870–1980." In *The Modern Caribbean*, ed. Franklin W. Knight and Colin A. Palmer, 85–110. Chapel Hill: U of North Carolina P, 1989.

Breslaw, Elaine G. *Tituba, Reluctant Witch of Salem: Devilish Indians and Puritan Fantasies*. New York: New York UP, 1996.

Breton, André. "Dans la vallée du monde." In *Clair de terre*, 77–8. 1923. Paris: Gallimard, 1966.

– "In the Valley of the World." In *Earthlight*, 69–70. Trans. Bill Zavatsky and Zack Rogow. Los Angeles: Sun and Moon, 1993.

Brooks, Peter. "The Law as Narrative and Rhetoric." In *Law's Stories: Narrative and Rhetoric in the Law*, ed. Peter Brooks and Paul Gewirtz, 14–22. New Haven: Yale UP, 1996.

Browning, Tod, dir. *Freaks*. 1932. Videocassette. Warner Studios, 1990.

Buck-Morss, Susan. *Hegel, Haiti, and Universal History*. Pittsburgh: U of Pittsburgh P, 2009.

Burac, Maurice, ed. *Guadeloupe, Martinique et Guyane dans le monde américain: Réalités d'hier, mutations d'aujourd'hui, perspectives 2000*. Paris: Karthala, 1994.

"Burning House of Love." *True Blood*. Dir. Alan Ball. 2008. HBO Home Video, 2009. DVD.

Burr, George Lincoln. *Narratives of the Witchcraft Cases*. New York: Barnes and Noble, 1959.

Busnot, Dominique. *Histoire du règne de Moulay Ismaïl*. Ed. Xavier Girard. 1714. Paris: Mercure de France, 2002.

Butler, Judith. *Bodies That Matter: On the Discursive Limits of "Sex."* New York: Routledge, 1993.

– *Gender Trouble: Feminism and the Subversion of Identity*. New York: Routledge, 1990.

– "Performative Acts and Gender Constitution: An Essay in Phenomenology and Feminist Theory." In *Performing Feminisms: Feminist Critical Theory and Theatre*, ed. Sue-Ellen Case, 270–82. Baltimore: Johns Hopkins UP, 1990.

– *Undoing Gender*. London: Routledge, 2004.

Cagnon, Maurice. *The French Novel of Quebec*. Boston: Twayne, 1986.

Calef, Robert. *More Wonders of the Invisible World: 1700*. Ed. Chadwick Hansen. Bainbridge, York Mail-Print, 1972.

Camus, Albert. *La peste*. 1947. Paris: Gallimard, 1972.

– *The Plague*. Trans. Stuart Gilbert. New York: A.A. Knopf, 1948.

Canguilhem, Georges. *Normal and the Pathological*. Trans. Carolyn R. Fawcett in collab. with Robert S. Cohen. New York: Zone, 1989.

– *Le normal et le pathologique*. 1966. Paris: PU de France, 2009.

Caplan, Marc. "Tituba was here, but 'im disappear.': Legends, History and the Novelistic Form in *I, Tituba, Black Witch of Salem* and *The Harder They Come*." In *African Literatures at the Millenium*, ed. Arthur D. Drayton, Omofolabo Ajayi-Soyinka, and I. Peter Ukpokodu, 154–76. Trenton: Africa World, 2007.

Caputo, John, and Mark Yount. "Institutions, Normalization, and Power." Introduction. In *Foucault and the Critique of Institutions*, ed. John Caputo and Mark Yount, 3–23. University Park: Pennsylvania State UP, 1993.

Carby, Hazel. *Cultures in Babylon: Black Britain and African America*. London: Verso, 1999.

Carruggi, Noëlle. *Maryse Condé: Rébellion et transgressions*. Paris: Karthala, 2010.

Castillo, David. *Baroque Horrors: Roots of the Fantastic in the Age of Curiosities*. Ann Arbor: U of Michigan P, 2010.

Cazenave, Odile. *Femmes rebelles: Naissance d'un nouveau roman africain au féminin*. Paris: L'Harmattan, 1996.

– "Gender, Age, and Narrative Transformations in *L'enfant de sable* by Tahar Ben Jelloun." *French Review* 64, 3 (1991): 437–50.

- *Rebellious Women: The New Generation of Female African Novelists*. Boulder: Lynne Rienner, 1999.

Certeau, Michel de. *L'écriture de l'histoire*. Paris: Gallimard, 1975.

- *The Writing of History*. Trans. Tom Conley. New York: Columbia UP, 1988.

Césaire, Aimé. *Cahier d'un retour au pays natal*. 1939. Paris: Présence africaine, 1983.

- *Discourse on Colonialism*. Trans. Joan Pinkham. 1972. New York: Monthly Review, 2000.

- *Discours sur le colonialisme*. 1955. Paris: Présence africaine, 2004.

- *Lyric and Dramatic Poetry, 1946–82*. Trans. Clayton Eshleman and Annette Smith. Charlottesville: UP of Virginia, 1990.

- *Notebook of a Return to the Native Land*. Trans. Clayton Eshleman and Annette Smith. Middletown: Wesleyan UP, 2001.

Chamoiseau, Patrick. *Texaco*. Paris: Gallimard, 1992.

Chancy, Myriam J.A. "Desecrated Bodies/Phantom Limbs: Post-Traumatic Reconstructions of Corporeality in Haiti/Rwanda." *Atlantic Studies: Literary, Cultural, and Historical Perspectives* 8, 1 (2011): 109–23.

Chanfrault, Bernard. "Figure du corps et problématique de l'oralité dans *L'enfant de sable* et *La nuit sacrée* de Tahar Ben Jelloun." Actes du colloque de littérature marocaine de langue française: Récits et discours, 9–11 March 1998. *Revue de la Faculté des Lettres et des Sciences humaines* 3 (1989, Université Cadi Ayyad of Marrakech): 41–69.

Charrad, Mounira M. *States and Women's Rights: The Making of Postcolonial Tunisia, Algeria, and Morocco*. Berkeley: U of California P, 2001.

"Charte de la langue française: 25 ans et pleine d'avenir." olf.gouv.qc.ca. "Ressources: Place publique." Office québécois de la langue française, n.d. Web. 23 February 2010.

- Advertisement . Office québécois de la langue française. 2002. "Charte langue française." YouTube.com. YouTube, 24 May 2007. Web. 23 February 2010.

Chebel, Malek. *Histoire de la circoncision: Des origines à nos jours*. Paris: Balland, 1992.

- *Le corps en Islam*. Paris: Quadrige, 1999. Rpt. of *Le corps dans la tradition au Maghreb*. Paris: Presses universitaires de France, 1984.

- *L'esprit de sérail: Perversions et marginalités sexuelles au Maghreb*. Paris: Lieu Commun, 1988.

- *L'esprit de sérail: Mythes et pratiques sexuels au Maghreb*. Paris: Payot et Rivages, 1995.

- *L'esprit de sérail. Mythes et pratiques sexuels au Maghreb*. Paris: Payot et Rivages, 2003.

- *L'imaginaire arabo-musulman*. Paris: PU de France, 1993.

– *L'islam et la raison: Le combat des idées*. Paris: Perrin, 2006.

Chemers, Michael M. "Le Freak, C'est Chic: The Twenty-First Century Freak Show as Theatre of Transgression." *Modern Drama* 46, 2 (2003): 285–304.

– *Staging Stigma: A Critical Examination of the American Freak Show*. New York: Palgrave Macmillan, 2008.

Chen, Ying. *Le mangeur*. Montreal: Boréal, 2006.

Chrétien, Simone, and Robert Brousse. *La montagne Pelée se revéille: Comment se prépare une éruption cataclysmique*. Paris: Société nouvelle des Editions Boubée, 1988.

Christiansen, Carol D. "The Lived Experience of Circumcision in Immigrant Somali Women: A Heideggerian Hermeneutic Analysis." Diss. U of Illinois at Chicago, 1995.

Cixous, Hélène. "The Laugh of the Medusa." Trans. Keith Cohen and Paula Cohen. *Signs* 1, 4 (1976): 875–93.

– "Le rire de la Méduse." In *Simone de Beauvoir et la lutte des femmes*, 39–54. Aix-en-Provence: L'Arc, 1975.

Cixous, Hélène, and Catherine Clément. *La jeune née*. Paris: Union Générale d'Éditions, 1975.

– *The Newly Born Woman*. Trans. Betsy Wing. Minneapolis: U of Minnesota P, 1986.

Clair, Colin. *Human Curiosities*. London: Abelard-Schuman, 1968.

Clarke, Adele E., Janet Shim, Sara Shostak, and Alondra Nelson. "Biomedicalising Genetic Health, Diseases and Identities." In *The Handbook of Genetics and Society: Mapping the New Genomic Era*, ed. Paul Atkinson, Peter E. Glasner, and Margaret M. Lock, 21–40. New York: Routledge, 2009.

Clinton, Catherine. *The Plantation Mistress: Woman's World in the Old South*. New York: Pantheon, 1982.

Coadou, Martine. *Serpent, menicou et … dorlis: Bestiaire symbolique martiniquais*. Petit-Bourg: Ibis Rouge, 2000.

Code noir, Ou recueil d'édits, déclarations et arrêts, concernant la discipline et le commerce des esclaves nègres des îles françaises de l'Amérique. 1685. fr.wikisource.org/wiki/Code_noir/1685. Code noir/1685, 17 October 2009. Web. 12 December 2009.

Cohen, Joshua, Matthew Howard, Martha C. Nussbaum, eds. *Is Multiculturalism Bad for Women? Susan Moller Okin with Respondents*. Princeton: Princeton UP, 1999.

Cojean, Annick. "A Port-au-Prince, des amputations par milliers…" *lemonde.fr*. *Le Monde*, 29 January 2010. Web. 15 February 2010.

– "En Haïti, 'les esprits savaient.'" lemonde.fr. *Le Monde*, 23 January 2010. Web. 15 February 2010.

Collard, Franck, and Evelyne Samama, eds. *Handicaps et sociétés dans l'histoire: L'estropié, l'aveugle, et le paralytique de l'Antiquité aux temps modernes*. Paris: L'Harmattan, 2010.

Condé, Maryse. *Histoire de la femme cannibale*. Paris: Mercure de France, 2003.

– *I, Tituba, Black Witch of Salem*. Trans. Richard Philcox. New York: Ballantine, 1994.

– "The Imaginary Caribbean." In *The Nation of the Other: Constructions of Nation in Contemporary Cultural and Literary Discourses*, ed. Anna Branach-Kallas and Katarzyna Wieckowska, 121–8. Torún: Wydawnictwo Uniwersytetu Mikolaja Kopernika, 2004.

– Interview. *Maryse Condé dévoile son cœur*. Dir. Susan Wilcox. Boulder: Full Duck Productions, 2003.

– Interview with Ann Armstrong Scarboro. "Afterword." In *I, Tituba, Black Witch of Salem*, trans. Richard Philcox, 198–213. New York: Ballantine, 1994.

– Interview with Maria Anagnostopoulou-Hielscher. "Parcours identitaires de la femme antillaise: Un entretien avec Maryse Condé." *Etudes francophones* 14, 2 (1999): 67–81.

– *Moi, Tituba, sorcière ... Noire de Salem*. Paris: Mercure de France, 1986.

– "Order, Disorder, Freedom, and the West Indian Writer." *Yale French Studies* 97 (2000) : 151–65.

– *La parole des femmes: Essai sur des romancières des Antilles de langue française*. Paris: L'Harmattan, 1993.

– "A Plural Life." Interview. In *Conversations with Maryse Condé*, by Françoise Pfaff, 1–33. Lincoln: U of Nebraska P, 1996. 1–33.

– "Retour à la Caraïbe et aux Amériques." Interview. In *Entretiens avec Maryse Condé*, by Françoise Pfaff, 85–113. Paris: Karthala, 1993.

– "Return to the West Indies and the Americas." Interview. In *Conversations with Maryse Condé*, by Françoise Pfaff, 56–77. Lincoln: U of Nebraska P, 1996.

– *Le roman antillais*. Vol. 1. Paris: Fernand Nathan, 1977.

– *Traversée de la Mangrove*. Paris: Mercure de France, 1989.

– "Vie plurielle." Interview. *Entretiens avec Maryse Condé*. By Françoise Pfaff. Paris: Karthala, 1993. 9–54.

– "The voyager in, the voyager out." In *Guadeloupe: Temps incertains*, ed. Marie Abraham and Daniel Maragnès, 250–9. Paris: Autrement, 2001.

Condé, Maryse, and Madeleine Cottenet-Hage, eds. *Penser la créolité*. Paris: Karthala, 1995.

Confiant, Raphaël. *Nuée ardente*. Paris: Mercure de France, 2002.

conjoinedtwins.med.sa. Kingdom of Saudi Arabia Conjoined Twins, n.d. Web. 6 January 2010.

"Conjoined Twins." *mayoclinic.com*. Mayo Clinic, 19 November 2008. Web. 1 March 2009.

"Contre la peur et l'agenouillement: Rèspé pou Travayè Manganao !" lkpgwa.wordpress.com. Journal des organisations membres du collectif L.K.P. Guadeloupe, 5 October 2009. Web. 1 March 2010.

Courtine, Jean-Jacques, and Claudine Haroche. *Histoire du visage: Exprimer et taire ses émotions, XVIe – début XIXe siècle*. Paris: Rivages, 1988.

Courtois, Edme-Bonaventure. *Papiers inédits trouvés chez Robespierre, Saint-Just, Payan, etc., supprimés ou omis par Courtois*. Paris: Baudouin frères, 1828.

Couser, G. Thomas. *Signifying Bodies: Disability in Contemporary Life Writing*. Ann Arbor: U of Michigan P, 2009.

"Curse of the Coffin." *CSI: Miami*. CBS. New York, 23 October 2006. Television.

Daily Kos. "Quebec Sovereignty Referendum." dkosopedia.com. dKosopedia, 17 April 2006. Web. 23 February 2010.

DalMolin, Eliane. *Cutting the Body: Representing Woman in Baudelaire's Poetry, Truffaut's Cinema, and Freud's Psychoanalysis*. Ann Arbor: U of Michigan P, 2000.

Damas, Léon Gontran. "Hoquet." *Pigments*. 1937. In *Pigments, édition définitive*, 33–6. Paris: Présence africaine, 1962.

Daston, Lorraine, and Katharine Park. *Wonders and the Order of Nature: 1150–1750*. New York: Zone, 1998.

Davis, Lennard J. *Bending over Backwards: Disability, Dismodernism, and Other Difficult Positions*. New York: New York UP, 2002.

– "Constructing Normalcy: The Bell Curve, the Novel, and the Invention of the Disabled Body in the Nineteenth Century." In *The Disability Studies Reader*, ed. Lennard J. Davis, 9–28. New York: Routledge, 1997.

– *Enforcing Normalcy: Disability, Deafness, and the Body*. London: Verso, 1995.

Davis, Natalie Zemon. *The Return of Martin Guerre*. Cambridge: Harvard UP, 1983.

Dayan, Colin (*see also* Dayan, Joan). *The Law Is a White Dog: How Legal Rituals Make and Unmake Persons*. Princeton: Princeton UP, 2011.

Dayan, Joan (*see also* Dayan, Colin). *Haiti, History, and the Gods*. Berkeley: U of California P, 1995.

Debates of the Senate (Hansard), 1st Session, 38th Parliament, vol. 142, issue

29. 1 February 2005. www.parl.gc.ca. Parliament of Canada, n.d. Web. 1 January 2010.

Deblaine, Dominique, Yamna Abdelkader, and Dominique Chancé, eds. *Transmission et théories des littératures francophones: Diversité des espaces et des pratiques linguistiques*. Actes du colloque international des 5, 6, et 7 avril 2006. Pessac: PU de Bordeaux/Pointe-à-Pitre: Jasor, 2008.

Déjeux, Jean. "Les romans de Tahar Ben Jelloun ou 'Le territoire de la blessure.'" In *Carrefour de cultures: Mélanges offerts à Jacqueline Leiner*, ed. Régis Antoine, 273–86. Tübingen: G. Narr, 1993.

de la Cruz, Bernard J., Jeannette Hacker, and Fouad R. Kandeel. "A History of the Penis: Images, Worship, and Practices." In *Male Sexual Dysfunction: Pathophysiology and Treatment*, ed. Fouad R. Kandeel, 3–10. New York: Informa Healthcare USA, 2007.

Delisle, Phillipe. "Aux sources de l'univers magico-religieux martiniquais: Esclavage et phobie des sorciers." *Cahiers d'Histoire* 41, 1 (1996): 61–76.

Denis, Angèle. "Corridors: Language as Trap and Meeting Ground." In *Talking about Identity: Encounters in Race, Ethnicity, and Language*, ed. Carl E. James and Adrienne Lynn Shadd, 133–45. Toronto: Between the Lines, 2001.

Denny, Frederick Matthewson, ed. *An Introduction to Islam*. 3rd ed. Upper Saddle River: Pearson Prentice Hall, 2006.

DeRosa, Robin. *The Making of Salem: The Witch Trials in History, Fiction and Tourism*. Jefferson: McFarland, 2009.

d'Esparbès, Georges, André Ibels, Maurice Lefèvre, and Georges Montorgueil. *Demi-cabots: Le café-concert, le cirque, les forains*. Paris: G. Charpentier and E. Fasquelle, 1896.

Deutscher, Penelope. "Autobiobodies: Nietszche and the Life-Blood of the Philosopher." *Parallex* 11, 3 (2005): 28–39.

Dickason, Olive Patricia. "The Sixteenth-Century French Vision of Empire: The Other Side of Self-Determination." In *Decentring the Renaissance: Canada and Europe in Multidisciplinary Perspective, 1500–1700*, ed. Germaine Warkentin and Carolyn Podruchny, 87–109. Toronto: U of Toronto P, 2001.

Dictionnaire de la langue française. Ed. Emile Littré. Paris: Gallimard/Hachette, 1957.

Dingli, Laurent. *Robespierre*. Paris: Flammarion, 2004.

Diprose, Rosalyn. *Corporeal Generosity: On Giving with Nietzsche, Merleau-Ponty, and Levinas*. Albany: State U of New York P, 2002.

Djebar, Assia. *Femmes d'Alger dans leur appartement*. Paris: Des femmes, 1980.

– *Women of Algiers in Their Apartment*. Trans. Marjolijn de Jager. Charlottesville: UP of Virginia, 1992.

Domecq, Jean-Philippe. *Robespierre, derniers temps*. Paris: Seuil, 1984.

Douville, Raymond, and Jacques Donat Casanova. *La vie quotidienne des Indiens du Canada à l'époque de la colonisation française*. Paris: Hachette, 1967.

Drainville, Bernard. "Lettre à Lucien Bouchard: La course vers la souveraineté." ledevoir.com. *Le Devoir*, 19 February 2010. Web. 23 February 2010.

– "Lettre ouverte de Bernard Drainville à Lucien Bouchard — 'M. Bouchard, nous continuerons jusqu'à l'indépendance!'" *Actualité*. partiquebecois.org. Parti Québécois, 19 February 2010. Web. 23 February 2010.

Drake, Samuel G. *The Witchcraft Delusion in New England*. Roxbury: W.E. Woodward, 1866.

Dreger, Alice Domurat. *One of Us: Conjoined Twins and the Future of the Normal*. Cambridge: Harvard UP, 2004.

Dubuisson, Colette, and Marie Nadeau. *Etudes sur la langue des signes québécoise*. Montréal: P de l'U de Montréal, 1993.

Dumur, Guy, ed. *Histoire des spectacles*. Paris: Gallimard, 1965.

Dunn, Katherine. *Geek Love*. New York: Vintage, 1989.

Durbach, Nadja. *Spectacle of Deformity: Freak Shows and Modern British Culture*. Berkeley: U of California P, 2010.

Duteil, Yves. "La langue de chez nous." *La langue de chez nous*. Audiogram, 1985. CD.

Duvivier, Julien, dir. *Pépé le Moko*. DisCina, 1937. The Criterion Collection, 2003.

Eagleton, Terry. *Literary Theory: An Introduction*. 2nd ed. Minneapolis: U of Minnesota P, 1996.

Eddouada, Souad. "Gender and the Concept of the Nation within the Context of the Moroccan Family Code." In *The Nation of the Other: Constructions of Nation in Contemporary Cultural and Literary Discourses*, ed. Anna Branach-Kallas and Katarzyna Wieckowska, 57–63. Torun: Wydawnictwo Uniwersytetu Mikolaja Kopernika, 2004.

El Dareer, Asma. *Woman, Why Do You Weep? Circumcision and Its Consequences*. London: Zed, 1982.

El Saadawi, Nawal. *Woman at Point Zero*. 1975. London: Zed, 1983.

Elliot, Missy "Misdemeanor." "Get Ur Freak On." By Missy Elliot and Tim "Timbaland" Mosley. *Miss E … So Addictive*. Elektra, 2001.

– "Get Ur Freak On." *Miss E … So Addictive*. Elektra, 2001. Music Video.

Prod. Tim "Timbaland" Mosley. youtube.com. You Tube, 30 June 2001. Web. 15 April 2009.

Elliott, Stuart. "Using Humor in a Campaign Supporting the Disabled." *New York Times*, 28 January 2010. Web. 1 February 2010.

Esposito, John. *The Oxford Dictionary of Islam*. Oxford: Oxford UP, 2003.

Eugenides, Jeffrey. *Middlesex*. New York: Picador, 2002.

eunuch.org. The Eunuch Archive, n.d. Web. 17 July 2009.

Fanon, Frantz. *Black Skin, White Masks*. Trans. Charles Lam Markmann. New York: Grove, 1967.

– *Peau noire, masques blancs*. 1952. Paris: Seuil, 1995.

Fayad, Marie. "Borges in Tahar Ben Jelloun's *L'enfant de sable*: Beyond Intertextuality." *French Review* 67, 2 (1993): 291–9.

Felman, Shoshana. *What Does a Woman Want? Reading and Sexual Difference*. Baltimore: Johns Hopkins UP, 1993.

Fernández Bravo, Alvaro. "Ambivalent Argentina: Nationalism, Exoticism, and Latin Americanism at the 1889 Paris Universal Exposition." *Nepantla: Views from the South* 2, 1 (2001): 115–39.

Fiedler, Leslie. *Freaks: Myths and Images of the Secret Self*. New York: Simon and Schuster, 1978.

– *Tyranny of the Normal: Essays on Bioethics, Theology and Myth*. Boston: David R. Godine, 1996.

Fignolé, Jean-Claude. *L'aube tranquille*. Paris: Seuil, 1990.

Findling, John E., and Kimberly D. Pelle, eds. *Historical Dictionary of World's Fairs and Expositions, 1851–1988*. New York: Greenwood, 1990.

Fisher, Lawrence E. *Colonial Madness: Mental Health in the Barbadian Social Order*. New Brunswick: Rutgers UP, 1985.

Flaubert, Gustave. *Madame Bovary: Mœurs de province*. 1856. Paris: Flammarion, 1986.

– *Madame Bovary: Provincial Ways*. Trans. Lydia Davis. New York: Viking, 2010.

Flaugh, Christian. "Identity Betrayed: Negotiations of the Freak in Tahar Ben Jelloun's *L'enfant de sable*." brown.edu. *Equinoxes* (Fall/Winter) 2003.

– "Of Colonized Mind and Matter: The Dis/Abilities of Negritude in Aimé Césaire's *Cahier d'un retour au pays natal*." *Journal of Literary and Cultural Disability Studies* 4, 3 (2010): 291–308.

– "On Normalities: Narratives of Bodies, Ability, and Freaks of Culture in Twentieth-century Francophone Literature." *Contemporary French and Francophone Studies/Sites* 10, 2 (2006): 217–25.

– "Operating Narrative: Words on Gender and Disability in Two Novels of Tahar Ben Jelloun." *Forum for Modern Language Studies* "Perspectives on Africa" 45, 5 (2009): 411–26.

Forth, Christopher E., and Ivan Crozier, eds. *Body Parts: Critical Explorations in Corporeality*. Lanham: Lexington, 2005.

Foucault, Michel. *Abnormal: Lectures at the Collège de France, 1974–1975*. Trans. Graham Burchell. New York: Picador, 2003.

– *Les anormaux: Cours au Collège de France, 1974–1975*. Paris: Gallimard/Seuil, 1999.

– *The Birth of Biopolitics: Lectures at the Collège de France, 1978–79*. Trans. Graham Burchell. New York: Palgrave Macmillan, 2008.

– *The Birth of the Clinic: An Archaeology of Medical Perception*. 1973. Trans. A. M. Sheridan Smith. New York: Pantheon, 1973.

– *Discipline and Punish: The Birth of the Prison*. Trans. Alan Sheridan. New York: Pantheon, 1977.

– *Histoire de la folie à l'âge classique*. 1961. Paris: Gallimard, 1972.

– *Histoire de la sexualité*. Vol. 1. Paris: Gallimard, 1976.

– *The History of Madness*. Trans. Jonathan Murphy and Jean Khalfa. London: Routledge, 2006.

– *The History of Sexuality*. Vol. 1. 1976. Trans. Robert Hurley. New York: Pantheon, 1978.

– *Naissance de la biopolitique: Cours au Collège de France, 1978–1979*. Paris: Seuil, 2004.

– *Naissance de la clinique: Une archéologie du regard médical*. Paris: PU de France, 1963.

– *Surveiller et punir: Naissance de la prison*. Paris: Gallimard, 1975.

Fox, Cora. "Authorising the Metamorphic Witch: Ovid in Reginald Scot's *Discoverie of Witchcraft*." In *Metamorphosis: The Changing Face of Ovid in Medieval and Early Modern Europe*, ed. Alison Keith and Stephen James Rupp, 165–78. Toronto: Centre for Reformation and Renaissance Studies, 2007.

Frankétienne. *Melovivi ou Le piège*. Paris: Riveneuve, 2010.

Frantz Fanon: Black Skin, White Mask. Prod. Mark Nash for the Arts Council of England. California Newsreel, 1995. Videocassette.

Freud, Sigmund. "L'inquiétante étrangeté." In *L'inquiétante étrangeté, et autres essais*, 213–63. 1919. Trans. Bertrand Féron. Paris: Gallimard, 1985.

– *Totem et tabou: Quelques concordances entre la vie psychique des sauvages et celle des névrosés*. 1913. Trans. Marielne Weber. Paris: Gallimard, 1992.

Frideres, James S. *Canada's Indians: Contemporary Conflicts*. Scarborough: Prentice-Hall of Canada, 1974.

Fulton, Dawn. *Signs of Dissent: Maryse Condé and Postcolonial Criticism*. Charlottesville: U of Virginia P, 2008.

Fuss, Diana. *Identification Papers*. New York: Routledge, 1995.

Gaensbauer, Deborah B. "Geography and Identity in Maryse Condé's *Dieu nous l'a donné*." *French Review* 74, 2 (2000): 287–95.

Gagné, Peter J. *King's Daughters and Founding Mothers: The* Filles du Roi, *1663–1673*. Pawtucket: Quintin, 2001.

Gagnon, Alain-G, and Raffaele Iacovino. *Federalism, Citizenship, and Quebec: Debating Multinationalism.* Toronto: U of Toronto P, 2007.

– "Interculturalism: Expanding the Boundaries of Citizenship." In *Québec: State and Society*, 3rd ed., ed. Alain-G. Gagnon, 369–88. Orchard Park: Broadview, 2004.

Galéry, Eunice. "*Les têtes à Papineau*: Comment peut-on être québécois?" *Etudes littéraires* 16, 2 (1983): 223–30.

Garber, Marjorie B. *Vested Interests: Cross-Dressing and Cultural Anxiety*. New York: Routledge, 1992.

Garland Thomson, Rosemarie. "Du prodige à l'erreur: Les monstres de l'Antiquité à nos jours." In *Zoos humains: Au temps des exhibitions humaines*, ed. Nicolas Bancel, Pascal Blanchard, Gilles Boëtsch, Eric Deroo, and Sandrine Lemaire, 38–48. Paris: La Découverte, 2004.

– *Extraordinary Bodies: Figuring Physical Disability in American Culture and Literature*. New York: Columbia UP, 1997.

– "Integrating Disability, Transforming Feminist Theory." In *Gendering Disability*, ed. Bonnie G. Smith and Beth Hutchison, 73–103. New Brunswick: Rutgers UP, 2004.

– "Introduction: From Wonder to Error – A Genealogy of Freak Discourse in Modernity." In *Freakery: Cultural Spectacles of the Extraordinary Body*, ed. Garland Thomson, 1–19. New York: New York UP, 1996.

– *Staring: How We Look*. Oxford: Oxford UP, 2009.

Garland Thomson, Rosemarie, ed. *Freakery: Cultural Spectacles of the Extraordinary Body*. New York: New York UP, 1996.

Gates, Henry Louis, Jr, ed. *"Race," Writing, and Difference*. Chicago: U of Chicago P, 1986.

Gates, Raquel J. "Reclaiming the Freak: Michael Jackson and the Spectacle of Identity." *Velvet Light Trap* 65 (2010): 3–4.

Gauch, Suzanne. "Telling the Tale of a Body Devoured by Narrative." *Differences: A Journal of Feminist Cultural Studies* 11, 1 (1999): 179–202.

Gaucher, Charles. "Le citoyen sourd: Du mouvement social à la communauté identitaire." *Développement humain, handicap et changement social* 15, 2 (2006): 34–45.

Genette, Gérard. *Palimpsestes: La littérature au second degré*. Paris: Seuil, 1982.
– *Palimpsests: Literature in the Second Degree*. Trans. Channa Newman and Claude Doubinsky. Lincoln: U of Nebraska P, 1997.
Gerber, David A, ed. *Disabled Veterans in History*. Ann Arbor: U of Michigan P, 2000.
"The Gift." *Law & Order: Criminal Intent*. NBC. New York, 12 October 2003. Television.
Gilman, Sander L. *Difference and Pathology: Stereotypes of Sexuality, Race, and Madness*. Ithaca: Cornell UP, 1985.
– *Making the Body Beautiful: A Cultural History of Aesthetic Surgery*. Princeton: Princeton UP, 1999.
Gilroy, Paul. *Against Race: Imagining Political Culture beyond the Color Line*. Cambridge: Belknap P of Harvard UP, 2000.
– *The Black Atlantic: Modernity and Double Consciousness*. Cambridge: Harvard UP, 1993.
Gisler, Antoine. *L'esclavage aux Antilles françaises (XVIIe–XIXe siècle [sic]): Contribution au problème de l'esclavage*. Paris: Karthala, 1981.
Glidden, Hope H. "The Face in the Text: Montaigne's Emblematic Self-Portrait (*Essais* III:12)." *Renaissance Quarterly* 46, 1 (1993): 71–97.
Glissant, Edouard. *Caribbean Discourse: Selected Essays*. Trans. J. Michael Dash. Charlottesville: UP of Virginia, 1989.
– *Le discours antillais*. 1981. Paris: Gallimard, 1997.
– *Poetics of Relation*. Trans. Betsy Wing. Ann Arbor: U of Michigan P, 1997.
– *Poétique de la relation*. Paris: Gallimard, 1990.
Glover, Kaiama. "Tituba's Fall: Maryse Condé's Counter-Narrative of the Female Slave Self." *Contemporary French and Francophone Studies* 15, 1 (2011): 99–106.
Gobineau, Arthur de. *Essai sur l'inégalité des races humaines*. 1853–55. 2nd ed. Paris: Firmin-Didot et Compagnie, 1884. gallica.bnf.fr. Gallica Bibliothèque numérique, n.d. Web. 11 February 2010.
Godbout, Jacques. *L'écrivain de province*. Paris: Seuil, 1991.
– *Hail Galarneau!* Trans. Alan Brown. Don Mills: Longman Canada, 1970.
– *Salut Galarneau!* Paris: Seuil, 1967.
– *Les Têtes à Papineau*. 1981. Montréal: Boréal, 1991.
Goellner, Sage. "Writing with the Past: Intertextual Representations in Algerian Francophone Literature." Diss. UW-Madison, 2005.
Gomez, Michael A. *Reversing Sail: A History of the African Diaspora*. Cambridge: Cambridge UP, 2005.

Gontard, Marc. *Le moi étrange: Littérature marocaine de langue française*. Paris: L'Harmattan, 1993.

Goodnight, James E. "Foreword." In *Operative Surgery Manual*, by Vijay P. Khatri and Juan A. Asenio, vii–viii. Philadelphia: Saunders, 2003.

Goolcharan-Kumeta, Wendy. *My Mother, My Country: Reconstructing the Female Self in Guadeloupean Women's Writing*. Oxford: Peter Lang, 2003.

Gordon, Rae Beth. *Dances with Darwin, 1875–1910: Vernacular Modernity in France*. Farnham: Ashgate, 2009.

– *Why the French Love Jerry Lewis: From Cabaret to Early Cinema*. Stanford: Stanford UP, 2001.

Gouges, Olympe de. *L'escalvage des noirs ou l'heureux naufrage*. Paris: Chez la Veuve Duchesne, 1792. gallica.bnf.fr. Gallica Bibliothèque numérique, n.d. Web. 1 April 2010.

– *Zamore et Mirza, ou l'heureux naufrage: Drame indien, en trois actes et en prose*. Paris: Chez l'Auteur et Chez Cailleau, 1788.

Grand dictionnaire universel du XIXe siècle. 1866–90. Geneva: Slatkine, 1982.

Graves Monroe, Amy. "'Ce n'est pas sorcier: La place du surnaturel dans l'œuvre de Simon Goulart." In *Simon Goulart: Un pasteur aux intérêts vaste comme le monde*, ed. Olivier Pot, 221–36. Geneva: Droz, 2012.

Grodzinsky, Yosef, and Andrea Santi. "The Battle for Broca's Region." *Trends in Cognitive Sciences* 12, 12 (2008): 474–80.

Grosrichard, Alain. *Structure du sérail: La fiction du despotisme asiatique dans l'occident classique*. Paris: Seuil, 1979.

Grosz, Elizabeth. "Intolerable Ambiguity: Freaks as/at the Limit." In *Freakery: Cultural Spectacles of the Extraordinary Body*, ed. Rosemarie Garland Thomson, 55–66. New York: New York UP, 1996. Rpt. of "Freaks: An Exploration of Human Anomalies," *Social Semiotics* 1, 2 (1991): 22–38.

– *Volatile Bodies: Toward a Corporeal Feminism*. Bloomington: Indiana UP, 1994.

– *Space, Time, and Perversion: Essays on the Politics of Bodies*. New York: Routledge, 1995.

Guide pratique du code de la famille. Rabat: Ministère de la justice, 2005.

Guessoum, Nidhal. "Une histoire déformée de la Raison en Islam: Critique de 'L'Islam et la Raison' de Malek Chebel (Ed. Perrin, 2005)." oumma.com. Oumma, 5 July 2006. Web. 26 July 2007.

Gutierrez, Ellen Turner. *The Reception of the Picaresque in the French, English, and German Traditions*. New York: Peter Lang, 1995.

Haiken, Elizabeth. *Venus Envy: A History of Cosmetic Surgery*. Baltimore: Johns Hopkins UP, 1997.

"Haiti's Disabled Find New Voice After Quake." terradaily.com. Terra Daily (AFP), 9 June 2010. Web. 13 June 2010.

Hajdukowski-Ahmed, Maroussia. "The Unique, Its Double and the Multiple: The Carnivalesque Hero in the Québécois Novel." *Yale French Studies* 65 (1983): 139–53.

Halberstam, Judith. *Skin Shows: Gothic Horror and the Technology of Monsters.* Durham: Duke UP, 1995.

Hale, Dana S. *Races on Display: French Representations of Colonized Peoples, 1886–1940.* Bloomington: Indiana UP, 2008.

Hall, Stuart. "Cultural Identity and Diaspora." In *Identity: Community, Culture, Difference*, ed. Jonathan Rutherford, 222–37. London: Lawrence and Wishart, 1990.

Hamel, Ernest. *Histoire de Robespierre, d'après des papiers de famille, les sources originales et des documents entièrement inédits.* Paris: Librairie internationale, 1865–67.

Hamon, Philippe. *Expositions: Littérature et architecture au XIXe siècle.* Paris: José Corti, 1989.

– *Expositions: Literature and Architecture in Nineteenth-Century France.* Trans. Katia Sainson-Frank and Lisa Maguire. Berkeley: U of California P, 1992.

"Handicapped Struggle to Be Included in Haiti's Reconstruction." haitiantimes.com. *HaitianTimes*, 11 June 2010. Web. 13 June 2010.

Handler, Jerome S. "Slave Medicine and Obeah in Barbados, Circa 1650 to 1834." *New West Indian Guide/Nieuwe West-Indische Gids* 74, 1/2 (2000): 57–90.

Handler, Jerome S., and JoAnn Jacoby. "Slave Medicine and Plant Use in Barbados." *Journal of the Barbados Museum and Historical Society* 41 (1993): 74–98.

Handler, Richard. *Nationalism and the Politics of Culture in Quebec.* Madison: U of Wisconsin P, 1988.

Hansen, Chadwick. Introduction. In *More Wonders of the Invisible World: 1700*, Robert Calef, v-xiv. Bainbridge, NY: York Mail-Print, 1972.

– "The Metamorphosis of Tituba, or Why American Intellectuals Can't Tell an Indian Witch from a Negro." *New England Quarterly* 47, 1 (1974): 3–12.

Hargreaves, Alec G., Charles Forsdick, and David Murphy, eds. *Transnational French Studies: Postcolonialism and littérature-monde.* Liverpool: Liverpool UP, 2010.

Harvey, Robert. "Purloined Letters: Intertextuality and Intersexuality in Tahar Ben Jelloun's *The Sand Child*." In *Articulations of Difference: Gender*

Studies and Writing in French, ed. Dominique D. Fisher and Lawrence R. Schehr, 226–45. Stanford: Stanford UP, 1997.

Hawley, John C. Introduction. In *Postcolonial, Queer: Theoretical Intersections*, 1–18. Albany: State U of New York P, 2001.

Hawthorne, Nathaniel. *The Scarlet Letter*. 1850. New York: Bantam, 1986.

– "Young Goodman Brown." 1835. In *American Gothic Tales*, ed. Joyce Carol Oates, 52–64. New York: Plume, 1996.

Hayes, Jarrod. "Looking for Roots among the Mangroves: Errances enracinées and Migratory Identities." *Centennial Review* 42, 3 (1998): 459–74.

– *Queer Nations. Marginal Sexualities in the Maghreb*. Chicago: U of Chicago P, 2000.

Hebouche, Nadra. "L'individu et l'identité nationale: l'échec de l'utopie collectiviste dans le roman francophone contemporain." Diss. State U of New York-Buffalo, 2012.

Hellou, Gisèle. *Complexité, systémique et herméneutique: Pour une philosophie pratique des soins intensifs*. Paris: L'Harmattan, 2009.

Hennessy, Rosemary. *Materialist Feminism and the Politics of Discourse*. New York: Routledge, 1993.

Hernlund, Ylva, and Bettina Shell-Duncan. "Transcultural Positions: Negotiating Rights and Culture." In *Transcultural Bodies: Female Genital Cutting in Global Context*, ed. Hernlund and Shell-Duncan, 1–45. New Brunswick: Rutgers UP, 2007.

Hess, Deborah M. *La poétique de renversement chez Maryse Condé, Massa Makan Diabaté et Édouard Glissant*. Paris: L'Harmattan, 2006.

Hevey, David. *The Creatures Time Forgot: Photography and Disability Imagery*. New York: Routledge, 1992.

Hewer, C.T.R. *Understanding Islam: An Introduction*. Minneapolis: Fortress, 2006.

Hill, Catherine Ann. "Slanted and Enchanted: Witches and Counter-Discursive Strategies in *Moi, Tituba sorcière … noire de Salem* by Maryse Condé, *Les Enfants du sabbat* by Anne Hebert, and *The Book of Secrets* by Fiona Kidman." Diss. Victoria U of Wellington, 1999.

Hobbes, Thomas. *Leviathan*. 1651. Oxford: Oxford UP, 1998.

Holiday, Billie. "Strange Fruit." 1939. By Abel Meeropol/Lewis Allen. Charly International Aps. Atlas, 1995.

Hoving, Isabel. "Love in the Third World: Two Caribbean Women Writers on Myths about the Relation between Sexuality and Race." *Thamyris: Mythmaking from Past to Present* 2, 2 (1995): 151–75.

"How Volcanoes Work." geology.sdsu.edu, n.d. How Volcanoes Work. Web. 5 March 2011.

Hughes, Bill. "What Can a Foucauldian Analysis Contribute to Disability Theory?" In *Foucault and the Government of Disability*, ed. Shelley Tremain, 78–92. Ann Arbor: U of Michigan P, 2005.

Huet, Marie-Hélène. *Monstrous Imagination*. Cambridge: Harvard UP, 1993.

Hugo, Victor. *L'homme qui rit*. 1869. Paris: Livre de Poche, 2002.

– *The Man Who Laughs*. Trans. n.n. Project Gutenberg. N.p., n.d. Web. 26 July 2010

– *Notre-Dame de Paris*. 1831. Paris: Garnier-Flammarion, 1967.

– *Les misérables*. 1862. Paris: Gallimard, 1999.

– *Les misérables*. Trans. n.n. Project Gutenberg. N.p., n.d. Web. 11 February 2010.

Hurbon, Laënnec. *Dieu dans le vaudou haïtien*. Paris: Payot, 1972.

"I Don't Wanna Know." *True Blood*. Dir. Alan Ball. 2008. HBO Home Video, 2009. DVD.

Ingres, Jean-Auguste-Dominique. *L'odalisque à l'esclave*. 1842. art.thewalters.org. The Walters Art Museum, n.d.. Web. 10 November 2009.

Ingstad, Benedicte, and Susan Reynolds Whyte. "Disability and Culture: An Overview." Introduction. In *Disability and Culture*, ed. Ingstad and Whyte, 3–32. Berkeley: U of California P, 1995.

"L'insertion socioprofessionnelle des déficients intellectuels." 2 December 2008. rekrute.com. Rekrute, 3 December 2008. Web. 26 July 2011.

Ionesco, Eugène. *La leçon*. 1951. In *La cantatrice chauve, anti-pièce; Suivi de La leçon, drame comique*, 103–90. Paris: Gallimard, 1972.

– *The Lesson*. Trans. Donald M. Allen. In *Four Plays*, 43–78. New York: Grove, 1958.

Ireland, Craig. *The Subaltern Appeal to Experience: Self-Identity, Late Modernity, and the Politics of Immediacy*. Montreal: McGill-Queen's UP, 2004.

"Isidore Geoffroy Saint-Hilaire." brittanica.com. Encyclopaedia Brittanica, n.d. Web. 23 July 2011.

Jackson, Michael. Interviews with Lisa Robinson. "The Boy Who Would Be King." *Vanity Fair*, September 2009, 292–301, 339–40.

Jackson, Shirley. *The Witchcraft of Salem Village*. New York: Random House, 1956.

Jacoby, Lars. "Airline: Conjoined QC Infants Count as 2 Passengers." azcentral.com. AZ Central, 3 October 2007. Web. 28 February 2008.

Jaenen, Cornelius J. *Friend and Foe: Aspects of French-Amerindian Cultural Contact in the Sixteenth and Seventeenth Centuries*. New York: Columbia UP, 1976.

James, Rick. "Super Freak." By James and Alonzo Miller. *Street Songs*. Motown, 1981. CD.

Jameson, Frederic. *Postmodernism, or, The Cultural Logic of Late Capitalism*. Durham: Duke UP, 1991.

Jenson, Deborah. *Beyond the Slave Narrative: Politics, Sex, and Manuscripts in the Haitian Revolution*. Liverpool: Liverpool UP, 2011.

– *Trauma and Its Representations: The Social Life of Mimesis in Post-revolutionary France*. Baltimore: Johns Hopkins UP, 2001.

Johnson, Melissa. "(Re-)Writing the Marginalized Body: Grace Nichols's *The Fat Black Woman's Poems*." In *Postcolonial Perspectives on Women Writers from Africa, the Caribbean, and the US*, ed. Martin Japtok, 209–25. Trenton: Africa World, 2003.

Jordan, David. *The Revolutionary Career of Maximilien Robespierre*. New York: Free, 1985.

"Joy as Cameroon Twins Separated." news.bbc.co.uk. BBC, 24 April 2007. Web. 1 March 2008.

Julien, Eileen. *African Novels and the Question of Orality*. Bloomington: Indiana UP, 1992.

Kadish, Doris Y. "Guadeloupean Women Remember Slavery." *French Review* 77, 6 (2004): 1181–92.

Kapferer, Bruce. *Beyond Rationalism: Rethinking Magic, Witchcraft and Sorcery*. New York: Berghahn, 2002.

Katrak, Ketu, H. *Politics of the Female Body: Postcolonial Women Writers of the Third World*. New Brunswick: Rutgers UP, 2006.

Kennan, George. *Le désastre de la Pelée: Un récit de voyage et d'observation à la Martinique (mai-juin 1902)*. Trans. Thierry Lesales. Matoury: Ibis Rouge, 2002.

– *The Tragedy of Pelée: A Narrative of Personal Experience and Observation in Martinique*. New York: Outlook, 1902.

Khady. *Mutilée*. In collaboration with Marie-Thérèse Cuny. Paris: Oh!, 2005.

Khatibi, Abdelkebir. *Maghreb pluriel*. Paris: Denoël, 1983.

Khuri, Fuad I. *The Body in Islamic Culture*. London: Saqi, 2001.

Kinsey, Alfred C. *Sexual Behavior in the Human Male*. Philadelphia: W.B. Saunders, 1948.

Kirby, Vicki. "Out of Africa: 'Our Bodies Ourselves?'" In *Female Circumcision and the Politics of Knowledge: African Women in Imperialist Discourses*, ed. Obioma Nnaemeka, 81–96. Westport: Praeger, 2005.

Korieh, Chima. "'Other' Bodies: Western Feminism, Race, and Representation in Female Circumcision Discourse." In *Female Circumcision and the*

Politics of Knowledge: African Women in Imperialist Discourses, ed. Obioma Nnaemeka, 111–32. Westport: Praeger, 2005.

Kourouma, Amadou. *Les soleils des indépendances*. 1968. Paris: Seuil, 1995.

– *The Suns of Independence*. Trans. Adrian Adams. London: Heineman, 1981.

Kratz, Corrine A. "Seeking Asylum, Debating Values, and Setting Precedents in the 1990s: The Cases of Kassindja and Abankwah in the United States." In *Transcultural Bodies: Female Genital Cutting in Global Context*, ed. Ylva Hernlund and Bettina Shell-Duncan, 167–201. New Brunswick: Rutgers UP, 2007.

Kristéva, Julia. *Histoires d'amour*. Paris: Denoël, 1983.

– *Les nouvelles maladies de l'âme*. Paris: Fayard, 1993.

– *Pouvoirs de l'horreur: Essai sur l'abjection*. Paris: Seuil, 1980.

Kruks, Sonia. *Retrieving Experience: Subjectivity and Recognition in Feminist Politics*. Ithaca: Cornell UP, 2001.

Kudlick, Catherine J. "Disability History: Why We Need Another 'Other.'" *American Historical Review* 108, 3 (2003): 763–93.

Kuppers, Petra. *Disability and Contemporary Performances: Bodies on Edge*. New York: Routledge, 2003.

– *The Scar of Visibility: Medical Performance and Contemporary Art*. Minneapolis: U of Minnesota P, 2007.

Kyoore, Paschal B. Kyiiripuo. *The African and Caribbean Historical Novel in French: A Quest for Identity*. New York: Peter Lang, 1996.

LaCom, Cindy. "'The Time Is Sick and Out of Joint': Physical Disability in Victorian England." *PMLA* 120, 2 (2005): 547–52.

Lacroix, Alfred. *La montagne Pelée et ses éruptions*. Paris: Masson, 1904.

– *La montagne Pelée après ses éruptions, avec observations sur les éruptions du Vésuve en 79 et en 1906*. Paris: Masson, 1908.

"Lacroix, Alfred." *Complete Dictionary of Scientific Biography*. Vol. 7. Detroit. Charles Scribner's Sons, 2008, 548–9. galenet.galegroup.com. Cengage Learning, n.d. Web. 9 September 2011.

Lalonde, Michèle. "Speak White." 1968. In *Défense et illustration de la langue québécoise: Suivie de prose et poèmes*, 37–40. Paris: Seghers/Laffont, 1979.

Lanctôt, Gustave. *Les Canadiens français et leurs voisins du sud*. Montreal: Bernard Valiquette, 1941.

"Langue des signes québécoise." fr.wikipedia.org. Wikipédia, 22 December 2009. 1 April 2010.

Lapouge, George Vacher de. *L'aryen: Son rôle social: Cours libre de science politique professé à l'Université de Montpellier (1889–1890)*. Paris: Librarie des Ecoles françaises d'Athènes et de Rome, 1899. babel.hathitrust.org. Hathi Trust Digital Library, n.d. Web. 1 April 2010.

Larrier, Renée B. *Autofiction and Advocacy in the Francophone Caribbean*. Gainesville: UP of Florida, 2006.

– *Francophone Women Writers of Africa and the Caribbean*. Gainesville: UP of Florida, 2000.

Lazreg, Marnia. *The Eloquence of Silence: Algerian Women in Question*. New York: Routledge, 1994.

– *Questioning the Veil: Open Letters to Muslim Women*. Princeton: Princeton UP, 2009.

Le Bris, Michel, and Jean Rouaud. "Pour une 'littérature-monde' en français." *Le Monde* 16 March 2007.

Le Bris, Michel, and Jean Rouaud, eds. *Pour une littérature monde*. Paris: Gallimard, 2007.

Leblanc, Allen. "Technoscience et normativité médicale." In *Compromis, dilemmes et paradoxes en éthique clinique*, ed. Jean-François Malherbe, 143–58. Namur: Artel/Montréal: Fides, 1999.

Lecomte, Nelly. *Le roman négro-africain des années 50 à 60: Temps et acculturation*. Paris: L'Harmattan, 1993.

Lefebvre, Thierry. "Comment fut soigné Cyparis." *Revue d'histoire de la pharmacie* 90, 336 (2002) : 678–9.

Léon, Joseph de. *Vie de Moulay Ismaïl, roi de Fès et de Maroc: D'après Joseph de Léon, 1708–1728, étude et édition*. 1743. Ed. Chantal de la Véronne. Paris: Librairie Orientaliste Paul Geuthner, 1974.

Leriche, René. *La philosophie de la chirurgie*. Paris: Flammarion, 1951.

Leroi, Armand Maris. *Mutants: On Genetic Variety and the Human Body*. New York: Viking, 2003.

Leti, Geneviève. *L'univers magico-religieux antillais: ABC des croyances et superstitions d'hier et d'aujourd'hui*. Paris: L'Harmattan, 2000.

Lévi-Strauss, Claude. *Le regard éloigné*. Paris: Plon, 1983.

Lifson, Robert. *Enter the Sideshow*. Bala Cynwyd: Mason, 1983.

Lindfors, Bernth. "Ethnological Show Business: Footlighting the Dark Continent." In *Freakery: Cultural Spectacles of the Extraordinary Body*, ed. Rosemarie Garland Thomson, 207–18. New York: New York UP, 1996.

Linton, Simi. *Claiming Disability: Knowledge and Identity*. New York: New York UP, 1998.

Lionnet, Françoise. "*Créolité* in the Indian Ocean: Two Models of Cultural Diversity." *Yale French Studies* 82 (1993): 101–12.

– *Postcolonial Representations: Women, Literature, Identity*. Ithaca: Cornell UP, 1995.

– "Women's Rights, Bodies, and Identities: The Limits of Universalism and the Legal Debate around Excision in France." In *Female Circumcision and*

the Politics of Knowledge: African Women in Imperialist Discourses, ed.
Obioma Nnaemeka, 97–110. Westport: Praeger, 2005. Rpt. Of "Identity,
Sexuality, and Criminality." *Contemporary French Civilization* 16 (1992):
294–307.

Lo, Marieme. "Paradoxical Embodiment of Mothering: Interrogating
Agency, the Discursive Framing and Social Construction of the Identities
of Women with Fistula." Gender and Disability Studies Forum. Cultures
and Texts Strategic Strength Faculty Advisory Committee Workshop.
Norton Hall, State U of New York-Buffalo. 3 March 2009.

Loi 22. L.Q. 1974, chap. 6. "Loi sur la langue officiélle." oqlf.gouv.qc.ca.
Office québécois de la langue française, n.d. Web. 4 May 2012.

Loi 101. L.R.Q. chap. C-11 (1977, chap. 5). "Charte de la langue française."
oqlf.gouv.qc.ca. Office québécois de la langue française, n.d. Web. 4 May
2012.

Loi 178. L.Q. 1988, chap. 54. "Repères et jalons historiques." oqlf.gouv.qc.ca.
Office québécois de la langue française, n.d. Web. 4 May 2012.

Loi 2005–102 du 11 février 2005 pour l'égalité des droits et des chances, la
participation et la citoyenneté des personnes handicapées. legifrance.
gouv.fr. LegiFrance, Le service public de la diffusion du droit, n.d. Web.
19 June 2010.

Loi 2005–158 du 23 février 2005 portant reconnaissance de la Nation et contribution nationale en faveur des Français rapatriés. legifrance.gouv.fr. Legi-
France, Le service public de la diffusion du droit, n.d. Web. 12 June 2009.

Longfellow, Henry Wadsworth. *Giles Corey of the Salem Farms*. In *The New-
England Tragedies*, 97–179. Boston: Boston, Ticknor and Fields, 1868.

Lopes, Rosaly M. *The Volcano Adventure Guide*. Cambridge: Cambridge UP,
2005.

Louder, Dean R., Christian Morissonneau, and Eric Waddell. Introduction.
In *Du continent perdu à l'archipel retrouvé: Le Québec et l'Amérique française*,
2–10. Quebec: P de l'U de Laval, 1983.

"Louis Auguste Sylbaris, alias Louis Cyparis, alias Cyparis, dit Sanson."
reve-lemanique.ch. N.p., n.d. Web. 27 July 2011.

Lyons, John D. *Before Imagination: Embodied Thought from Montaigne to
Rousseau*. Stanford: Stanford UP, 2005.

Lyotard, Jean-François. *La condition postmoderne: Rapport sur le savoir*. Paris:
Minuit, 1979.

– *The Postmodern Condition: A Report on Knowledge*. Trans. Geoff Benning-
ton and Brian Massumi. Minneapolis: U of Minnesota P, 1984.

Maazaoui, Abbes. "L'Enfant de sable et La Nuit sacrée ou le corps tragique."
French Review 69, 1 (1995): 68–77.

Maguire, Gregory. *Wicked: The Life and Times of the Wicked Witch of the West.* 1995. New York: HarperCollins, 1996.

Maillet, Antonine. *Pélagie.* Trans. Philip Stratford. Garden City: Doubleday, 1982.

– *Pélagie-la-charette.* Paris: B. Grasset, 1979.

Malena, Anne. *The Negotiated Self: The Dynamics of Identity in Francophone Caribbean Narrative.* New York: Peter Lang, 1990.

Malti-Douglas, Fedwa. *Power, Marginality, and the Body in Medieval Islam.* Burlington: Ashgate, 2001.

Mangin, Charles. *La force noire.* Paris: Hachette, 1910.

Manzor-Coats, Lillian. "Of Witches and Other Things: Maryse Condé's Challenges to Feminist Discourse." *World Literature Today* 67, 4 (1993): 737–44.

Marcotte, Gilles. *Le roman à l'imparfait: Essais sur le roman québécois d'aujourd'hui.* Montréal: La Presse, 1976.

Marcuse, Herbert. *One-Dimensional Man: Studies in the Ideology of Advanced Industrial Society.* Boston: Beacon, 1964.

Mardorossian, Carine M. "From Fanon to Glissant: A Martinican Geneaology." *Small Axe* 13, 3 30 (2009): 12–24.

– *Reclaiming Difference: Caribbean Women Rewrite Postcolonialism.* Charlottesville: U of Virginia P, 2005.

Marks, Deborah. *Disability: Controversial Debates and Psychosocial Perspectives.* New York: Routledge, 1999.

Marmon, Shaun. *Eunuchs and Sacred Boundaries in Islamic Society.* New York: Oxford UP, 1995.

Marrouchi, Mustapha. "Breaking Up/Down/Out of the Boundaries: Tahar Ben Jelloun." *Research in African Literatures* 21, 4 (1990): 71–83.

– "My Aunt Is a Man: *Ce "je"-là est multiple.*" *Comparative Literature* 54, 4 (2002): 325–56.

Marshall, Elaine. "Crane's 'The Monster' Seen in Light of Robert Lewis's Lynching." *Nineteenth-Century Literature* 51, 2 (1996): 205–24.

Martin, Ernest. *Histoire des monstres: Depuis l'antiquité jusqu'à nos jours.* Paris: C. Reinwald, 1880.

Martin, Grant. "Delta Requires Two Seats for Conjoined Twins." gadling.com. AOL Travel, 5 October 2007. Web. 28 February 2008.

Martin, Jean-Clément. *La Terreur: Part maudite de la Révolution.* Paris: Gallimard, 2010.

"Martinique 1902–2002: Documents." stpierre1902.org. Martinique 1902–2002, 21 August 2010, rev. 6 May 2011. Web. 26 July 2011.

Mather, Cotton. "The Trial of Bridget Bishop." In *The Wonders of the Invisible*

World: Narratives of the Witchcraft Cases: 1648–1706, ed. George Lincoln
    Burr, 223–9. New York: Barnes and Noble, 1959.
Maupassant, Guy de. "La mère aux monstres." 1883. In *Contes Fantastiques
    Complets*, 145–51. Paris: Marabout, 2000.
– "A Mother of Monsters." In *The Entire Original Maupassant Short Stories*.
    Trans. Albert M.C. McMaster, A.E. Henderson, Mme Quesada, and others.
    Project Gutenberg. N.p., n.d. Web. 26 July 2010.
Mauriès, Patrick. *Cabinets de curiosités*. Paris: Gallimard, 2002.
– *Cabinets of Curiosities*. New York: Thames and Hudson, 2002.
Maximin, Daniel. *L'isolé soleil*. Paris: Seuil, 1981.
– *Lone Sun*. Trans. Nidra Poller. Charlottesville: UP of Virginia, 1989.
– *Soufrières*. Paris: Seuil, 1987.
McClintock, Anne. "The Angel of Progress: Pitfalls of the Term 'Post-colo-
    nialism.'" In *Colonial Discourse and Post-Colonial Theory: A Reader*, ed.
    Patrick Williams and Laura Chrisman, 291–304. New York: Columbia UP,
    1994.
McClintock, Anne, Aamir Mufti, and Ella Shohat, eds. *Dangerous Liaisons:
    Gender, Nation, and Postcolonial Perspectives*. Minneapolis: U of Minnesota
    P, 1997.
McRuer, Robert. *Crip Theory: Cultural Signs of Queerness and Disability*. New
    York: New York UP, 2006.
– "Reflections on Disability in Haiti." In *Disabling Postcolonialism*, ed. Stuart
    Murray and Clare Barker. *Journal of Literary and Cultural Disability Studies*
    4, 3 (2010): 327–32.
Mephon, Harry P. *Corps et société en Guadeloupe: Sociologie des pratiques de
    compétition*. Rennes: PU de Rennes, 2007.
Merchant, Carolyn. "Secrets of Nature: The Bacon Debates Revisited."
    Journal of the History of Ideas 69, 1 (2008): 147–62.
Merleau-Ponty, Maurice. *Phénoménologie de la perception*. Paris: Gallimard,
    1945.
– *Le visible et l'invisible*. Paris: Gallimard, 1964.
Mernissi, Fatima. *Beyond the Veil: Male-Female Dynamics in a Modern Muslim
    Society*. Cambridge: Schenkman, 1975.
– *Beyond the Veil: Male-Female Dynamics in Modern Muslim Society*. Rev. ed.
    Bloomington: Indiana UP, 1987.
– "The Meaning of Spatial Boundaries." In *Feminist Postcolonial Theory:
    A Reader*, ed. Reina Lewis and Sara Mills, 489–501. New York: Routledge,
    2003.
– *Sexe, idéologie, Islam*. Trans. Diane Brower and Anne-Marie Pelletier. Paris:
    Tierce, 1983.

Mességué, Maurice, et André Gayot. *Ce soir le diable viendra te prendre: La sorcellerie aux Antilles*. Paris: Robert Laffont, 1968.

"Michael Jackson Autopsy Report." thesmokinggun.com. The Smoking Gun, n.d. Web. 25 June 2010.

"Michael Jackson Is Dead." latimesblogs.latimes.com. *Los Angeles Times*, 25 June 2009. Web. 25 June 2010.

"Michael Jackson, 50, Is Dead." artsbeat.blogs.nytimes.com. *New York Times*, 25 June 2009. Web. 25 June 2010.

Michel, Claudine. "Of Worlds Seen and Unseen: The Educational Character of Haitian Vodou." In *Haitian Vodou: Spirit, Myth, and Reality*, ed. Patrick Bellegarde-Smith and Claudine Michel, 32–45. Bloomington: Indiana UP, 2006.

Micone, Marco. "Speak What." *Jeu: Revue de théâtre* 50 (1989): 83–5.

Miles, Steven H. *The Hippocratic Oath and the Ethics of Medecine*. Oxford: Oxford UP, 2004.

Miles, M. "Signing in the Seraglio: Mutes, Dwarfs, and Jestures at the Ottoman Court 1500–1700." *Disability and Society* 15, 1 (2000): 115–34.

Miller, Arthur. *The Crucible*. 1953. New York: Penguin, 1995.

Miller, Christopher L. *The French Atlantic Triangle: Literature and Culture of the Slave Trade*. Durham: Duke UP, 2008.

Miller, Dean A. "Some Psycho-Social Perceptions of Slavery." *Journal of Social History* 18, 4 (1985): 587–605.

Miller, Paul Allen. "Toward a Post-Foucauldian History of Discursive Practices." *Configurations* 7, 2 (1999): 211–25.

Miron, François. *Etude des phénomènes volcaniques: Tremblements de terre, éruptions volcaniques, la cataclysme de la Martinique 1902*. Paris: Ch. Béranger, 1903.

Mishra, Vijay, and Bob Hodge. "What is Post(-)colonialsim?" *Colonial Discourse and Post-Colonial Theory: A Reader*, ed. Patrick Williams and Laura Chrisman, 276–90. New York: Columbia UP, 1994.

Mitchell, David T. "Narrative Prosthesis." *Disability Studies: Enabling the Humanities*, ed. Sharon L. Snyder, Brenda Jo Brueggemann, and Rosemarie Garland Thomson, 15–30. New York: Modern Language Association, 2002.

Mitchell, David T., and Sharon L. Snyder, eds. *The Body and Physical Difference: Discourses of Disability*. Ann Arbor: U of Michigan P, 1997.

– "The Eugenic Atlantic: Race, Disability, and the Making of an International Eugenic Science, 1800–1945." *Disability and Society* 18, 7 (2003): 843–64.

– *Narrative Prosthesis: Disability and the Dependencies of Discourse*. Ann Arbor: U of Michigan P, 2000.

Mitchell, Margaret. *Gone with the Wind*. 1936. Motion picture edition. New York: Macmillan, 1940.

Monière, Denis. *Les Enjeux du Référendum*. Montréal: Québec / Amérique, 1977.

Montaigne, Michel de. *The Complete Essays of Montaigne*. Trans. Donald M. Frame. 1948. Stanford: Stanford UP, 1958.

– *Les essais de Michel de Montaigne*. 1588. Ed. Pierre Villey. Re-ed. and pref. by V.-L. Saulnier. 3rd ed. Vol. 2. Paris: Presses universitaires de France, 1978.

Montbrun, Christian. *Les Petites Antilles avant Christophe Colomb: Vie quotidienne des Indiens de la Guadeloupe*. Paris: Karthala, 1984.

Montilus, Guérin C. "Vodun and Social Transformation in the African Diasporic Experience: The Concept of Personhood in Haitian Vodun Religion." In *Haitian Vodou: Spirit, Myth, and Reality*, ed. Patrick Bellegarde-Smith and Claudine Michel, 1–6. Bloomington: Indiana UP, 2006.

Montvalon, Jean-Baptiste de. "Colonisation: La loi sera réécrite." *Le monde*, 6 January 2006.

Moreau, Jean-Michel. "C'est à ce prix que vous mangez du sucre en Europe." Illustration, chap. 19 of François Voltaire's *Candide* in *Œuvres complètes de Voltaire*. 1787. Paris, Bibliothèque nationale. scholarsresource.com. Web. 1 April 2010.

Morgan, Jennifer. *Laboring Women: Reproduction and Gender in New World Slavery*. Philadelphia: U of Pennsylvania P, 2004.

Morgan, Peter. *Fire Mountain: How One Man Survived the World's Worst Volcanic Disaster*. New York: Bloomsbury, 2003.

"The Moroccan Family Code (*Moudawana*) of February 5, 2004." Trans. 2005. hrea.org. Human Rights Education Associates, n.d. Web. 15 August 2010.

"The Moroccan Twins Aziza [sic] and Saeedah Leave the NGHA." conjoinedtwins.med.sa. Kingdom of Saudi Arabia Conjoined Twins, 16 August 2009. Web. 7 January 2010.

Morrison, Amanda. "Cuerpos latinoamericanos: La discapacidad fundacional en la novela hispanoamericana, 1847–1958." Diss. State U of New York-Buffalo, 2010.

Morrison, Toni. *Beloved*. 1987. New York: Signet, 1991.

Morton, Emma. "Man, 30, Gives Birth to His 'Twin.'" thesun.co.uk. *Sun*, 8 May 2009. Web. 12 December 2009.

Morton, Samuel George. *Crania Americana: A Comparative View of the Skulls of Various Aboriginal Nations of North and South America*. Philadelphia: J. Dobson, 1839.

Moudawana (Loi no. 70.03 portant Code de la famille). Bulletin Officiel n° 5358 du 2 ramadan 1426 (6 octobre 2005): 667. Original version in Arabic, 2004.

Moudileno, Lydie. *L'écrivain antillais au miroir de sa littérature: Mises en scène et mise en abyme du roman antillais*. Paris: Karthala, 1997.

Moura, Jean-Marc. *Littératures francophones et théorie postcoloniale*. Paris: PU de France, 1999.

Mudimbe, V.Y. *The Invention of Africa: Gnosis, Philosophy, and the Order of Knowledge*. Bloomington: Indiana UP, 1988.

– *L'odeur du père: Essai sur des limites de la science et de la vie en Afrique noire*. Paris: Présence africaine, 1982.

Munro, Martin, ed. *Haiti Rising: Haitian History, Culture and the Earthquake of 2010*. Kingston: U of the West Indies P, 2010.

Murdoch, H. Adlai. *Creole Identity in the French Caribbean Novel*. Gainesville: UP of Florida, 2001.

– "Border Crossings: *Francophonie*, Postcolonialism, and Caribbean/African Studies." In *African Literatures at the Millenium*, ed. Arthur D. Drayton, Omofolabo Ajayi-Soyinka, and I. Peter Ukpokodu, 300–7. Trenton: Africa World, 2007.

Murray, Stuart. *Autism*. New York: Routledge, 2011.

– "Autism Functions/The Function of Autism." *Disability Studies Quarterly* 30, 1 (2010): n.p. Web. 9 November 2011.

– *Representing Autism: Culture, Narrative, Fascination*. Liverpool: Liverpool UP, 2008.

Nack Ngue, Julie. "The Body of Survival, the Body Composite: Testimony and the Problematics of Integral Healing in Ken Bugul's *Le Baobab fou*." In *Emerging Perspectives on Ken Bugul: From Alternative Choices to Oppositional Practices*, ed. Ada Uzoamaka Azodo and Jeanne-Sarah de Larquier, 53–79. Trenton: Africa World, 2009.

– "Colonial Discourses of Disability and Normalization in Contemporary Francophone Immigrant Narratives: Bessora's *53 cm* and Fatou Diome's *Le Ventre de l'Atlantique*." *Wagadu: A Journal of Transnational Women's and Gender Studies* 4 (2007): 35–47.

– *Critical Conditions: Illness and Disability in Francophone African and Caribbean Women's Writing*. Lanham: Lexington, 2012.

Nancy, Jean-Luc. *La communauté désœuvrée*. Paris: Christian Bourgeois, 1986.

– *The Inoperative Community.* Trans. Peter Connor. Minneapolis: U of Minnesota P, 1991.

Nékrouf, Younès. *Une amitié orageuse: Moulay Ismaïl et Louis XIV.* Paris: Albin Michel, 1987.

Nesbitt, Nick. *Voicing Memory: History and Subjectivity in French Caribbean Literature.* Charlottesville: U of Virginia P, 2003.

Newby, Gordon. *A Concise Encyclopedia of Islam.* Oxford: Oneworld, 2002.

Ngwa Niba, Francis. "Cameroon's Conjoined Twins Help Spread Islam." news.bbc.co.uk. BBC, 19 April 2010. Web. 11 February 2010.

Nicholson, Desmond V. *The Story of the Arawaks in Antigua and Barbuda.* London: Linden, 1983.

Nield, Ted. "Le cachot de Cyparis." 10 October 2010. geolsoc.org.uk. The Geological Society of London, n.d. Web. 26 July 2011.

Nietzsche, Friedrich. *The Gay Science.* 1882. Trans. Josefine Nauckhoff. Ed. Bernard Williams. Cambridge: Cambridge UP, 2001.

Novén, Bengt. *Les mots et le corps: Etude des procès d'écriture dans l'œuvre de Tahar Ben Jelloun.* Uppsala: Uppsala UP, 1996.

Obank, Margaret. "The Woman of Sand and Wind." *Banipal: Magazine of Modern Arab Literature* 8 (2000): 23–4.

Oberlé, Thierry. "Maroc: Plébiscite confirmé pour la nouvelle Constitution." lefigaro.fr. *Le Figaro,* 1 July 2011. Web. 25 July 2011.

Oberlin, Christophe. *Manuel de chirurgie du membre supérieur.* Amsterdam: Elsevier, 2000.

Olsen, Fred. *On the Trail of the Arawaks.* Norman: U of Oklahoma P, 1974.

Olsen, Steve. "The Genetic Archaeology of Race." *Atlantic Monthly* 287, 4 (2001): 69–80.

"Operation." Entry I, Def. 3.a. *Oxford English Dictionary.* N.p. dictionary.oed.com. Web. 1 April 2009.

"Opération." Def. 2. *Dictionnaire de l'Académie française.* 9th ed. N.p. atilf.atilf.fr. Web. 1 April 2009.

– Entry A. *Le Trésor de la langue française.* N.p. cnrtl.fr. Web. 1 April 2009.

Organization of African Unity. African Charter on Human and Peoples' Rights ("Banjul Charter"). 27 June 1981, CAB/LEG/67/3 rev. 5, 21 I.L.M. 58 (1982).

Organization of American States. Inter-American Convention on the Elimination of All Forms of Discrimination against Persons with Disabilities. 7 June 1999, AG/RES. 1608 (XXIX-O/99).

Orlando, Valérie K. *Francophone Voices of the "New" Morocco in Film and Print: (Re)presenting a Society in Transition.* New York: Palgrave Macmillan, 2009.

Osteen, Mark. "Autism and Representation: A Comprehensive Introduction." In *Autism and Representation*, ed. Mark Osteen, 1–47. New York: Routledge, 2008.

Ouzri, Abdelwahed. *Le théâtre au Maroc: Structures et Tendances.* Casablanca: Toubkal, 1997.

Palermo, Lynn E. "Identity under Construction: Representing the Colonies at the Paris *Exposition Universelle* of 1889." In *The Color of Liberty: Histories of Race in France*, ed. Sue Peabody and Tyler Stovall, 285–301. Durham: Duke UP, 2003.

Paré, Ambroise. *Des monstres et prodiges.* 1573. Geneva: Droz, 1971.

– *On Monsters and Marvels.* Trans. Janis L. Pallister. Chicago: U of Chicago P, 1982.

"Paria." Entry A. *Le Trésor de la langue française.* N.p. cnrtl.fr. Web. 15 August 2008.

"Paria: Le succès d'un mot." "Figures d'exclus," *Magazine littéraire*, 334 (1995): 46.

"Pariah." Entry A. *Oxford English Dictionary.* N.p. dictionary.oed.com. 15 August 2008.

Patel, Geeta. "Home, Homo, Hybrid: Translating Gender." In *A Companion to Postcolonial Studies*, ed. Henry Schwarz and Sangeeta Ray, 410–27. Malden: Blackwell, 2000.

Paterson, Janet M. *Postmodernism and the Quebec Novel.* Trans. David Homel and Charles Phillips. Toronto: U of Toronto P, 1994.

Peterson, Carla. *Moments postmodernes dans le roman québécois.* Ottawa: U of Ottawa P, 1990.

– "Le surnaturel dans *Moi, Tituba sorcière … Noire de Salem* de Maryse Condé et *Beloved* de Toni Morrison." In *L'œuvre de Maryse Condé: A propos d'une écrivaine politiquement incorrecte*, Actes du colloque sur l'œuvre de Maryse Condé, 14–18 mars 1995, 91–104. Paris: L'Harmattan, 1996.

Petry, Anne. *Tituba of Salem Village.* New York: Cromwell, 1964.

Peyronie, François de la. *Mémoires de l'académie royale de chirurgie.* 1731. Paris: Charles Osmont, 1743.

Peyrouton, Marcel. *Histoire générale du Maghreb: Algérie – Maroc – Tunisie: Des origines à nos jours.* Paris: Albin Michel, 1966.

Phillips, Tom. "Haiti Earthquake Creating a Generation of Amputees, Doctors Warn." guardian.co.uk. *Guardian*, 1 March 2009. Web. 15 February 2010.

Piette, Alain. "Les langues à Papineau: Comment le texte national se fait littérature." *Voix et Images: Littérature québecoise* 9, 3 (1984): 113–27.

Pineau, Gisèle, and Marie Abraham. *Femmes des Antilles: Traces et Voix.* Paris: Stock, 1998.

Pitts-Taylor, Victoria. *Surgery Junkies: Wellness and Pathology in Cosmetic Culture*. New Brunswick: Rutgers UP, 2007.

potomitan.net. Poto Mitan, 2009. 1 April 2010.

Powell, Timothy B. "Introduction: Re-Thinking Cultural Identity." In *Beyond the Binary: Reconstructing Cultural Identity in a Multicultural Context*, ed. Powell, 1–13. New Brunswick: Rutgers UP, 1999.

"Préparons activement la mobilisation générale à compter du jeudi 5 février." cgt-martinique.fr. Confédération générale du travail de la Martinique, n.d. Web. 1 March 2010.

"The Prison Cell of Ludger Sylbaris." atlasobscura.com. Atlas Obscura, 2011. Web. 28 July 2011.

Prince, Gerald. *Narrative as Theme: Studies in French Fiction*. Lincoln: U of Nebraska P, 1992.

– "Towards a Normative Criticism of the Novel." *Genre* 2, 1 (1969): 1–8.

Purkiss, Diane. *The Witch in History: Early Modern and Twentieth-Century Representations*. New York: Routledge, 1996.

Quayson, Ato. *Calibrations: Reading for the Social*. Minneapolis: U of Minnesota P, 2003.

– *Aesthetic Nervousness: Disability and the Crisis of Representation*. New York: Columbia UP, 2007.

– "Looking Awry: Tropes of Disability in Postcolonial Writing." In *Relocating Postcolonialism*, ed. David Theo Goldberg and Ato Quayson, 217–30. Oxford: Blackwell, 2002.

– *Postcolonialism: Theory, Practice or Process?* Cambridge: Polity, 2000.

Qur'an. Trans. M.H. Shakir. Elmhurst: Tahrike Tarsile Qur'an, Inc., 1983. U of Michigan Digital Library Project, 2000. Web. 15 April 2009.

Reeser, Todd. *Masculinities in Theory: An Introduction*. Malden: Blackwell, 2010.

Reeser, Todd, and Lewis Seifert, eds. *"Entre hommes": French and Francophone Masculinities in Culture and Theory*. Newark: U of Delaware P, 2008.

Regosin, Richard L. *The Matter of My Book: Montainge's* Essais *as the Book of the Self*. Berkeley: U of California P, 1977.

Renner, Bernd. "A Monstrous Body of Writing?: Irregularity and the Implicit Unity of Montaigne's 'Des boyteux.'" *French Forum* 29, 1 (2004): 1–20.

"Reproduction." Entry 1, Def. E. *Oxford English Dictionary*. N.p. dictionary.oed.com. Web. 1 April 2009.

– Entry D, Def. 1. *Le Trésor de la langue française*. N.p. cnrtl.fr. Web. 1 April 2009.

Retamar, Roberto Fernández. *Caliban and Other Essays*. Trans. Edward Baker. Minneapolis: U of Minnesota P, 1989.

Reyes-Santos, Irmary. "Witch or Feminist – Anowa and Tituba: A Comparative Study of Two Postcolonial Female Characters." In *African Diasporas: Ancestors, Migrations and Borders*, ed. Robert Cancel and Winifred Woodhull, 115–23. Trenton: Africa World, 2008.

Rhys, Jean. *Wide Sargasso Sea*. 1966. New York: W.W. Norton, 1999.

Ringrose, Kathryn M. *The Perfect Servant: Eunuchs and the Social Construction of Gender in Byzantium*. Chicago: U of Chicago P, 2003.

"Ritual." *Law & Order: Special Victims Unit*. NBC. New York, 3 Feb. 2004. Television.

Rodríguez, Emilio Jorge. *Haiti and Trans-Caribbean Literary Identity/Haití y la transcaribeñidad literaria*. Trans. María Teresa Ortega. Philipsburg: House of Nehesi, 2011.

Rogers, Linda J., and Beth Blue Swadener. *Semiotics and Dis/ability: Interrogating Categories of Difference*. Albany: State U of New York P, 2001.

"Le roi de la pop, Michael Jackson, est mort." lemonde.fr. *Le Monde*, 25 June 2009. Web. 25 June 2010.

Rosello, Mireille. "Contamination et pureté: Pour un protocole de cohabitation." *L'Esprit Créateur* 37, 3 (1997): 3–13.

– *Littérature et identité créole aux Antilles*. Paris: Karthala, 1992.

Rosenblatt, Roger. "Carefully Taught." *Family Circle*, 18 February 1992, 152.

Rouzel, Joseph. *Ethnologie du feu: Guérisons populaires et mythologie chrétienne*. Paris: L'Harmattan, 1996.

Roy, Oliver, and Antoine Sfeir, eds. *The Columbia World Dictionary of Islamism*. Trans. John King. New York: Columbia UP, 2007.

Russo, Karen. "Little Lakshmi Takes First Steps." abcnews.go.com. ABC News, 18 February 2008. Web. 6 February 2010.

Sadkowski, Piotr. "Questioning National Identities: The 'Wars of Languages' in *Les Têtes à Papineau* by Jacques Godbout and *Le Siège de Bruxelles* by Jacques Neirynck." In *The Nation of the Other: Constructions of Nation in Contemporary Cultural and Literary Discourses*, ed. Anna Branach-Kallas and Katarzyna Wieckowska, 149–58. Torún: Wydawnictwo Uniwersytetu Mikolaja Kopernika, 2004.

Safran, William. "Diasporas in Modern Societies: Myths of Homeland and Return." *Diaspora* 1, 1 (1991): 83–99.

Said, Edward W. *Orientalism*. New York: Pantheon, 1978.

Saint-Hilaire, Etienne Geoffroy. *Philosophie anatomique: Des monstruosités humaines*. Paris: J.B. Baillière, 1822. archive.org. Internet Archive, 2001. Web. 14 July 2011.

Saint-Hilaire, Isidore Geoffroy. *Histoire générale et particulière des anomalies de l'organisation chez l'homme et les animaux*. Paris: J.B. Ballière, 1832. archive.org. Internet Archive, 2001. Web. 6 January 2011.

Sala-Molins, Louis. *Le code noir, ou, Le calvaire de Canaan*. Paris: PU de France, 1987.

"Salem Witch Trials." The History Channel. New York: A and E Television Networks, 1998. Videocassette.

Sanday, Peggy Reeves. *Fraternity Gang Rape: Sex, Brotherhood, and Privilege on Campus*. New York: New York UP, 1990.

Sartre, Jean-Paul. *Huis clos*. 1944. In *Huis clos*, suivi de *Les mouches*, 7–95. Paris: Gallimard, 1947.

– *No Exit*. Trans. Stuart Gilbert. In *No Exit* and *The Flies*, 1–61. New York: A.A. Knopf, 1947.

Saunders, Rebecca. "Decolonizing the Body: Gender, Nation and Narration in Tahar Ben Jelloun's 'L'enfant de sable.'" *Research in African Literatures* 37, 4 (2006): 136–60.

Savage-Smith, Emilie. "Attitudes Toward Dissection in Medieval Islam." *Journal of the History of Medicine and Allied Sciences* 50, 1 (1995): 67–110.

Scarry, Elaine. *The Body in Pain: The Making and Unmaking of the World*. New York: Oxford UP, 1987.

Scarth, Alwyn. *La catastrophe: The Eruption of Mount Pelée, the Worst Volcanic Eruption of the Twentieth Century*. Oxford: Oxford UP, 2002.

Schalock, Robert L., Ruth A. Luckasson, and Karrie A. Shogren. "The Renaming of *Mental Retardation*: Understanding the Change to the Term *Intellectual Disability*." *Intellectual and Developmental Disabilities* 45, 2 (2007): 116–24.

Schneider, William H. *An Empire for the Masses: The French Popular Image of Africa, 1870–1900*. Westport: Greenwood, 1982.

Scholz, Piotr O. *Eunuchs and Castrati: A Cultural History*. Trans. John A. Broadwin and Shelley L. Frisch. 1999. Princeton: Markus Wiener, 2001.

Schor, Naomi. "The Crisis of French Universalism." *Yale French Studies* 100 (2001): 43–64.

Sedgwick, Eve Kosofsky. *Epistemology of the Closet*. Berkeley: U of California P, 1990.

"72 Hours after the Successful Separation of the Moroccan Conjoined Twins Azizah and Saeedah." conjoinedtwins.med.sa. Kingdom of Saudi Arabia Conjoined Twins, 23 June 2009. Web. 7 January 2010.

Sharpe, Matthew D. "Maghrebi Migrants and Writers: Liminality, Trangres-
sion and the Transferal of Identity." *Dialectical Anthropology* 29, 3–4 (2005):
397–421.

Sharpley-Whiting, T. Denean. *Black Venus: Sexualized Savages, Primal Fears,
and Primitive Narratives in French*. Durham: Duke UP, 1999.

Shelley, Mary Wollstonecraft. *Frankenstein; or, The Modern Prometheus*. 1818.
Cambridge: Cambridge UP, 1998.

Shelton, Marie-Denise. "Condé: The Politics of Gender and Identity." *World
Literature Today* 67, 4 (1993): 717–22.

Shepherd, Verene A. *Women in Caribbean History: The British-Colonised Territories*. Kingston: Ian Randle, 1999.

"Siamese Twins and Separation: Saudi Arabia's Kingdom of Humanity."
americanbedu.com. American Bedu, 28 July 2008. Web. 11 February 2010.

Siebers, Tobin. *Disability Aesthetics*. Ann Arbor: U of Michigan P, 2010.

– *Disability Theory*. Ann Arbor: U of Michigan P, 2008.

"Signature de conventions de partenariat." *Bilan semestriel, janvier-juin* 2008,
26. fhandicap.ma. Centre National Mohammed VI des Handicapés, n.d.
Web. 26 July 2011.

Simek, Nicole. *Eating Well, Reading Well: Maryse Condé and the Ethics of
Interpretation*. Amsterdam: Rodopi, 2008.

Simonin, Anne. "The Terror as a Legal Fiction." In *Fiction and The Frontiers
of Knowledge in Europe, 1500–1800*, ed. Richard Scholar and Alexis Tadié,
123–39. Farnham: Ashgate, 2010.

Skloot, Rebecca. *The Immortal Life of Henrietta Lacks*. New York: Crown,
2010.

Smith, André. *L'universe romanesque de Jacques Godbout*. Montréal: Aquila
Limitée, 1976.

Smith, Arlette M. "The Semiotics of Exile in Maryse Condé's Fictional
Works." *Callaloo* 14, 2 (1991): 381–8.

Smith, Michelle. "Reading in Circles: Sexuality and/as History in 'I, Tituba,
Black Witch of Salem.'" *Callaloo* 18, 3 (1995): 602–7.

Snyder, Sharon L., Brenda Jo Brueggemann, and Rosemarie Garland Thomson, eds. *Disability Studies: Enabling the Humanities*. New York: Modern
Language Association, 2002.

Songolo, Aliko. *Aimé Césaire: Une poétique de la découverte*. Paris: L'Harmattan, 1985.

– "Présentation." "Littératures francophones: Un corp(u)s étranger?" *Présence
francophone* 60 (2003): 5–11.

Sontag, Susan. *Regarding the Pain of Others*. New York: Picador, 2003.

Soter, Steven. "Sifting Truth from Pelée's Ashes: How the Real Causes of a

Famous Disaster, Long Misunderstood, Became Key Elements in the Modern Science of Volcanology." *Natural History* 111, 8 (2002): 76–7.

Spear, Thomas C. "Carnivalesque Jouissance: Representations of Sexuality in the Francophone West Indian Novel." Trans. Richard D. Reitsma. *Jouvert: A Journal of Postcolonial Studies* 2, 1 (1998): 22 paragraphs.

Springfield, Consuelo López, ed. *Daughters of Caliban: Caribbean Women in the Twentieth Century*. Bloomington. Indiana UP, 1997.

Stanley, Alessandra. "Disabled and Seeking Acceptance in Fashion." *New York Times*, 1 December 2009, 4.

Starkey, Marion L. *The Devil in Massachusetts: A Modern Inquiry into the Salem Witch Trials*. New York: Alfred A. Knopf, 1949.

Stevenson, Garth. *Community Besieged: The Anglophone Minority and the Politics of Quebec*. Montreal: McGill-Queen's UP, 1999.

Stiker, Henri-Jacques. *Corps infirmes et sociétés: Essais d'anthropologie historique*. Paris: Aubier Montaigne, 1982. 3rd ed. Paris: Dunod, 2005.

– *A History of Disability*. Trans. William Sayers. Ann Arbor: U of Michigan P, 1999.

– *Les fables peintes du corps abîmé: Les images de l'infirmité du XVIe au XXe siècle*. Paris: Cerf, 2006.

Stoddard, Eve W. "A Serious Proposal for Slavery Reform: Sarah Scott's *Sir George Ellison*." *Eighteenth-Century Studies* 28, 4 (1995): 379–96.

Stone, John H., ed. *Culture and Disability: Providing Culturally Competent Services*. Thousand Oakes: Sage, 2005.

Strain, Ellen. "Exotic Bodies, Distant Landscapes: Touristic Viewing and Popularized Anthropology in the Nineteenth Century." *Wide Angle* 18, 2 (1996): 70–100.

Suárez, Isabel Carrera. "The Americas, Postcoloniality and Gender: New World Witches in Maryse Condé and Lucía Guerra." In *Post/Imperial Encounters: Anglo-Hispanic Cultural Relations*, ed. Juan E. Tazón Salces and Isabel Carrera Suárez, 137–53. Amsterdam: Rodopi, 2005.

Sunan Abu Dawud. Trans. Ahmad Hasan. Lahore: Sh. Muhammad Ashraf, 1984.

"Survived Mt. Pelee's Fire." *New York Times*. 25 February 1903. query.nytimes.com. *New York Times*, n.d. Web. 26 July 2011.

Sutherland, Anne. "The Body as a Social Symbol among the Rom." In *The Anthropology of the Body*, ed. John Blacking, 375–90. London: Academic, 1977.

Swan, Jim. "Disabilities, Bodies, Voices." In *Disability Studies: Enabling the Humanities*, ed. Sharon L. Snyder, Brenda Jo Brueggemann, and Rosemarie Garland Thomson, 283–95. New York: Modern Language Association, 2002.

Tabar, Luc-René. "Le maudit miraculé." In *Le maudit miraculé*. 4–27. Fort-de-France: Désormeaux, 2002.

Taffin, Dominique, comp. *"Le pays du volcan": Sources de l'histoire de Saint-Pierre de la Martinique et de sa région, XVIIe-XXe siècles*. Fort-de-France: Conseil général de la Martinique, 2006.

Taraborrelli, J. Randy. *Michael Jackson: The Magic, the Madness, the Whole Story, 1958–2009*. New York: Grand Central, 2009.

Taylor, Charles. *Sources of the Self: The Making of the Modern Identity*. Cambridge: Harvard UP, 1989.

– "Les valeurs inhérentes de la nation." *Cahiers du PÉQ* 16 (1999): 12–17.

Tazi, Nadia. "Le désert perpétuel: Visages de la virilité au Maghreb." In *La virilité en Islam*, ed. Fethi Benslama and Nadia Tazi, 27–58. Paris: L'Aube, 1998.

Tétu, Michel. *Qu'est-ce que la francophonie?* Vanves: Hachette, 1997.

Thomas, Gordon, and Max Morgan Witts. *The Day the World Ended*. New York: Stein and Day, 1969.

Thompson, C.J.S. *The Mystery and Lore of Monsters: With Accounts of Some Giants, Dwarfs, and Prodigies*. London: Williams and Norgate, 1930. New York: Citadel, 1970.

Tlatli, Soraya. *La folie lyrique: Essai sur le surréalisme et la psychiatrie*. Paris: L'Harmattan, 2004.

– *Le psychiatre et ses poètes: Essai sur le jeune Lacan*. Paris: Tchou, 2000.

Todorov, Tzvetan. *The Fantastic: A Structural Approach to a Literary Genre*. Trans. Richard Howard. Cleveland: P of Case Western Reserve U, 1973.

– *Introduction à la littérature fantastique*. Paris: Seuil, 1970.

– "'Race,' Writing, and Culture." Trans. Loulou Mack. In *"Race," Writing, and Difference*, ed. Henry Louis Gates, Jr, 370–80. Chicago: U of Chicago P, 1986.

Tonda, Joseph. *La guérison divine en Afrique centrale (Congo, Gabon)*. Paris: Karthala, 2002.

"Traditions et Croyances." guadeloupetraditions.fre.fr. Croyances et Sorcelleries. N.p., n.d. Web. 14 June 2006.

Tremain, Shelley. "Foucault, Governmentality, and Critical Disability Theory: An Introduction." In *Foucault and the Government of Disability*, ed. Shelley Tremain, 1–24. Ann Arbor: U of Michigan P, 2005.

Le Trésor de la langue française. N.p. cntrl.fr. Web. 1 April 2009.

Turner, Patricia. *Ceramic Uncles and Celluloid Mammies: Black Images and Their Influence on Culture*. New York: Anchor, 1994.

The Union Act. An Act to Reunite the Provinces of Upper and Lower Canada and for the Government of Canada, Statutes of Great Britain (1840) 4 Vict., chapter 35. 23 July 1840. solon.org. Ottawa Internet Exchange, 20 February 1996. Web. 12 December 2009.

UN General Assembly. *Convention on the Rights of Persons with Disabilities*. New York, 13 December 2006, A/RES/61/106, Annex I.

Ursulet, Léo. *Le désastre de 1902 à la Martinique: L'éruption de la montagne Pelée et ses conséquences*. Paris: L'Harmattan, 1997.

Vallières, Pierre. *Nègres blancs d'Amérique: Autobiographie précoce d'un "terroriste" québécois*. Paris: François Maspero, 1969.

– *Un Québec Impossible*. Montréal: Québec / Amérique, 1977.

"Vancouver: Le Canada a affiché tout son mépris envers les francophones, accuse Marois." ledevoir.com. *Le Devoir*, 15 February 2010. Web. 23 February 2010.

Veillette, Diane, comp. *État de la situation de la langue des signes québécoise en enseignement: Rapport de recherche et pistes de solution proposées par l'Office des personnes handicapées du Québec. Synthèse*. Drummondville: Office des personnes handicapées du Québec, 2005.

Vergès, Françoise. "Post-Scriptum." *Relocating Postcolonialism*, ed. David Theo Goldberg and Ato Quayson, 349–58. Oxford: Blackwell, 2002.

Vialet, Michèle E. "'Connais-toi toi-même': Identité et sexualité chez Maryse Condé." *Nouvelles écritures féminines* 118 (1994): 70–6.

Voltaire, François-Marie Arouet. *Œuvres complètes de Voltaire*. Ed. Pierre Augustin Caron de Beaumarchais, Jean-Antoine-Nicolas de Caritat, marquis de Condorcet, and Jacques Joseph Marie Decroix. Kehl: Société littéraire-typographique, 1785–89.

Wade, Mason, ed. *La Dualité canadienne: Essais sur les relations entre Canadiens français et Canadiens anglais. Canadian Dualism: Studies of French-English Relations*. Quebec: PU Laval, 1960. Toronto: U of Toronto P, 1960.

Wagram, Mylène, and Luc-René Tabar. *Cyparis, seul au monde*. In *Le maudit miraculé* by Luc-René Tabar, 36–77. Fort-de-France: Désormeaux, 2002.

Walker, Alice. *The Color Purple*. New York: Harcourt Brace Jovanovich, 1982.

Welch, Pedro L.V., with Richard A. Goodridge. *"Red" and Black Over White: Free Coloured Women in Pre-Emancipation Barbados*. Bridgetown: Carib Research and Publications, 2000.

Wesseling, H.L. *Divide and Rule: The Partition of Africa, 1880–1914*. Trans. Arnold J. Pomerans. Westport: Praeger, 1996.

Wilson, Elizabeth. "Sorcières, sorcières: 'Moi, Tituba, sorcière … Noire de Salem', révision et interrogation." In *L'œuvre de Maryse Condé: A propos d'une écrivaine politiquement incorrecte*, 104–25. Actes du Colloque sur l'œuvre de Maryse Condé, 14–18 March 1995. Paris: L'Harmattan, 1996.

Wu, Cynthia. "The Siamese Twins in Late-Nineteenth-Century Narratives of Conflict and Reconciliation." *American Literature* 80, 1 (2008): 29–55.

Xavier, Subha. "Littératures diasporique, migrante ou monde: Questions terminologiques et théoriques." Mémoire, diasporas, et formes du roman francophone contemporain. Department of French Studies, University of Waterloo. Walper Terrace Hotel, Kitchener, Ontario. 29 April 2011.

– "Mehdi Charef and the Politics of French Immigration." *French Review* 84, 2 (2010): 328–40.

Young, Robert J. C. *Colonial Desire: Hybridity in Theory, Culture and Race*. London: Routledge, 1995.

– *The Struggle for Quebec*. Montreal: McGill-Queen's UP, 1999.

Zanzana, Habib. "Gender, Body, and the Erasure of the Feminine in Tahar Ben Jelloun's L'Enfant de sable." *Romance Languages Annual* (RLA) 10, 1 (1998): 194–8.

Zebrowski, Ernest, Jr. *The Last Days of St. Pierre: The Volcanic Disaster That Claimed Thirty Thousand Lives*. New Brunswick: Rutgers UP, 2002.

Zola, Emile. *Germinal*. 1885. Paris: Gallimard, 1999.

– *Germinal*. Trans. Roger Pearson. New York: Penguin Books, 2004.

Zolf, Larry. "Speak White." CBC, 2 March 2007. vigile.net. Vigile, n.d. Web. 25 February 2010.

Zvan, Katja. "The Politics of the Reform of the New Family Law (the Moudawana)." MPhil thesis. St. Antony's College (U of Oxford), 2007. oucs.ox.ac.uk. Oxford University Computing Services, n.d. Web. 3 Janurary 2010.

Index